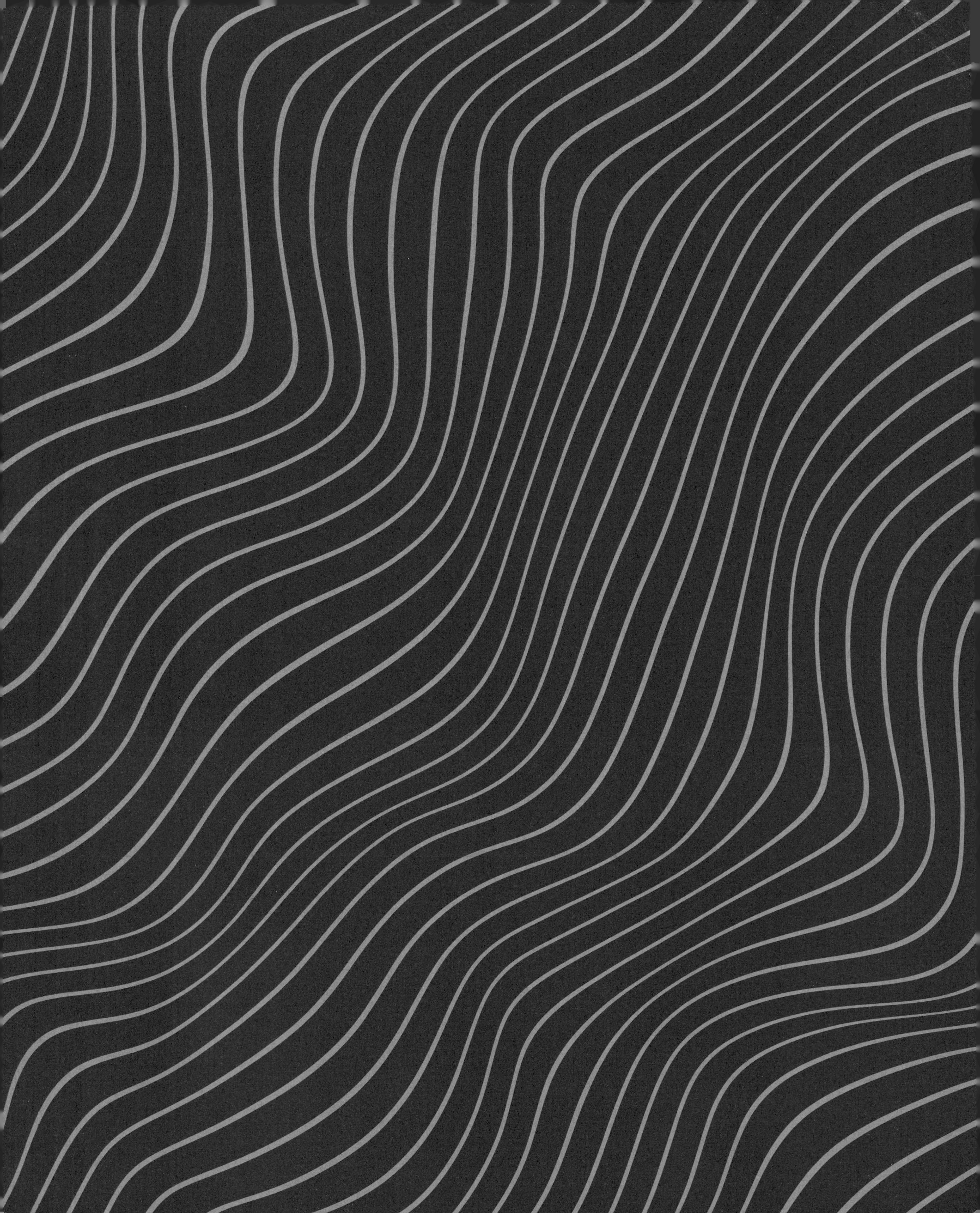

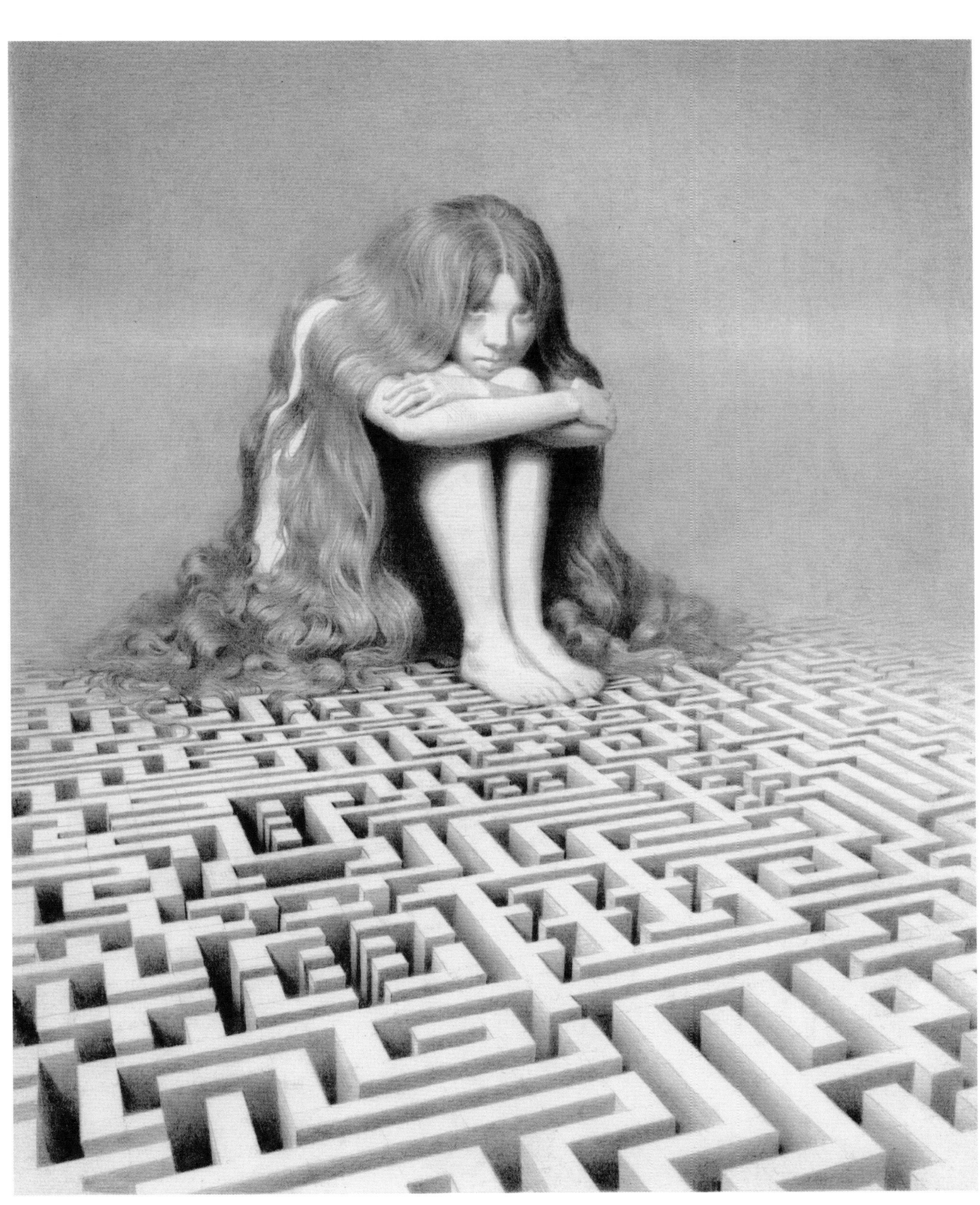

Mind is A Maze

2021

Miles Johnston

LIMINALITY

WORKS 2016–2024

PARAGON BOOKS

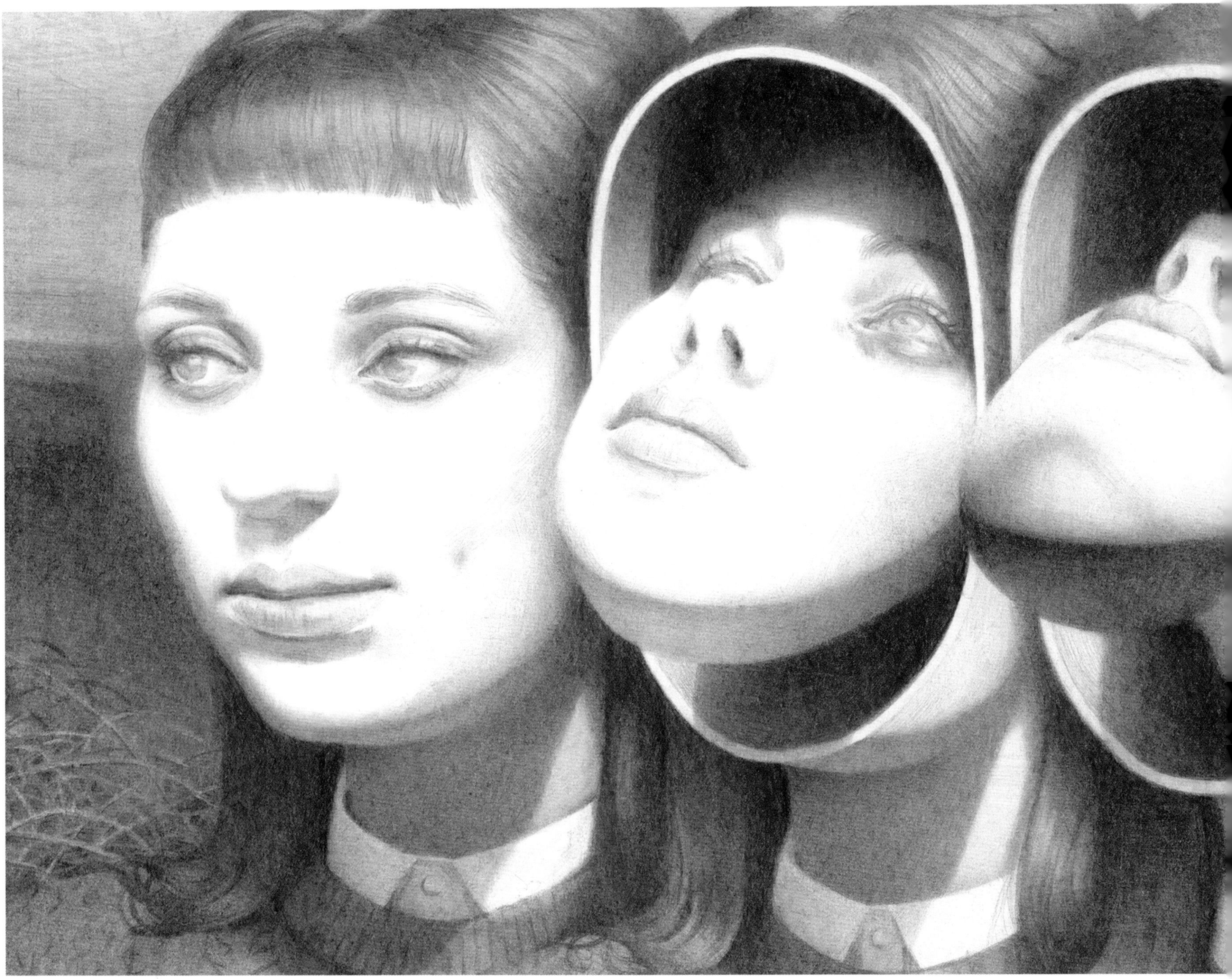

Miles Johnston—Liminality

WORKS 2016–2024

Hardcover Edition
2200 copies
First printing
November, 2024

ISBN: 978-1-952251-32-0

Published by Paragon Books.
Designed by Shaun Roberts.
Proofread & edited by Katherine Hamilton.

The text was set with Goudy Oldstyle designed by Frederic W. Goudy, Morris Fuller Benton, and Quarto designed by Hoefler & Co.
Printed on 200 gsm matte art paper.

Printed in China.

Paragon Books
929 Camelia St.
Berkeley, CA 94710
paragon-books.com

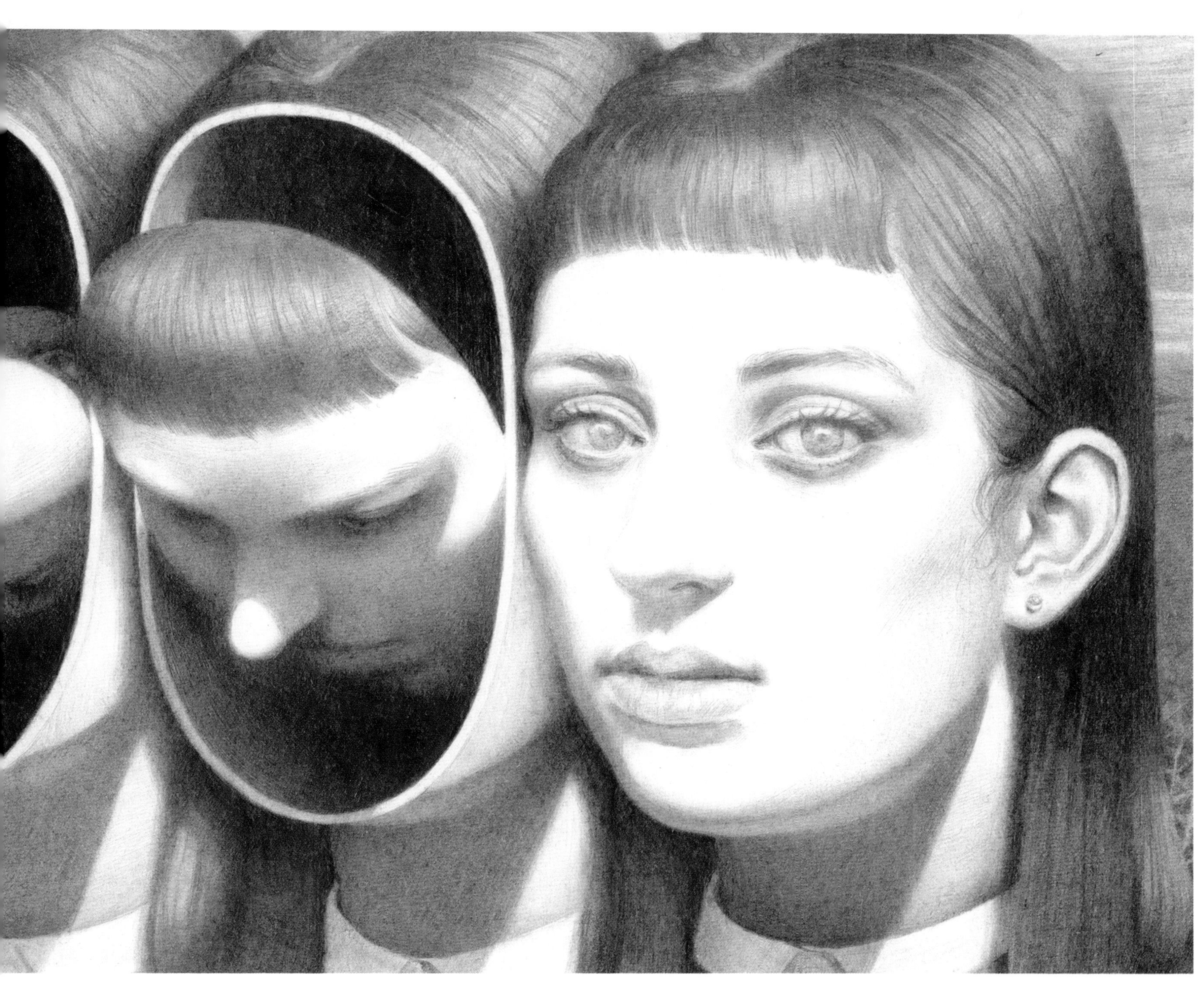

Persona Revolution (detail)
2018

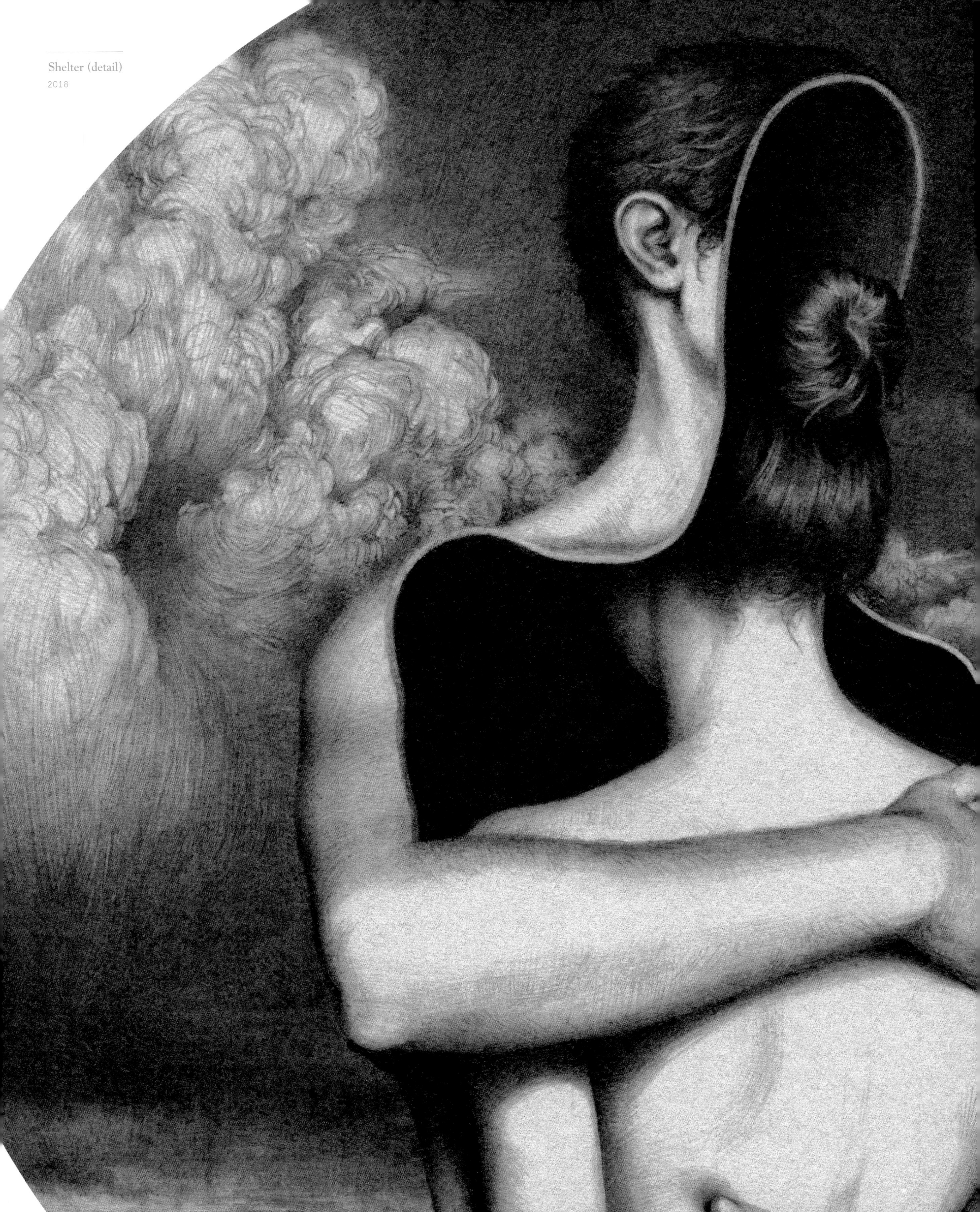

Shelter (detail)
2018

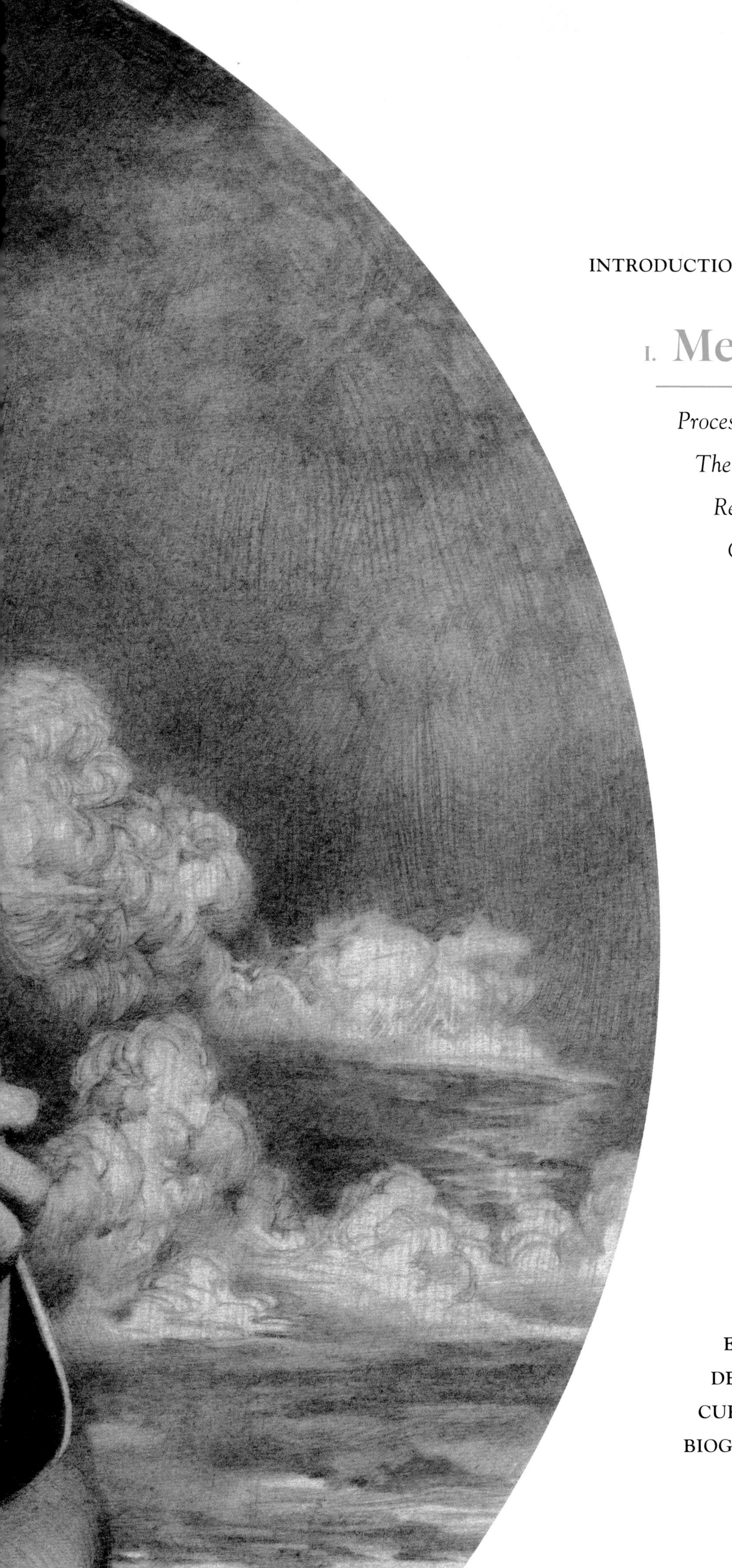

Contents

Introduction

I never set out to become an artist. For as long as I can remember, I've always loved to draw and create; I found great satisfaction in making things, but I never really envisioned myself painting for a living. Even from a young age when asked by adults if I would grow up to be an artist, I remember answering that I was going to pursue something more realistic. Somehow I seem to have become less jaded on this point as I've grown older. My mum helped to foster a love of creative pursuits, always encouraging me and my brother to draw, write, and make things, and for that I am deeply grateful.

When I was a teenager I had the great fortune of stumbling upon an exciting online forum, the now defunct *conceptart.org*, which was filled with a mixture of aspiring amateurs and professional artists from the entertainment industry. As a thirteen year old fully saturated in video games and movies, the idea that I could sharpen my skills to the point that people would actually pay me to design things for them was incredibly motivating. There is a widespread misconception that drawing occupies some special category of human knowledge, where some people simply have it and others do not. It was through the internet that I came to understand that it was just another skill that could be studied, practiced, and developed. All of my prior schooling was imposed from the outside, but this represented the first time I proactively sought out new knowledge of my own accord, and the feeling was very different.

It's always unnerving to see how easily things could have turned out differently in hindsight. It was summer 2006 when I first made the leap from lurking to posting on the message board. I discovered that a large majority of the users painted digitally using a graphics tablet and had constructed this naive idea in my head that as soon as I got my hands on one, I too would be producing art like all the people I was discovering and looking up to. When I did finally get a tablet that year for Christmas, the revelation of just how bad I was at painting, how little I knew, was crushing and my interest kind of waned. It was only the following summer, for reasons I no longer remember, that I rededicated myself to practice—this time for good.

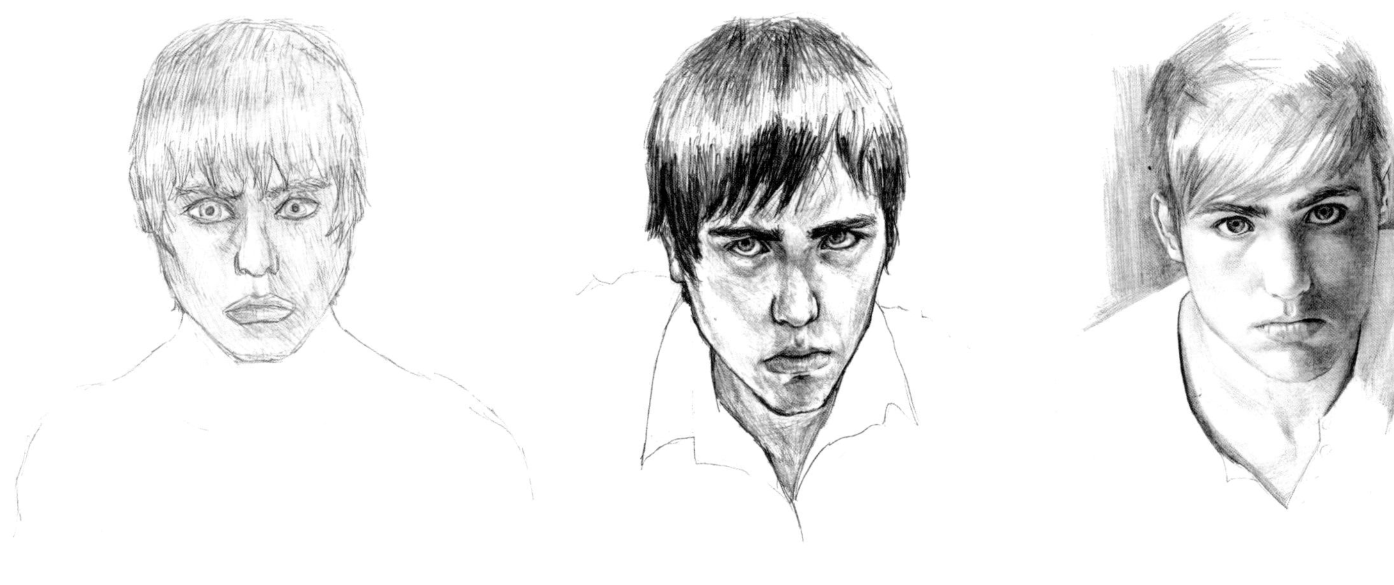

Miles Johnston self-portrait at ages 14, 15, & 17

Looking back, I feel a mixture of gratitude and surprise at how intensely I threw myself into everything. From 2007 onwards, I dedicated a huge chunk of my free time to practice. I always had a knack for drawing but it was by no means obvious that it would end up as my livelihood. I think that I was driven by more than just a positive motivation to achieve something. Like many I always experienced a lot of fear about my future from a young age. I went through several periods of being obsessed with the idea that I must have some horrible undiscovered illness. The thought of growing old terrified me and I simply couldn't imagine myself as an adult, it seemed impossible. My fears were the basics: old age, sickness and death. Dedicating myself to art so intensively allowed me to develop a positive relationship to the future for the first time. The passage of time was no longer just a relentless march into the unknown, but now each passing week brought new knowledge, new abilities and something to look forward to. It came with a feeling of being part of a secret community, filled with characters that dominated my mental landscape but were unknown to the wider culture.

Despite the intense inner feelings that were driving my practice, none of this was really showing up in the actual substance of the artwork I produced. I would dismiss the very label of an "artist" as pretentious, I wanted to be a hyper-skilled hired gun. The goal was to be able to draw anything from imagination in order to work as a concept artist or illustrator, bringing to life the ideas of others. I always had an intense relationship with artwork in general, it just never occurred to me that I could be attempting to produce work of the same kind. I derived a lot of meaning from music, movies, and books; they functioned almost as a secular religion. They were how I would find a way to talk about the things that really meant something to me with those around me, a way to explore life's big questions and play with my developing identity. Eventually the schism between these two outlooks had to collapse, but that didn't happen until later on during my studies at an atelier.

After I finished school I went to study at the Swedish Academy of Realist Art in 2011. The program almost entirely consisted of drawing from life, specifically figure drawing, cast drawing, and still life. After years of balancing my artistic practice with my school studies, the chance to fully immerse myself in drawing all day every day was thrilling. I had developed the discipline and the hunger to focus for hours on end and this began the most intense period of my artistic development. I genuinely don't think I could work the kind of schedule I did as an art student

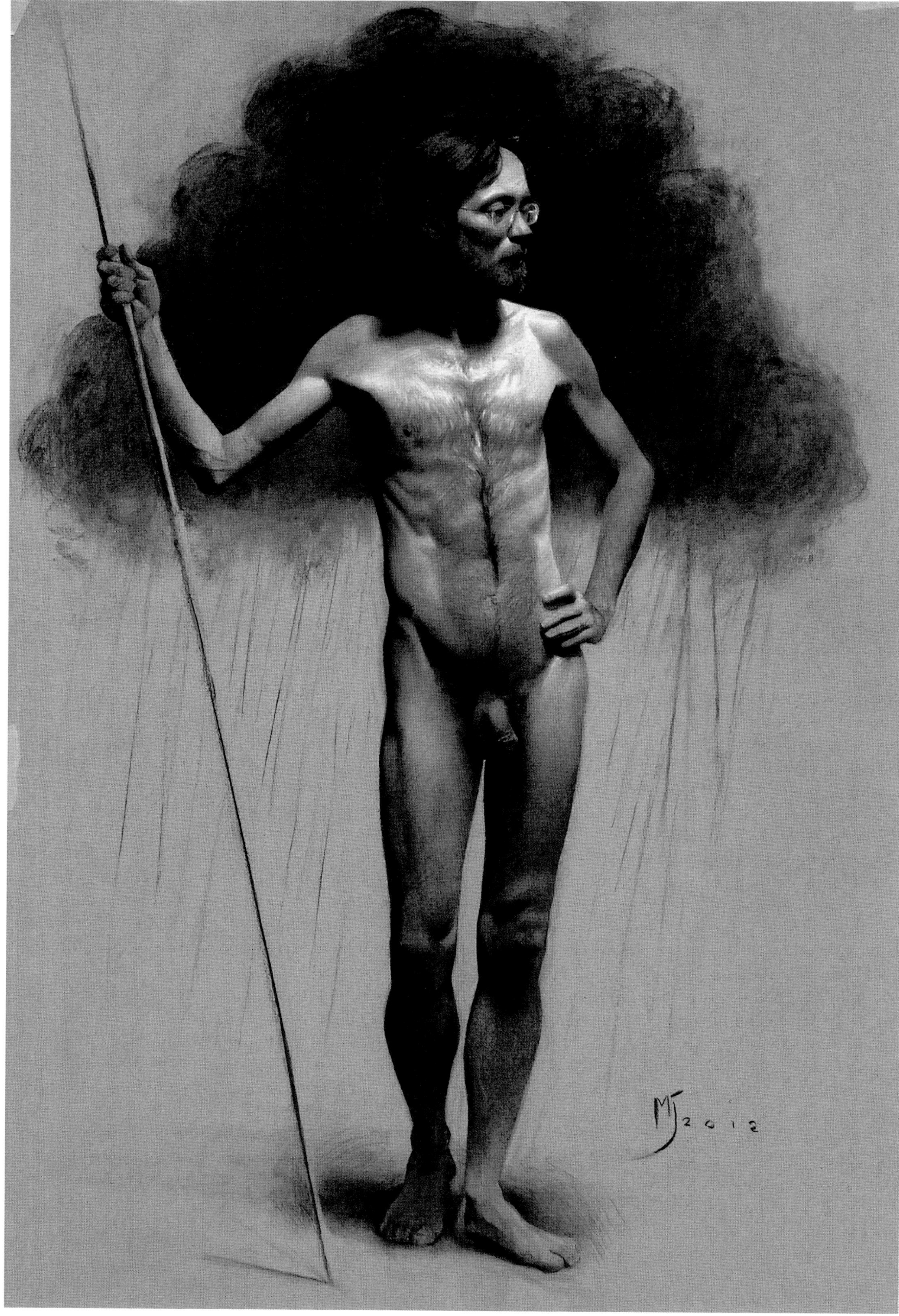

Figure Study, 2012

anymore. I would draw from life for up to 8 hours everyday, and then go home in the evenings to do personal work and small commissions. I really look back on this period of my life with fondness—it's where I cemented some of my lifelong friendships.

We would also organize trips as a school to visit different cities in Europe to see great paintings in person. It was during this time that something shifted in me internally and I realized that I no longer had any interest in working in the entertainment industry. To be a great concept artist is to be part of a team working together to realize a larger vision. You are an essential component of a workflow producing a separate larger project together. I realized that what I wanted was to make drawings and paintings that were standalone statements in and of themselves.

I started to experiment with allowing more of my own identity to come out in the things I was making. For the longest time I had created work that consisted of what I thought other people wanted from me. Works that belonged in a portfolio, or would be likely to appeal to potential buyers or clients. I experimented with taking the embarrassing and pathetic sides of myself that had come out during a recent break up and trying to comically depict them as these grotesque, horny, possessive goblin creatures. I know it seems ridiculous, but it was actually a huge step for me as an artist to realize that I could make work about the things that I actually thought about in my day to day life. I also started to play around with producing dream-like stream of consciousness works where I would allow imagery that felt evocative to emerge naturally onto the paper. As someone who had always felt tethered to producing art that was meant to fulfill some explicit purpose, it was liberating to just draw for my own amusement again.

By the time I graduated from the atelier, I had been drawing for almost 10 years and had built a decent foundational ability. I was living in London doing small bits of freelance to (barely) pay the bills, bouncing around between clients. It is probably due to a character flaw of mine that I found myself unable to really produce anything great when commissioned. I seemed to lack the motivation to summon the best parts of myself towards anyone else's projects. However, the idea of living off of my personal work still felt remote and inaccessible. I had this idea that if I could build up a really successful illustration career, then at some point I would have enough financial security and skills to pivot towards doing my own thing. It slowly dawned on me that this was simply another narrative I had built up to avoid just trying to do the thing that I really wanted to do.

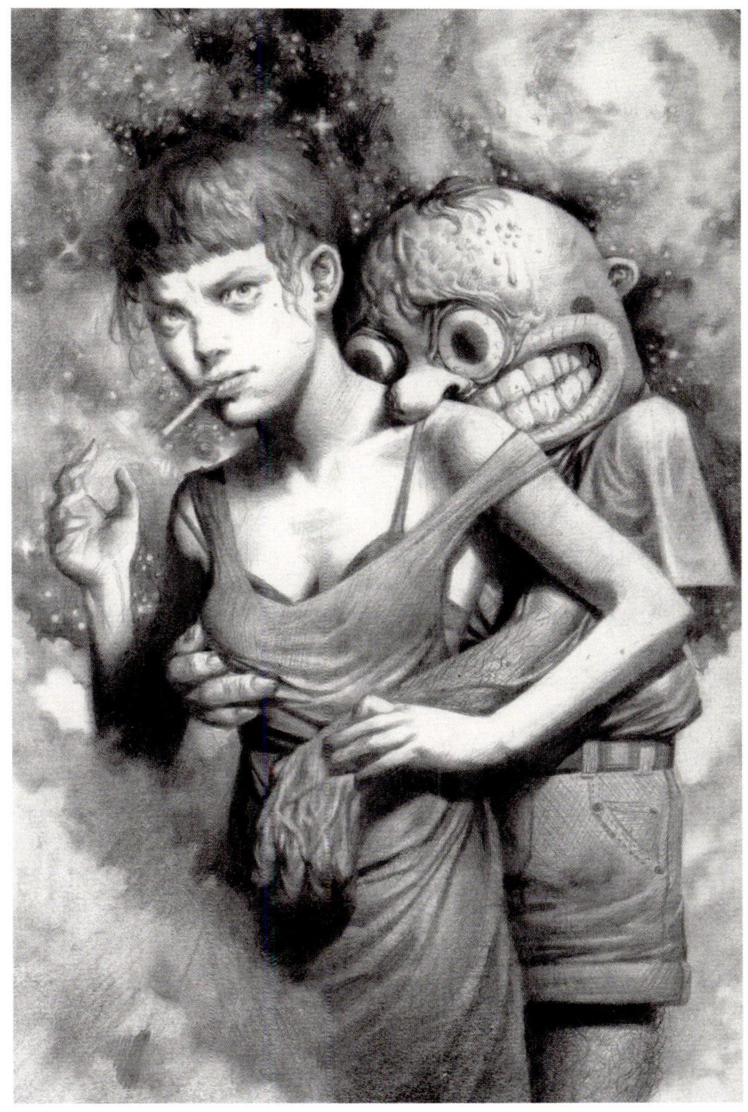

Sketchbook page, 2014

Through some turbulence in my personal life, I found myself moving around frequently, and decided to visit my old school in Sweden in late 2015. Originally, I planned to stay for just one month, but as the month drew to an end I asked if they could accommodate me in the school building with a studio space in exchange for part time work as a teacher. This allowed me to drop all of my freelance work and I gave myself a year to try doing nothing but focusing on my personal projects. After a decade of laying down the groundwork, this was the first time I had ever

“I want everyone who feels the pull to express themselves, to say something, to know the joys of developing and nurturing that side of yourself.”

dedicated months at a time to creating my own work with no distractions. Things snowballed faster than I had dared to imagine they could.

This book will cover from that point onwards, when I discovered and honed the kind of work that I really wanted to make—something that could be an outlet for me to express what mattered to me. It has all been possible thanks to people like you, reading this book. I can’t express enough my gratitude for having shown any interest at all in what I do, and I hope to keep providing you with artwork for many years to come.

Almost another decade later, I find myself writing this brief summary of my artistic life so far. It is hard to sum up such a big chunk of my life in a few short words and a lot of thought has been dedicated to trying to retell what I can as honestly as I can recall. It is my sincere wish to communicate to you the joy and meaning that art has brought to my life, and if that message can be of any use to you it is my greatest wish that you can hear it. I want everyone who feels the pull to express themselves, to say something, to know the joys of developing and nurturing that side of yourself. I hope that it can bring the same richness to your life. I am now standing on the other side of the most seismic shift in my life so far. Two years ago my wonderful partner Saga gave birth to our two children Hilma and Ofelia, to whom this book is primarily dedicated. When they are older I hope that there is something in here that can allow them to know a piece of me a little better.

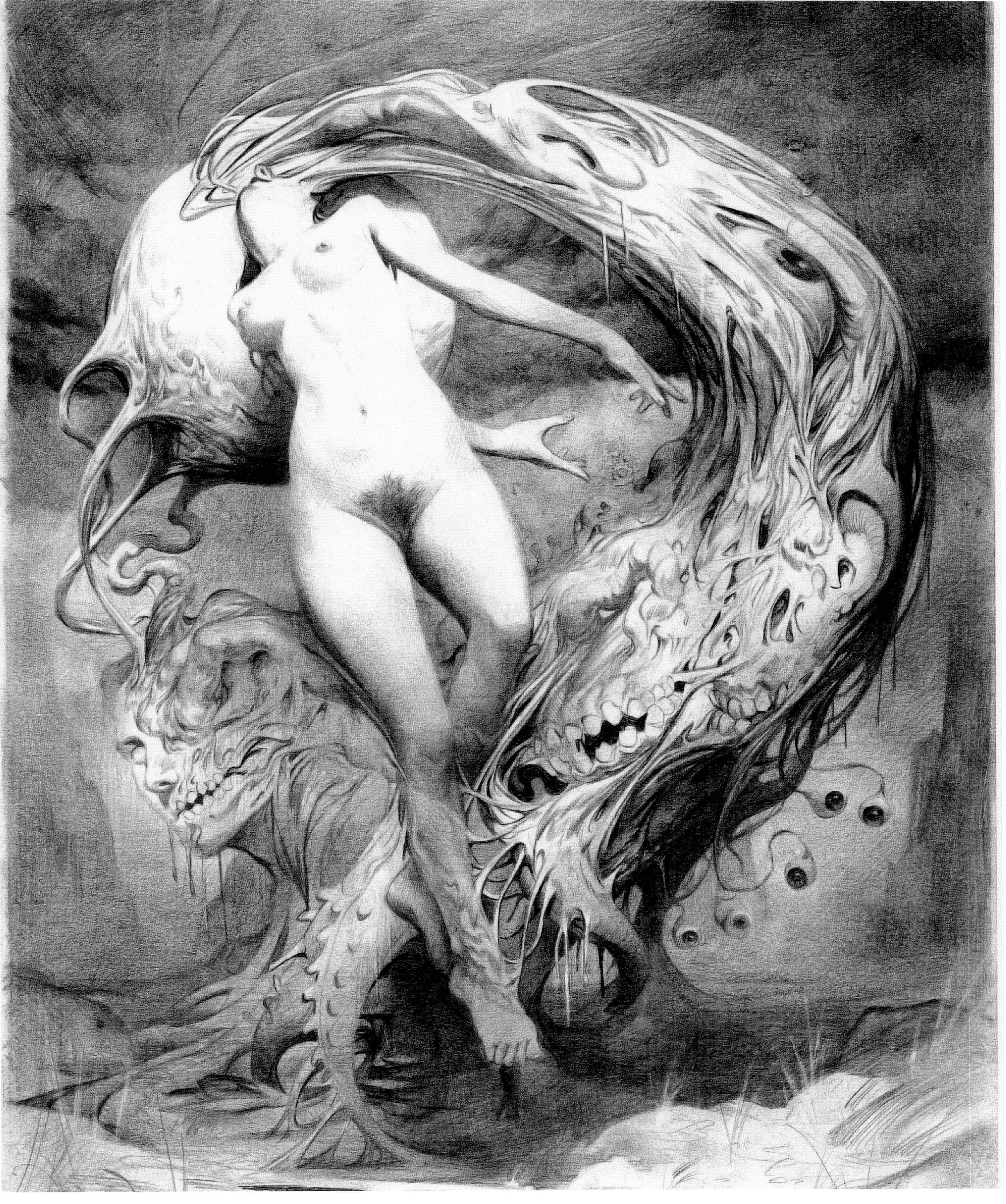

Growth, 2013

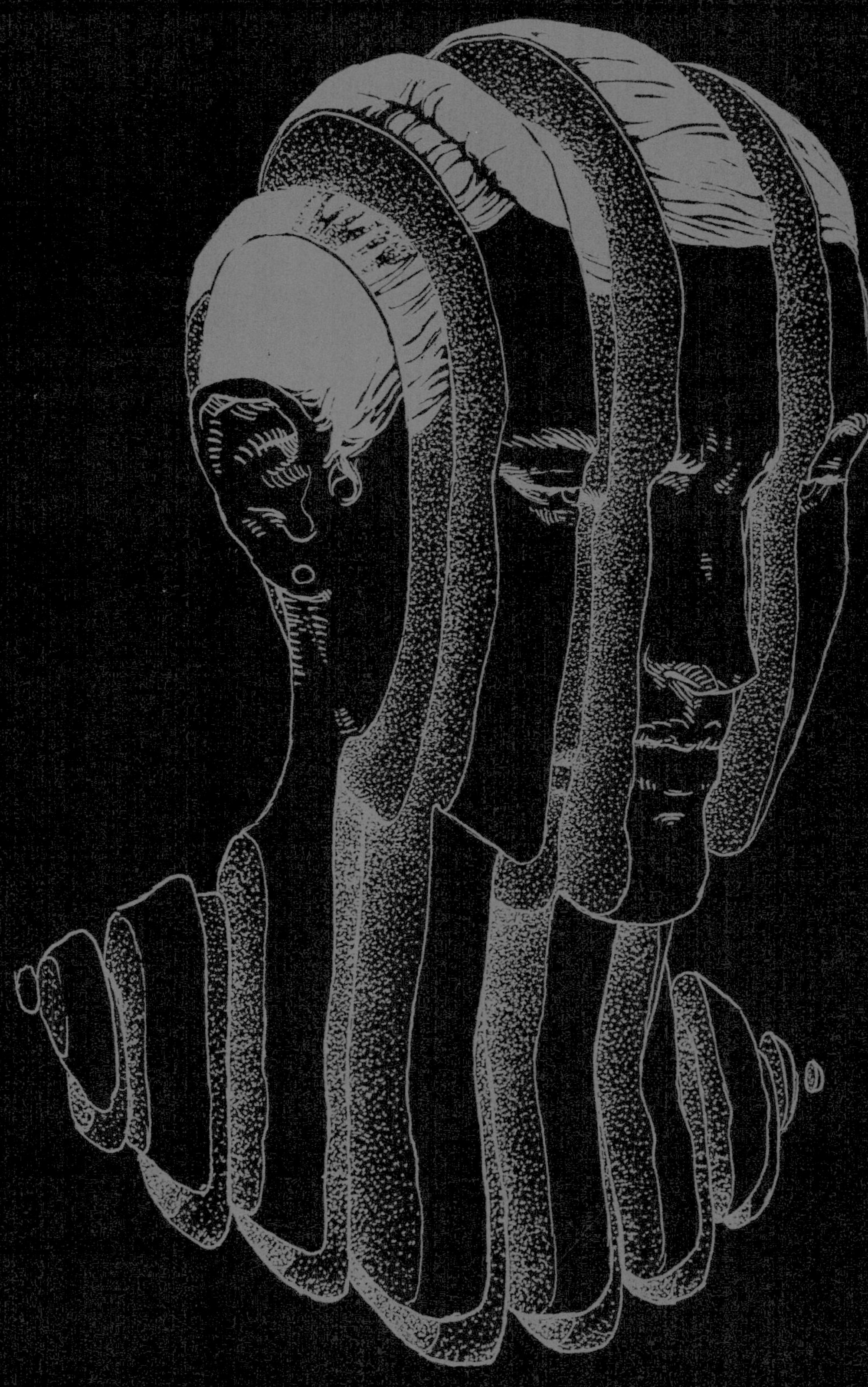

Segmented
2019

I

Mechanics

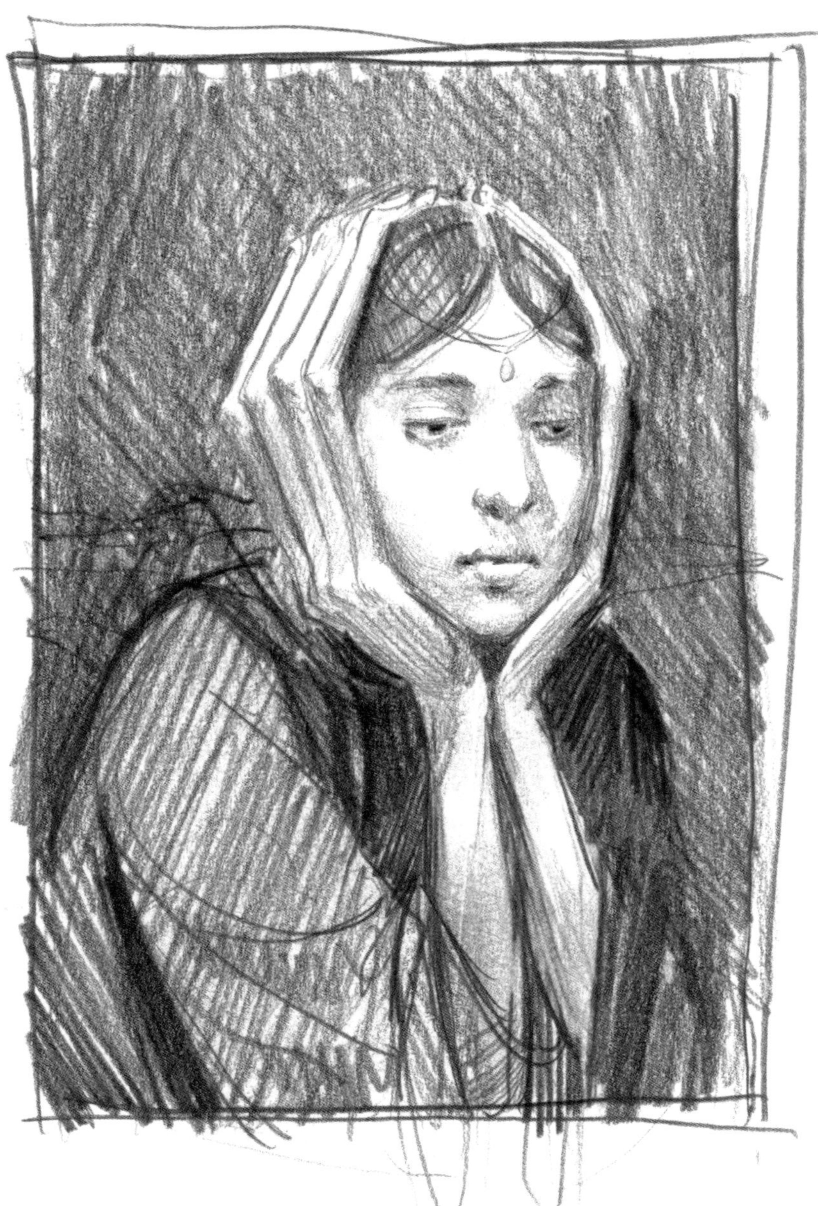

"I don't see my images in my head before I draw them, instead I respond to simple impulses that arise in the process of drawing."

Process & Play

Melancholia + Study
2020

I think that "*Melancholia*" serves as an interesting jumping off point to talk about how the creative process often doesn't look how we expect it to. This drawing, which came to mean a lot of different things to me, evolved out of asking myself the totally absurd question *"what if I made the fingers longer?"*

I was sketching one evening and started playing around with someone sitting with their head in their hands. It is a pose that has a simple, symmetrical beauty to it, and for me carries a compelling sense of introspection. I don't see my images in my head before I draw them. Instead I respond to simple impulses that arise in the process of drawing e.g. *"Oh this pose looks interesting, she seems lost in thought; I've always liked how the fingers bend different amounts based on how the fingertips conform to the shape of the skull, I wonder how that would look if the fingers were much longer."* As soon as I experimented with the idea, I knew I was on to something interesting. Most importantly, I didn't know why. For reasons I couldn't yet articulate, the nature of the surreal distortions used were forming a relationship with the body language and pose to hint at a new undiscovered meaning.

I think that one of the best ways to enhance your creative output is to demystify the process a little. Once you have fostered a high level of technique, creativity isn't quite as dramatic looking as you expect. It is playful and simple but surprisingly difficult to achieve. For me the complexity develops throughout the process, not in a flash of inspiration at the beginning.

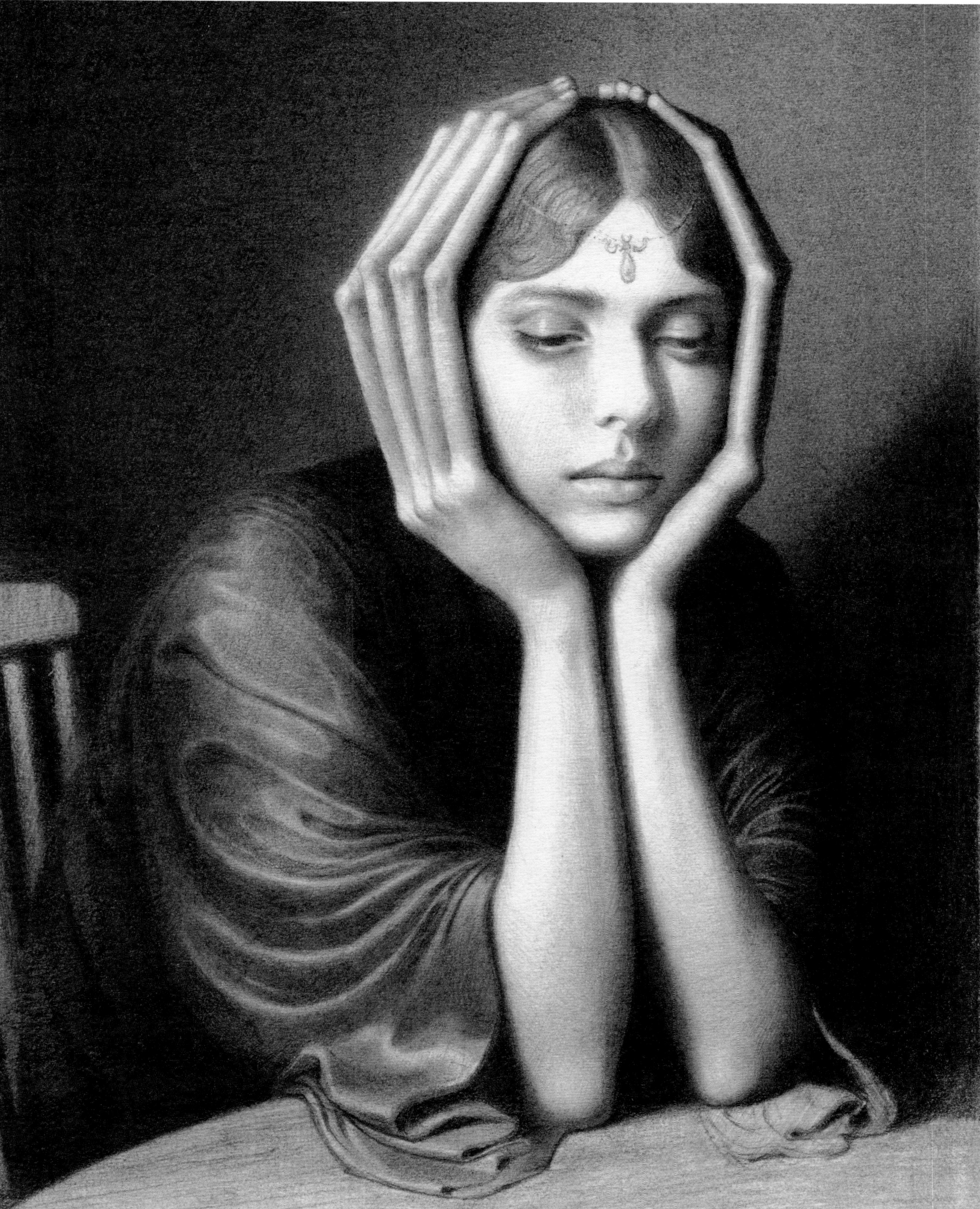

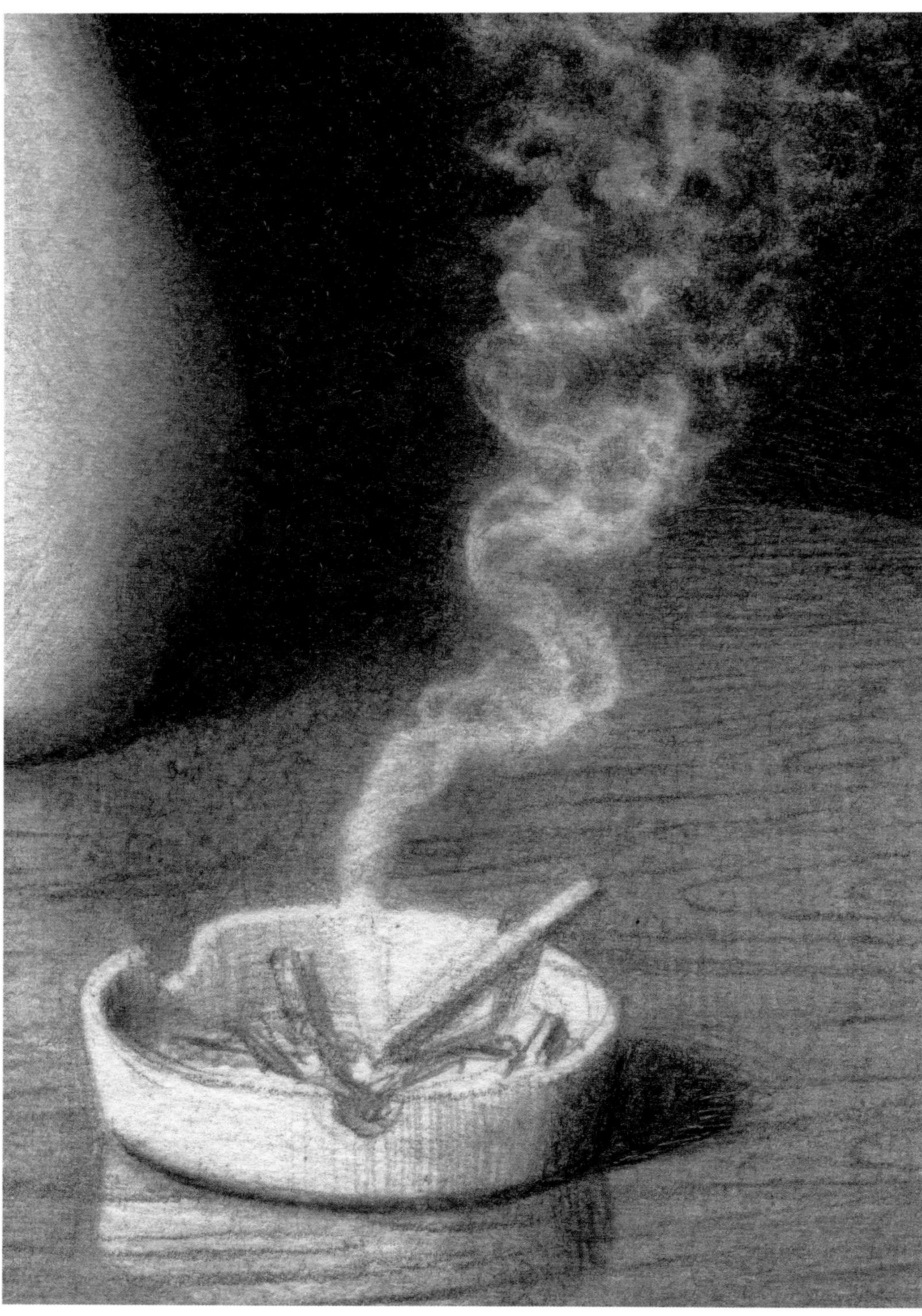

Contemplation
2020

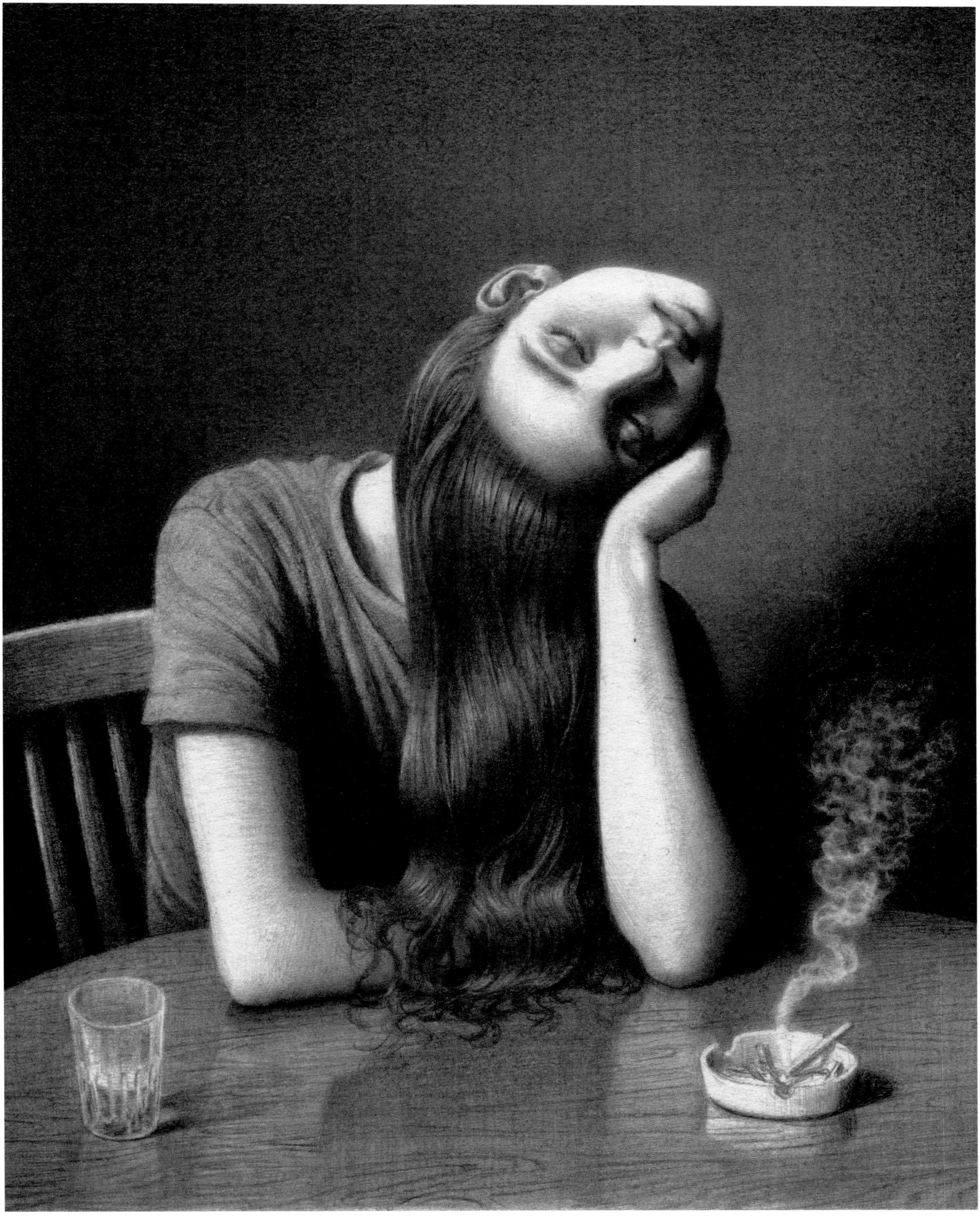

Nostalgia
2020

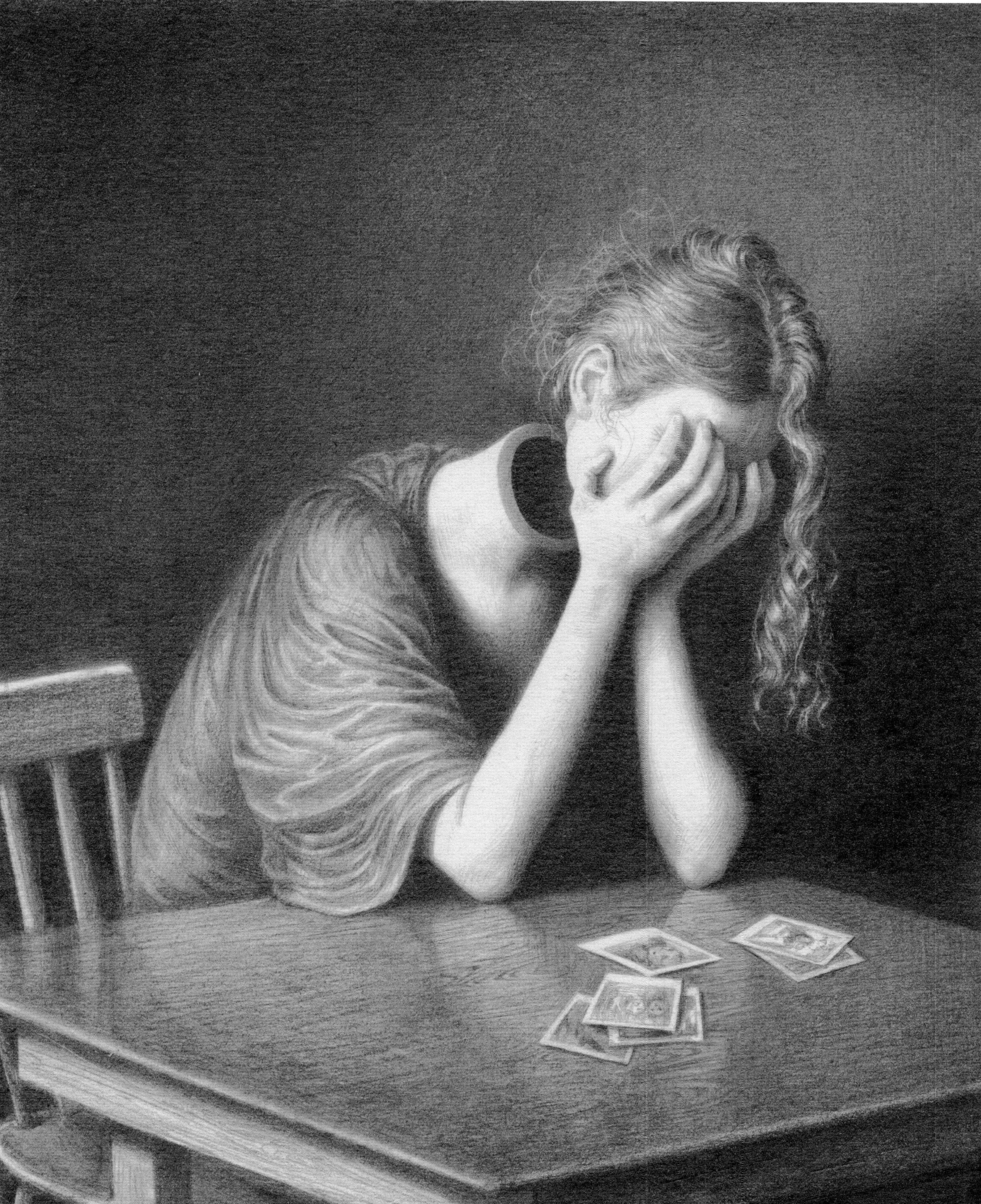

The Impossible, in Vivid Detail

One of my earliest artistic memories was seeing the works of M.C. Escher. I was most drawn towards his famous impossible spatial distortions. Images that defy fundamental geometrical constraints, physics or other natural laws. Yet within the confines of an image, he had the power to realize the impossible in vivid detail.

This idea of depicting the impossible with clarity is something that runs through all my works. In my figurative work I am often trying to deny or ignore the actual biological internal workings of the body, instead playing with the body as an object of perception. The intent is never for them to appear violent or horrific. I am aiming for a cleanness and softness that should make it clear the image is metaphorical.

These drawings are attempts to visualize the shared metaphorical language with which we experience our own bodies. When we are terrified, we do not perceive the excretion of cortisol into the blood, or the literal physiological changes happening in the body. Instead we experience them through an internal language of metaphor, it feels like tingling in our hands, or our stomach dropping, our heartbeat in our throat. The way I distort and manipulate figures translates feelings in the body into a vivid visual representation of those moments. Ideally, the exact specifics should remain open to interpretation, I am not so much trying to communicate any one particular experience as I am creating images that are ripe for interpretation.

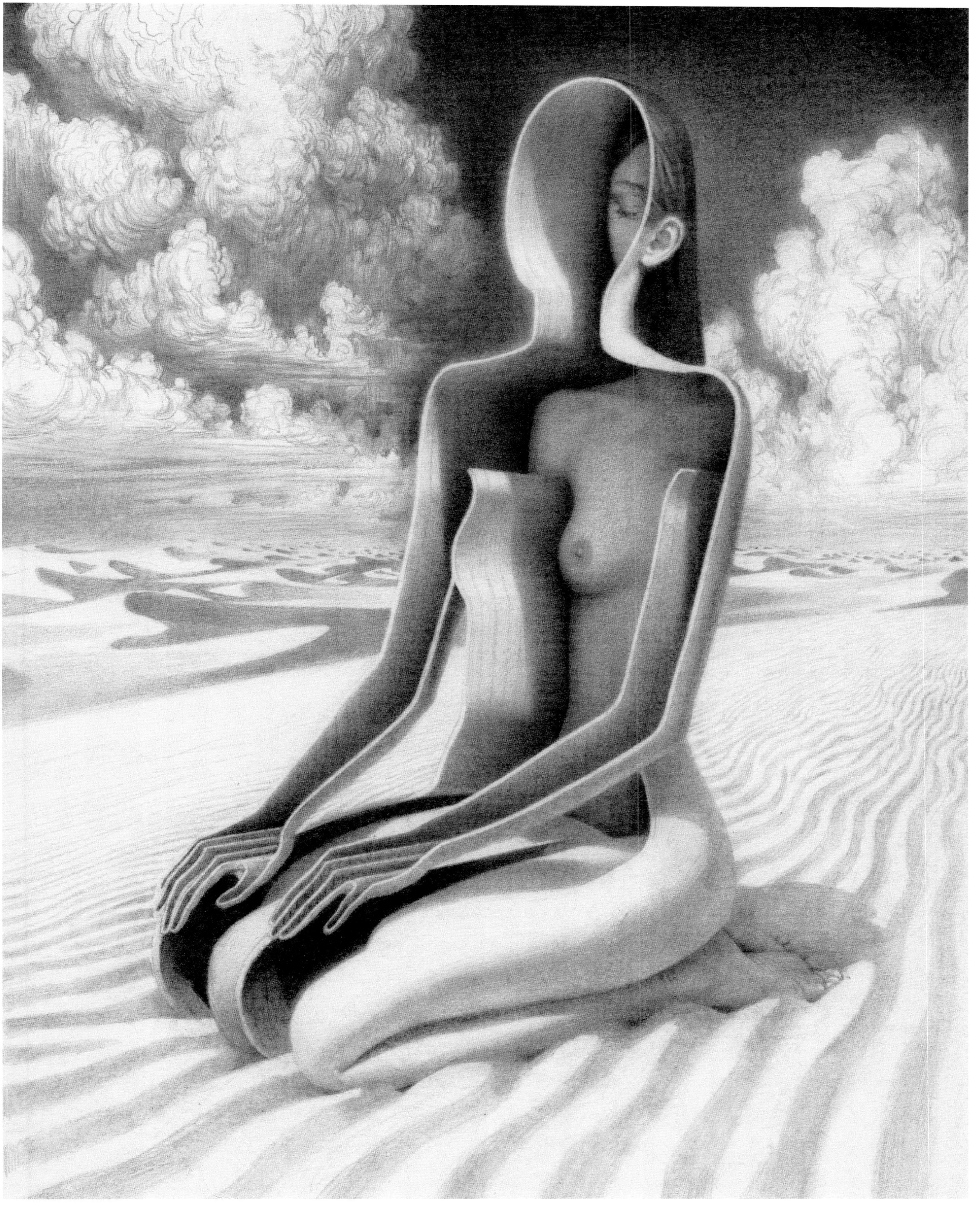

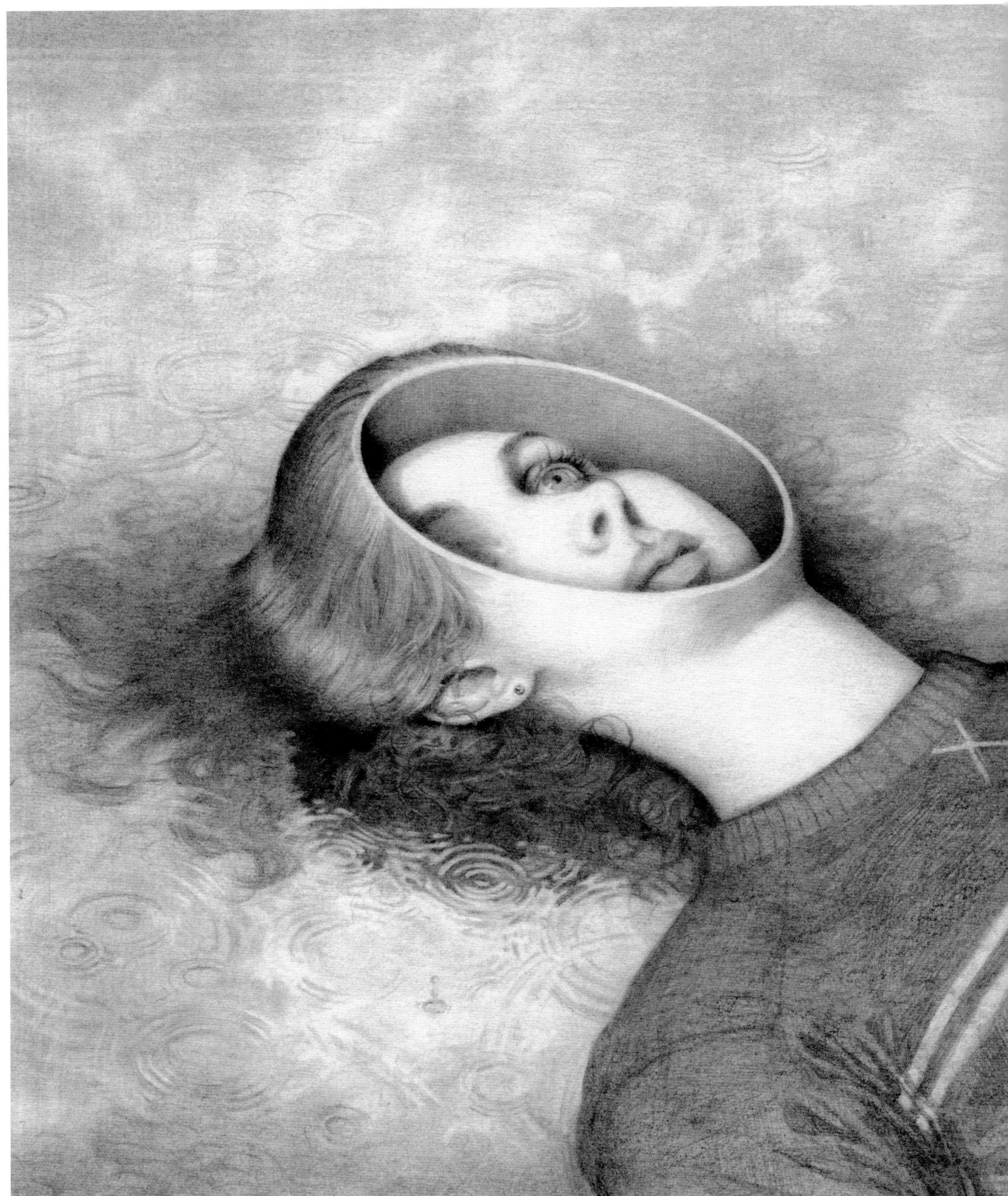

Withdrawal
2017

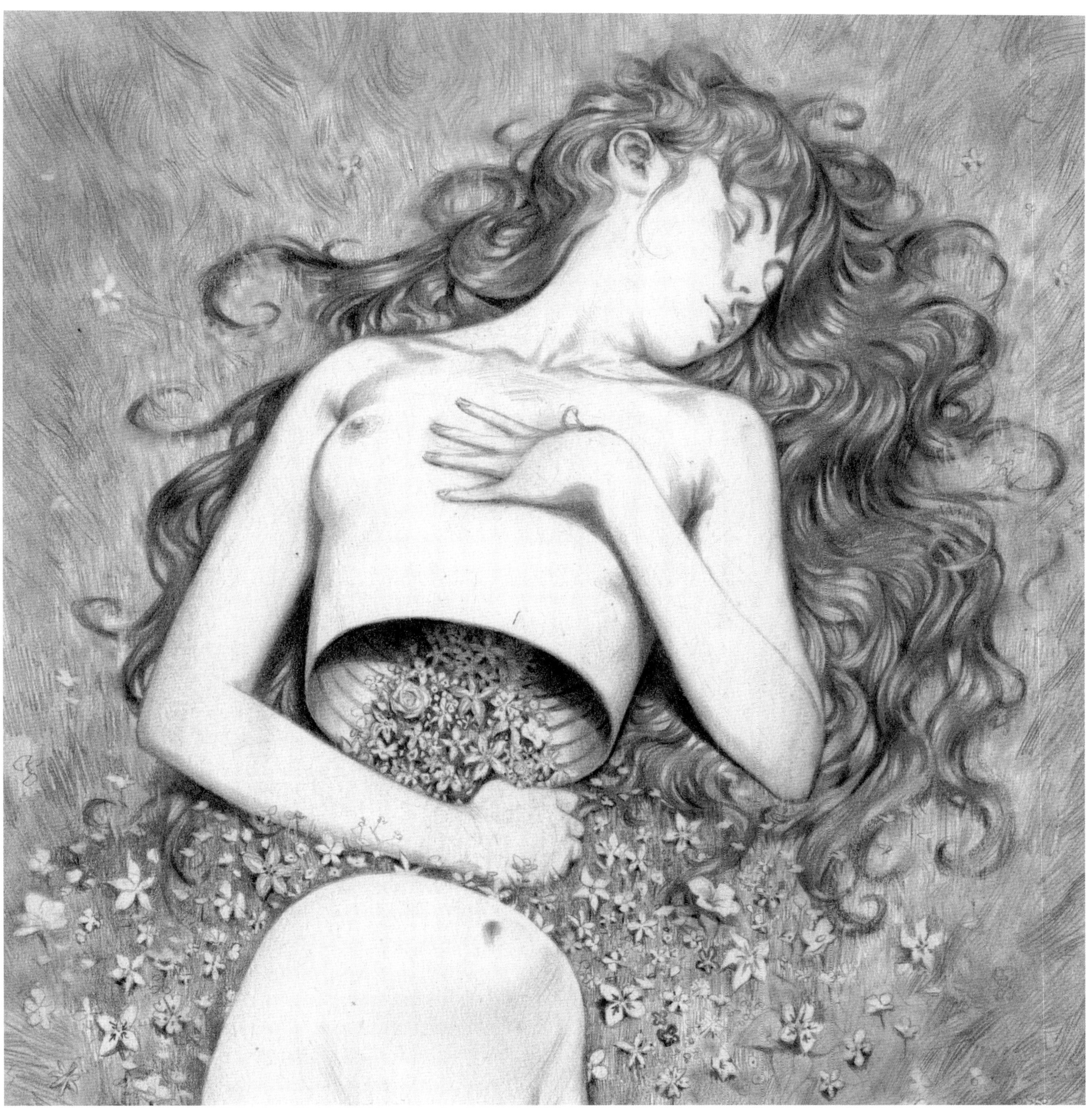

Hollow
2016

Disturbance + Study
2017

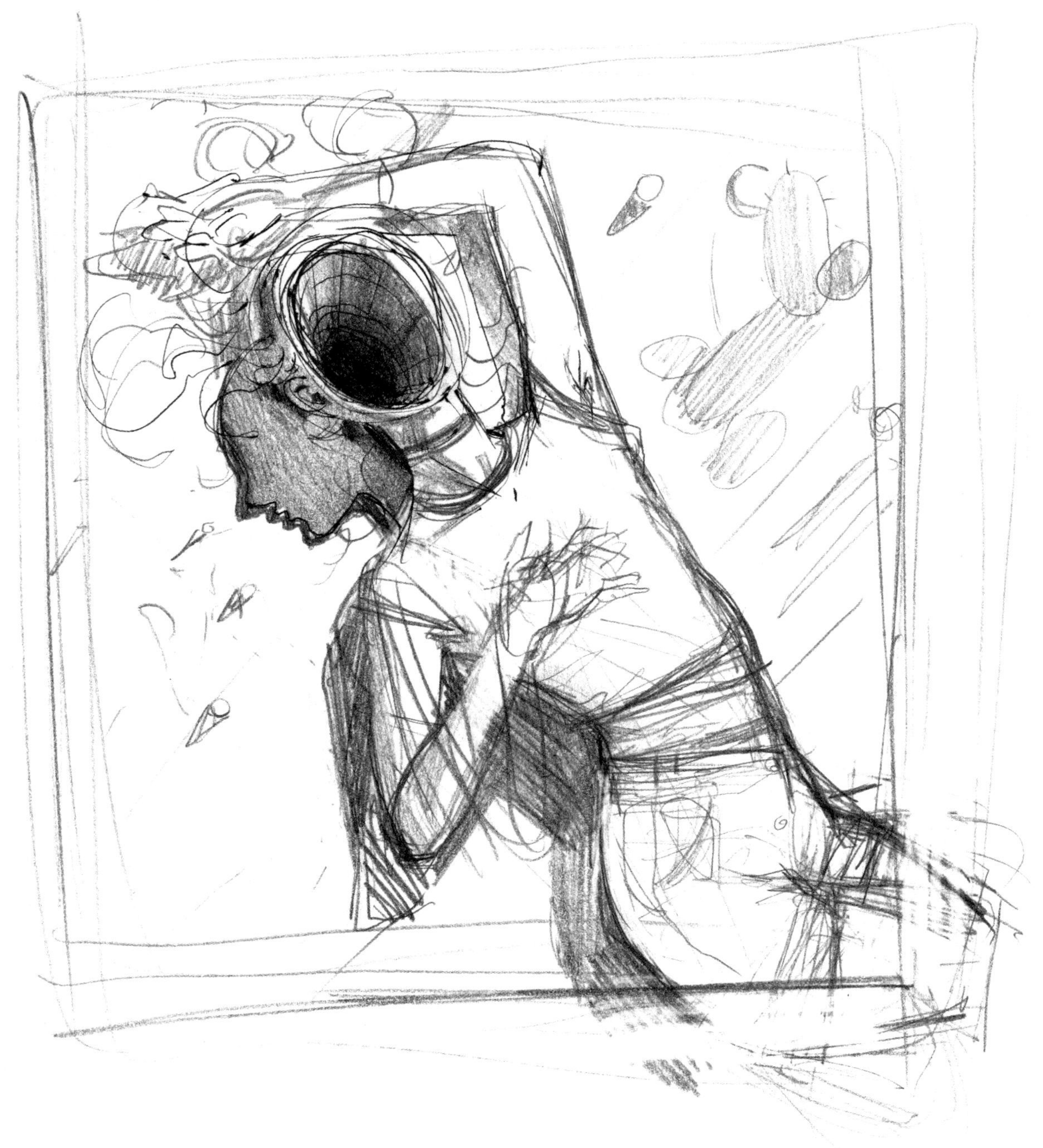

I spend a lot of time observing small phenomena in my day to day life, transient effects of light and shadow, patterns of erosion or weathering. I like to try and model in my head why things look the way they look in a particular moment. *Why does the moss grow on this part of the wall, why do the leaves build up here but not here?* The answers point to a deeper truth, that nothing looks the way it does arbitrarily. Everything in the world is a process. Things are loaded with information, they give us clues about the context in which we find them and their own histories if we know how to read them. I find meaning in appreciating the beauty of the small specifics of our reality and when creating a composition I try to pick things that support the psychological space I am trying to transport the viewer to.

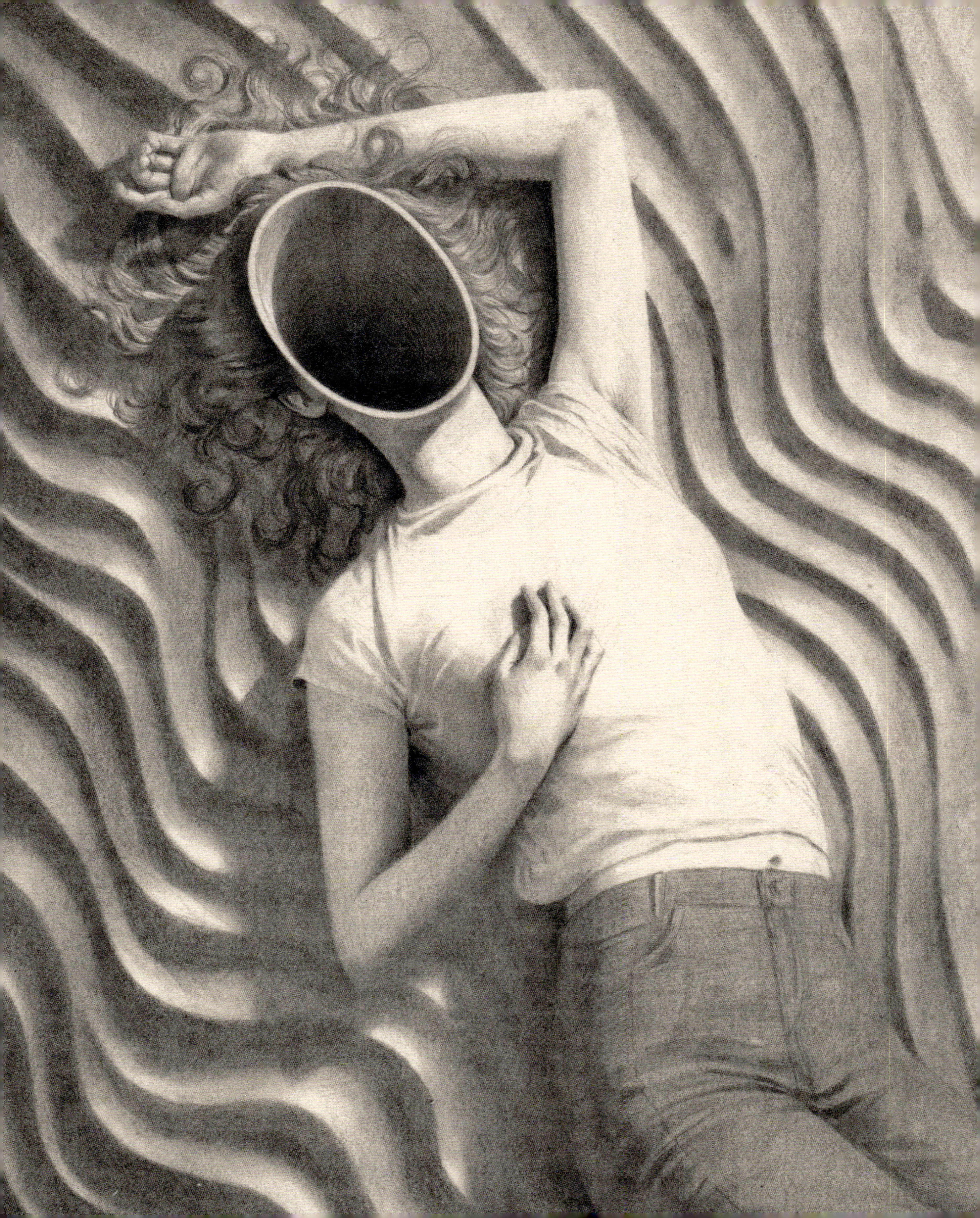

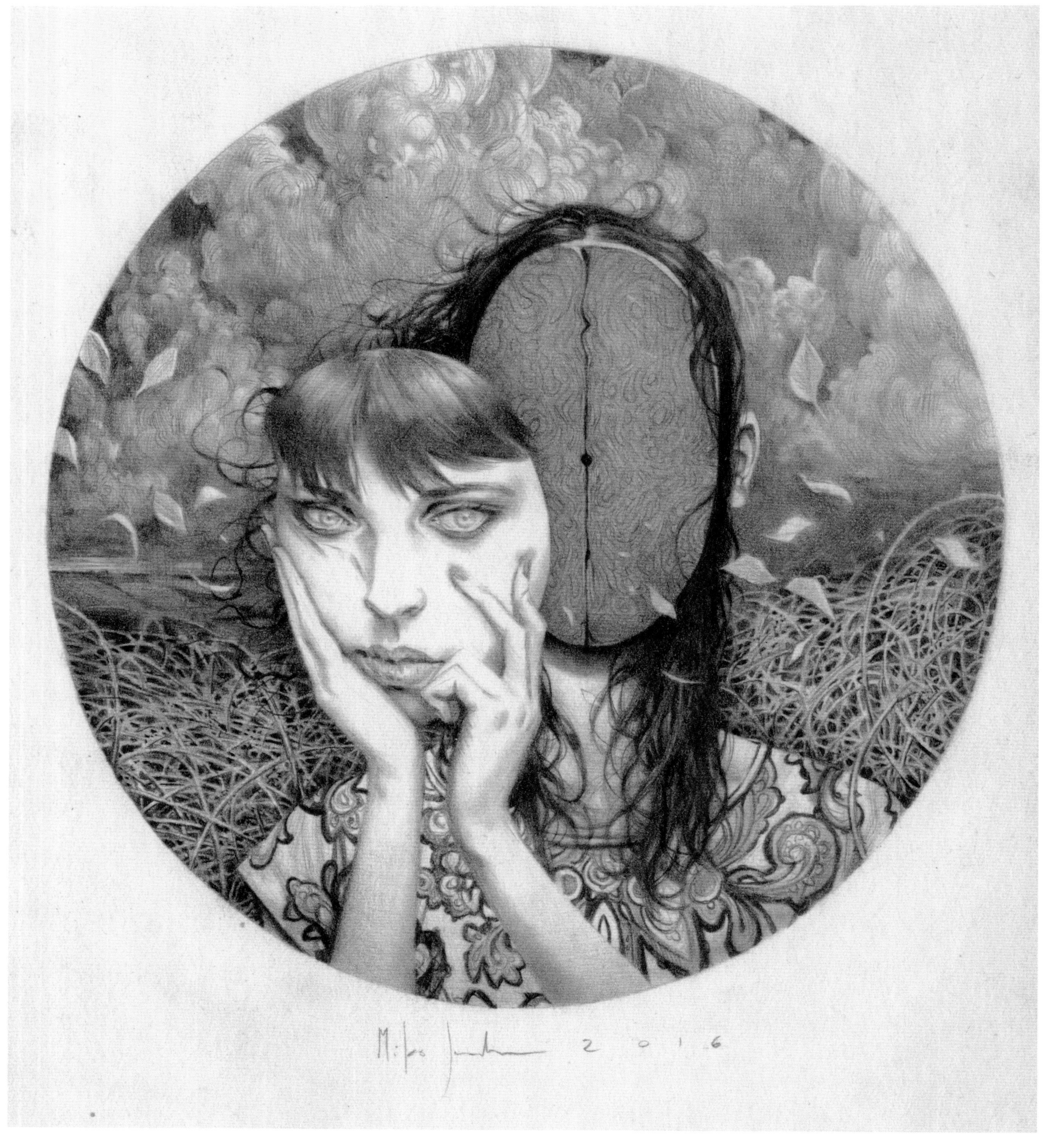

Introspection
2016

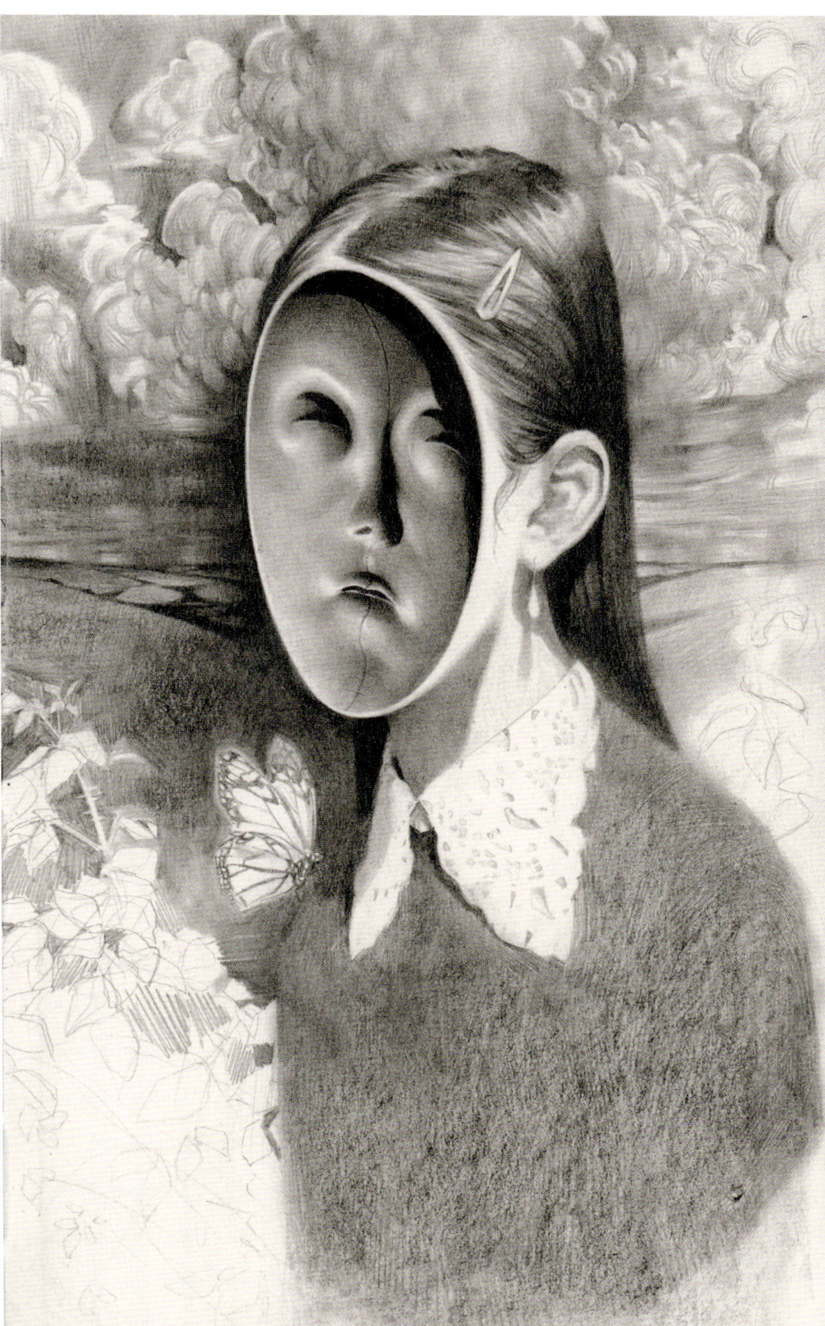

Receiver
2016

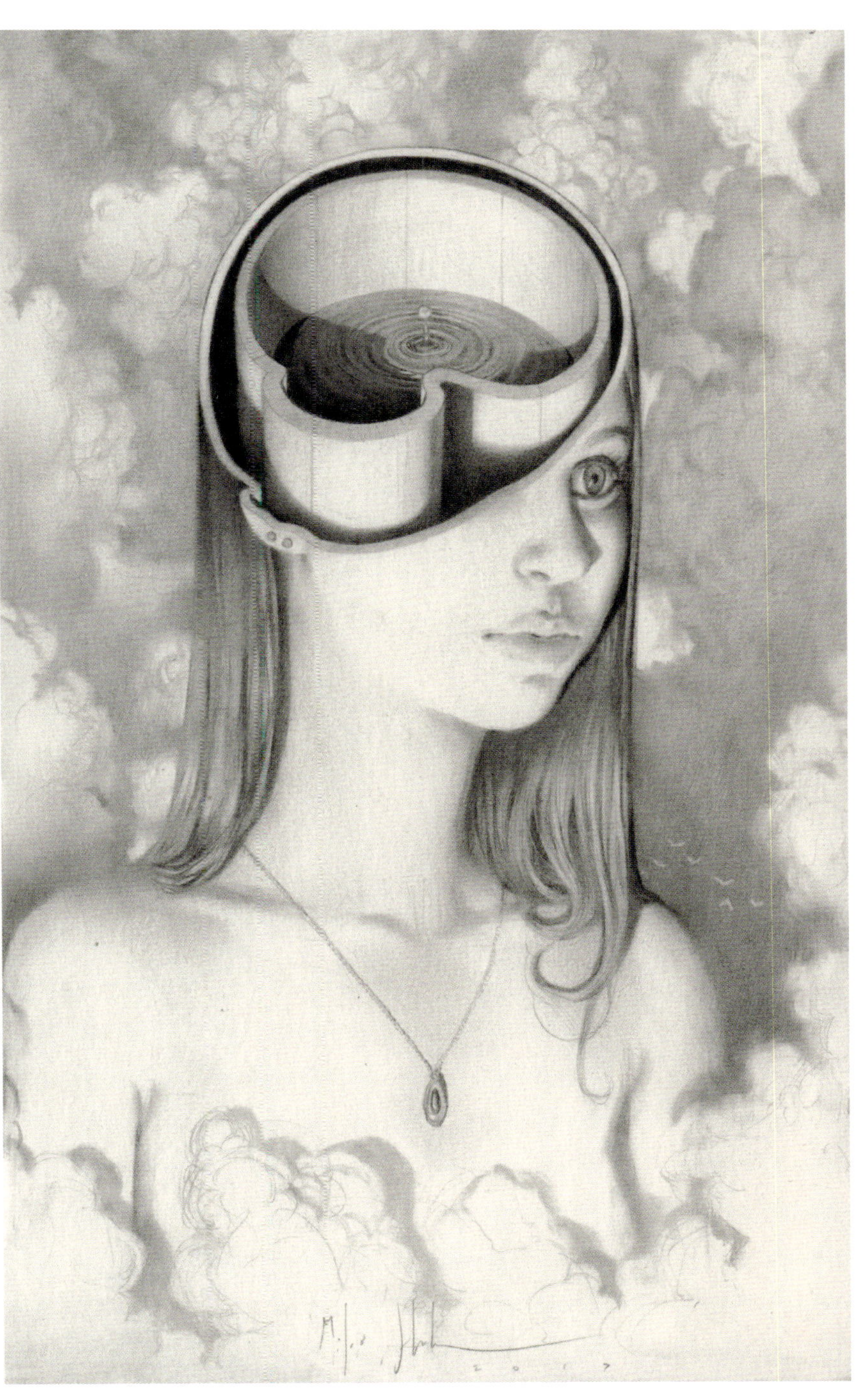

Drained
2017

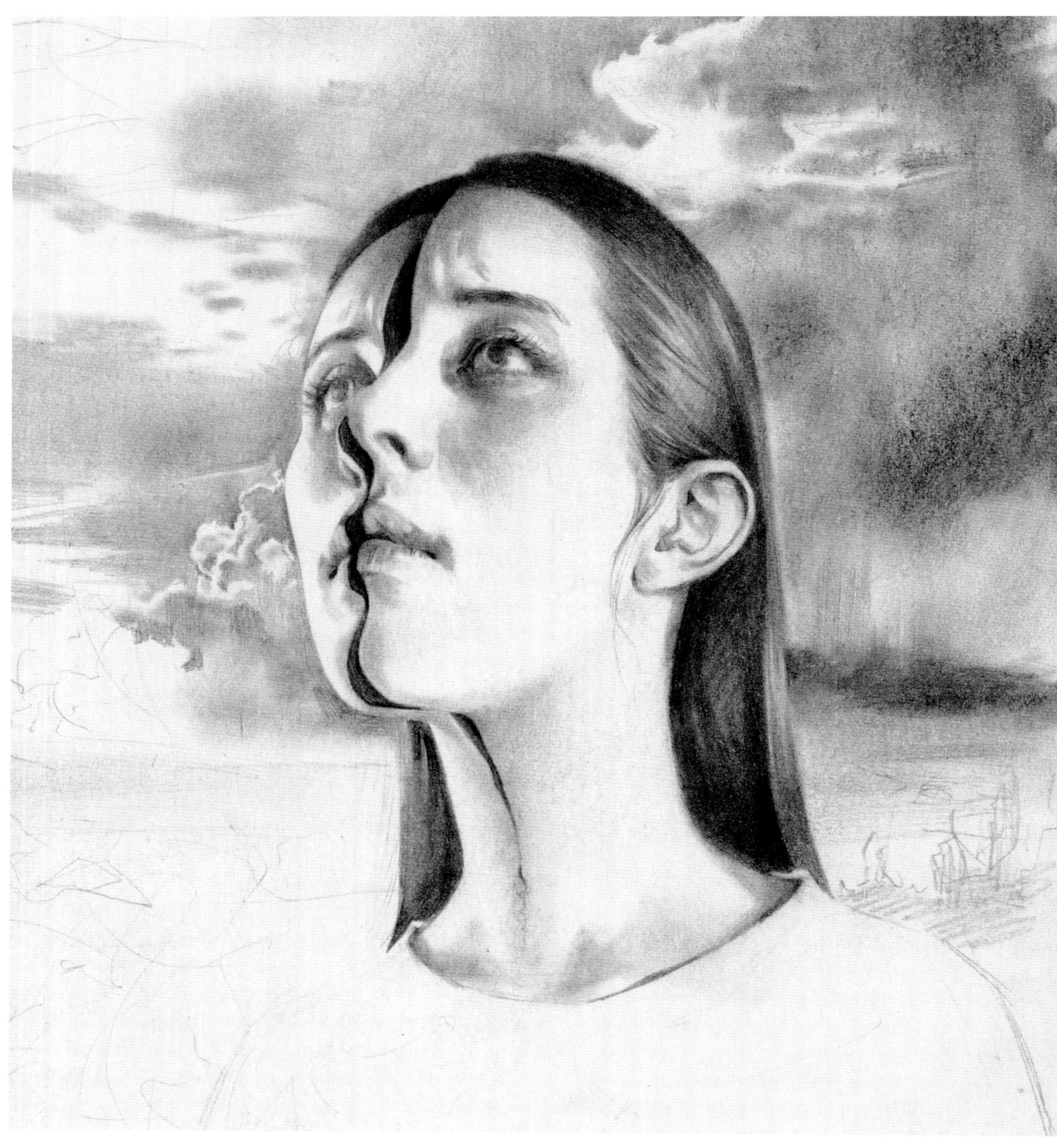

Vertical Misalignment
2016

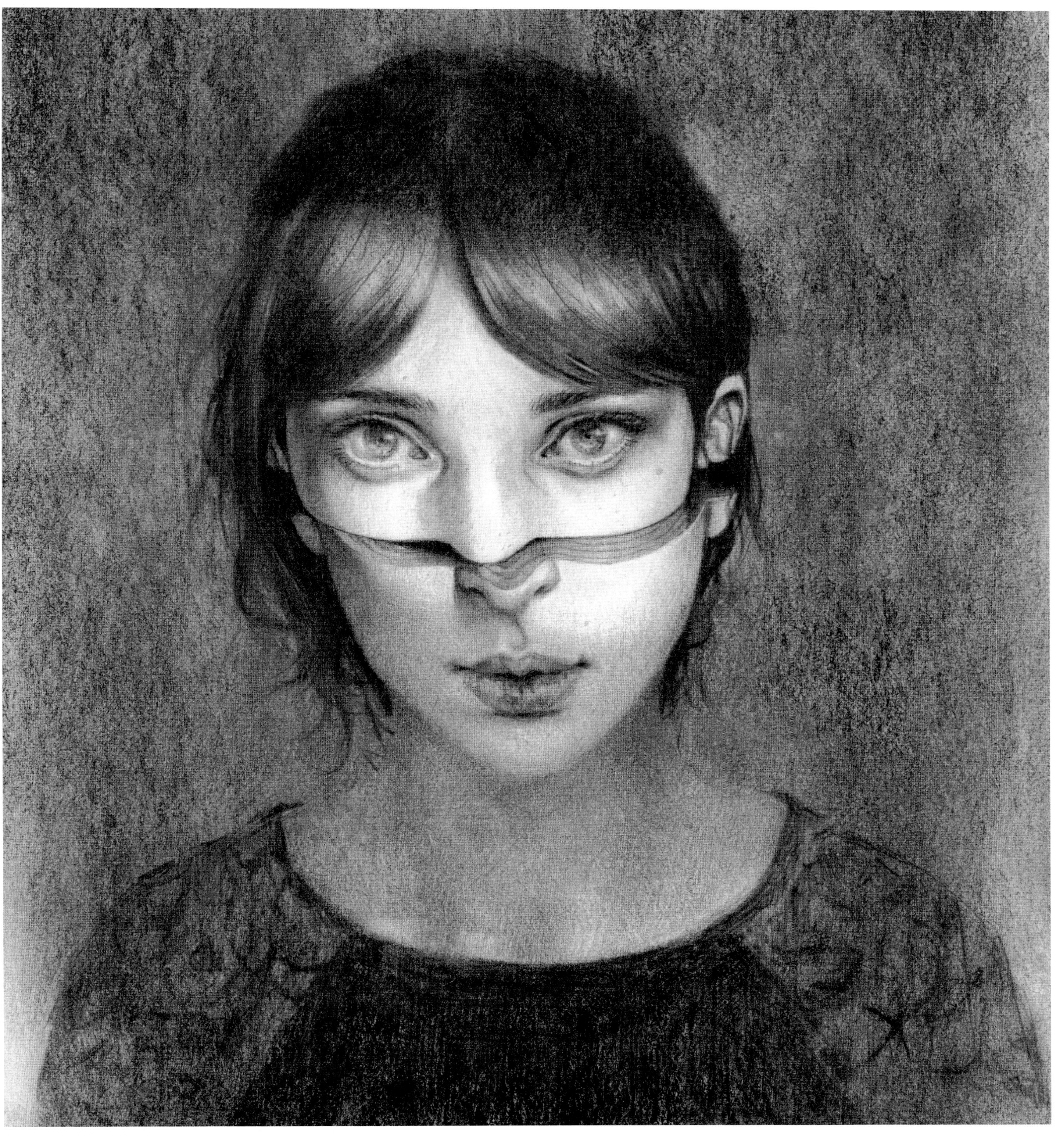

Horizontal Misalignment
2016

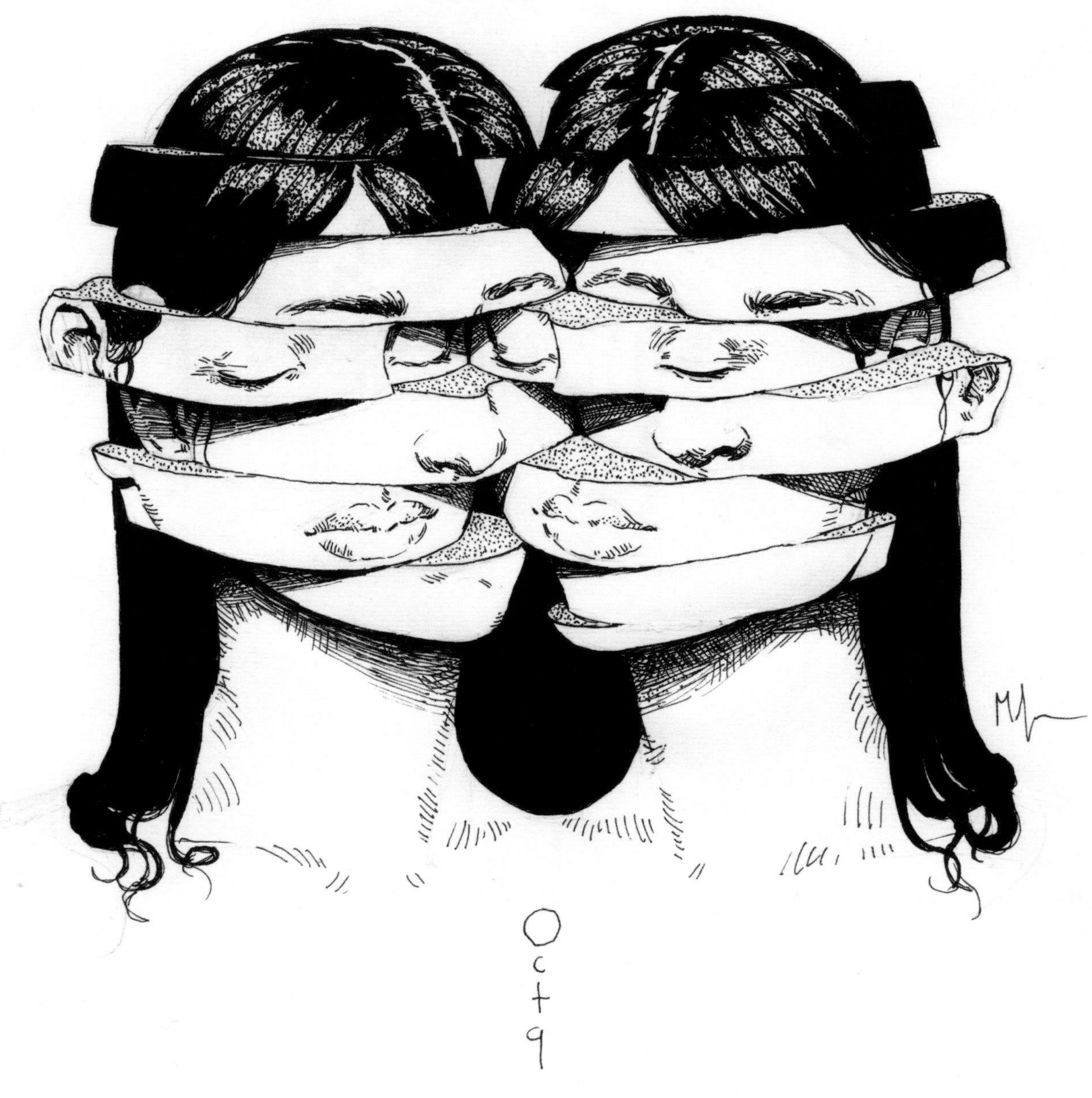

Splice
2018

Liminal
2018

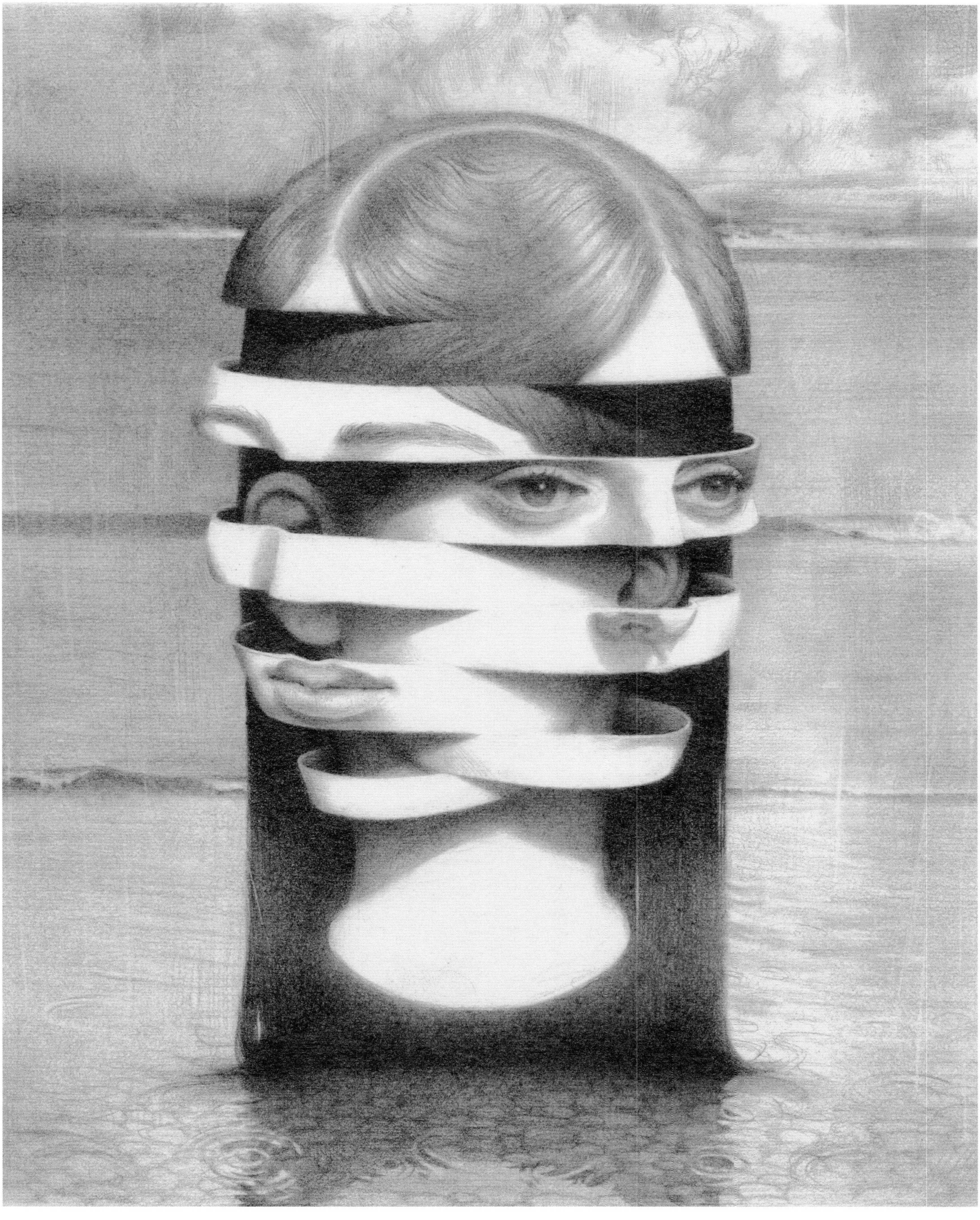

Rings
2017

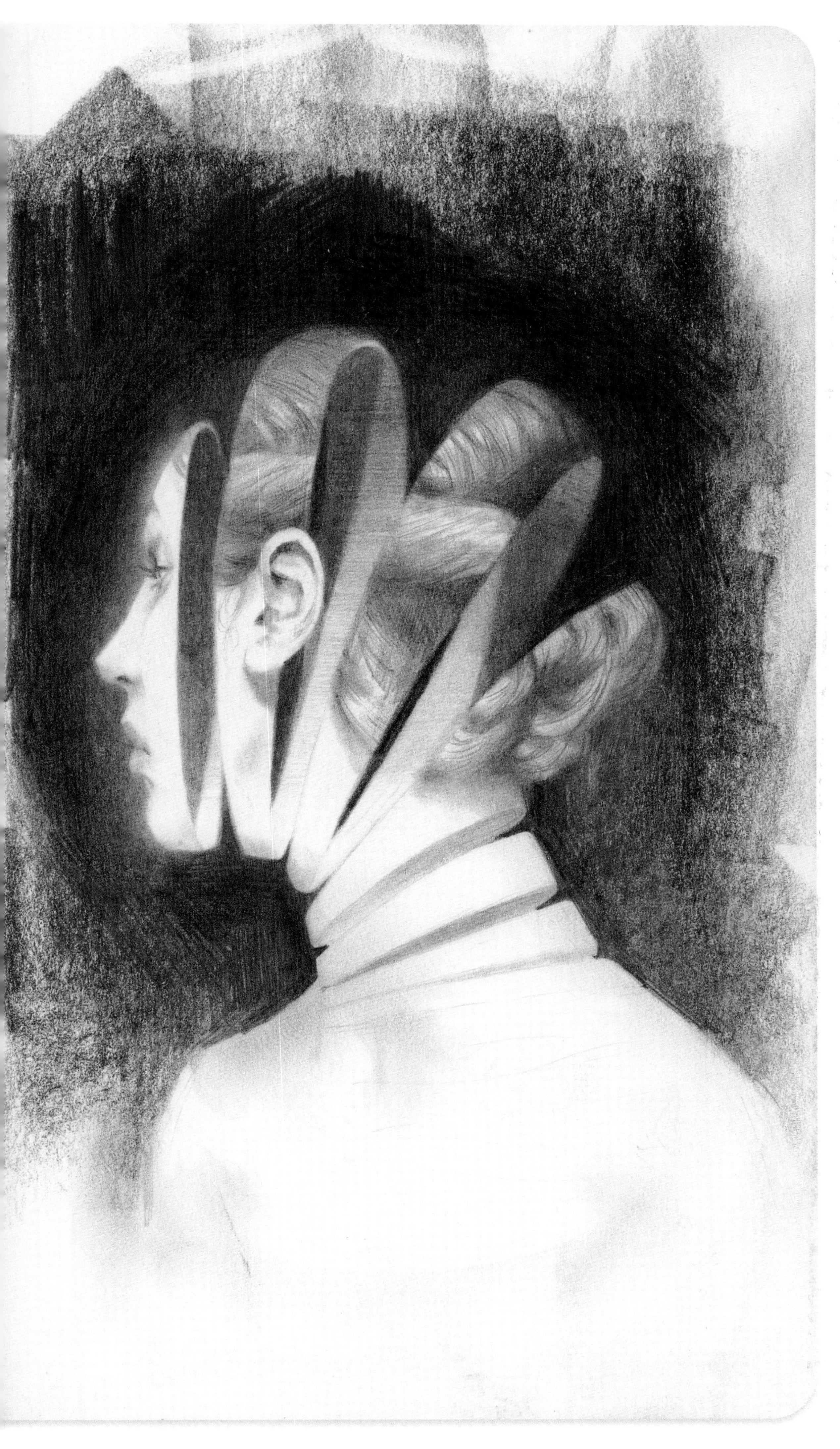

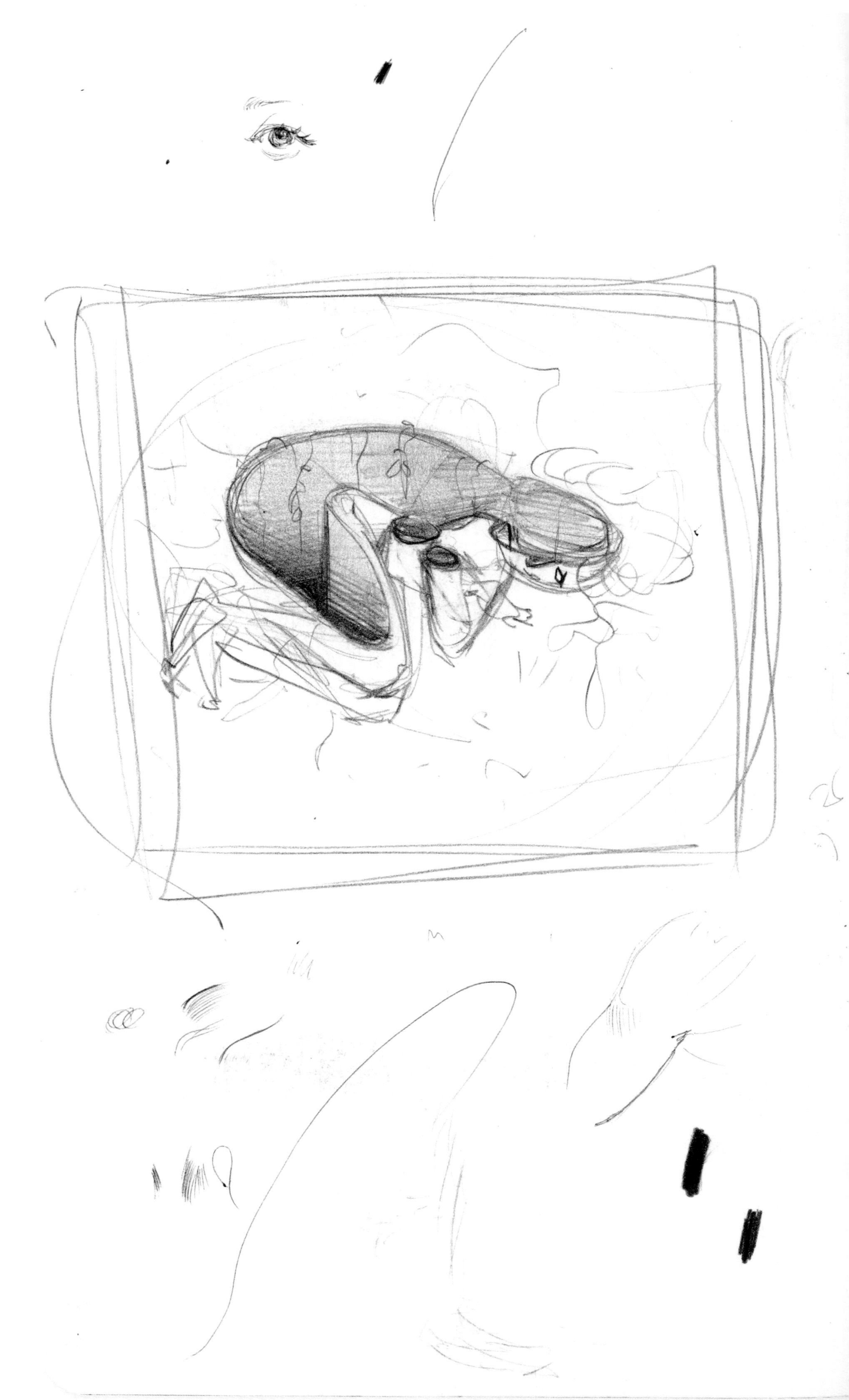

Studies for Inside Outside
2017

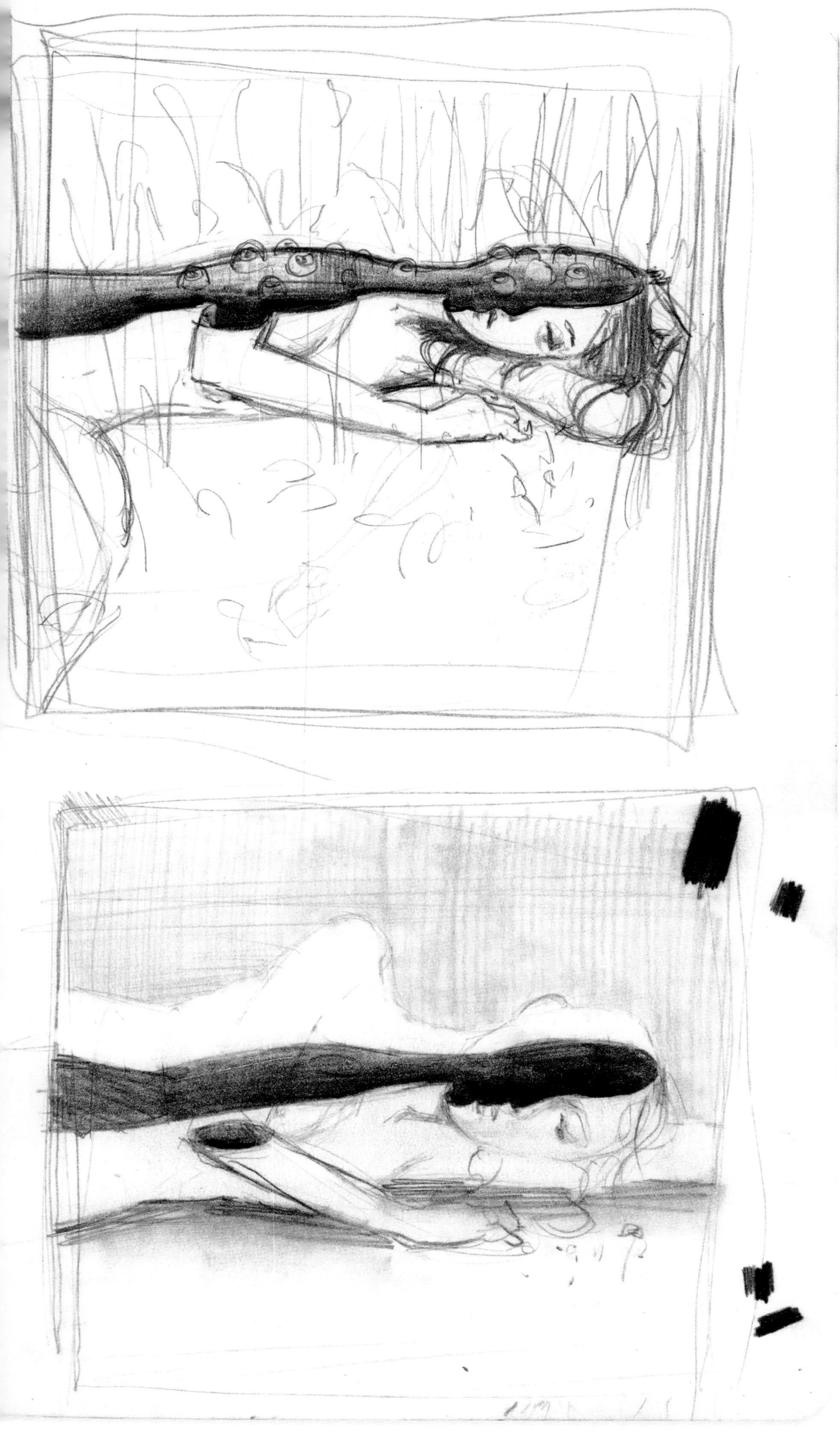

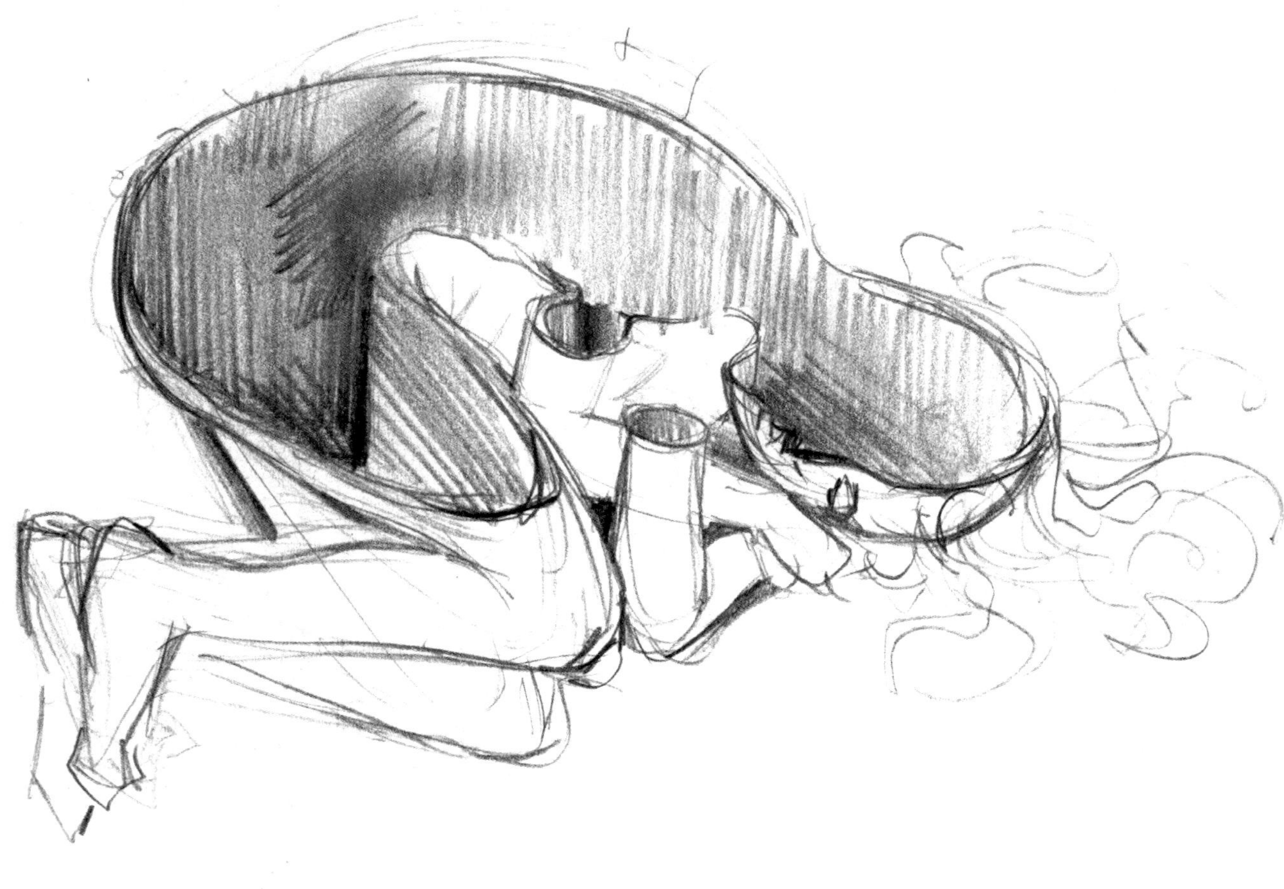

Inside Outside + Study

2017

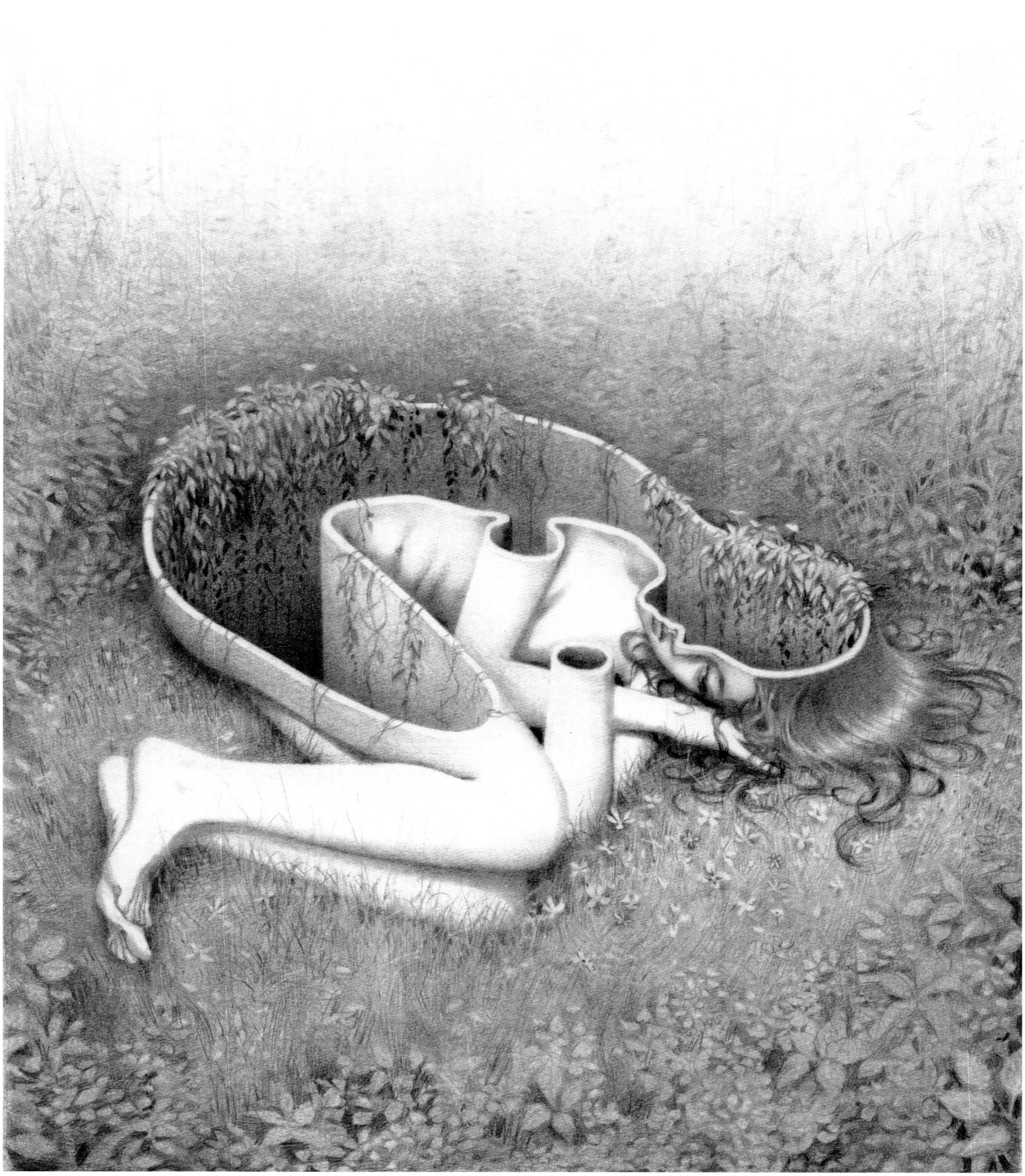

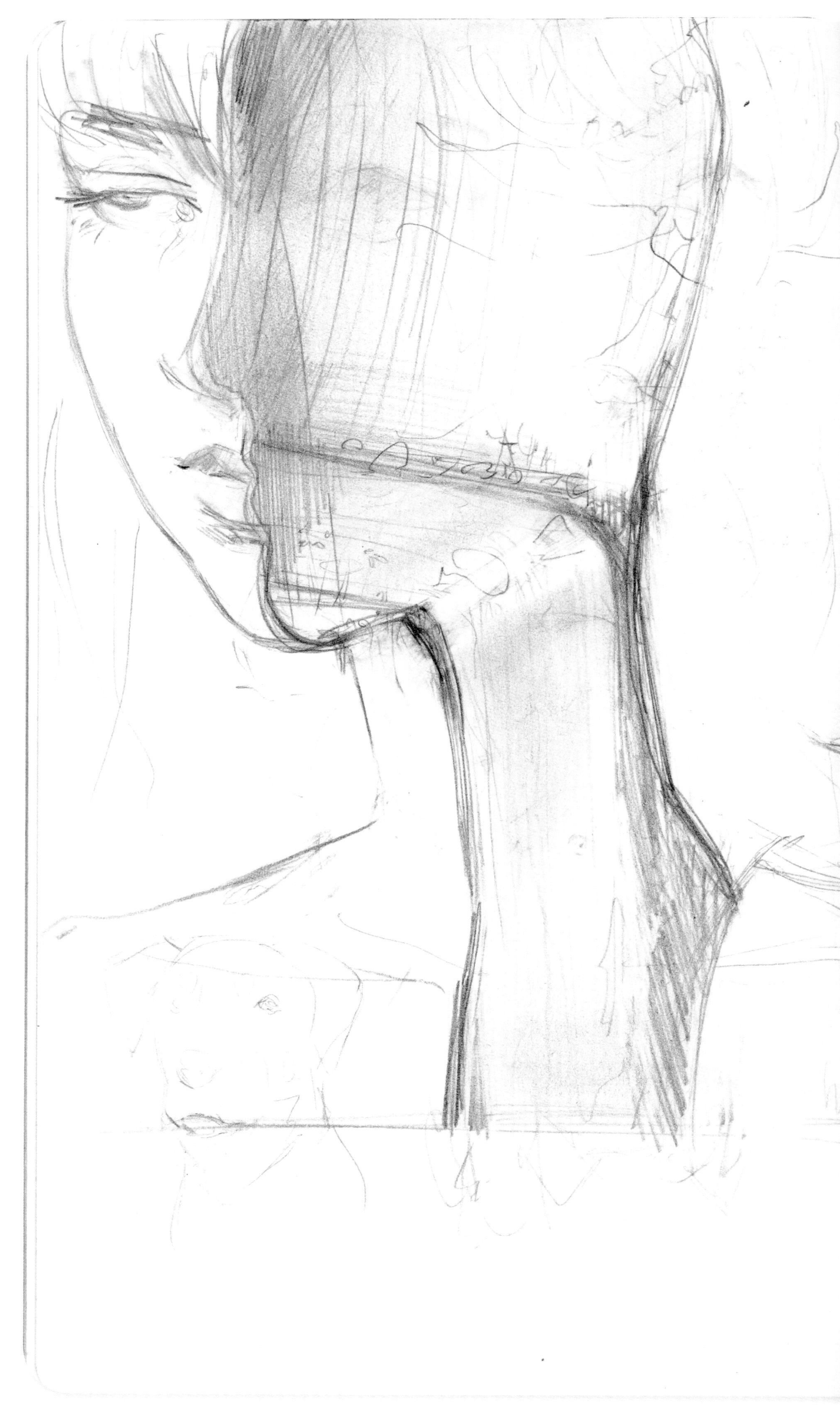

Studies for Overflow
2017

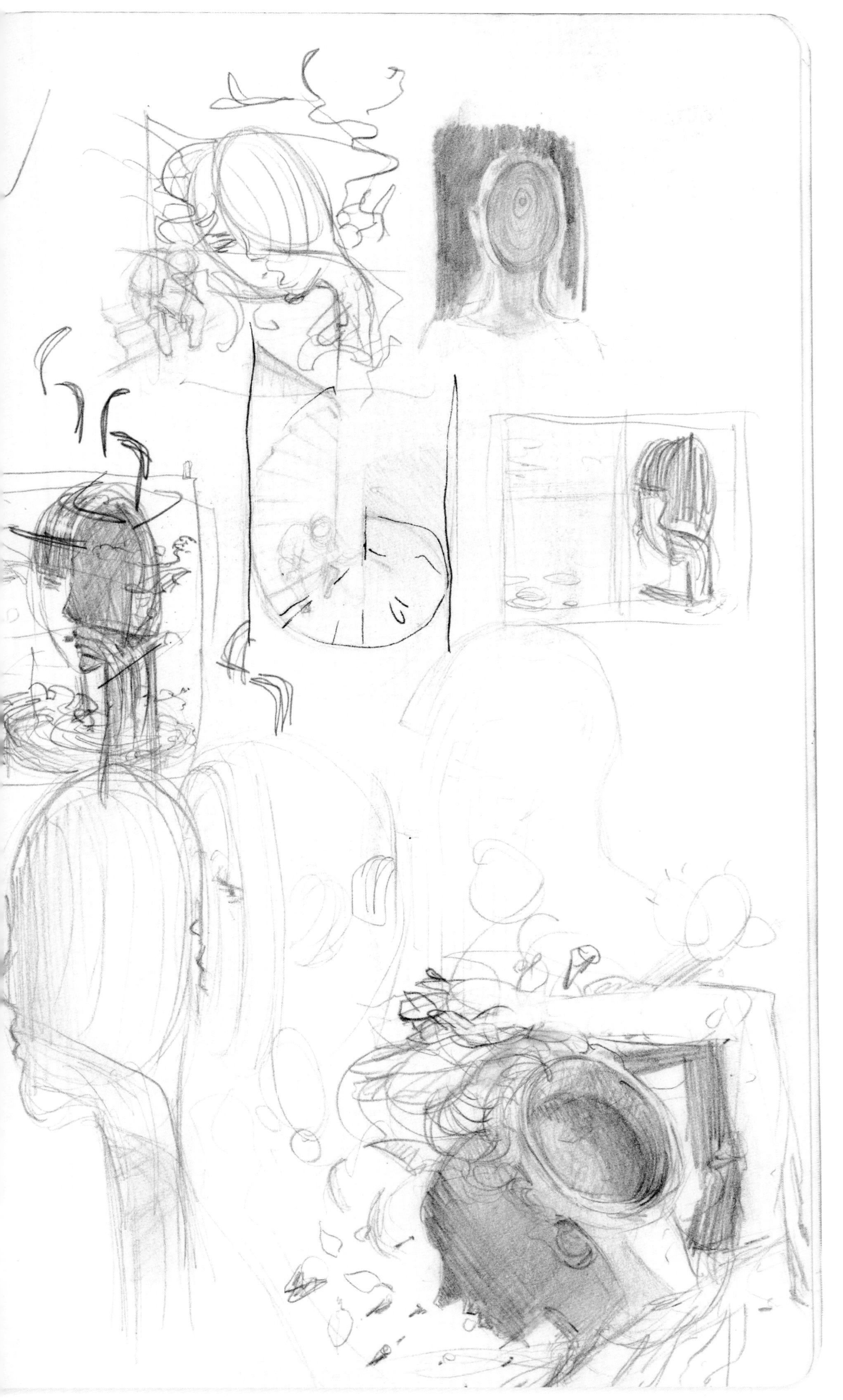

Overflow
2017

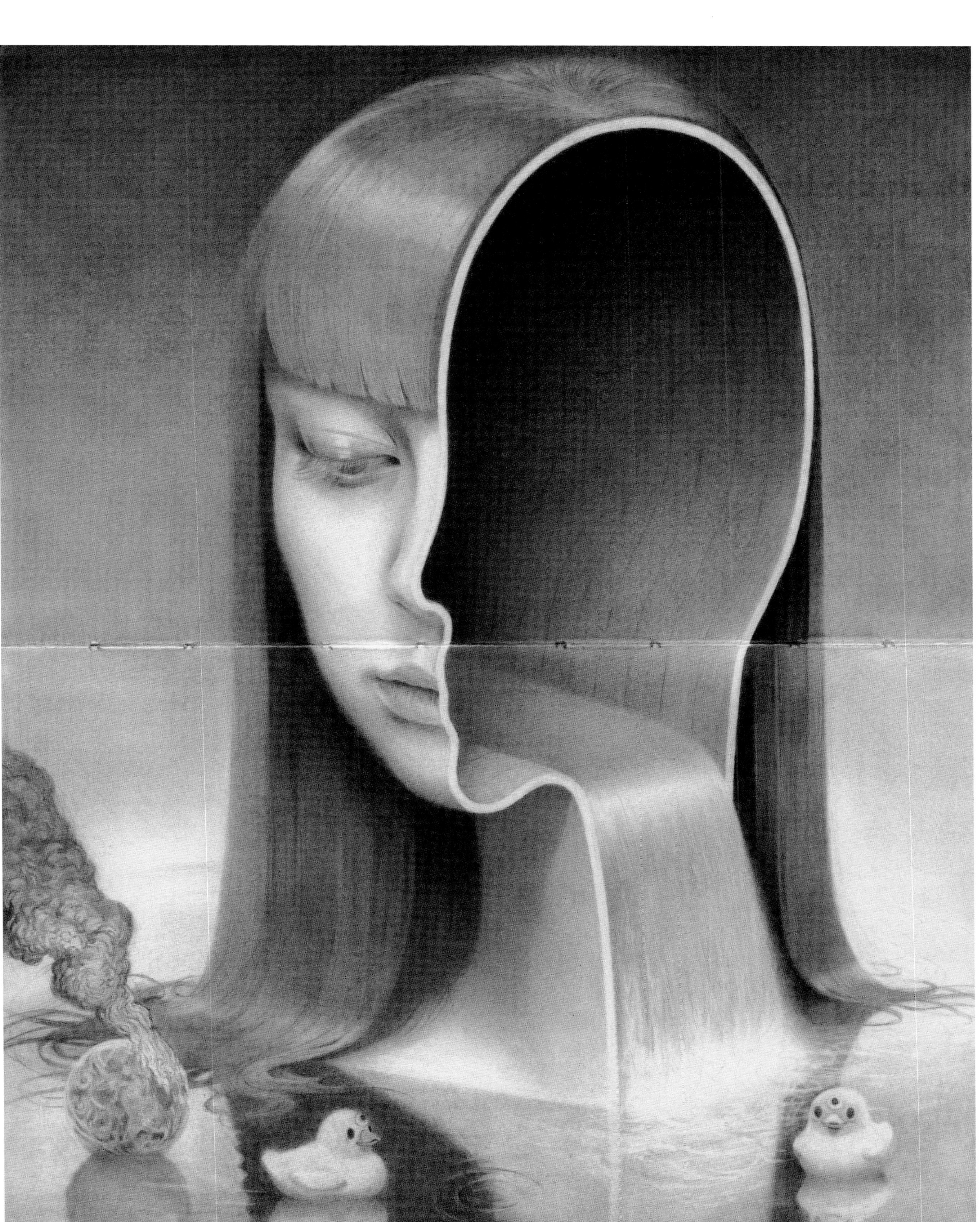

“Every single choice in a work of art is loaded with intention, conscious or unconscious.”

Recursion

Recursion is a theme in my work that is driven primarily from the visual spectacle. Something about the repetition of the same form and its slow rotation or transformation in scale is inherently compelling. It fascinates me like the first time I stepped into an elevator with mirrors on both sides and saw my reflection repeating into infinity. The subject has a movement that begs for interpretation. For a long while I wondered if it made a work of art inherently shallow to begin from a place of pure visual interest. I think this arises from a common misconception about what it means for artwork to have depth. For something to be “deep,” a lot of people expect to be able to say something about the work which produces a kind of aha moment, where the puzzle pieces click together and the real meaning is revealed. In my view, this dichotomy between the surface and the depth, the form and the content, is false. The meaning is so deeply embedded in the technical execution that they are inseparable. Every single choice in a work of art is loaded with intention, conscious or unconscious. It all reveals something of its creator.

There is definitely value in talking about a work of art: hearing a little bit about the

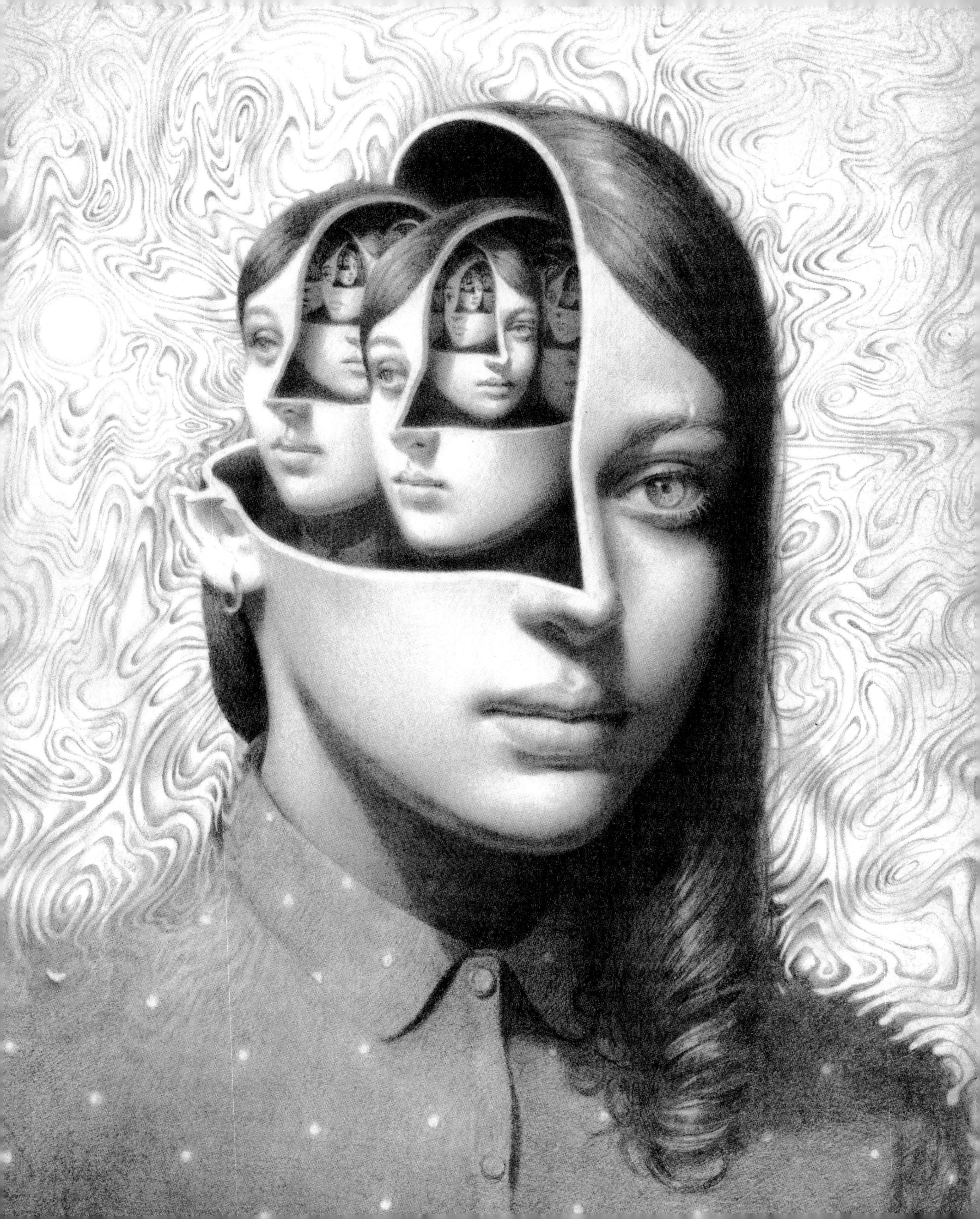

artist's intentions or an insightful critical analysis can sometimes reveal interesting context. But in the end, it is important not to confuse writing or thought about a work of art with the work itself. I sometimes feel like trying to describe what a drawing is about would be like asking a musician to explain an instrumental passage of music. The work is surely inspired by a myriad of thoughts and feelings, which the musician could elaborate on. But fundamentally if you want to understand the music all you have to do is pay attention and listen. If what I wanted to say could be expressed in words, I would express it in words.

A game is being played, of all of the infinite possibilities that could be beheld, the artist has chosen to present this. *How does it make me feel, what kinds of associations, memories, feelings and thoughts arise when confronted with this object?* None of these need to be congealed into a consistent narrative, it is about the constellation of reactions which arise in its presence.

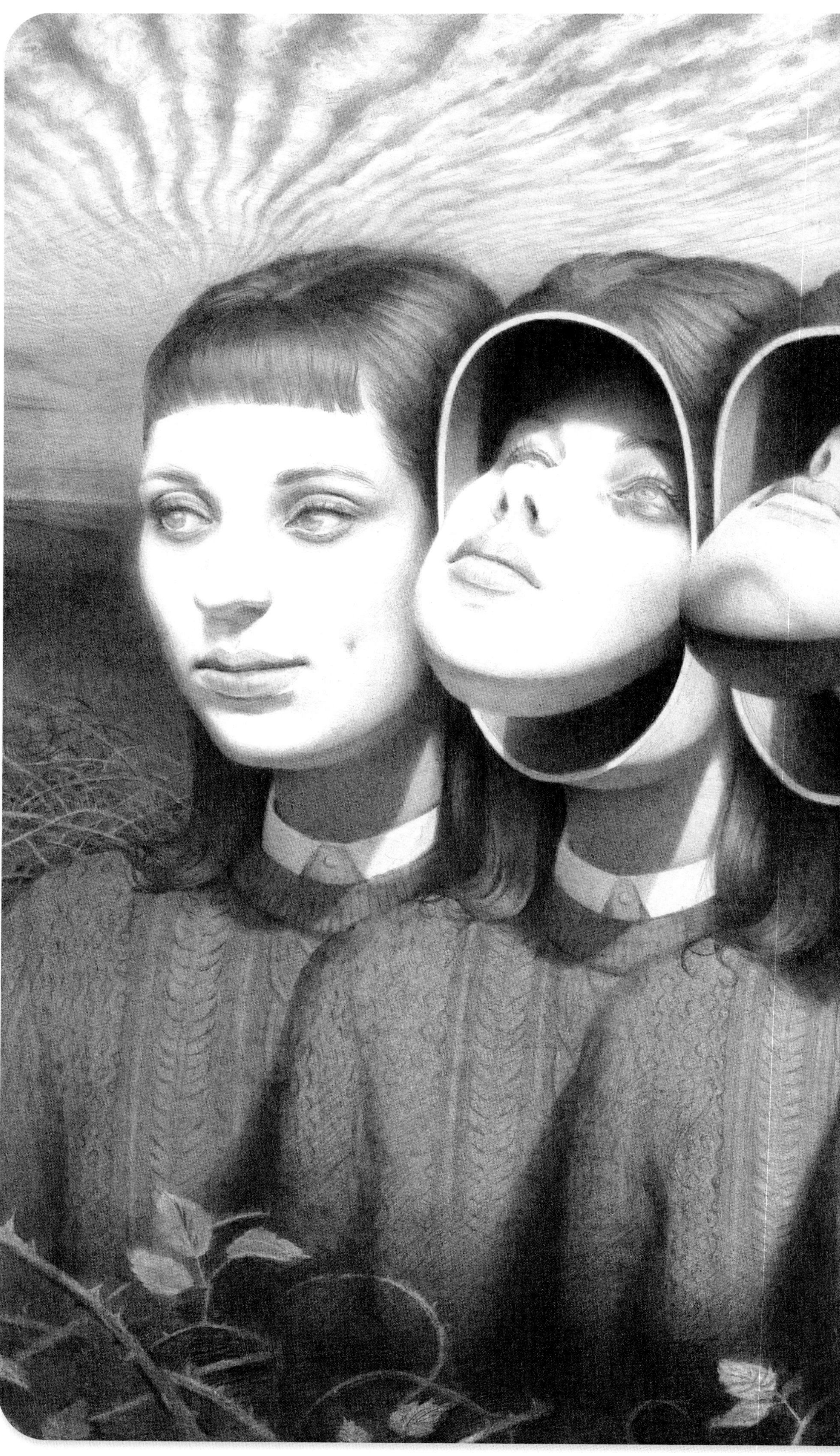

Persona Revolution
2018

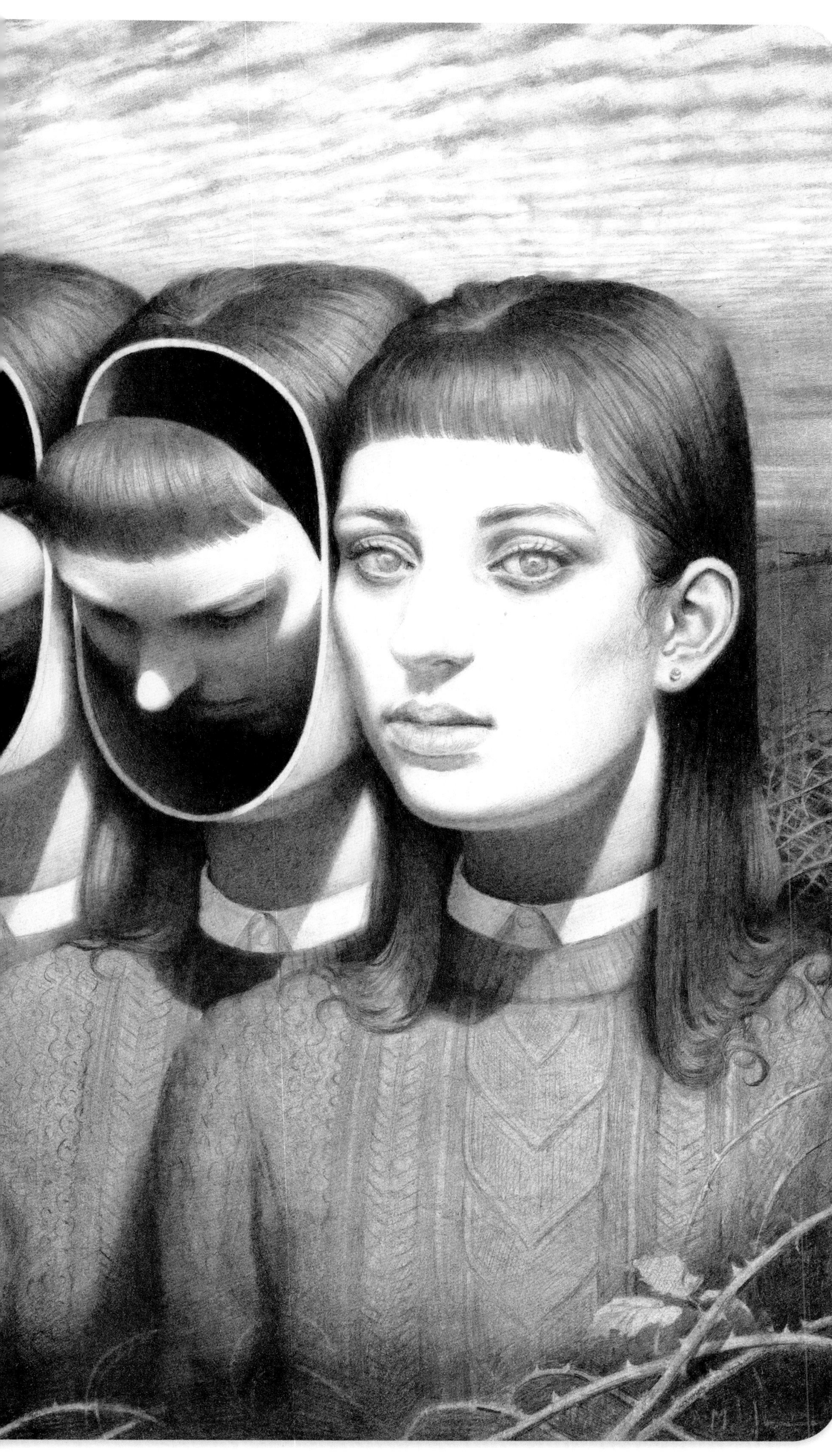

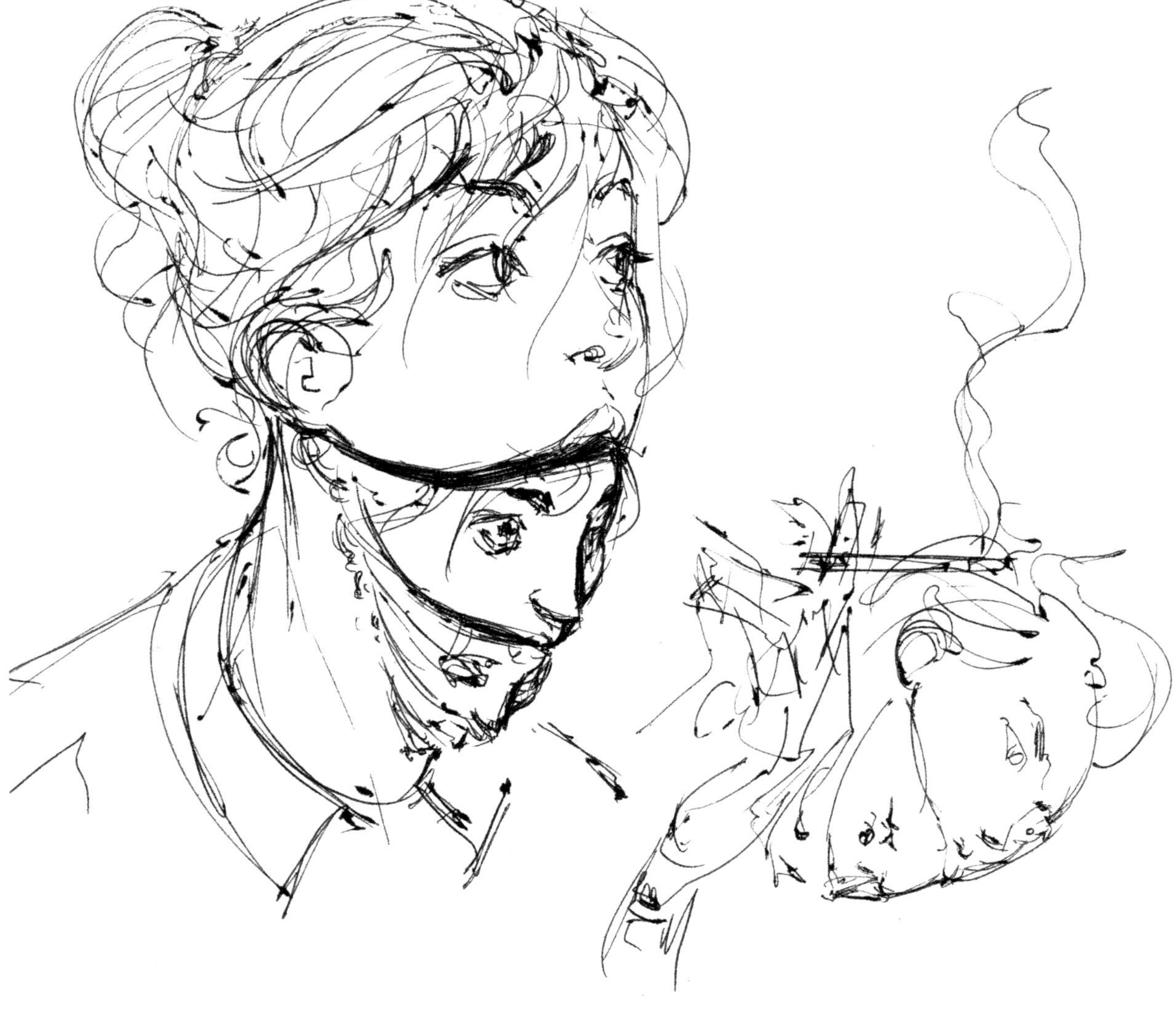

Thought Loops + Study
2016

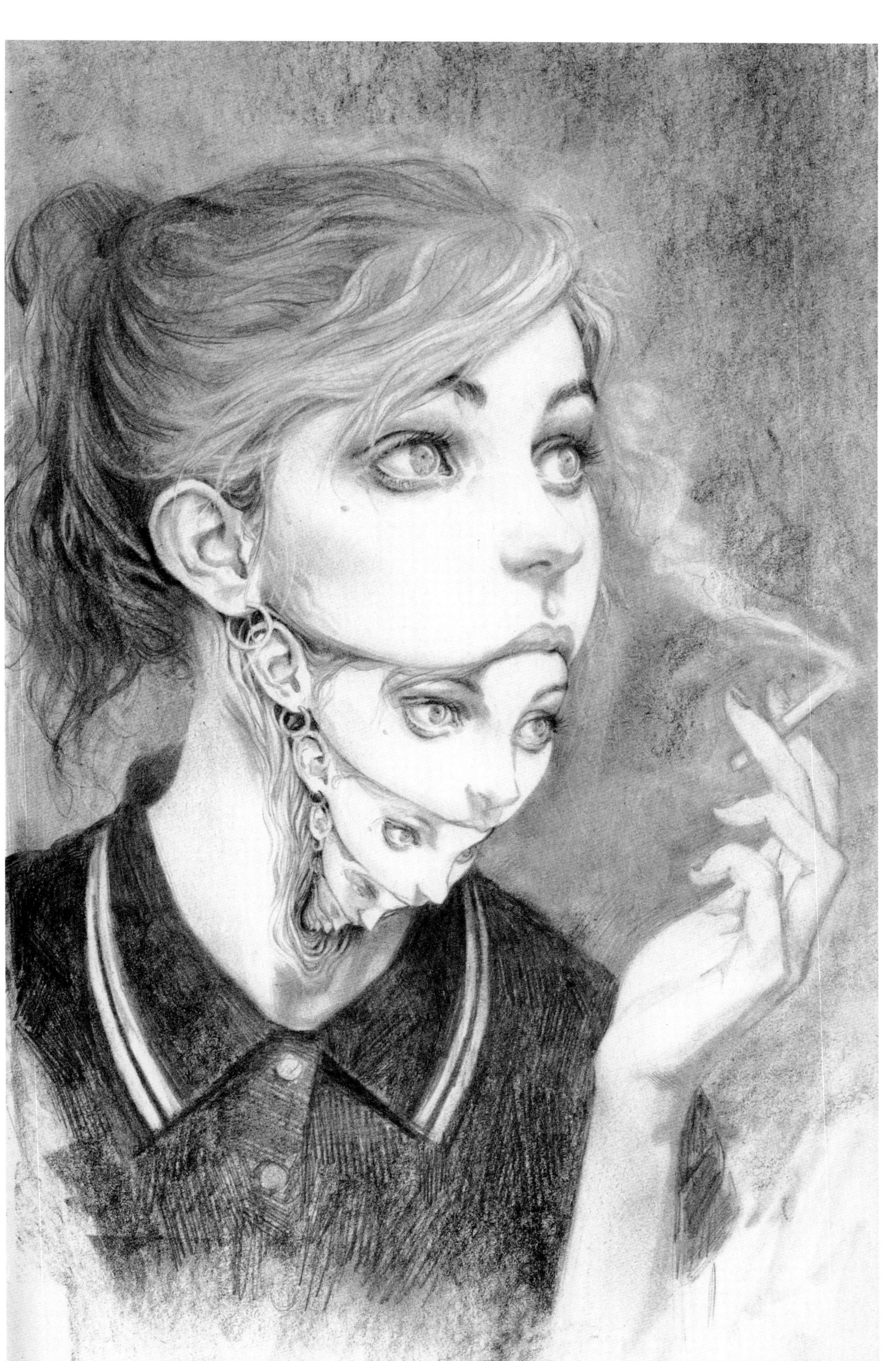

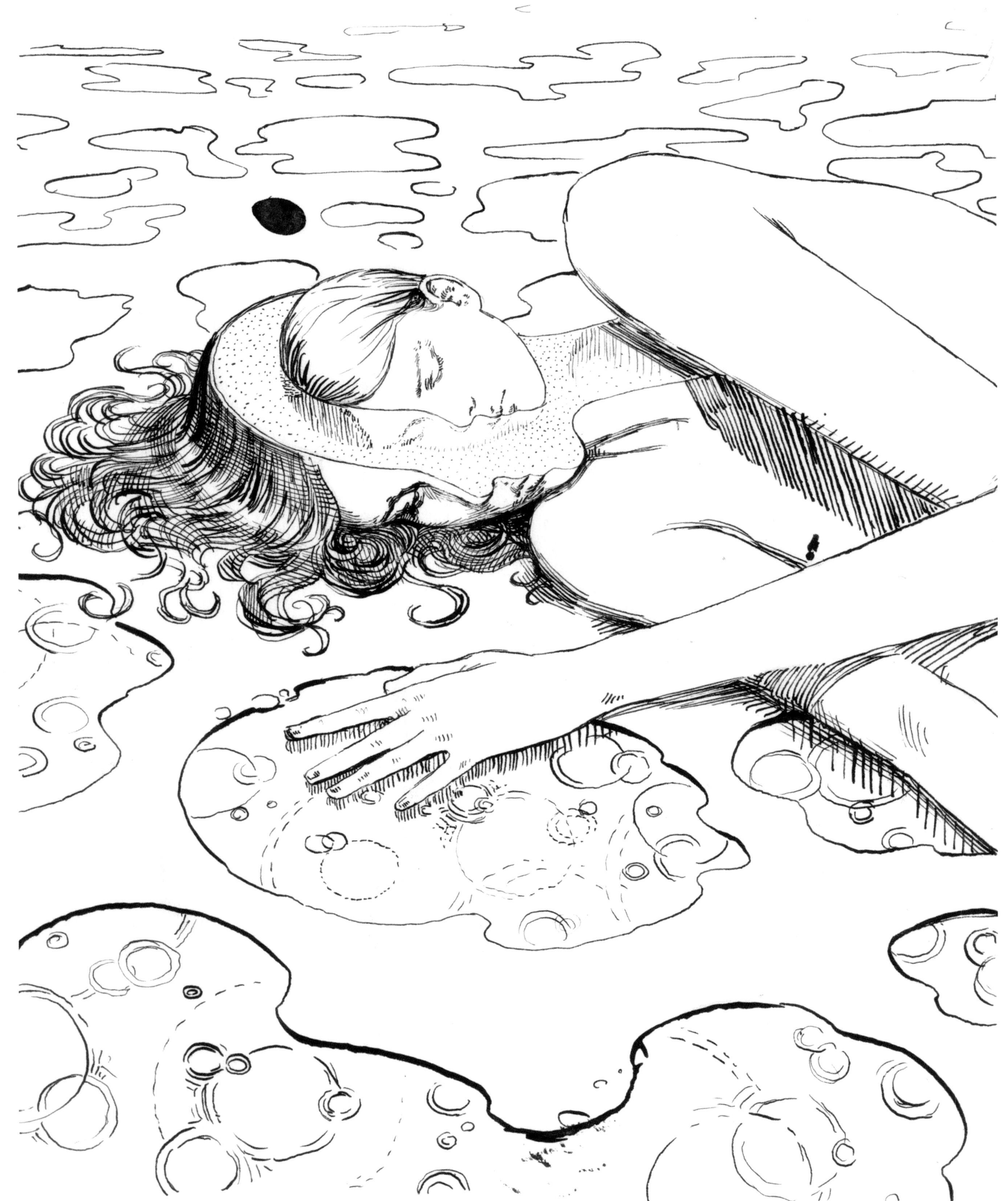

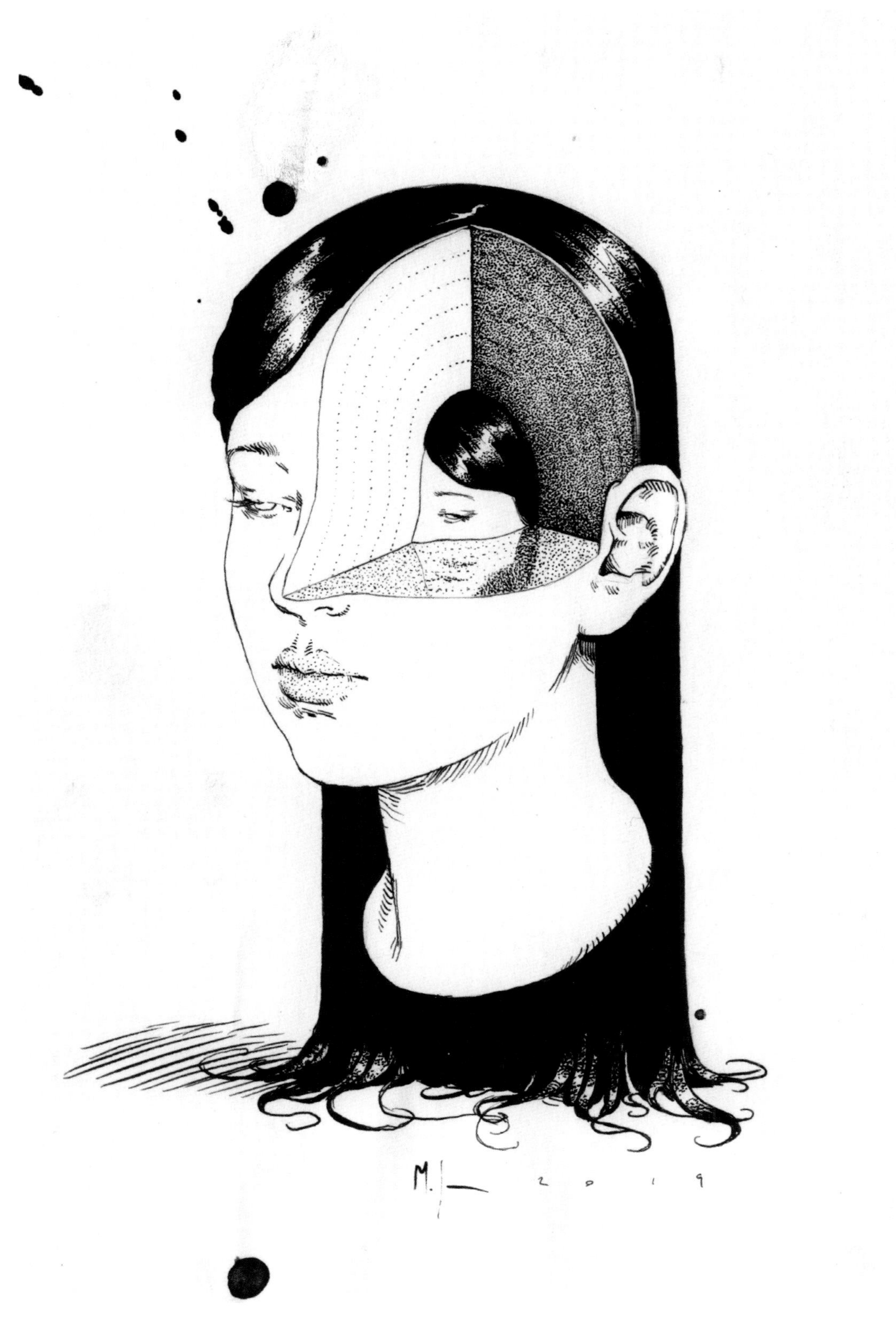

Three of a Kind
2019

Quarter Retraction
2019

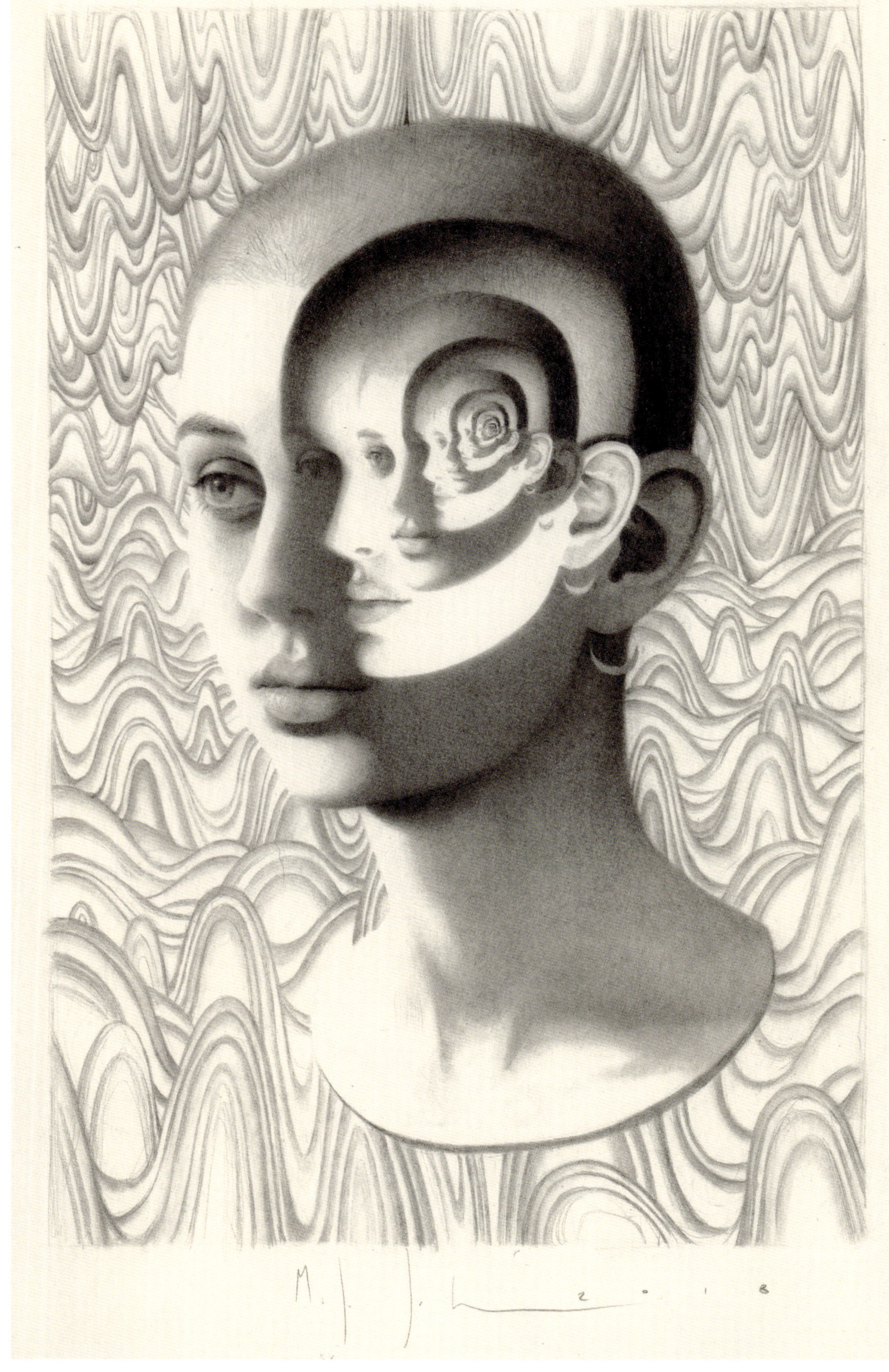

Dichotomy
2018

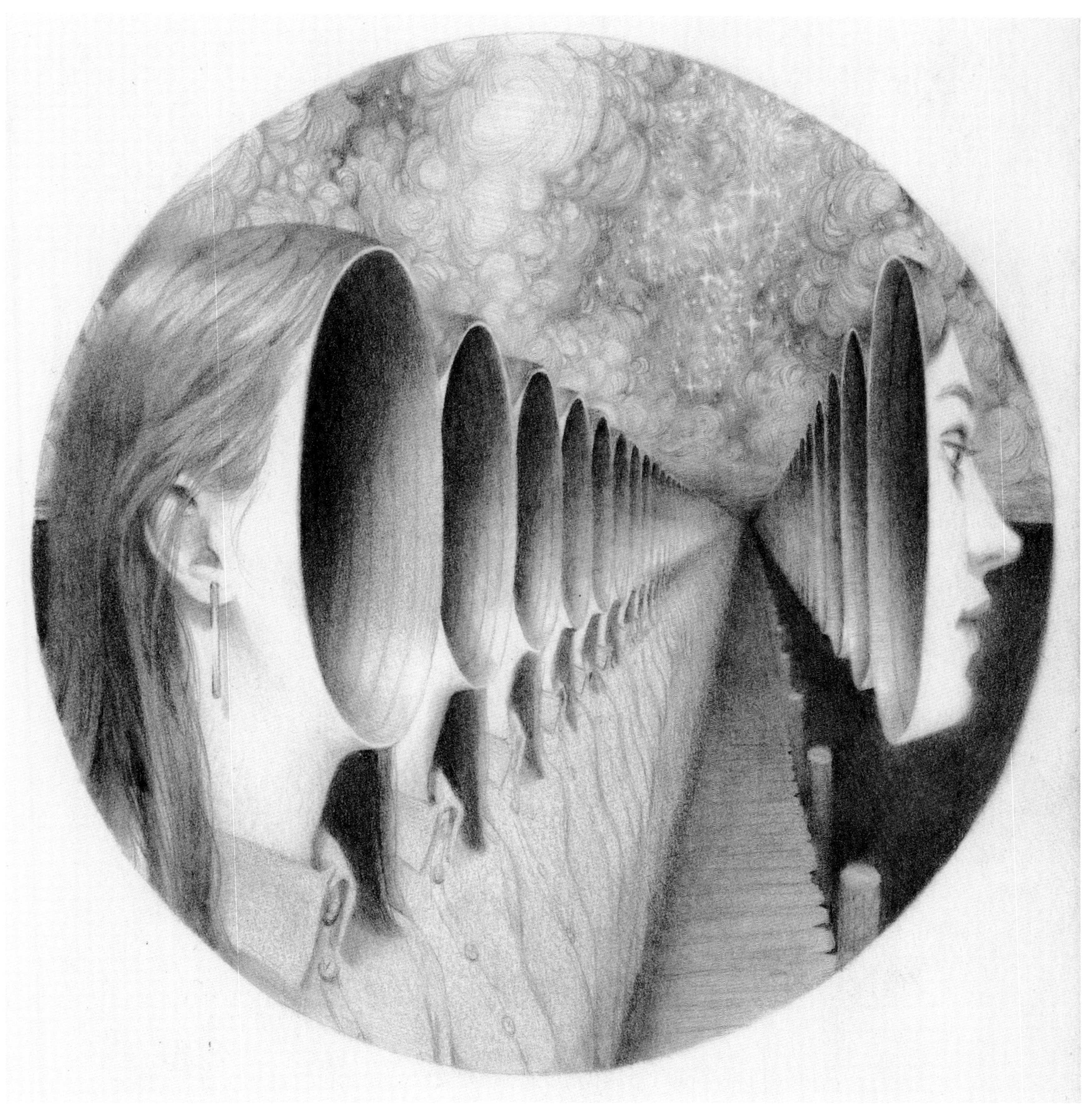

Mode of Ignoring
2017

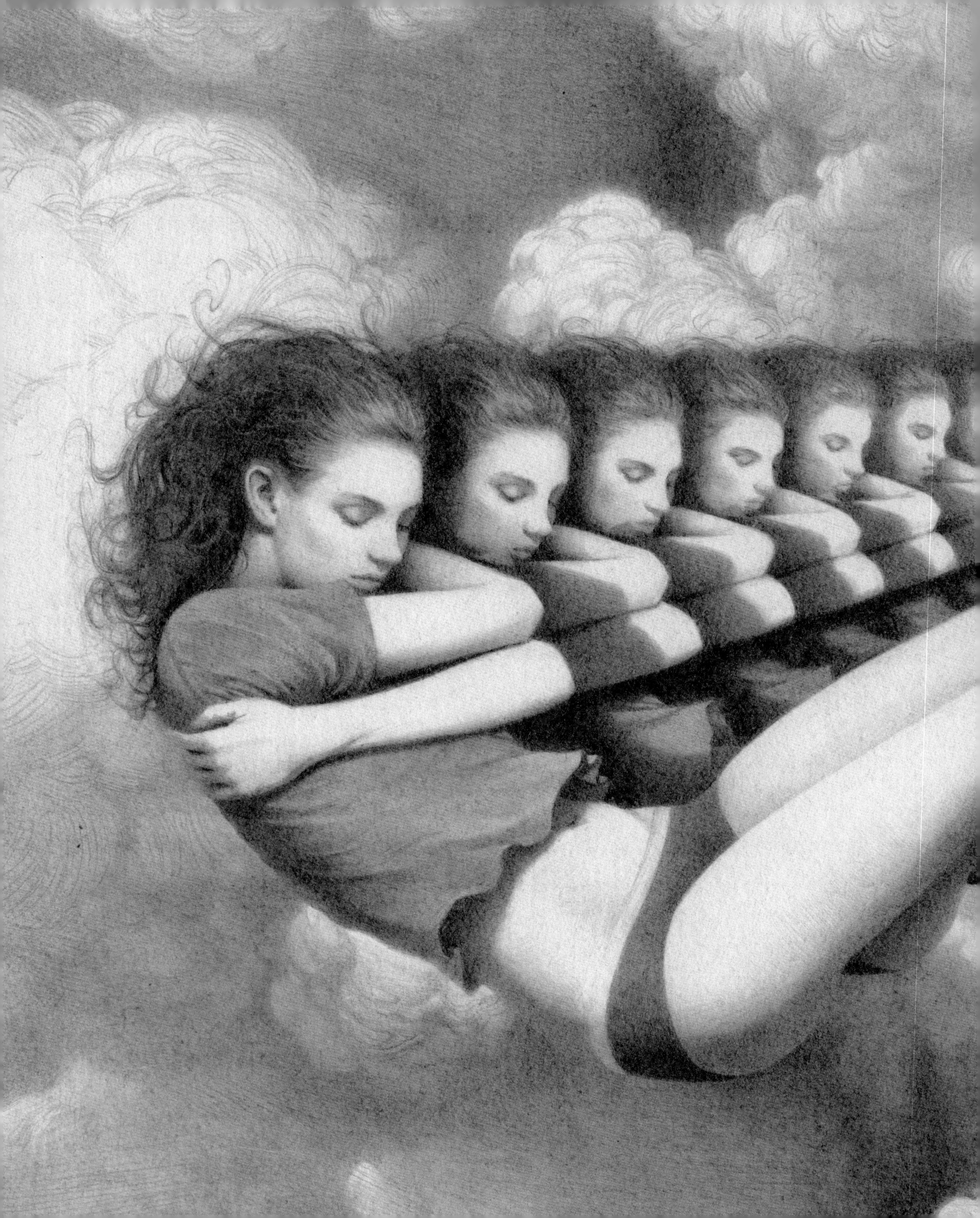

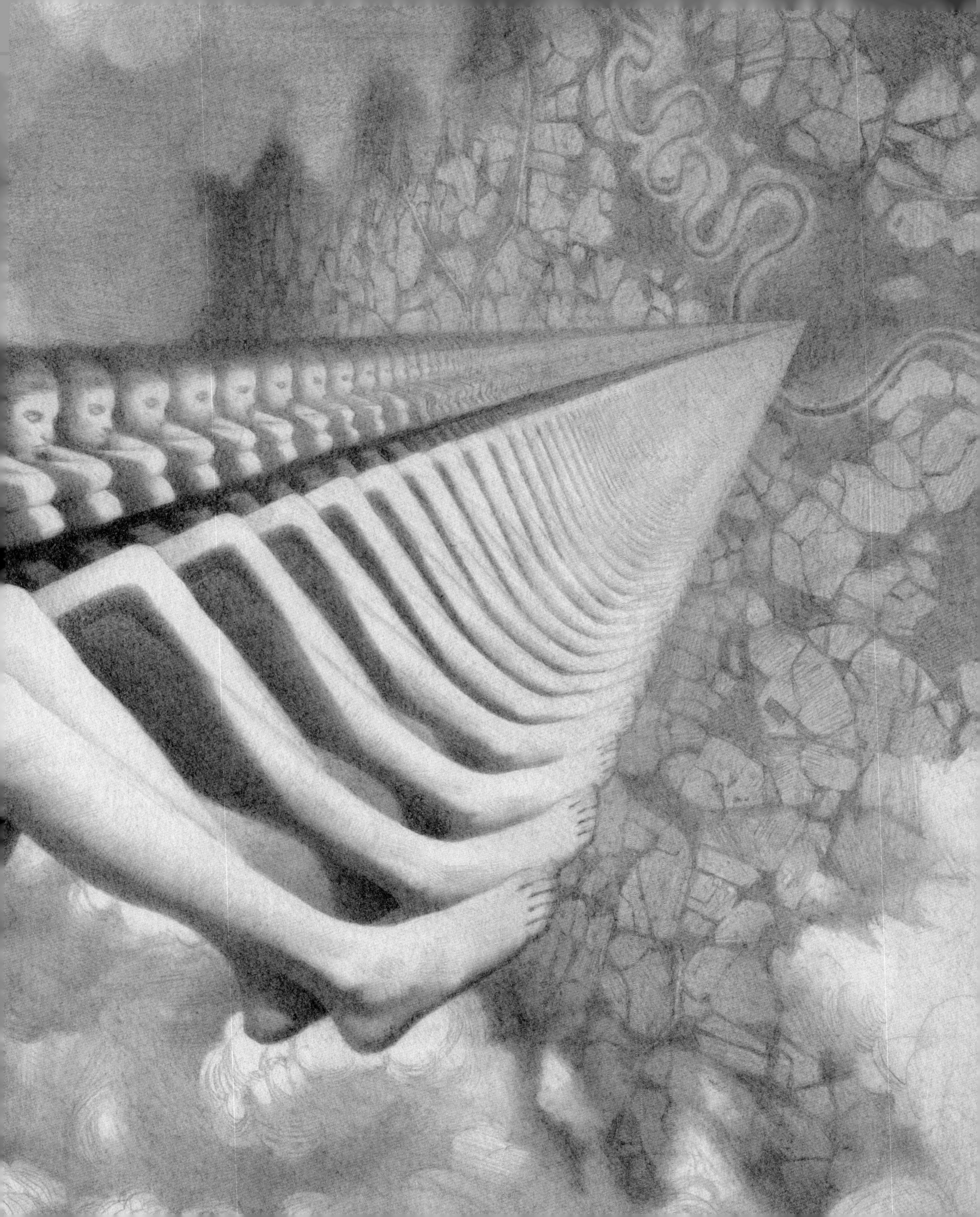

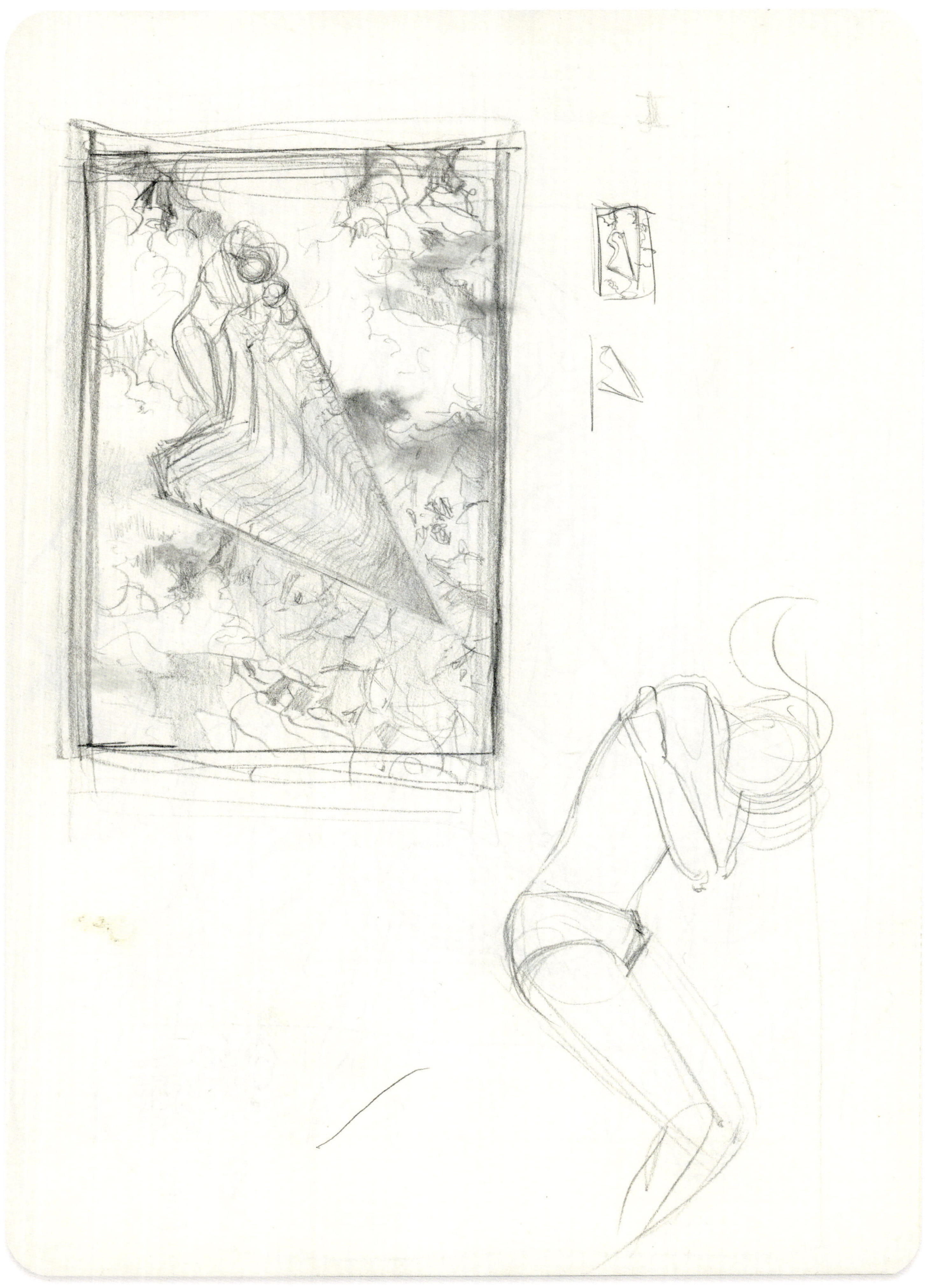

Projection + Studies
2018

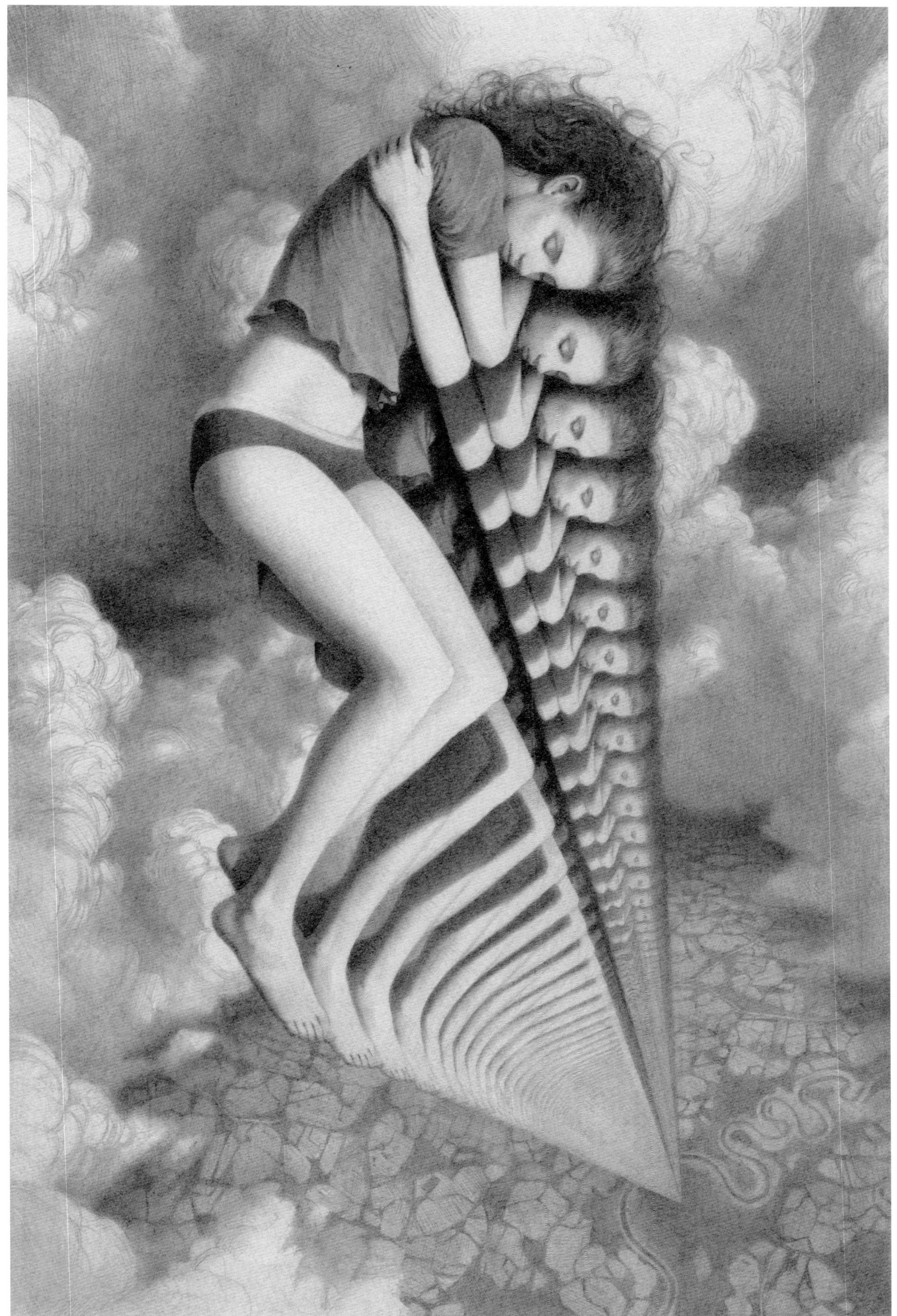

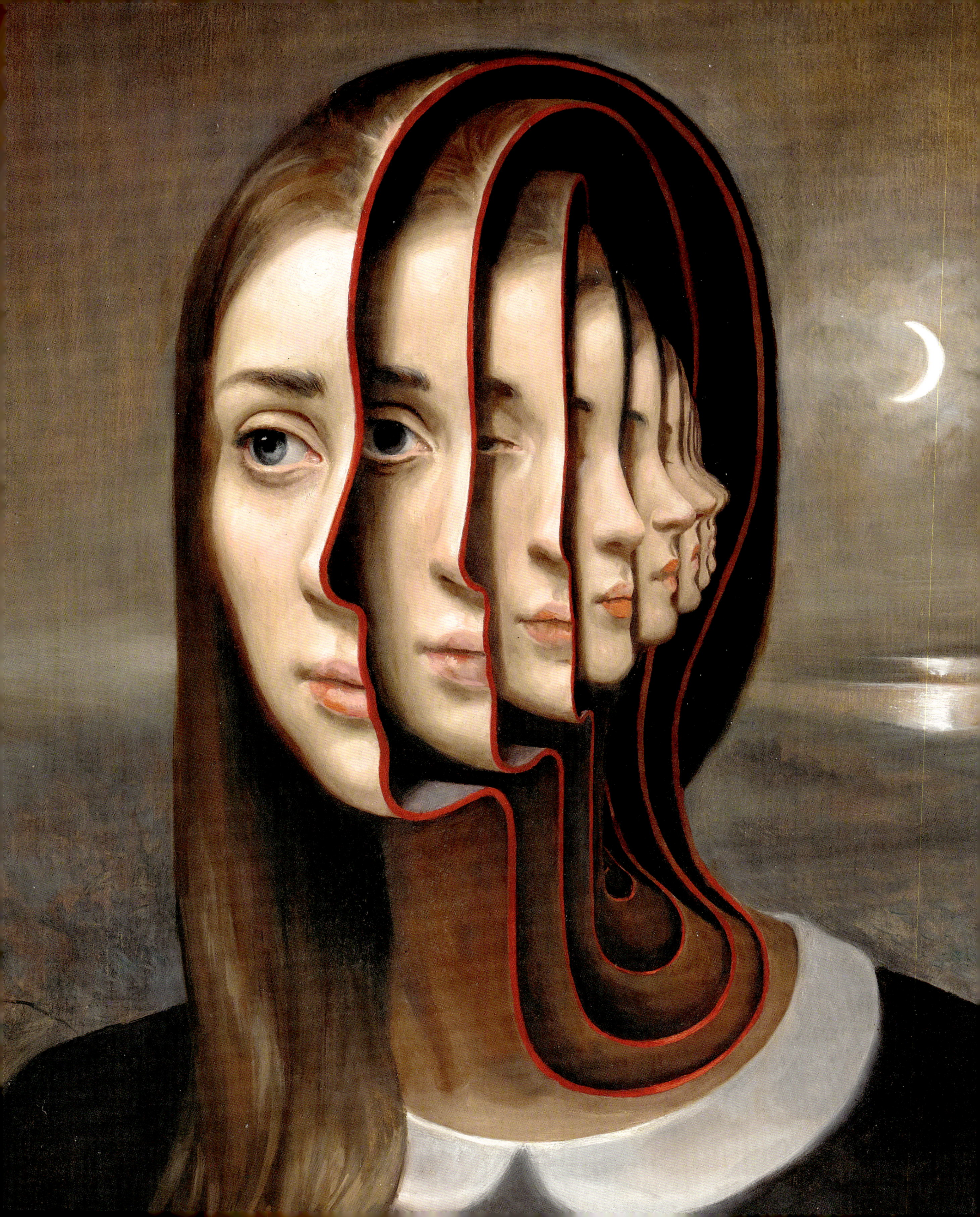

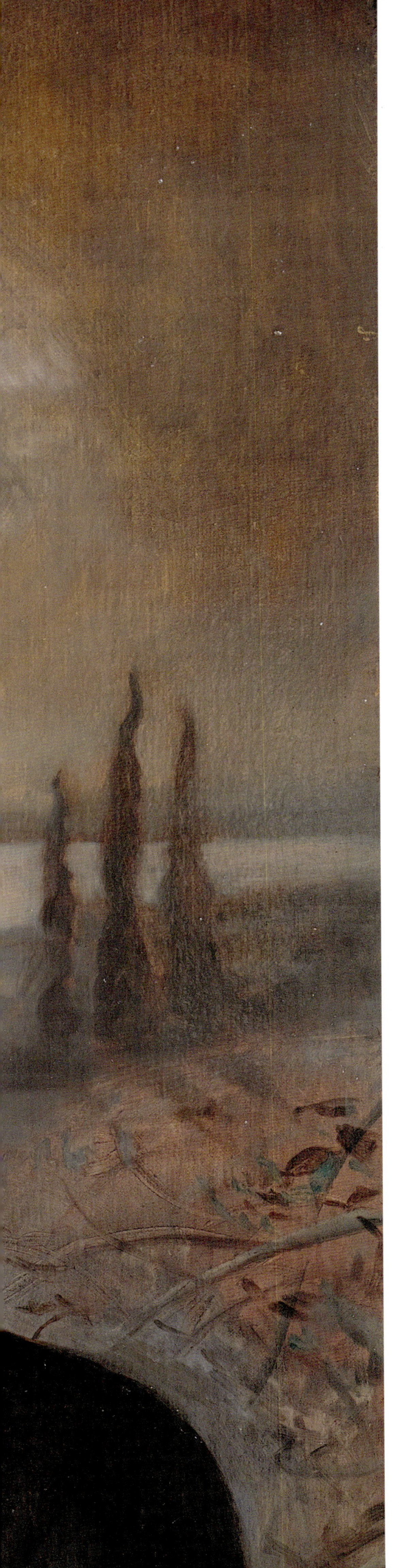

Retrospection (detail)
2018

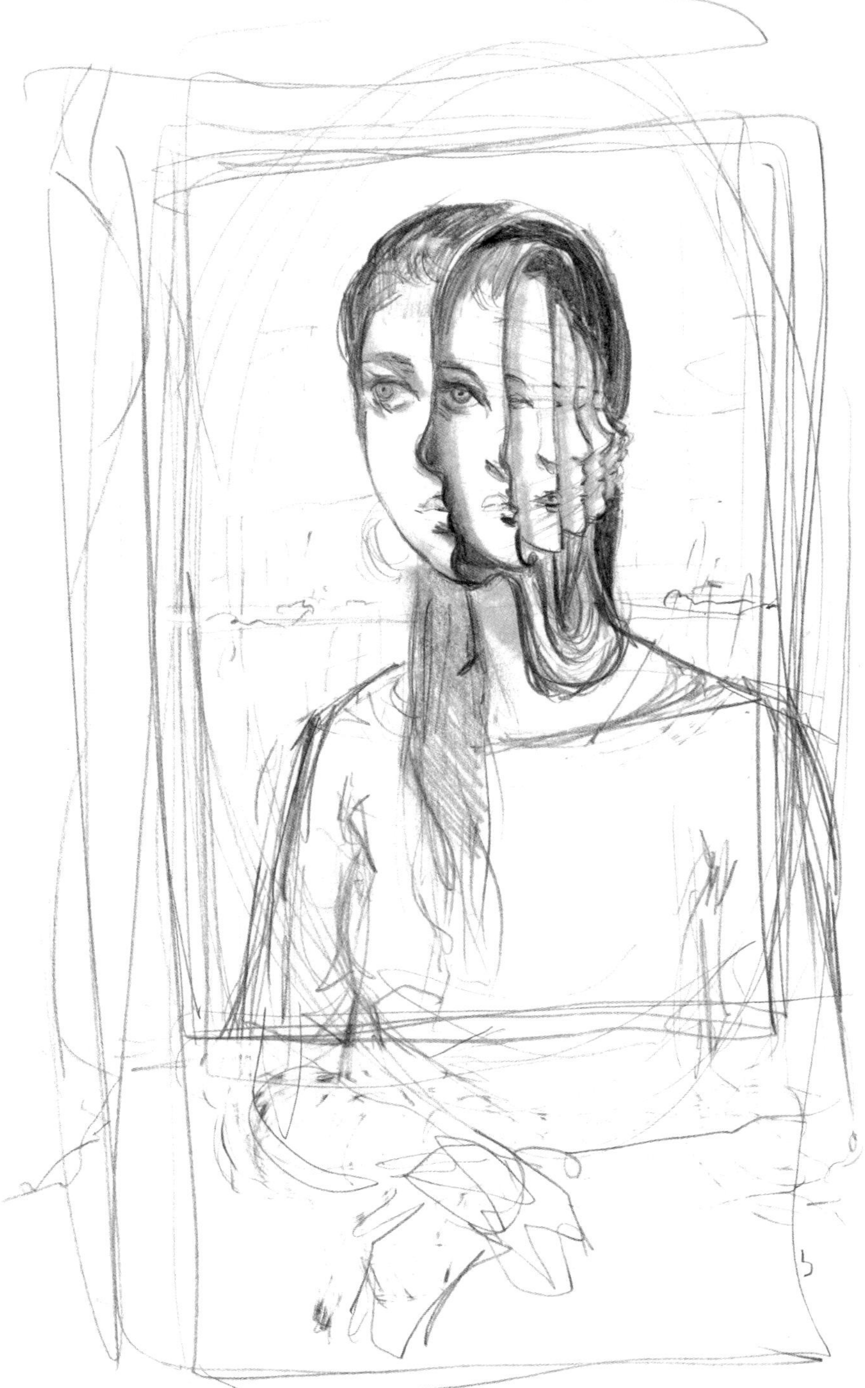

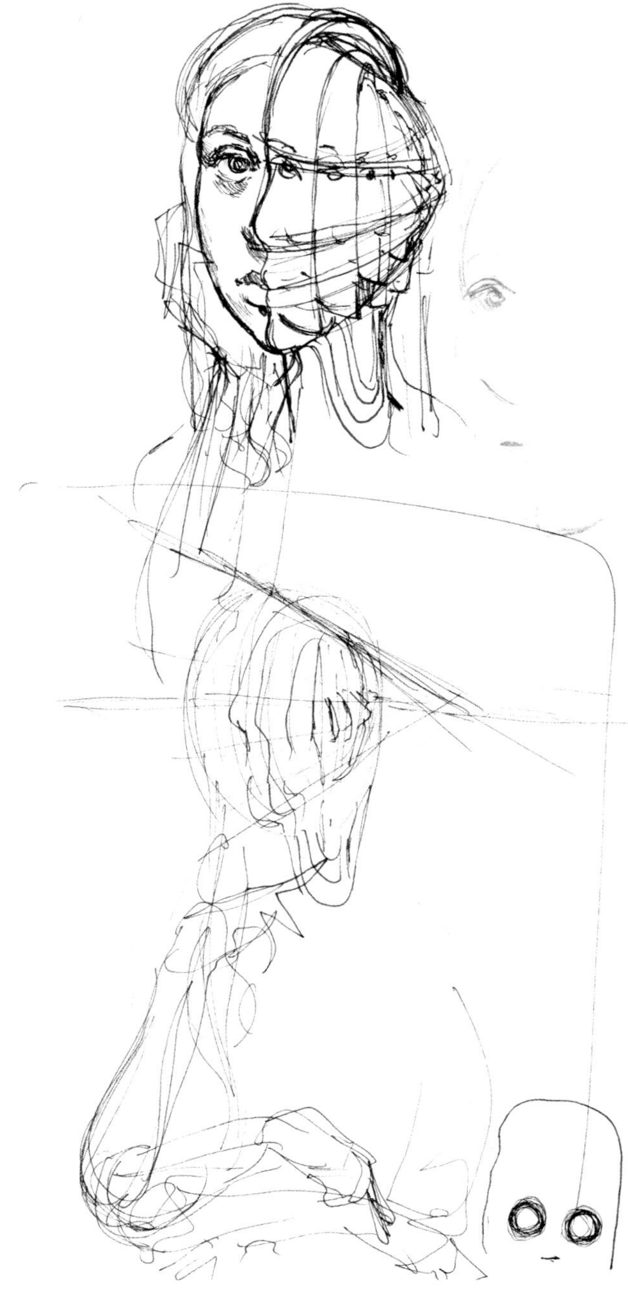

Retrospection + Studies

2018

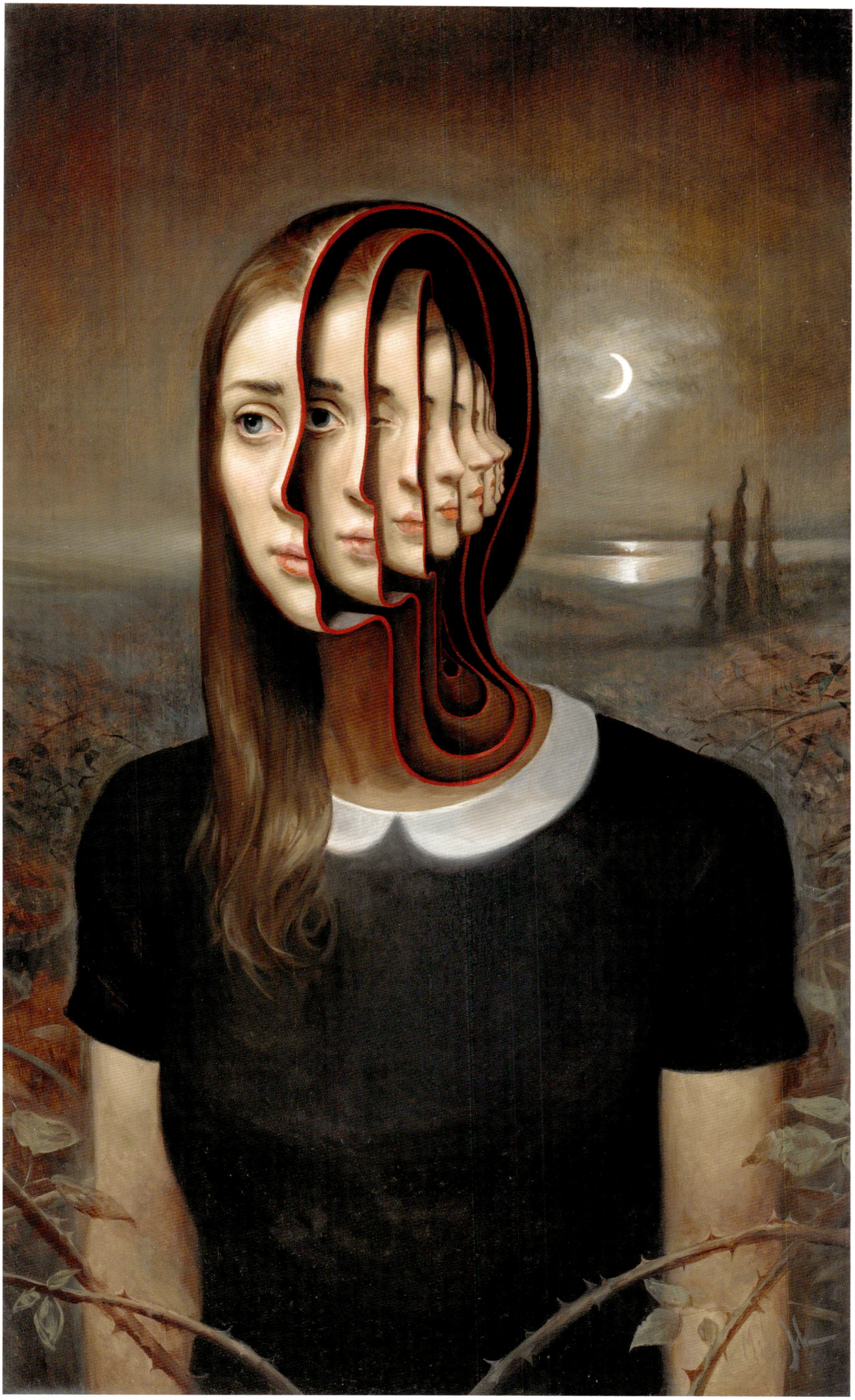

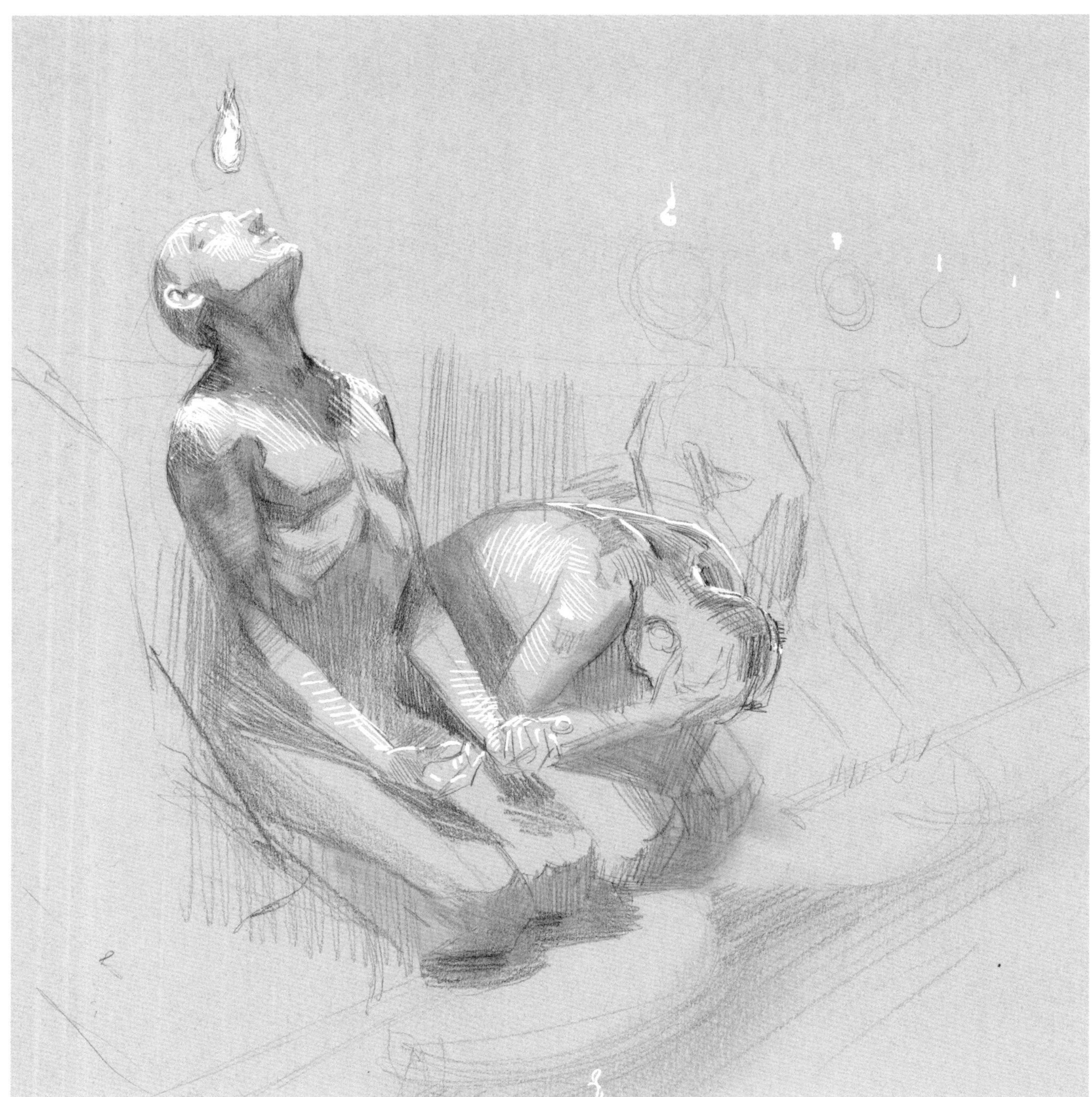

Extinguished + Study
2021

Odd One Out

Sometimes, rather than starting from a specific emotion or story that I want to portray, I build an image up from a simple attentional hook. The images in this section all utilize an 'odd one out' framework. The qualities of a subject, such as its size, direction, or form, appear more significant when placed against their opposite. When you have a composition filled with one type of thing contrasted by one single exception, our desire to project meaning onto the world immediately kicks in to try and build a narrative to explain the image.

You can follow in the sketches that led to "*Countercurrent*", how I built up from an extremely primitive sketch featuring a bunch of heads facing one way with a single portrait facing us. I followed an intuitive thread, experimenting with adding and removing elements that lead to the discovery of the final composition. As the work develops, I use an emerging feeling as a compass to make all of the many choices that go into making a painting. Through this process I discover what the image is about. Even with a sketch chosen, you still have an almost infinite amount of choices to make during the execution of a painting. *Where is the light coming from? How high is the waterline? How fast is the water flowing? What sort of colour palette should I use?* etc. The challenge is to not make

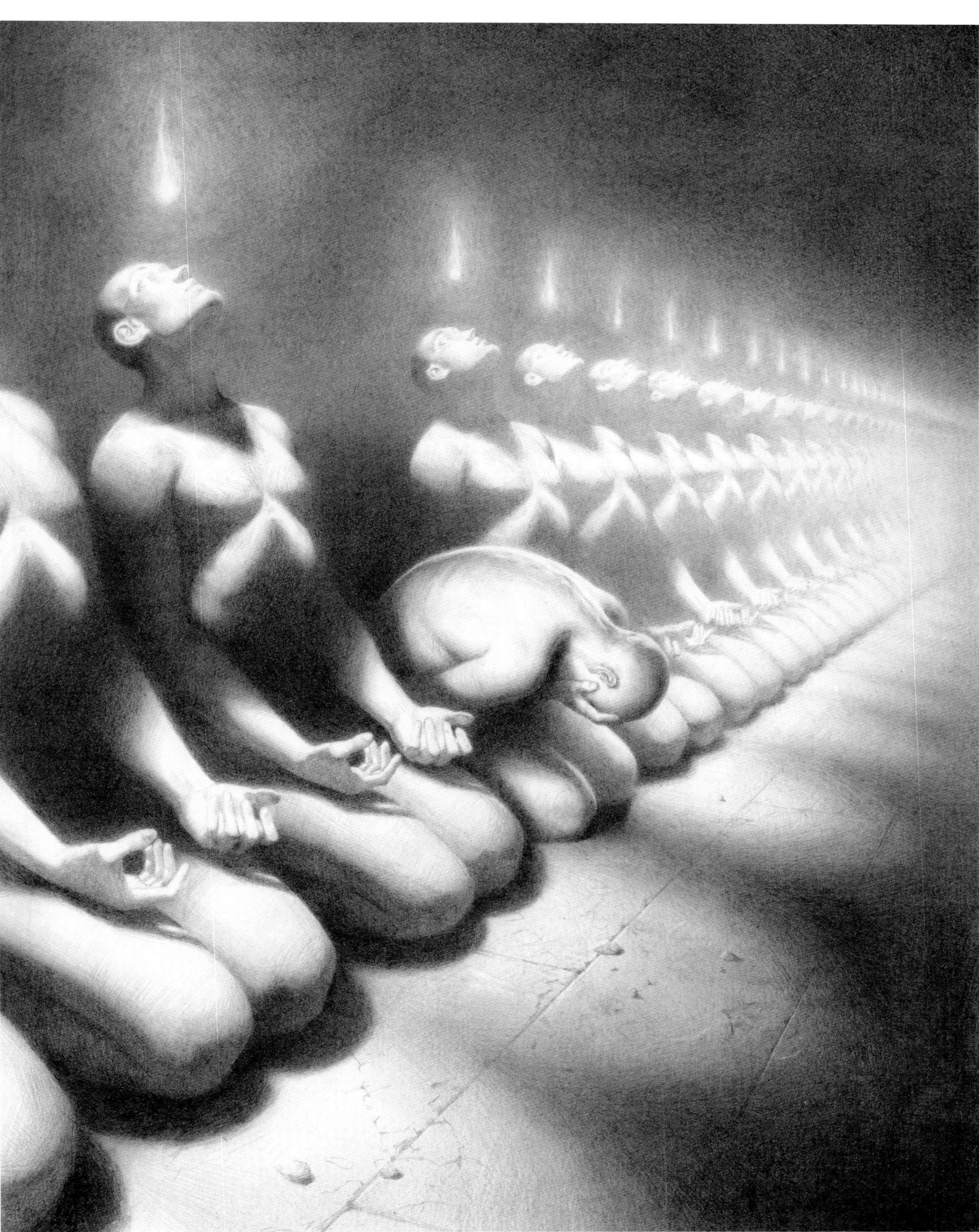

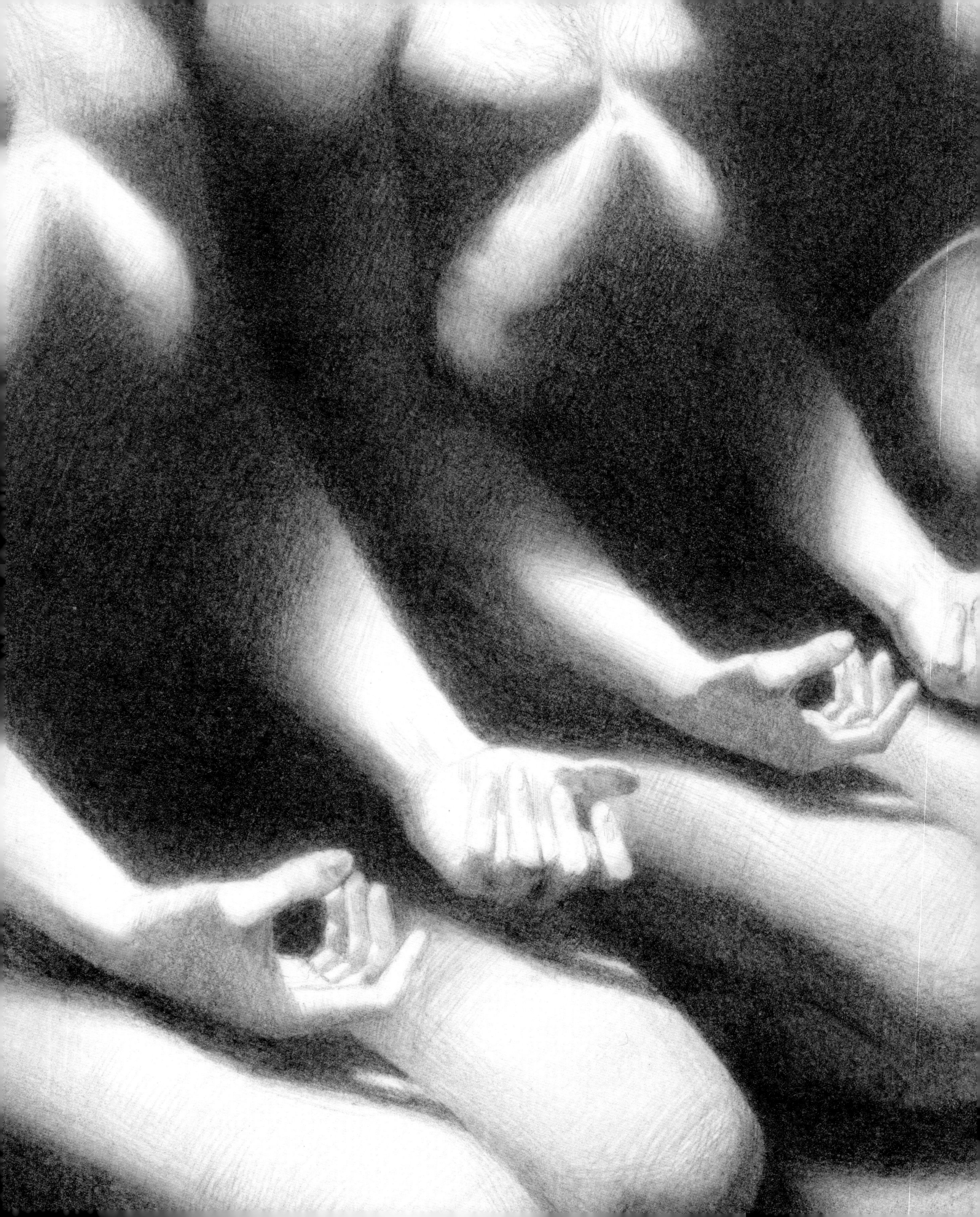

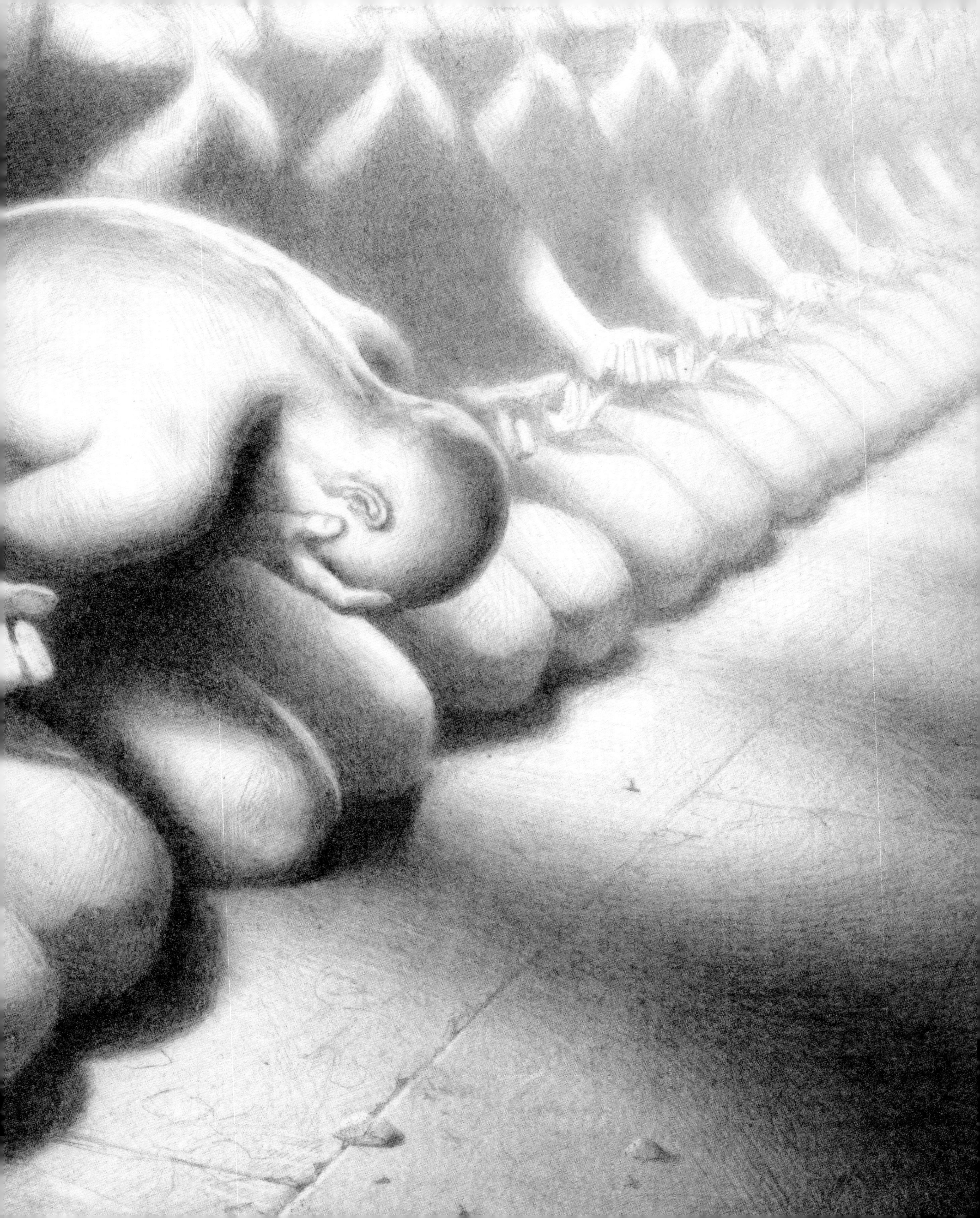

any of these choices arbitrarily, as all of them are opportunities to distill and strengthen the idea, to make it resonant and super real.

There is no logical way to make these choices, it is entirely an intuitive process, but far from random. It is a sense that can be developed. I am constantly reminding myself that it is my job to make sure nothing becomes boring or arbitrary, every piece of the painting should be soaked with intention.

All of these choices can't possibly be made ahead of time, we simply cannot imagine things to the fidelity required to have them pre-made. That is what keeps me interested in a painting as I work on it for weeks and sometimes months. The process of solving the very analytical and technical craftsmanship problems of a painting, guided by the emotional, intuitive, feeling-driven reason for making the painting, is one I find endlessly satisfying. I enjoy the absurdity of the whole thing, the sheer effort to create an object that will be inevitably torn apart by time and forgotten one day. I think of it like making sandcastles on the beach as a kid, but at a slower timescale. It is a statement of our humanness to struggle to find meaning in an impermanent world.

Countercurrent
2020

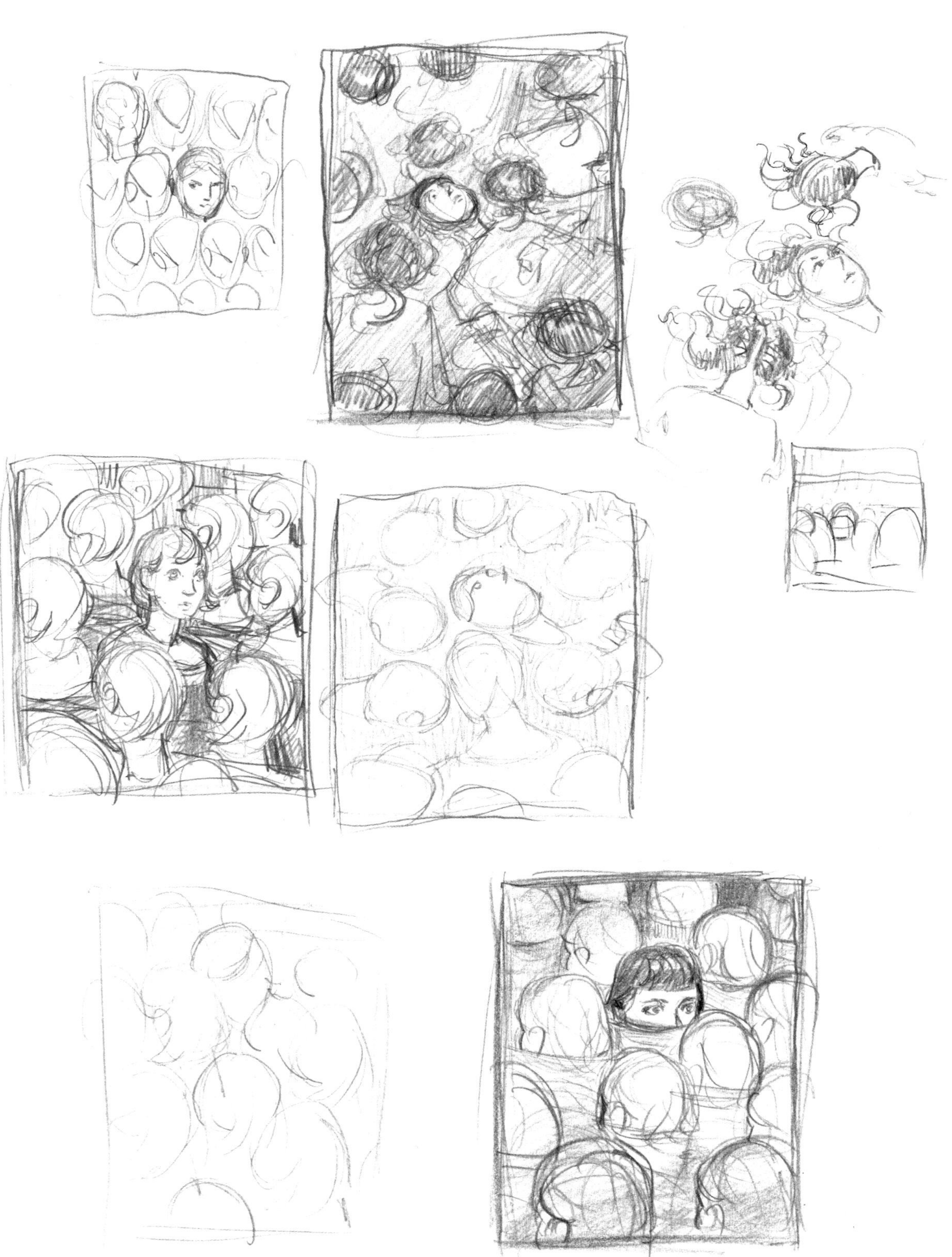

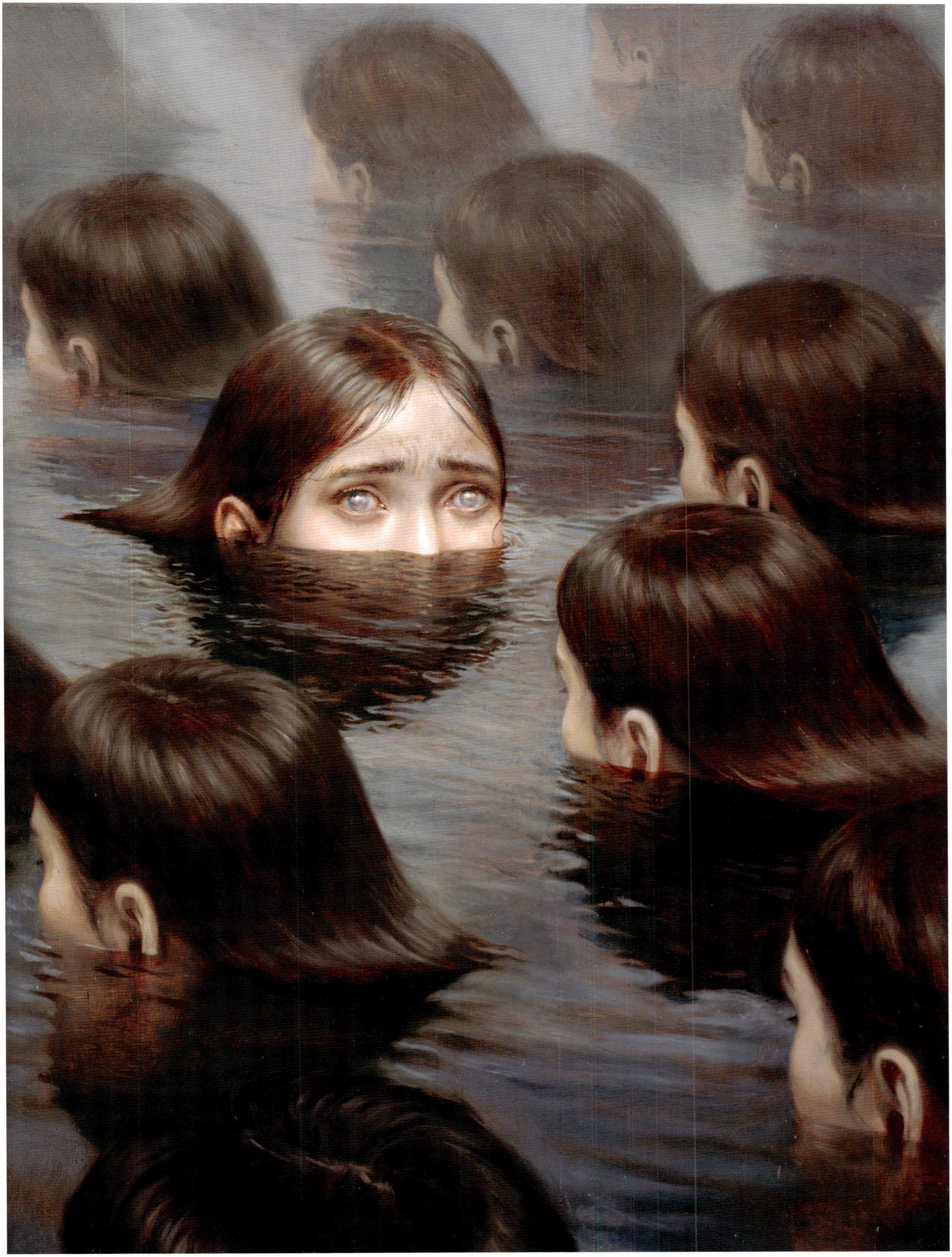

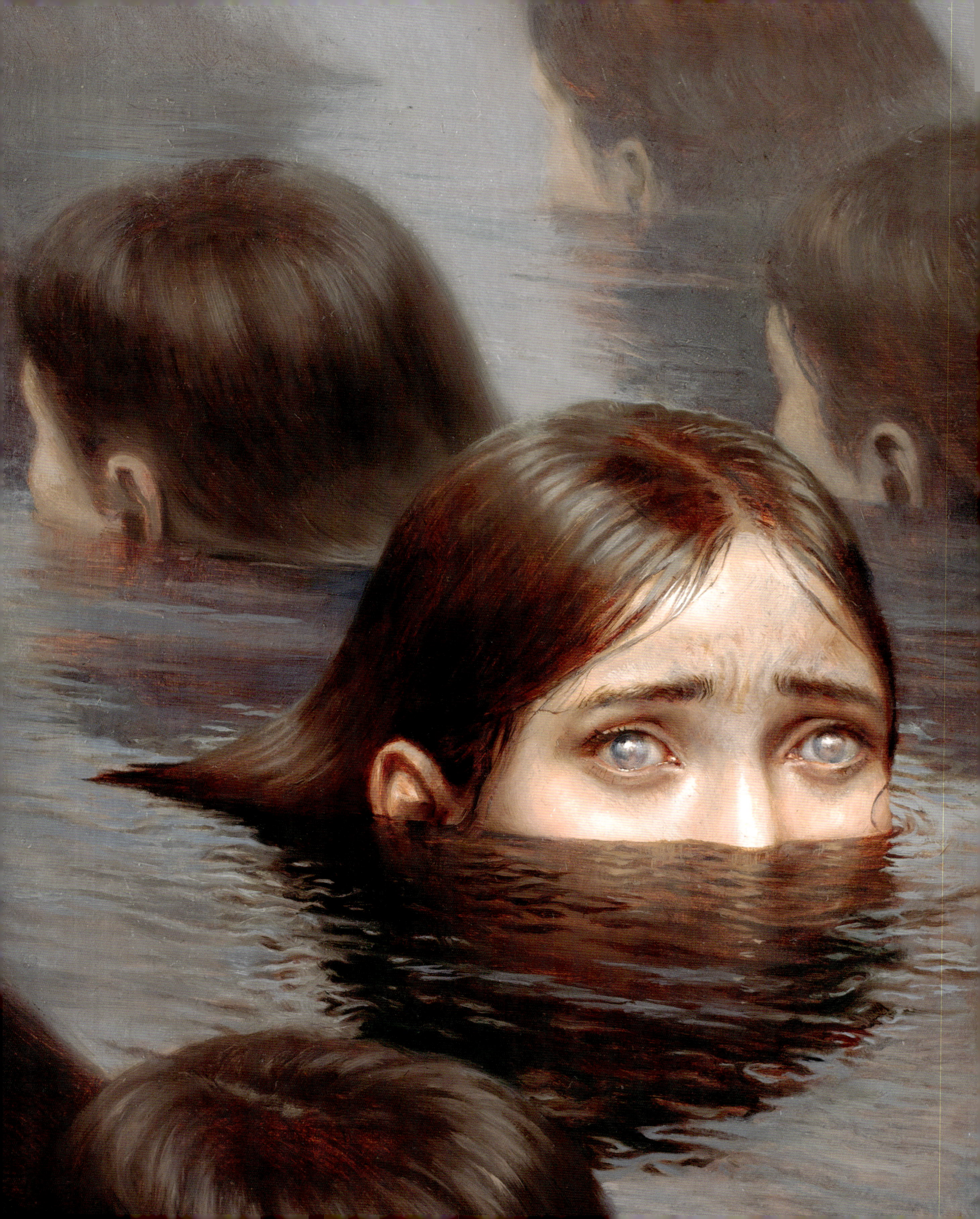

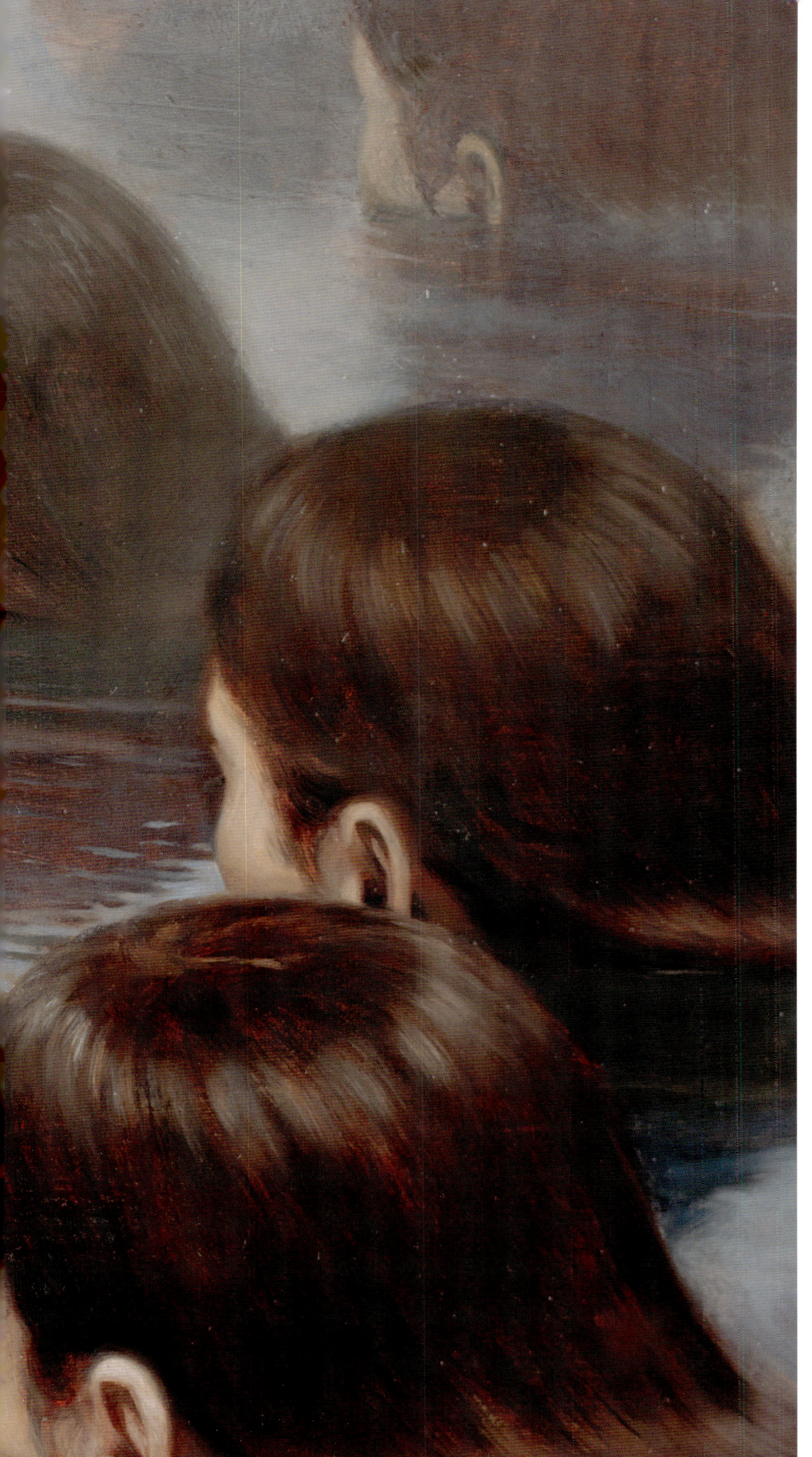

Countercurrent (detail)
2020

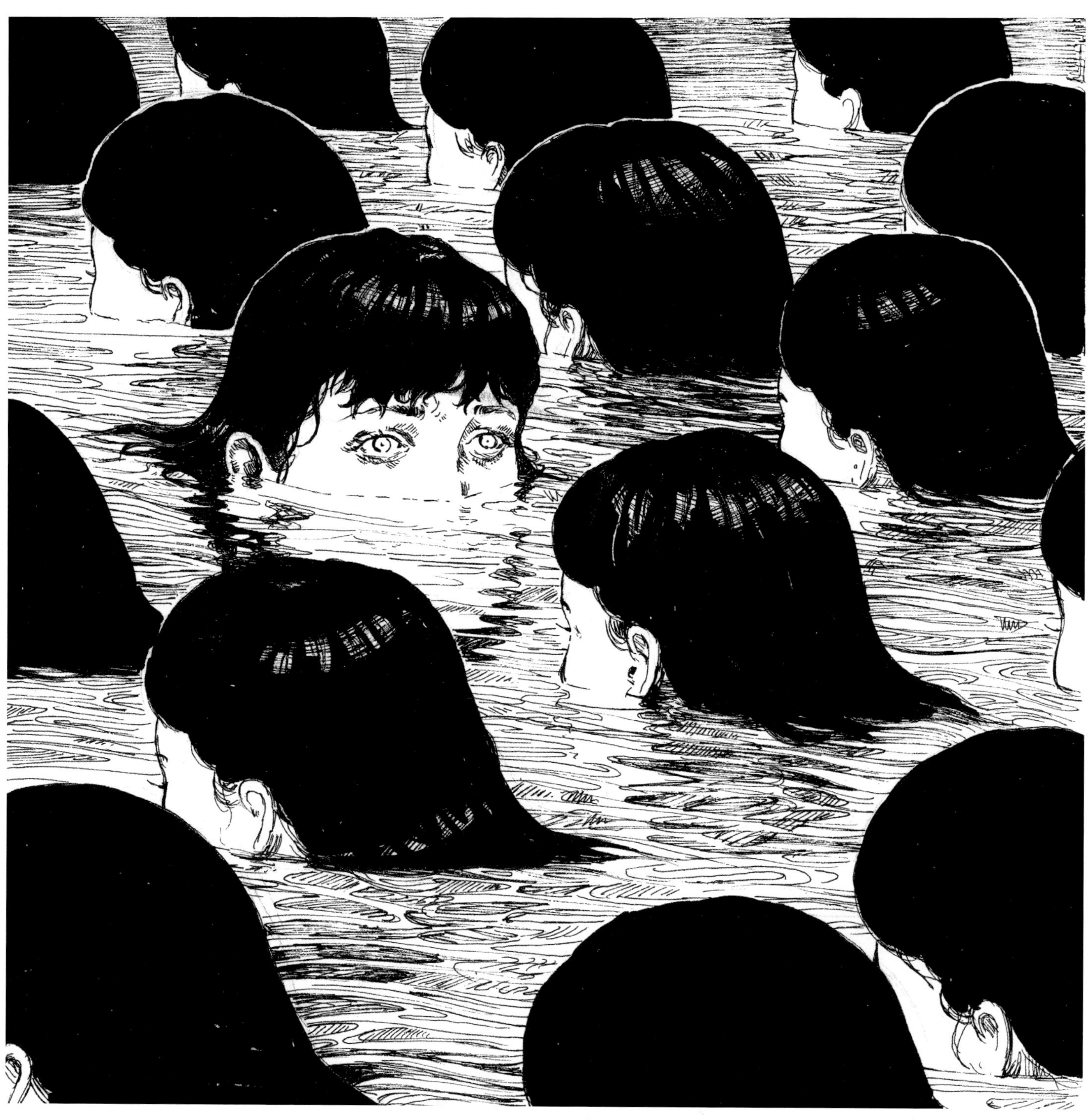

Countercurrent (Ink)
2018

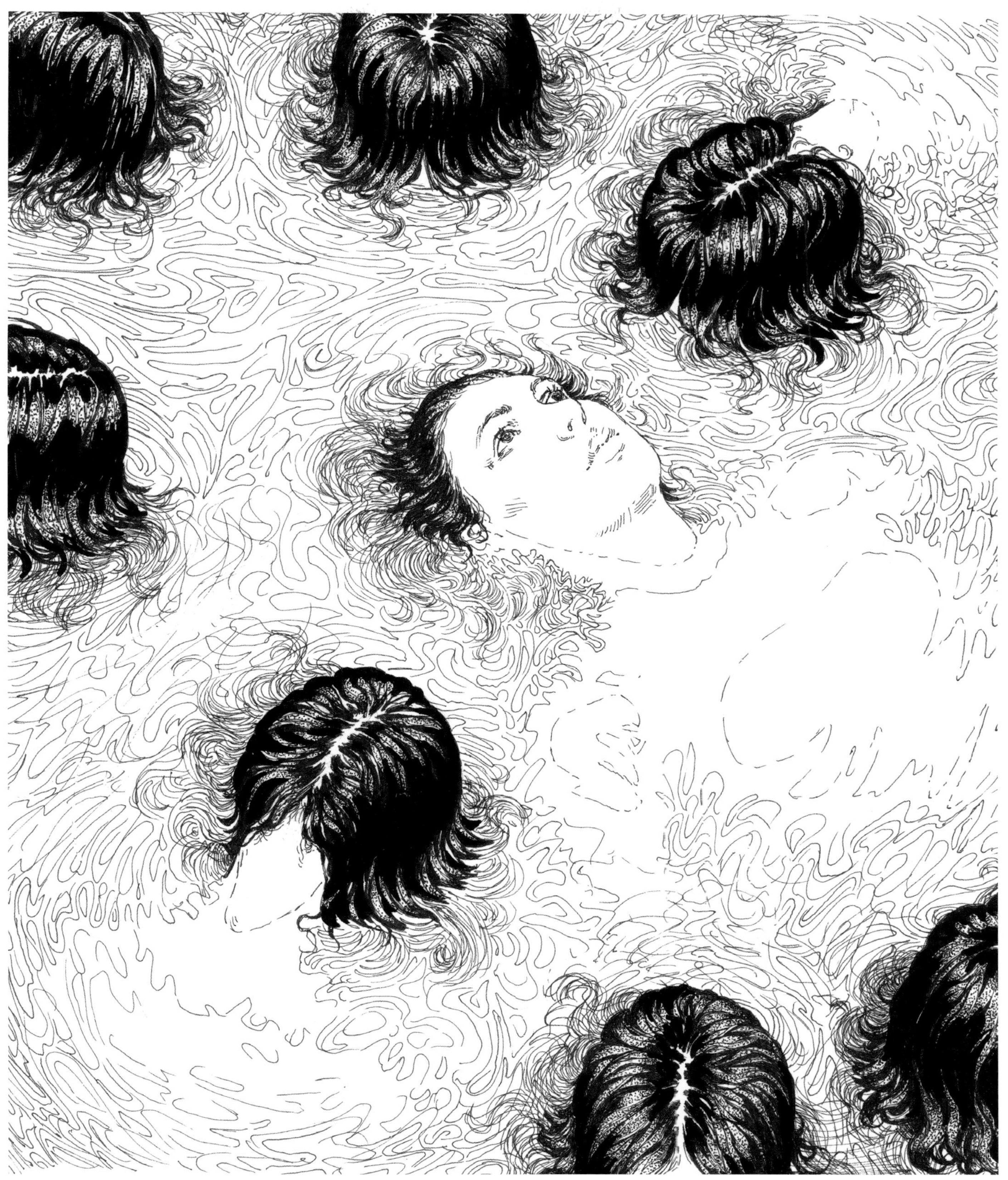

Survivorship Bias
2018

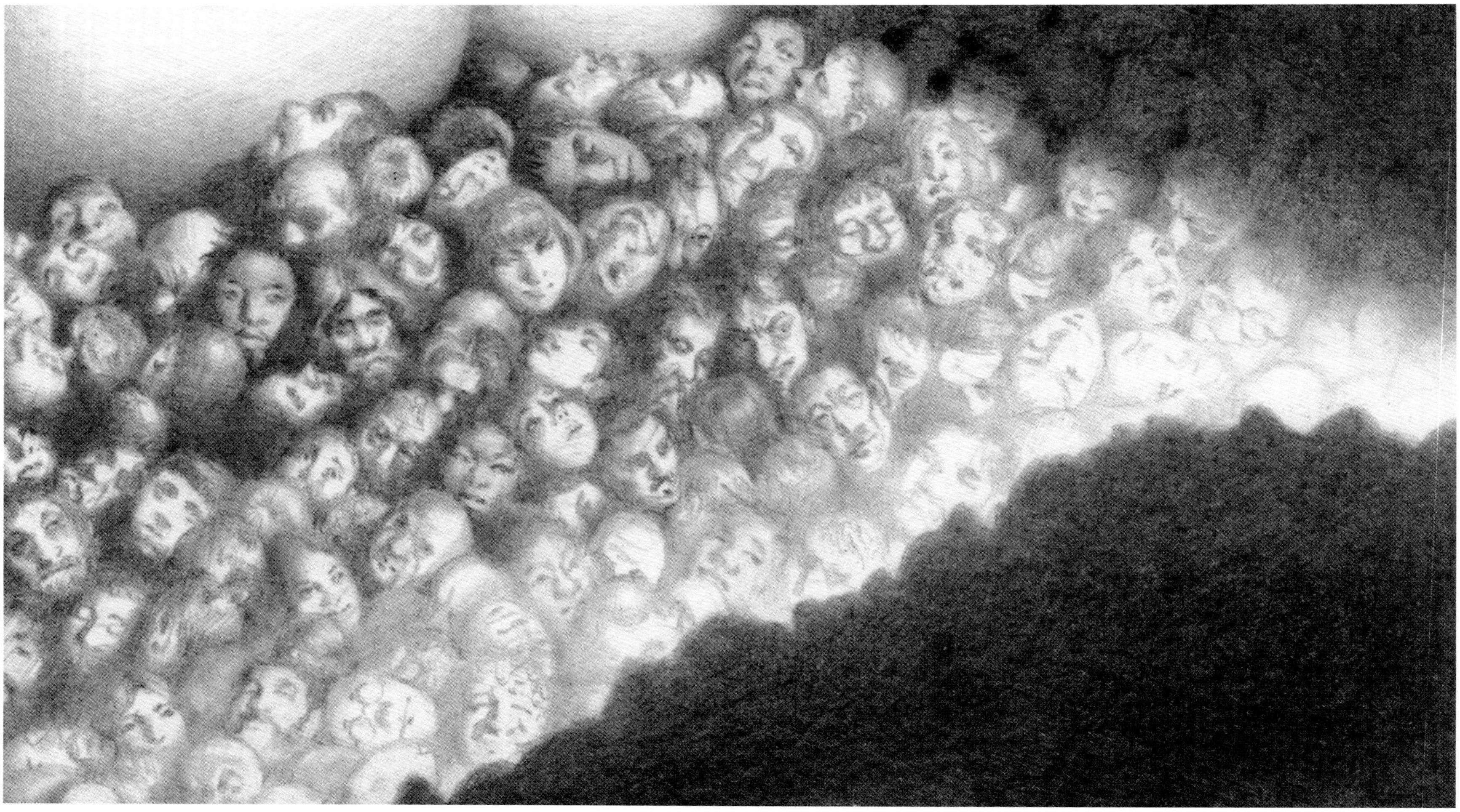

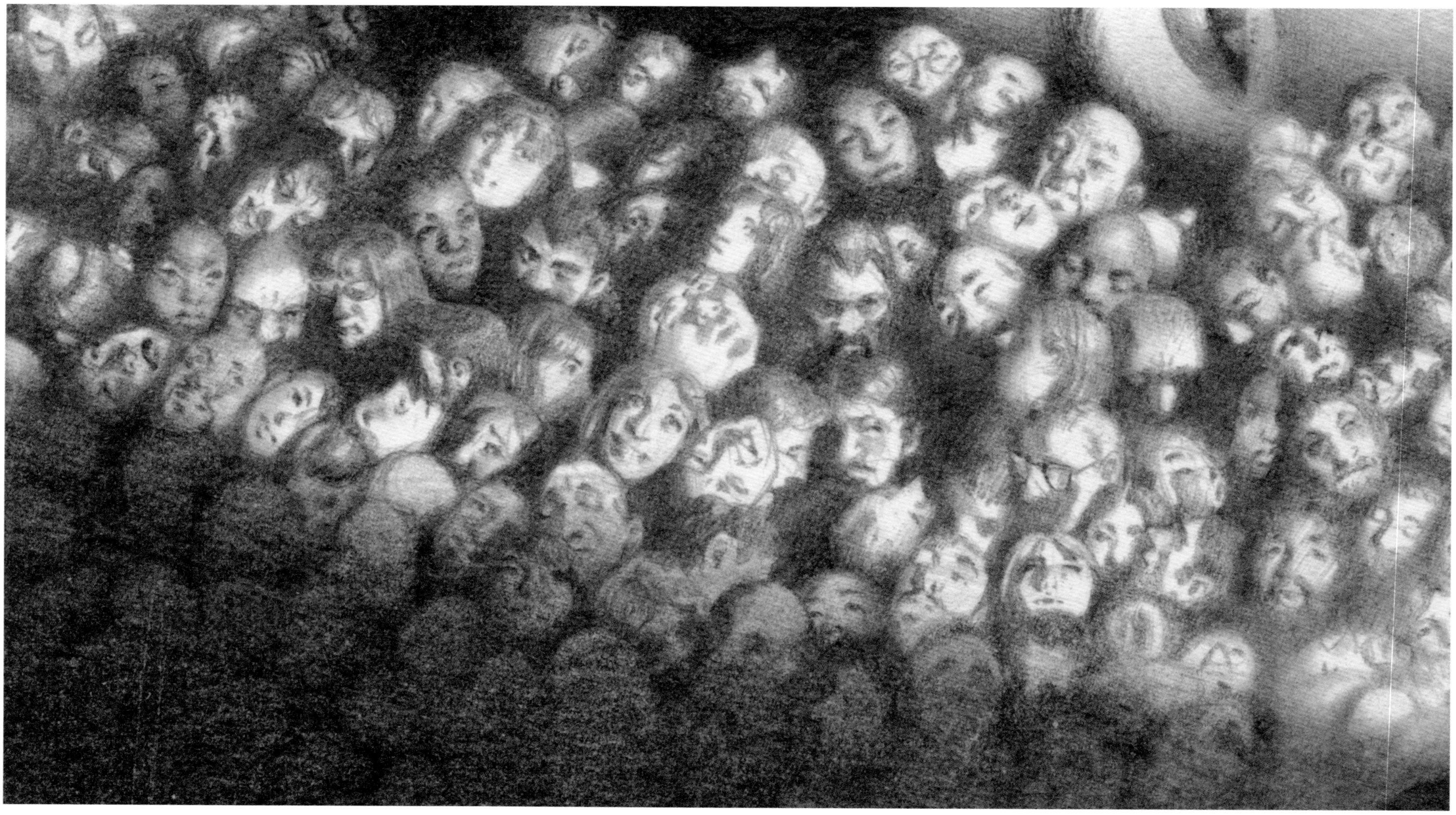

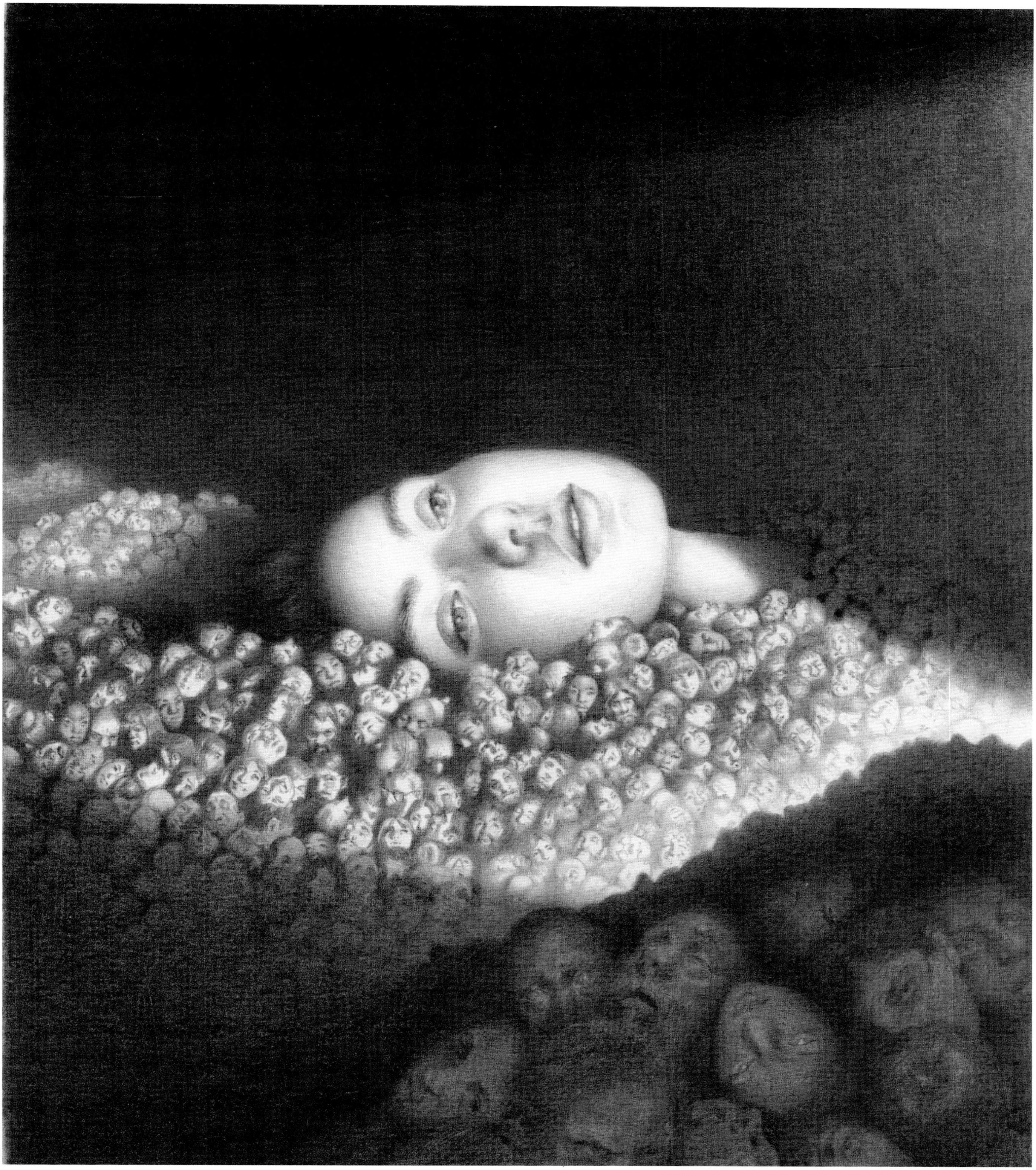

Collective Unconscious + Details

2020

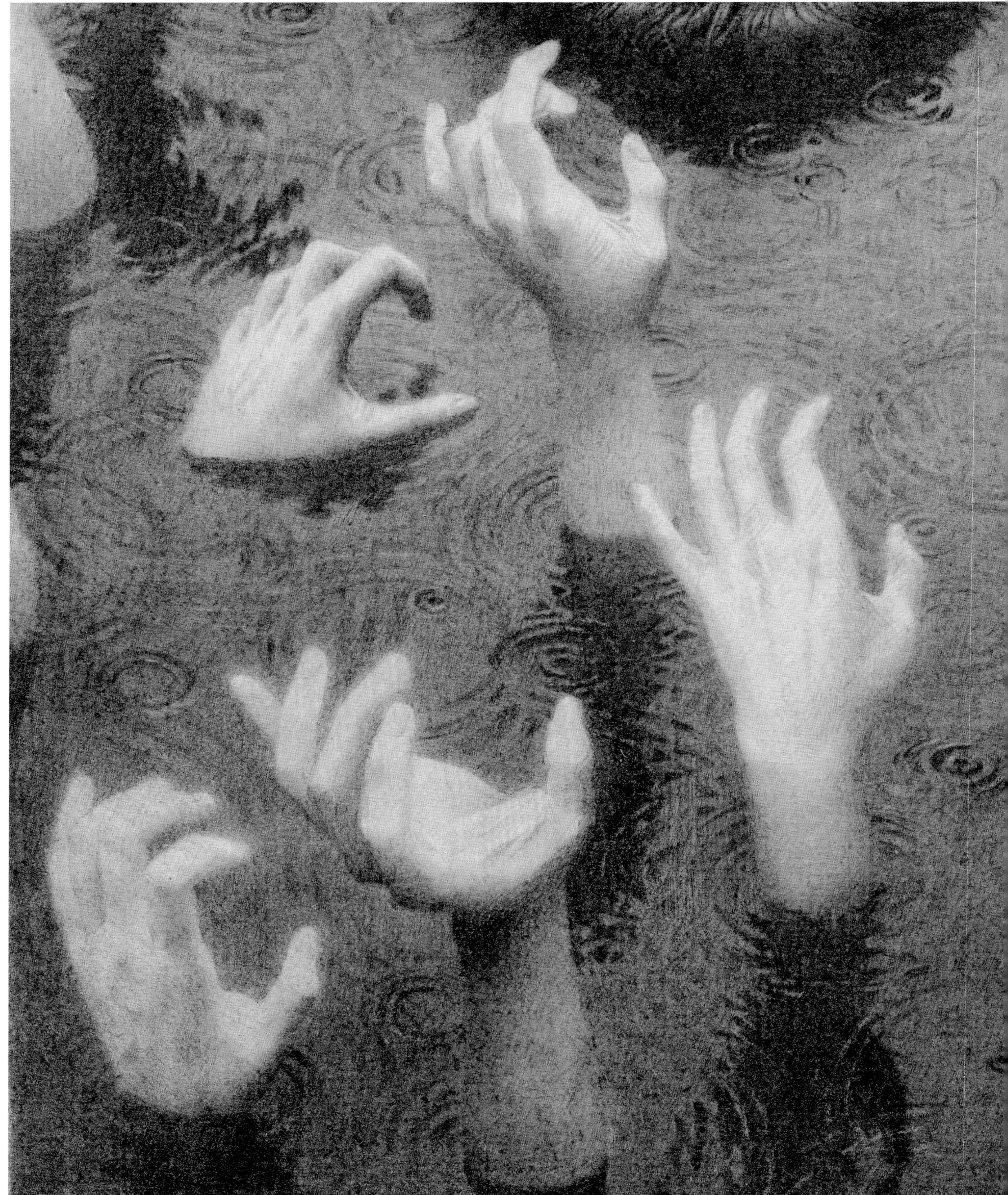

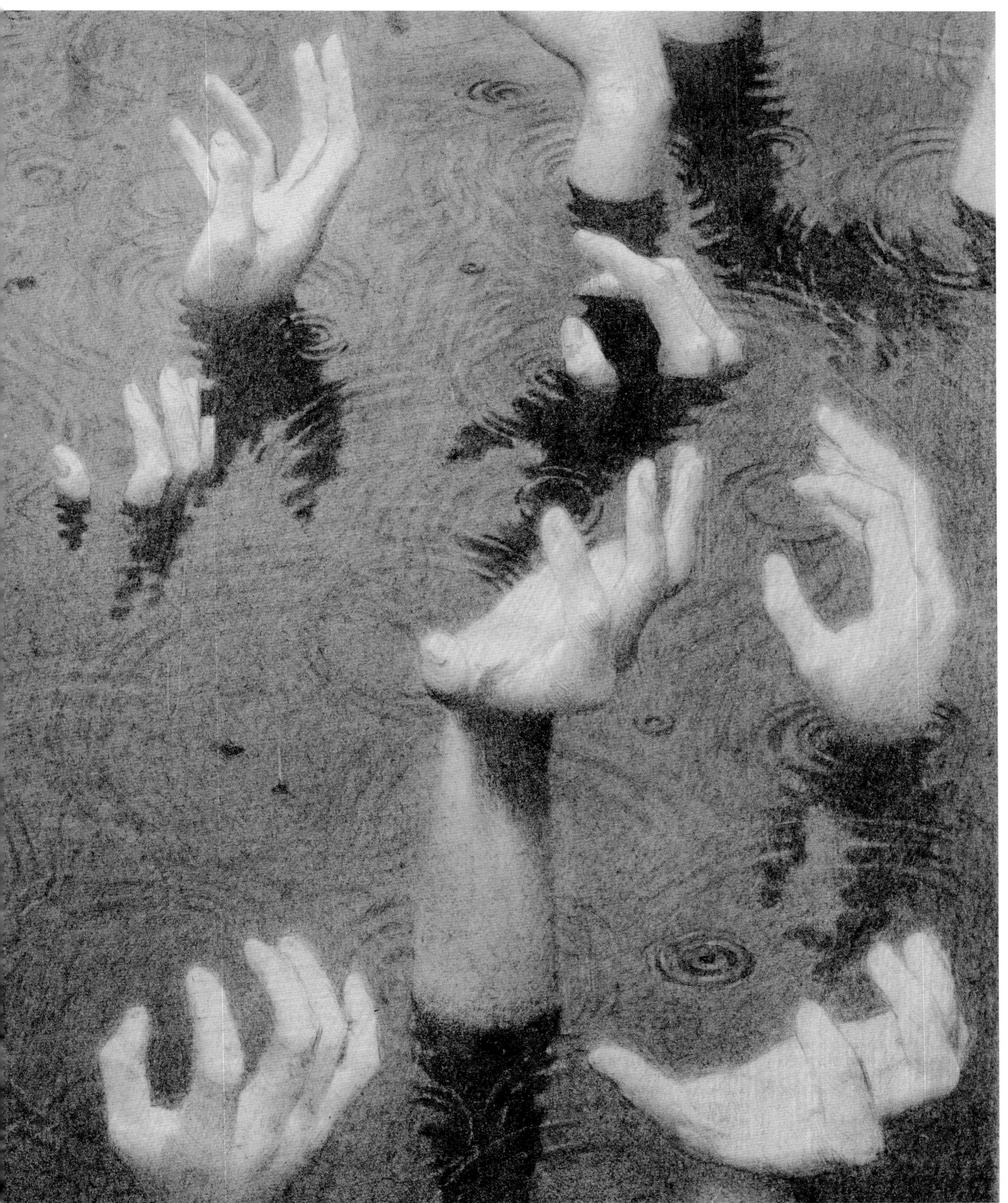

I make so much of my finished work in pencil, a medium that has historically been primarily used for sketching. To find inspiration for how to make compelling and polished black and white images, I often end up looking at etchings, engravings, and black and white photography. I took a lot of inspiration for this image from the work of a Finnish photographer, Pentti Sammallahti. His work is composed of these gorgeous, rich, subtle tones that I find hauntingly beautiful. I like to cram in a ton of detail in an understated way that almost disappears when you step back. Many many hours were spent drawing the rain patterns on the water, different ripples intersecting and interfering with each other, yet they should all merge together so that the hands and figure don't get lost in the noise.

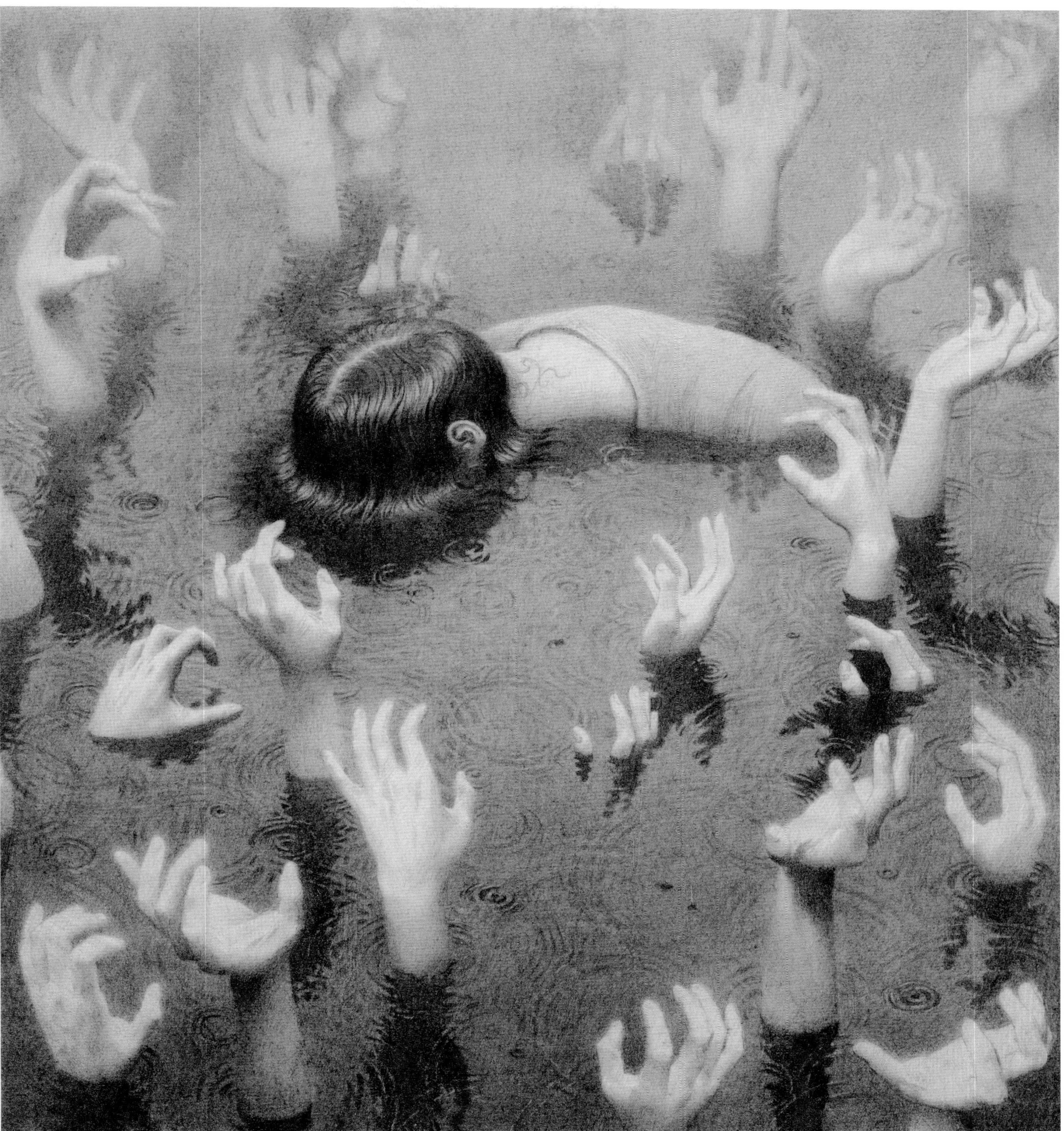

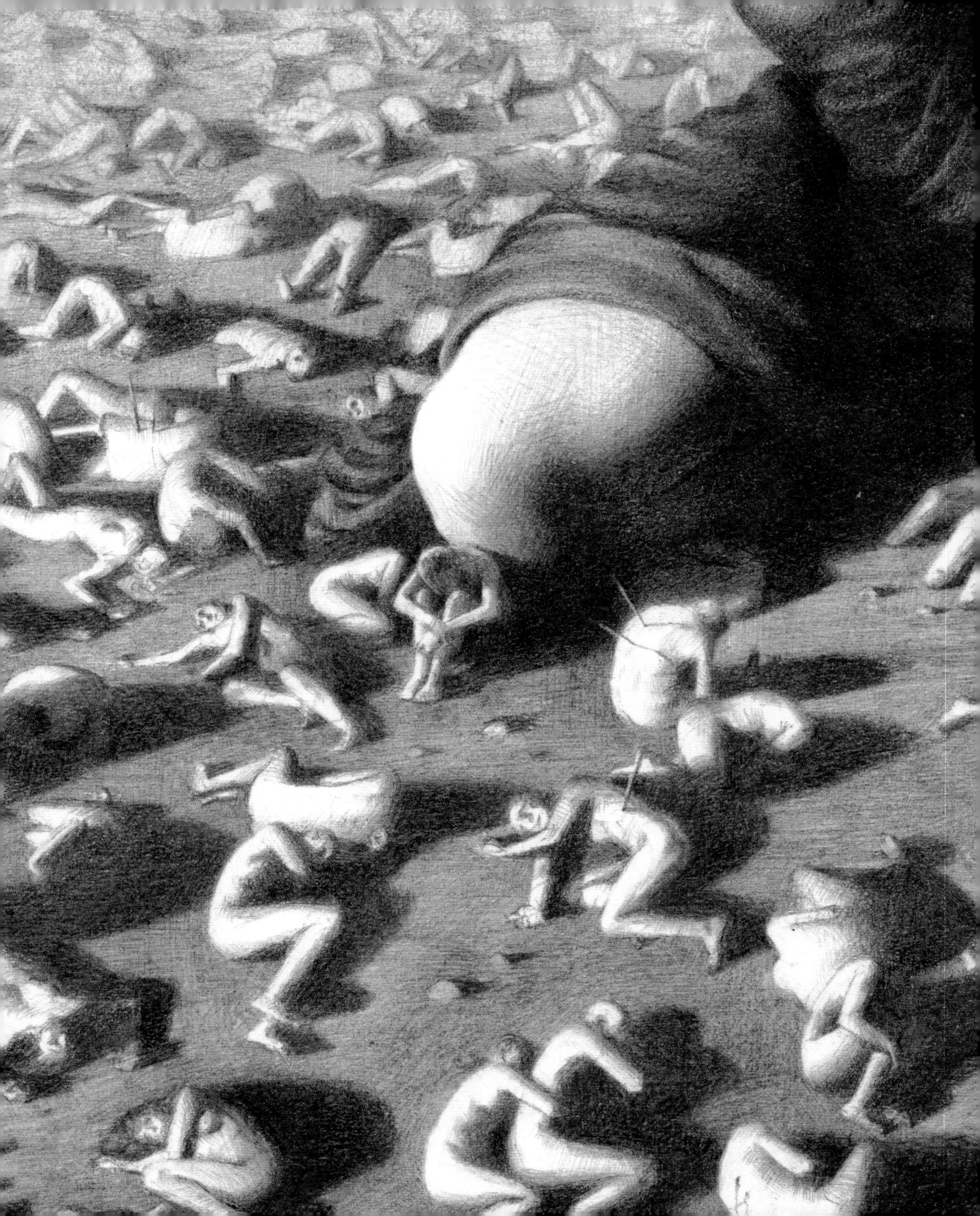

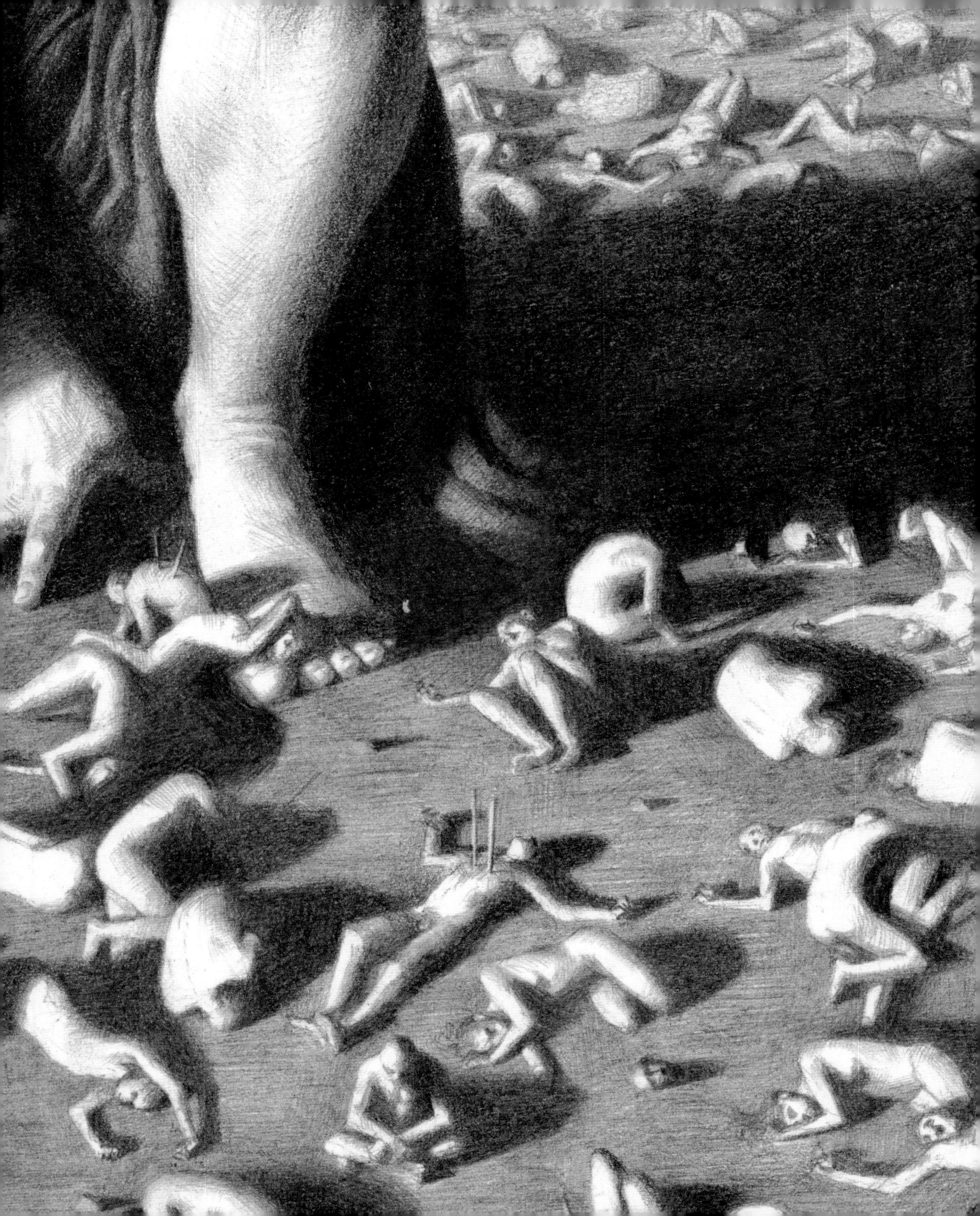

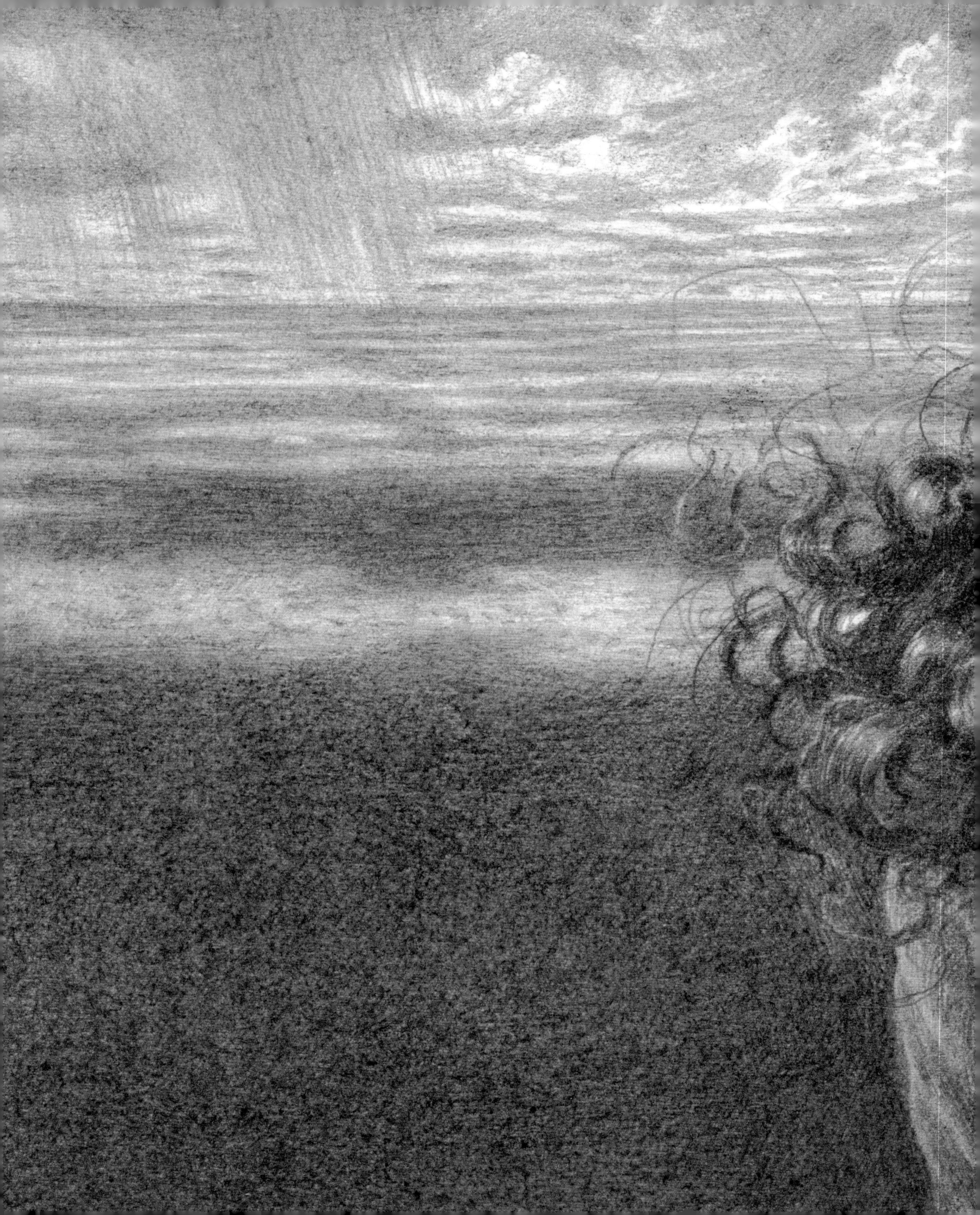

II

Morphology

“To make artwork about something is a devotional practice, a genuine sacrifice of our very precious finite time and attention.”

Art as Personal Therapy

Since my process is driven in an intuitive exploratory way, it tends to gravitate towards the feelings that still require my processing to reach a form of acceptance. A core principle to the ethos of my work is to depict elements of my experience in an honest, non-judgemental way. I find that there is always a subtle temptation to try and anticipate what your work will signal to the audience. This comes with an internal pressure to create something that will cast you in a positive light. I have found it is much more interesting to simply allow myself to be completely open about the full range of thoughts and feelings that I have been through. All of this together tends towards a bias to depicting some of the more difficult elements of my life.

Catharsis is ultimately what I am looking for. Life inevitably brings us experiences that are deeply painful and difficult. I suppose I am striving for a means to find something redemptive that can be distilled from these moments. I find it adds immense meaning in my life to transform the raw material of experience into something beautiful. Taking some of my pain and turning it into an opportunity for connection with other people is an activity that I find intrinsically rewarding. It feels natural in the same way that I don’t question whether sitting in the sun and feeling its warmth on my skin is worthwhile—it is somehow self justifying.

This form of honesty allows for the work to emerge in a more natural way. It is easy

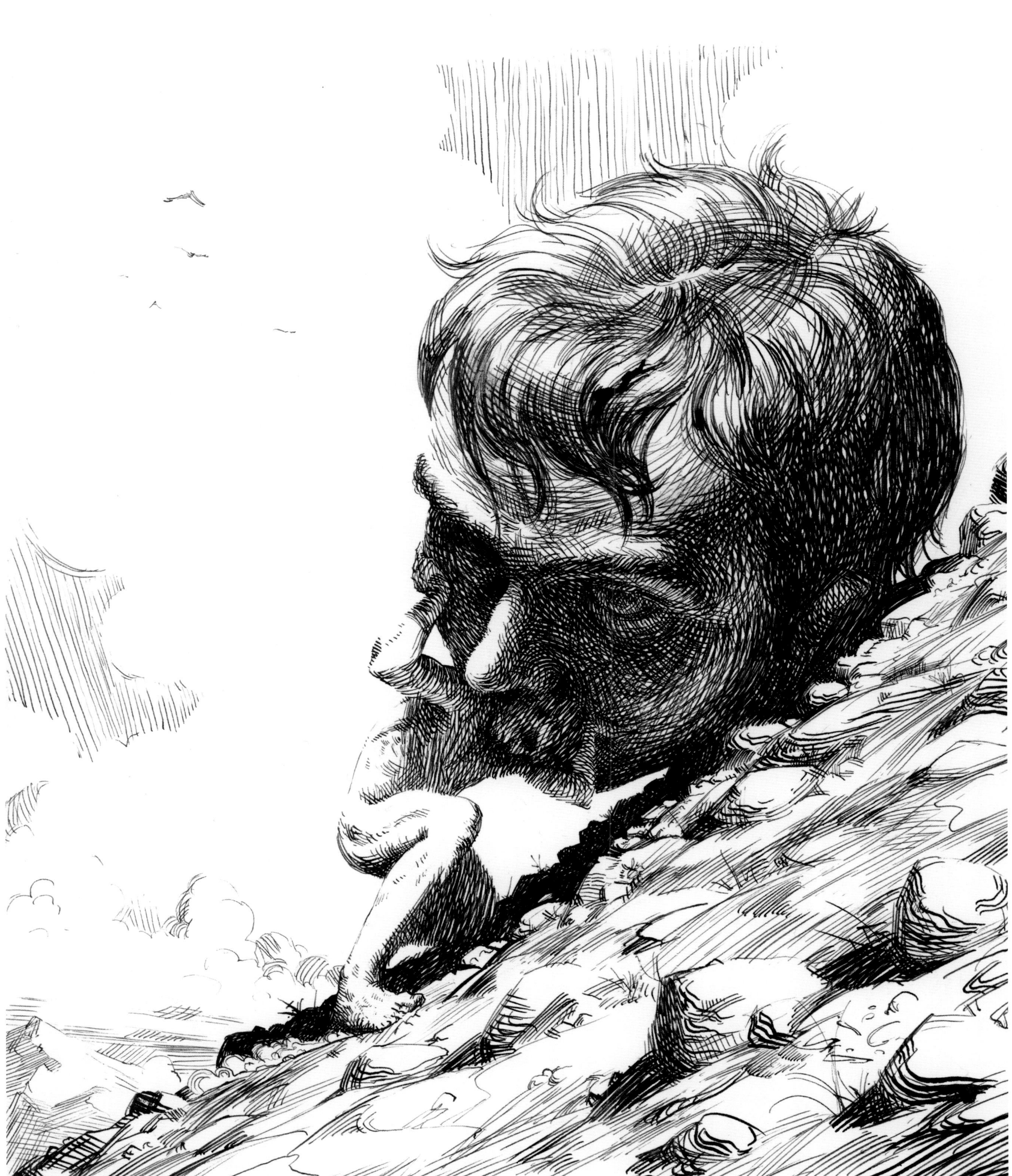

to wonder, what do I have to say about anything? A lot of the time, I simply feel confused, disconnected, overwhelmed or uninspired. Allowing myself to simply express those feelings in my artwork, to give them the validity and respect of allowing them to become the subject of a work of art means you can never run out of ideas. It is also common to worry that devoting your attention to these difficult emotions will somehow fortify them, whereas I believe the opposite is true. I find it easier to let go of things if I first acknowledge them. To make artwork about something is a devotional practice, a genuine sacrifice of our very precious finite time and attention. I believe that making art communicates an inherent optimism, no matter how dark the subject matter. Underneath the symbolism in the piece is the implied message that the artist believed that it was worth going through the effort of bringing this object into being.

Ego
2019

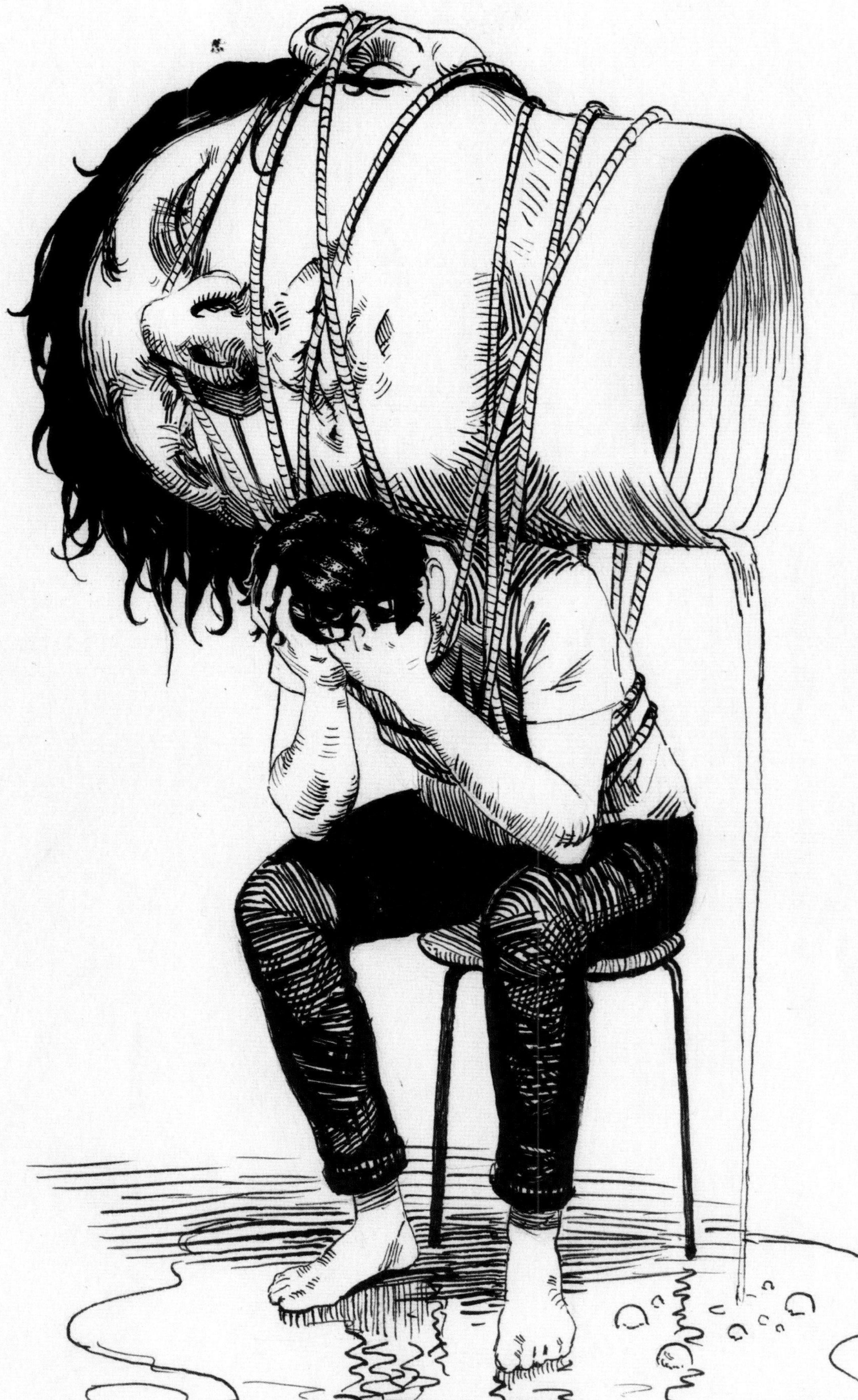

Stuck

2023

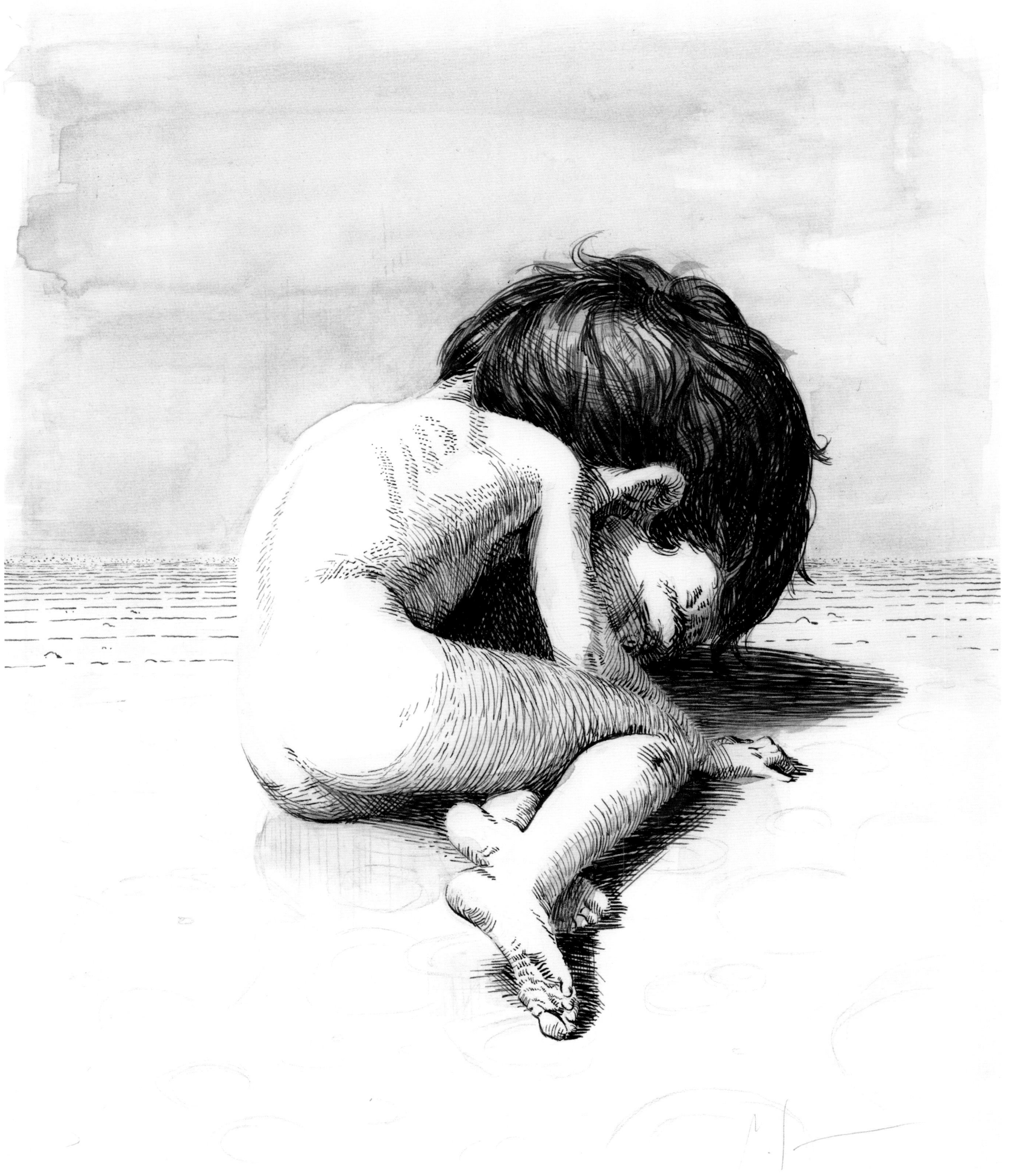

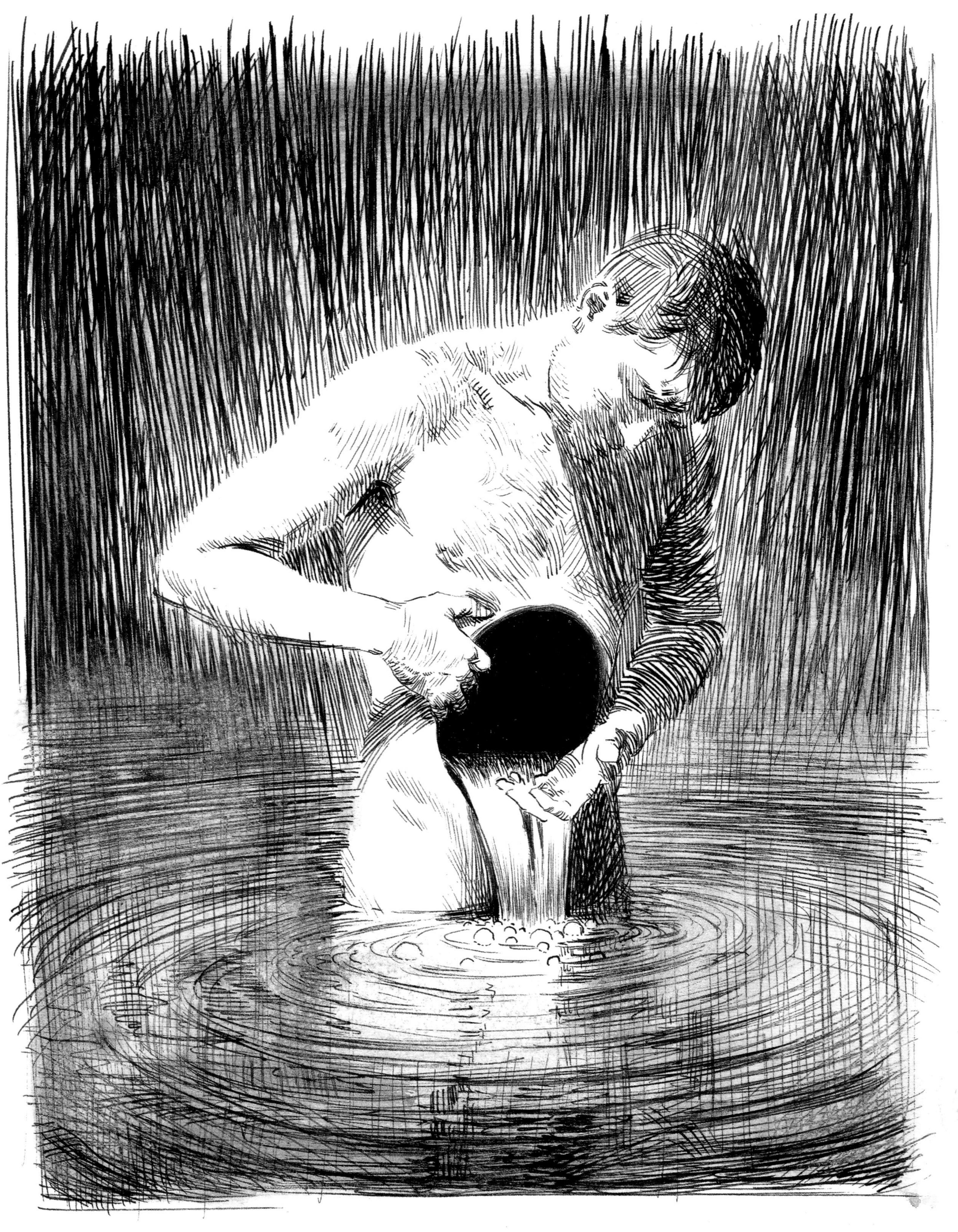

Empty Craving
2019

Beast of Burden
2019

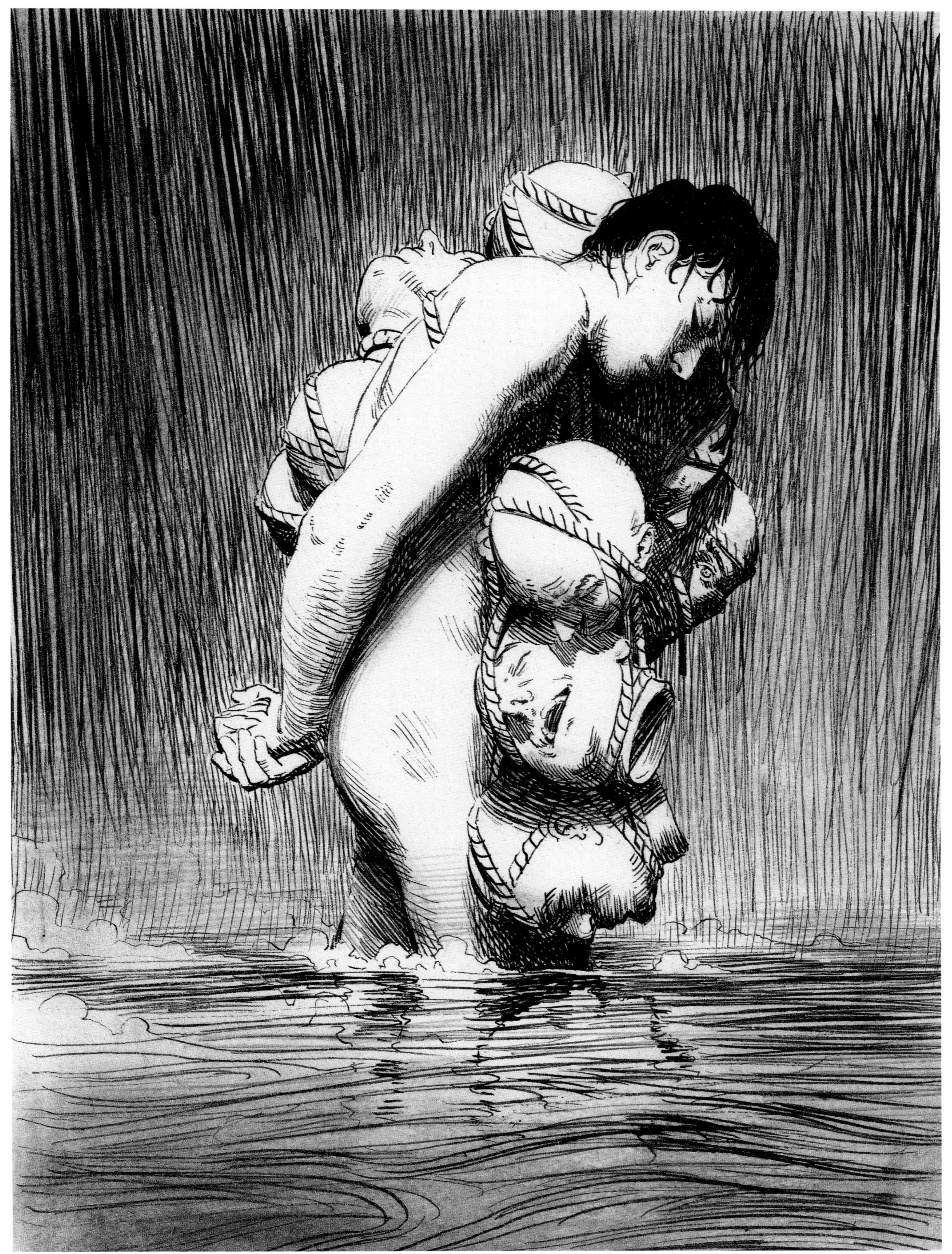

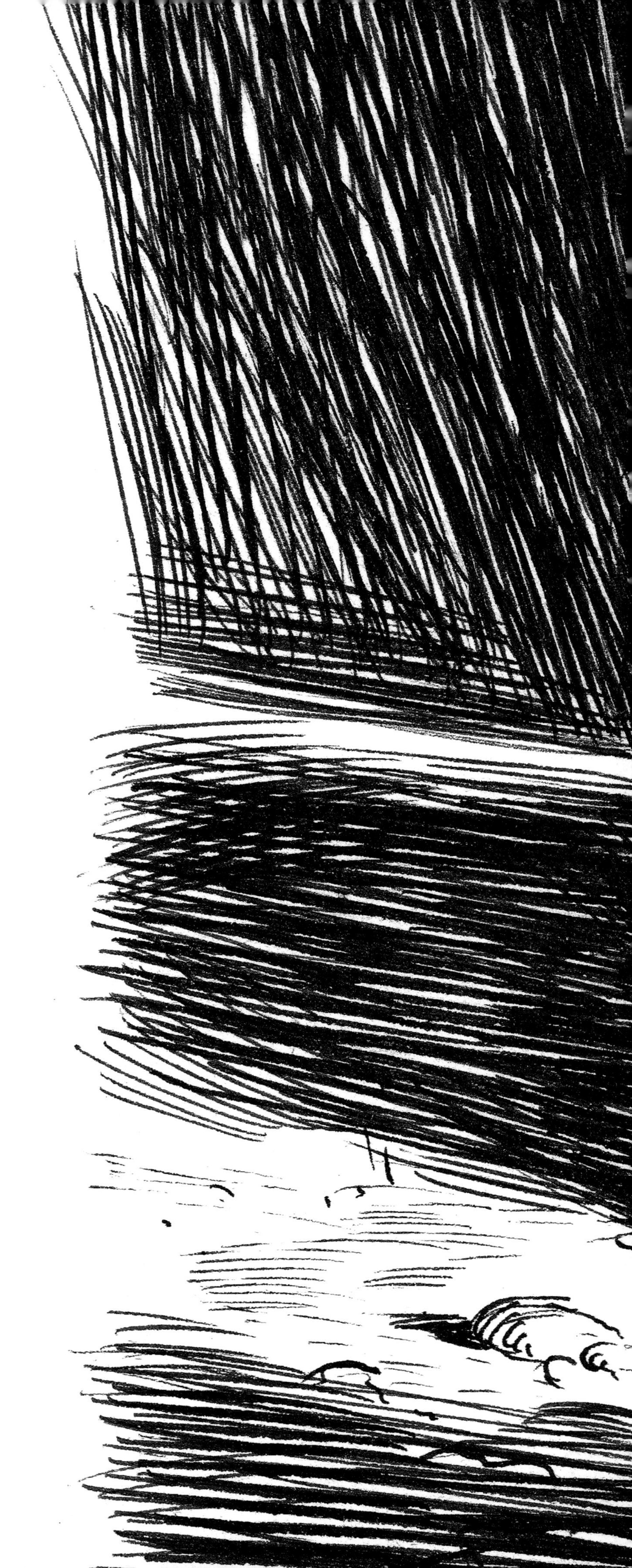

Empathy
2019

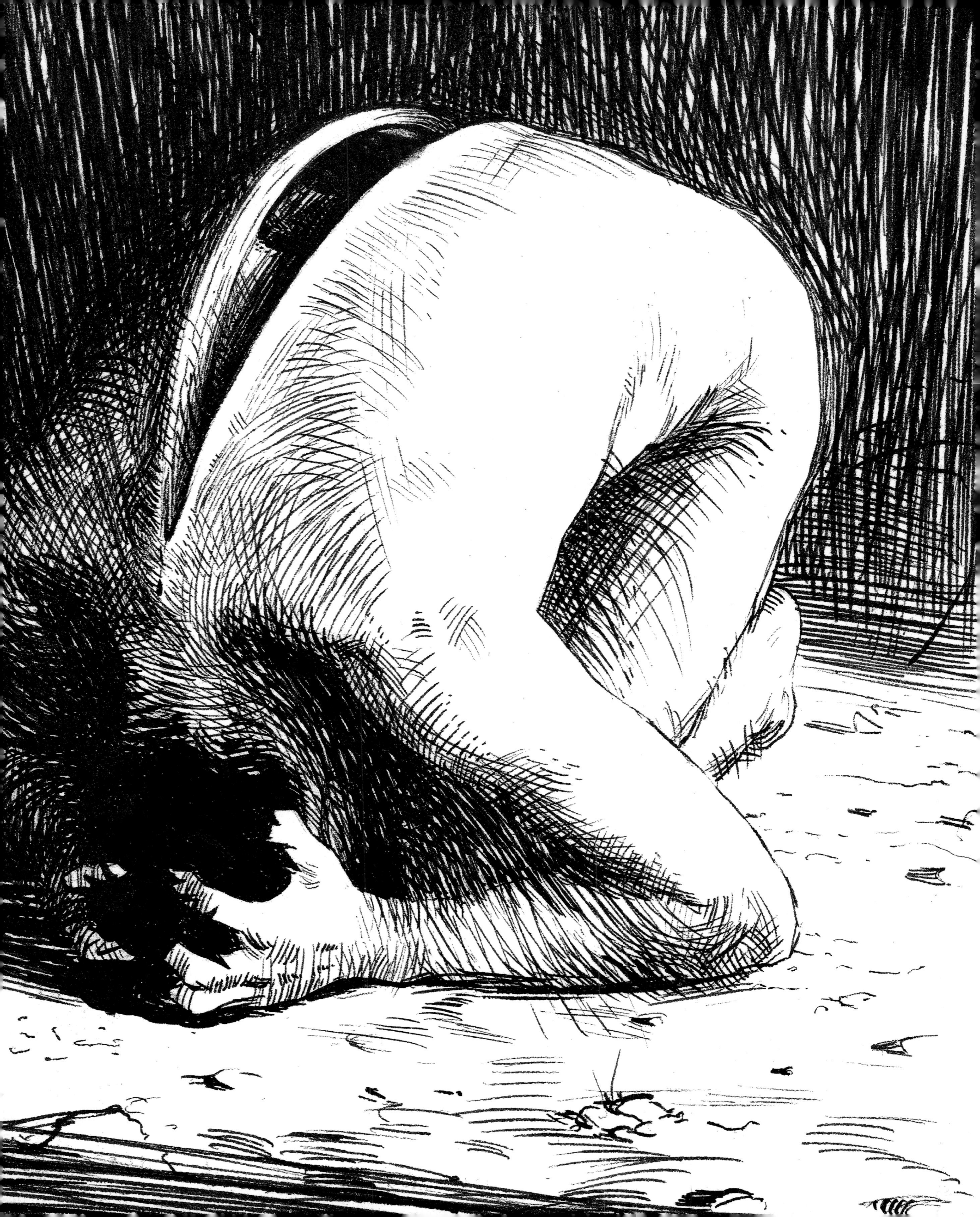

Eye Sea You + Study
2017

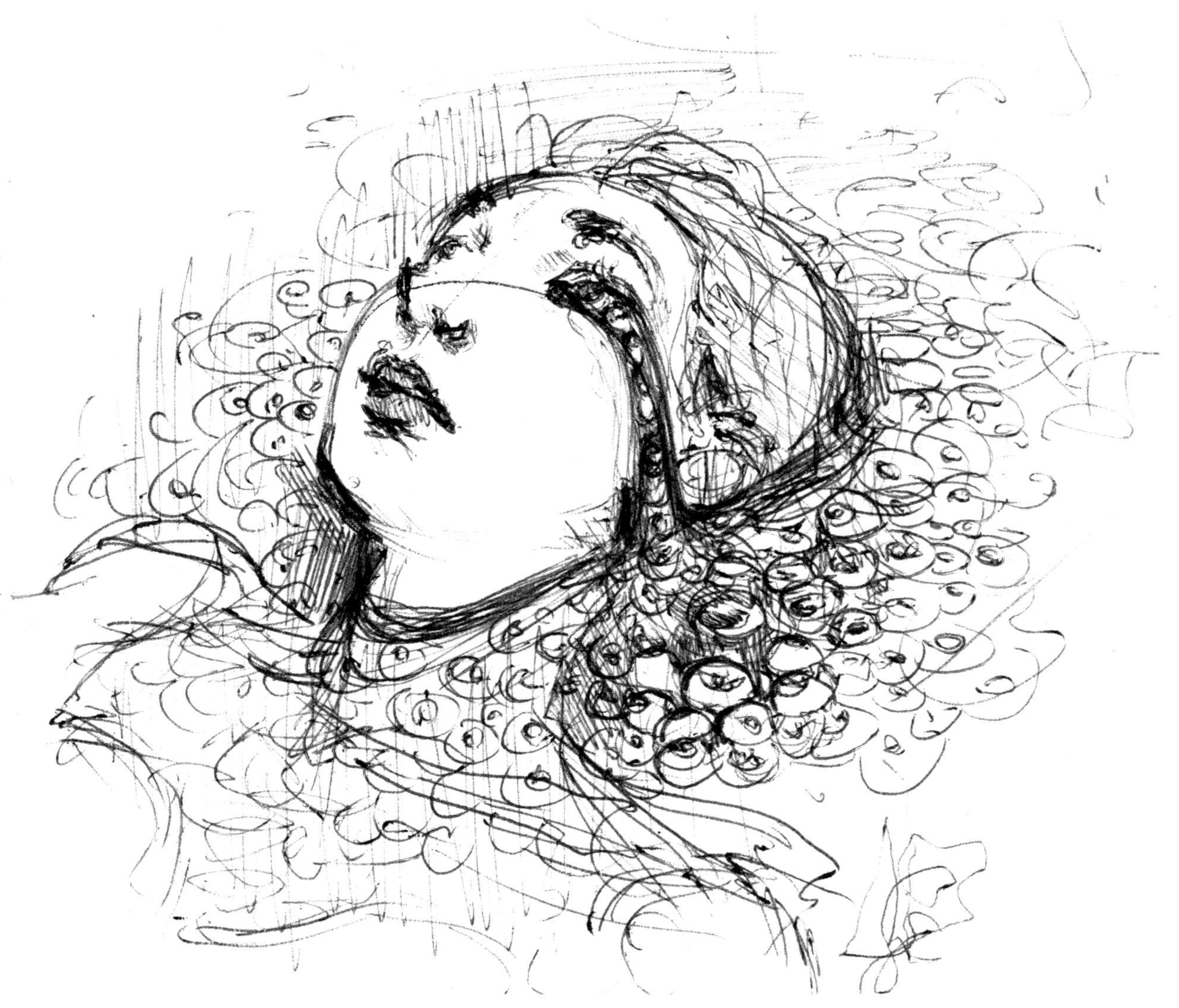

Absurdity

Isn't all of this completely absurd? It really is miraculous that we are able to tolerate the strangeness of reality at all. It seems the more we learn about our situation, the weirder it gets. From the mind-numbingly complicated cellular processes in our bodies to the vast cosmic kaleidoscope we exist within, life is happening on scales of space and time we can barely comprehend. And yet here we are, in the thin fragile skin of an atmosphere on a rock, as thinking apes, with the circus of culture and history pulling us to and fro. How is it that we so often feel that things are mundane, normal, boring?

Like a dream, we just find ourselves in our life, caught up in our current worries and goals. It never ceases to be odd to me that our memory just blurs and fails at a certain point of looking back. I don't remember how I got here, what it was like to go through the inverse of dying, to be born. There was a point at which I didn't exist, and yet here I am now totally caught in the midst of a human life. Do you ever wake from sleep and have that split second of remembering, *oh yeah, this thing, me, this is still going on huh?*

I have always enjoyed the way in which art can serve as an opportunity for us to take a step back and remember our childlike curiosity and awe about the world. Some of this work is my way of venting those feelings of amazement and confusion at all of it. Quite honestly, I find life terrifying, but the act of not turning away from it and instead leaning into my curiosity seems to help. I don't want to forget what an incredible opportunity it is to exist.

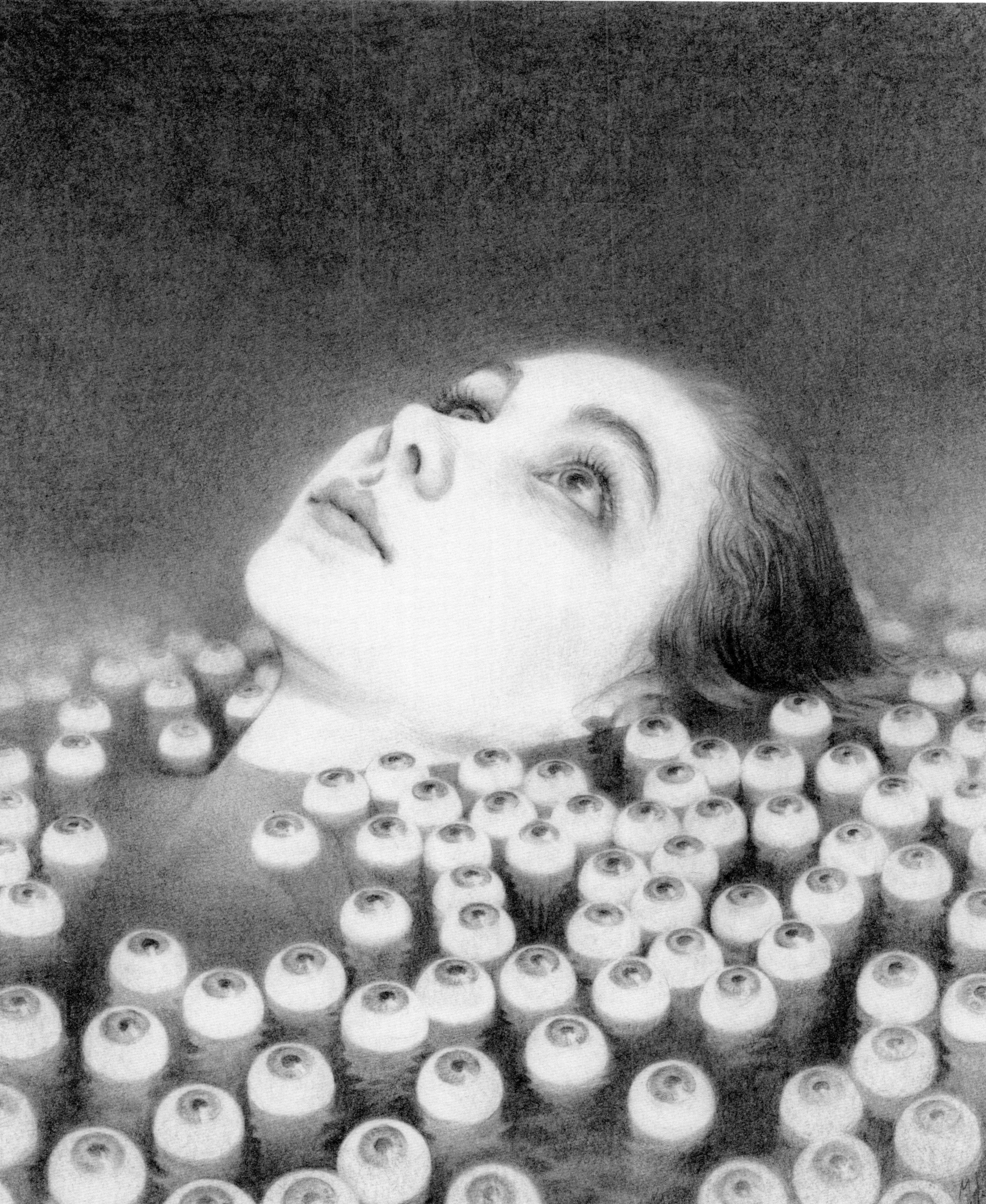

Inner Eye
2019

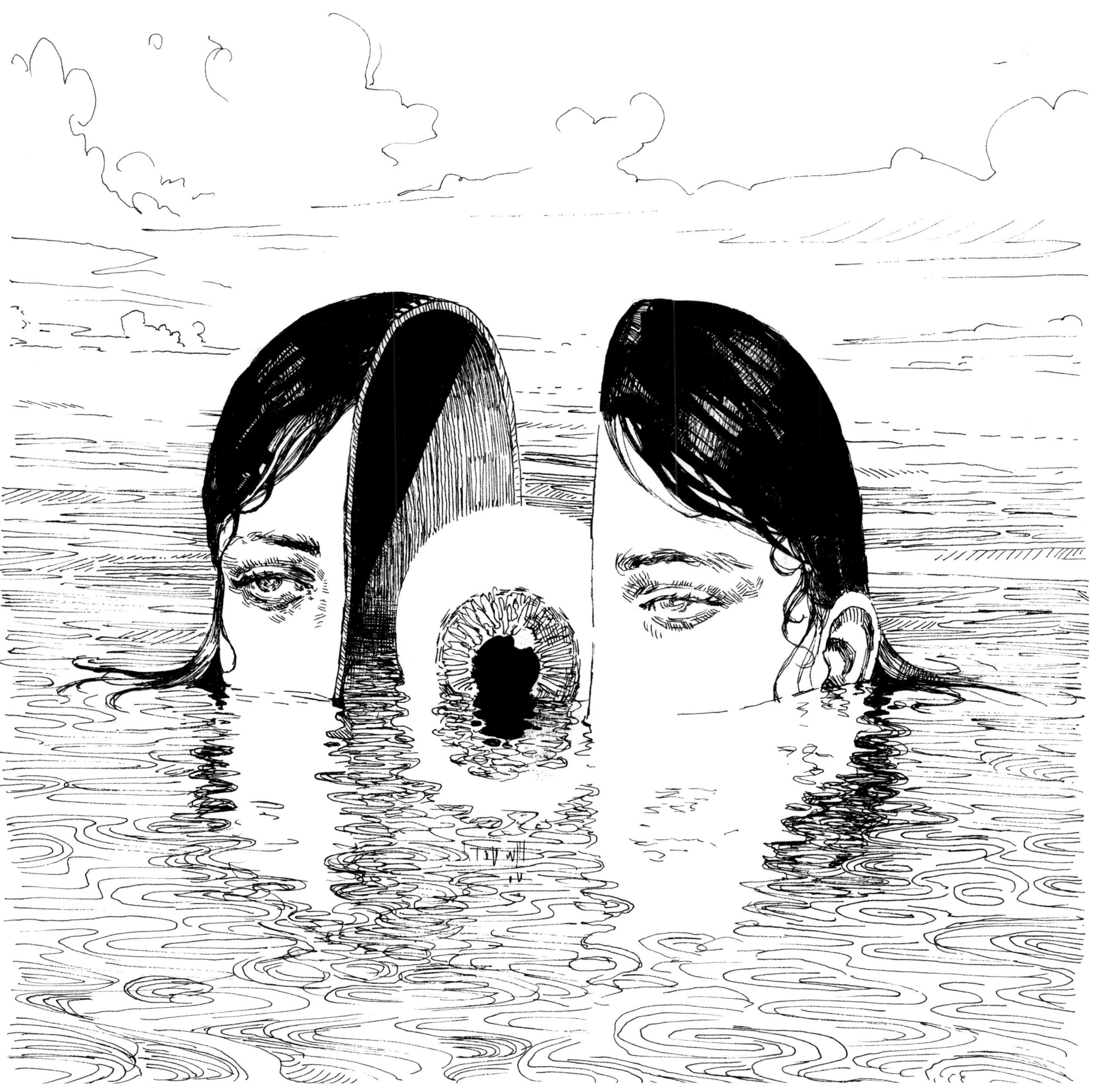

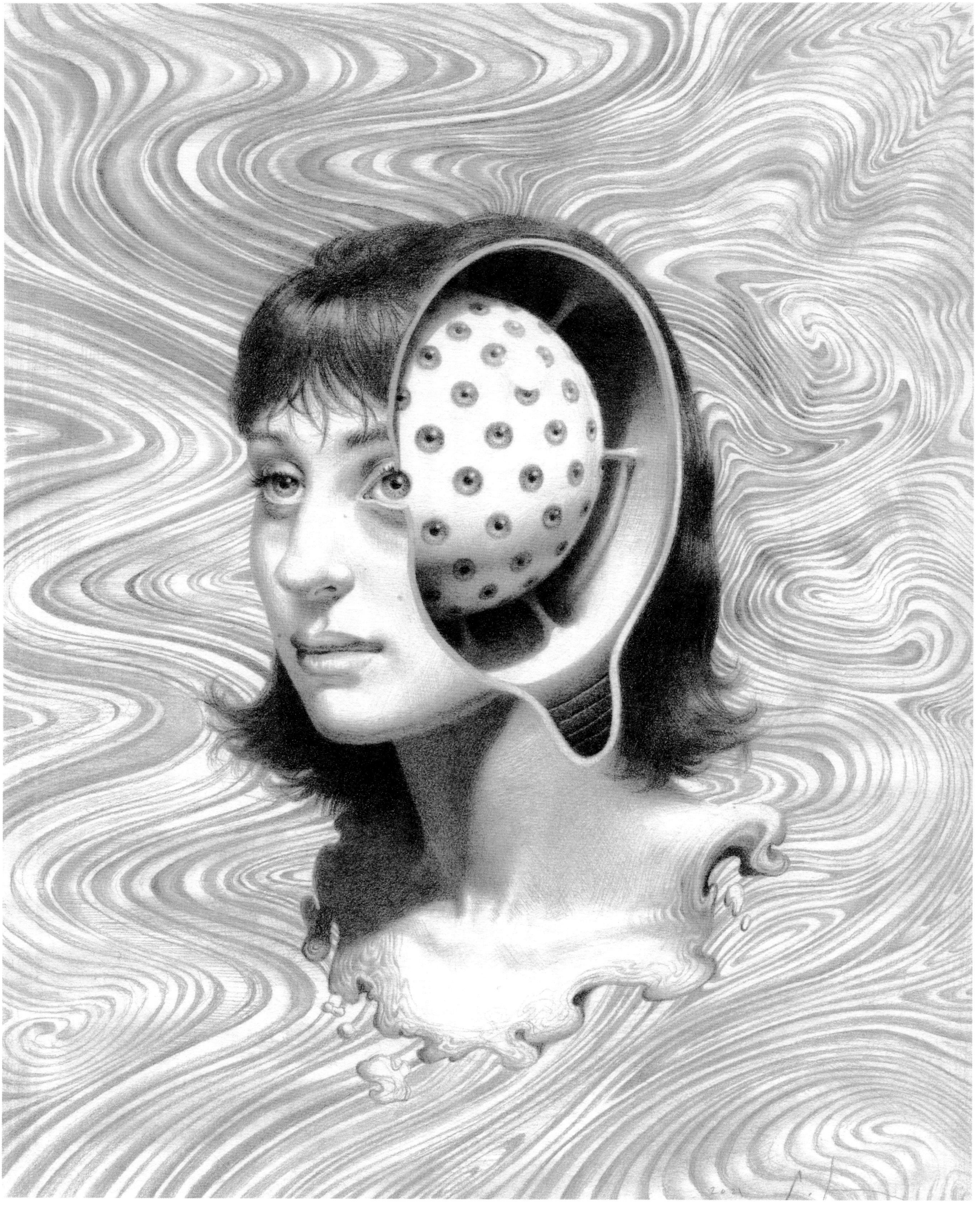

Blossom
2019

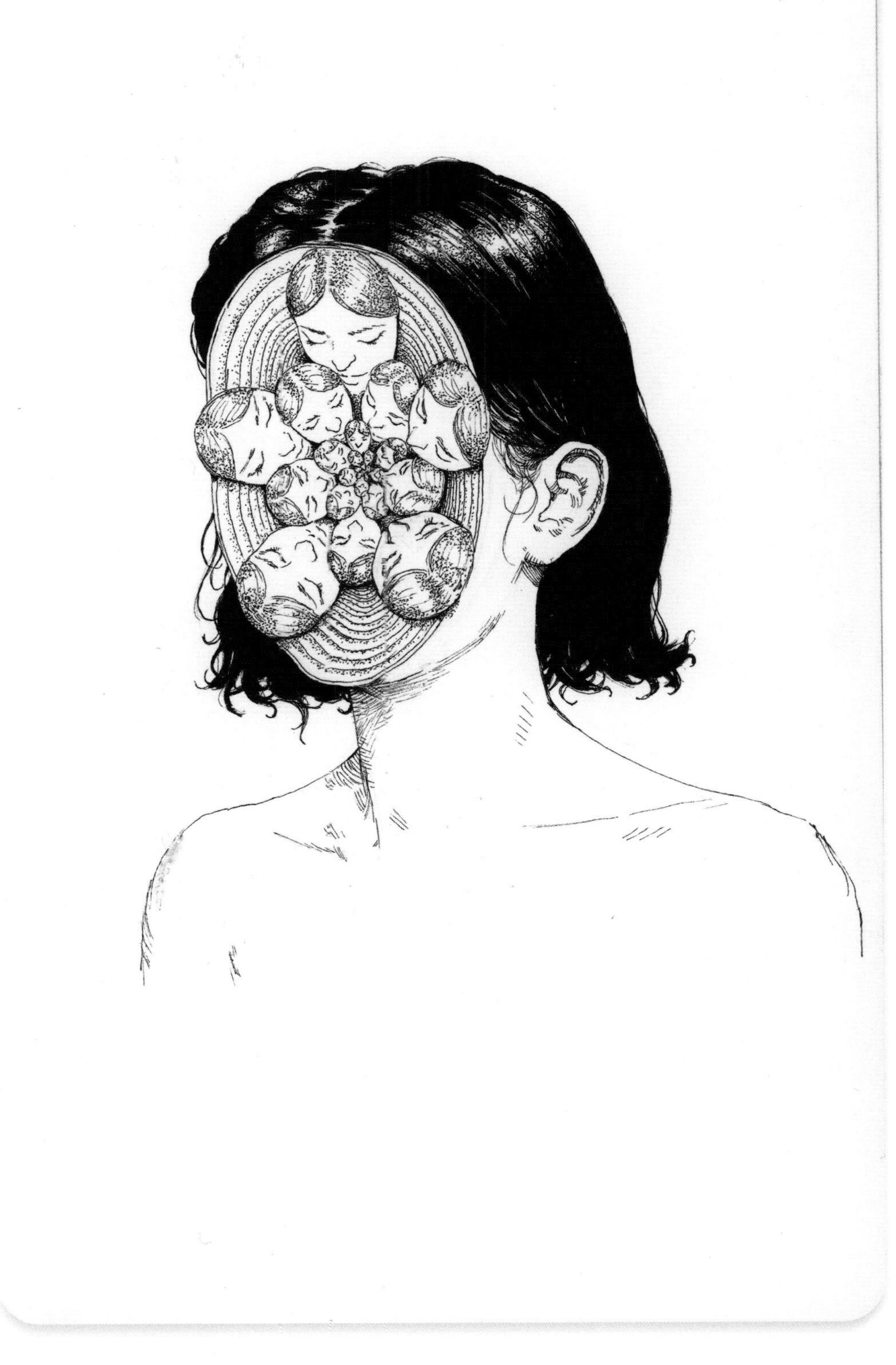

Anatomy of The Eyeball
2021

Watcher

2019

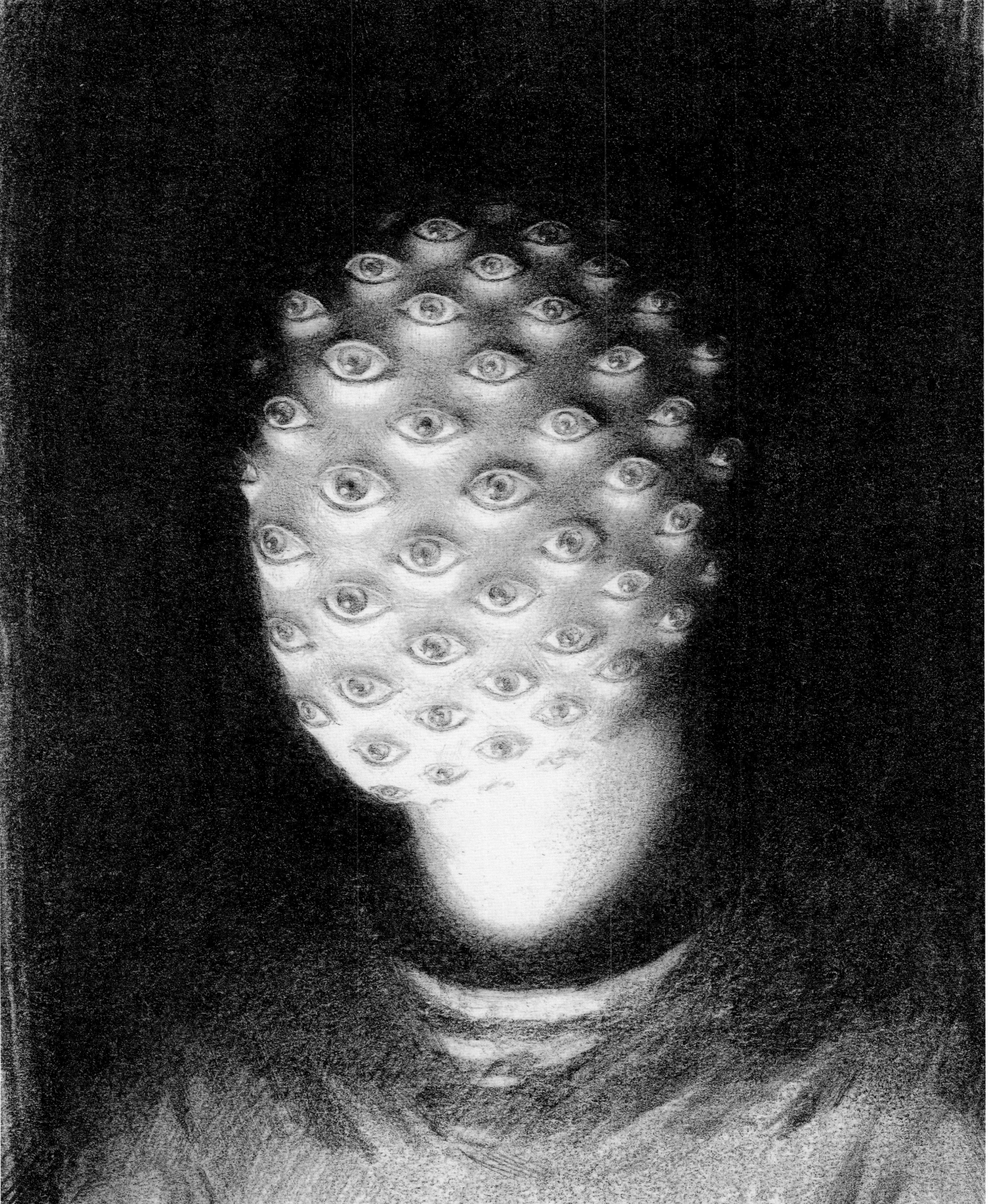

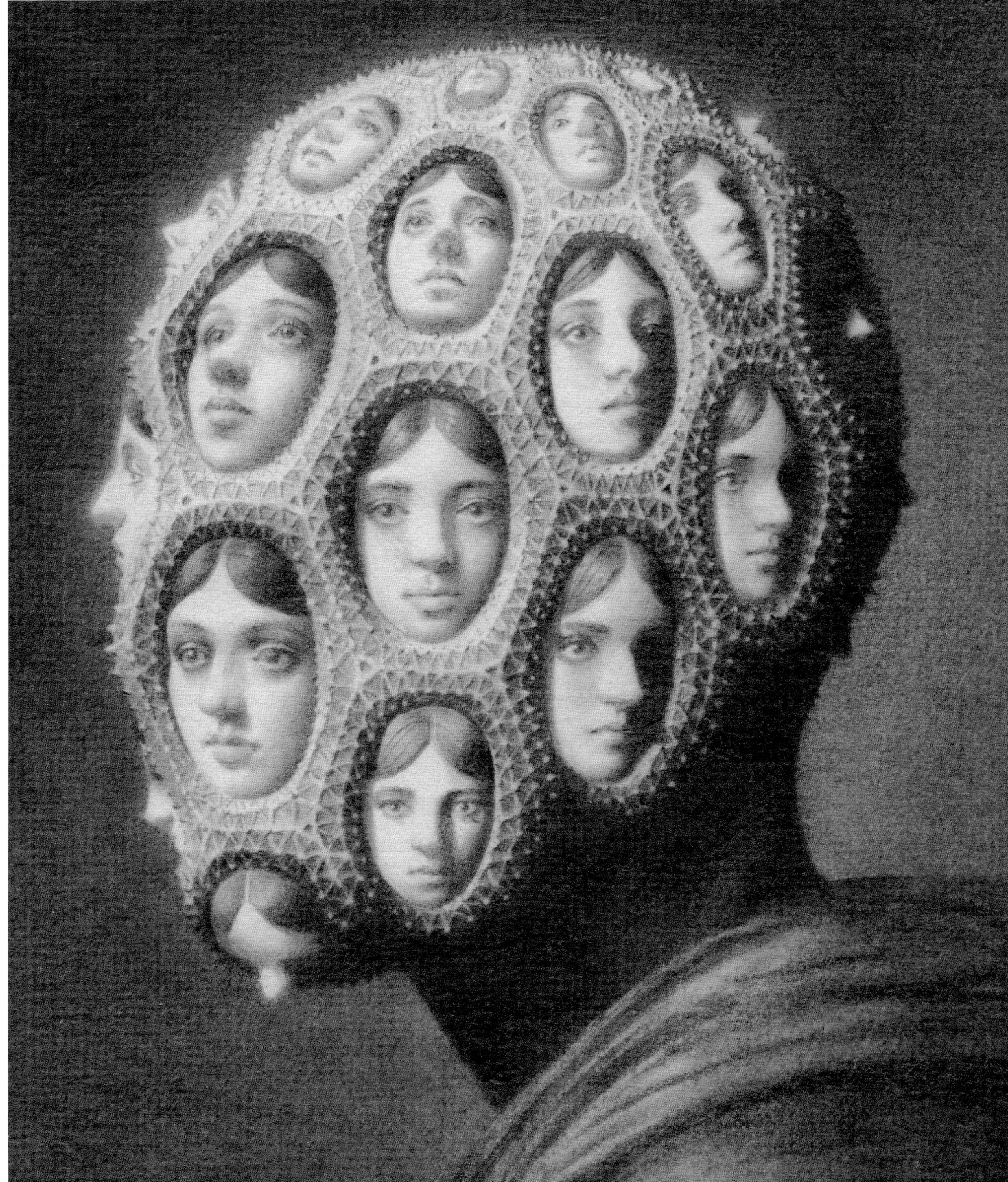

Panopticon (detail)
2020

The texture of the head between the many faces here is inspired by that found on starfish. I've always been fascinated by the way textures are accentuated as forms when they turn away from the light. The pockets of shadow deepen and merge with the shadow side of the form and the raised sections peek above like mountains and treetops catching the last light in the setting sun. Often, I forget about the subject that I am drawing and get lost in the thrill of light and form, a language in and of itself imbued with meaning that can't be expressed verbally. Working within the language of realism feels like worshipping nature, something always present as an undercurrent in my work. Behind the conceptual and psychological symbolism, my work is a love letter to reality.

Cube Head
2022

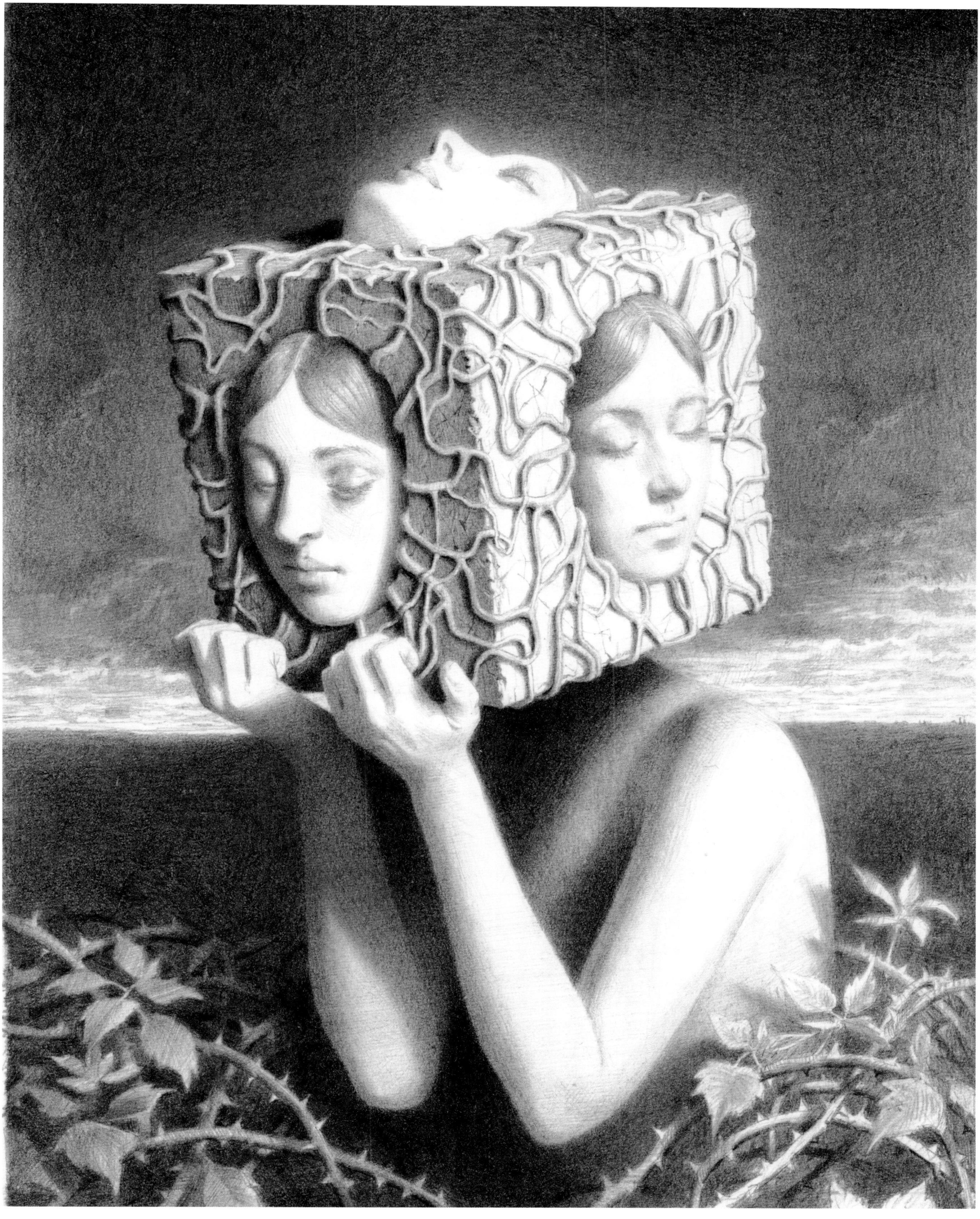

Handman

2024

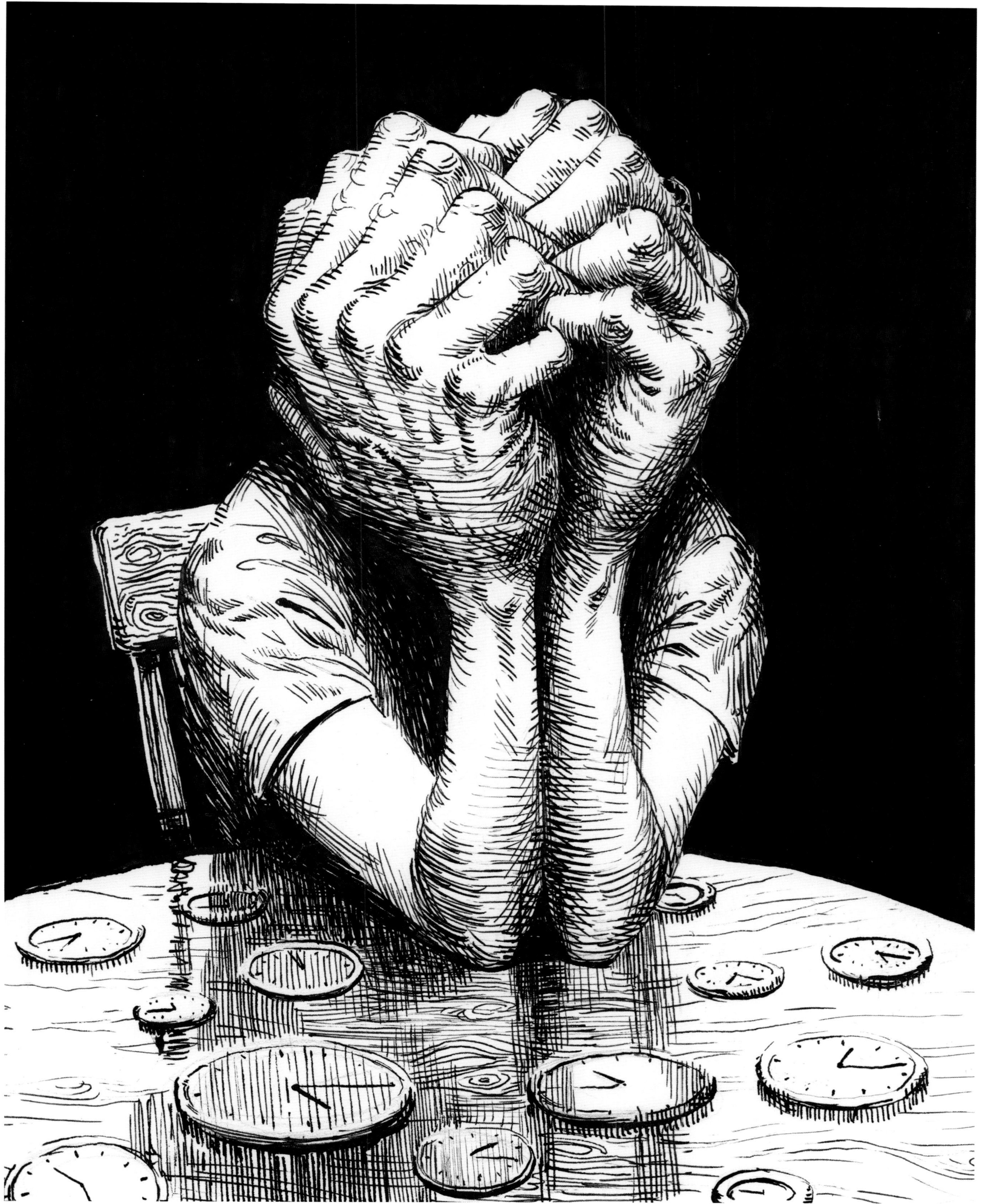

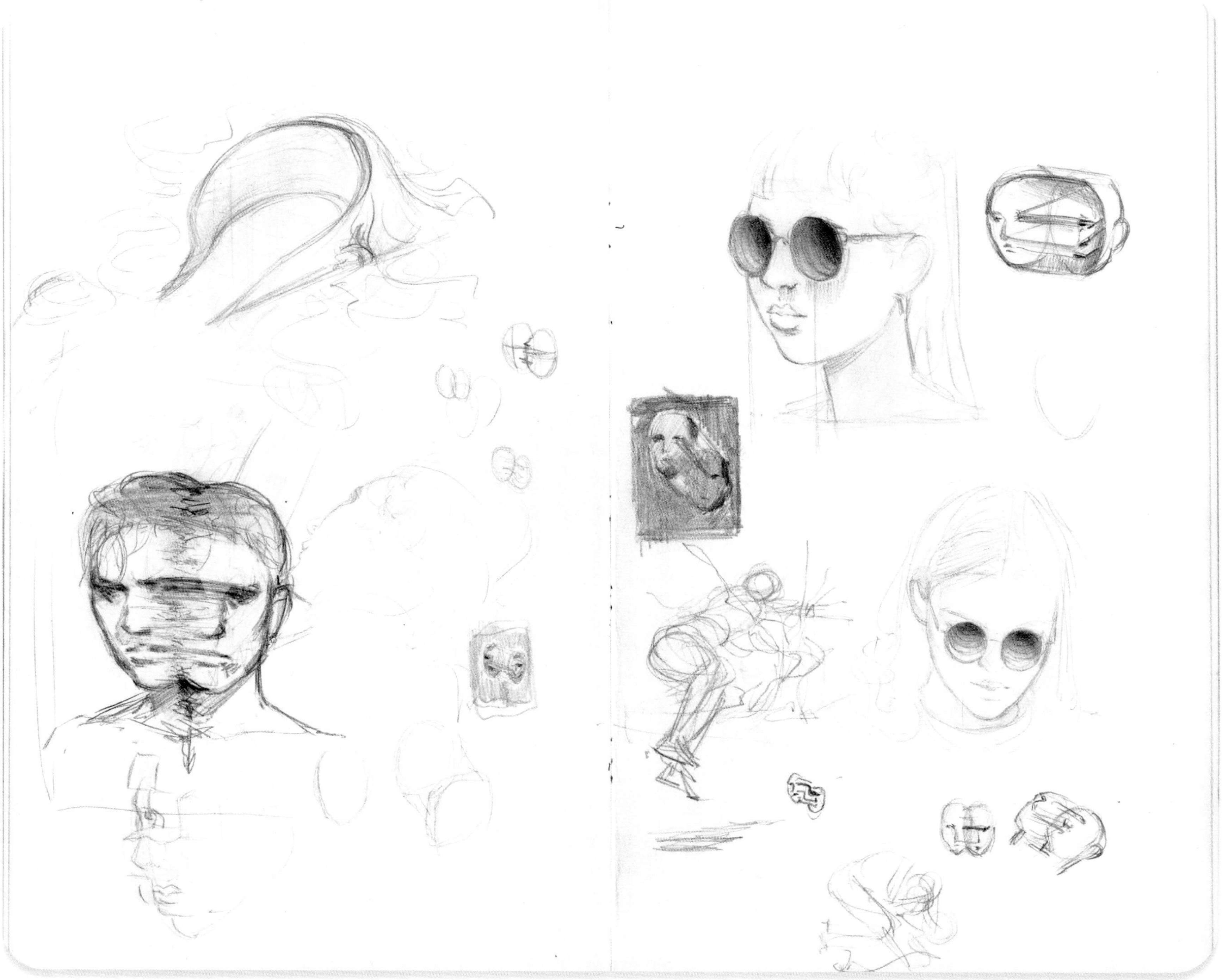

Mitosis + Studies

2018

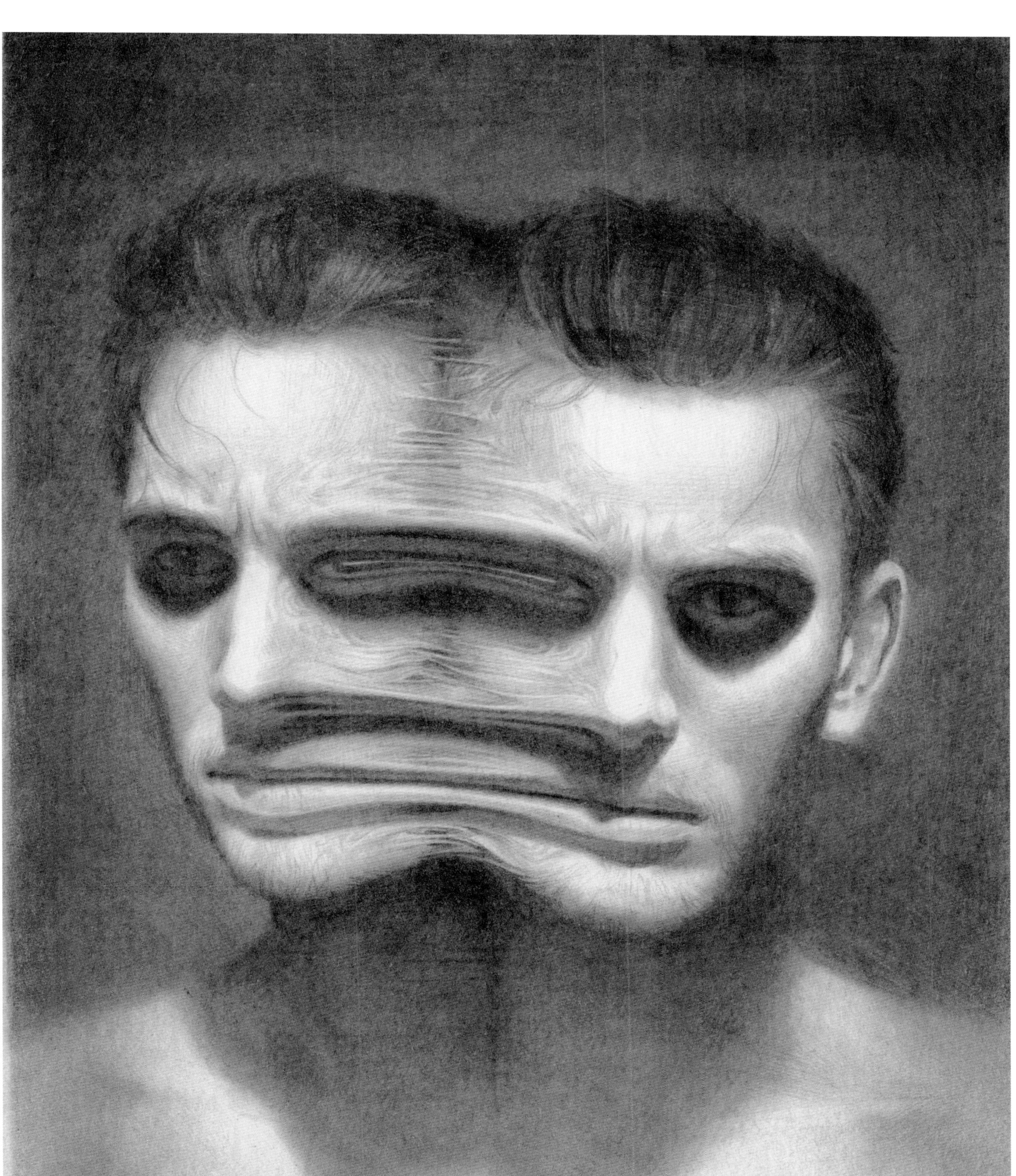

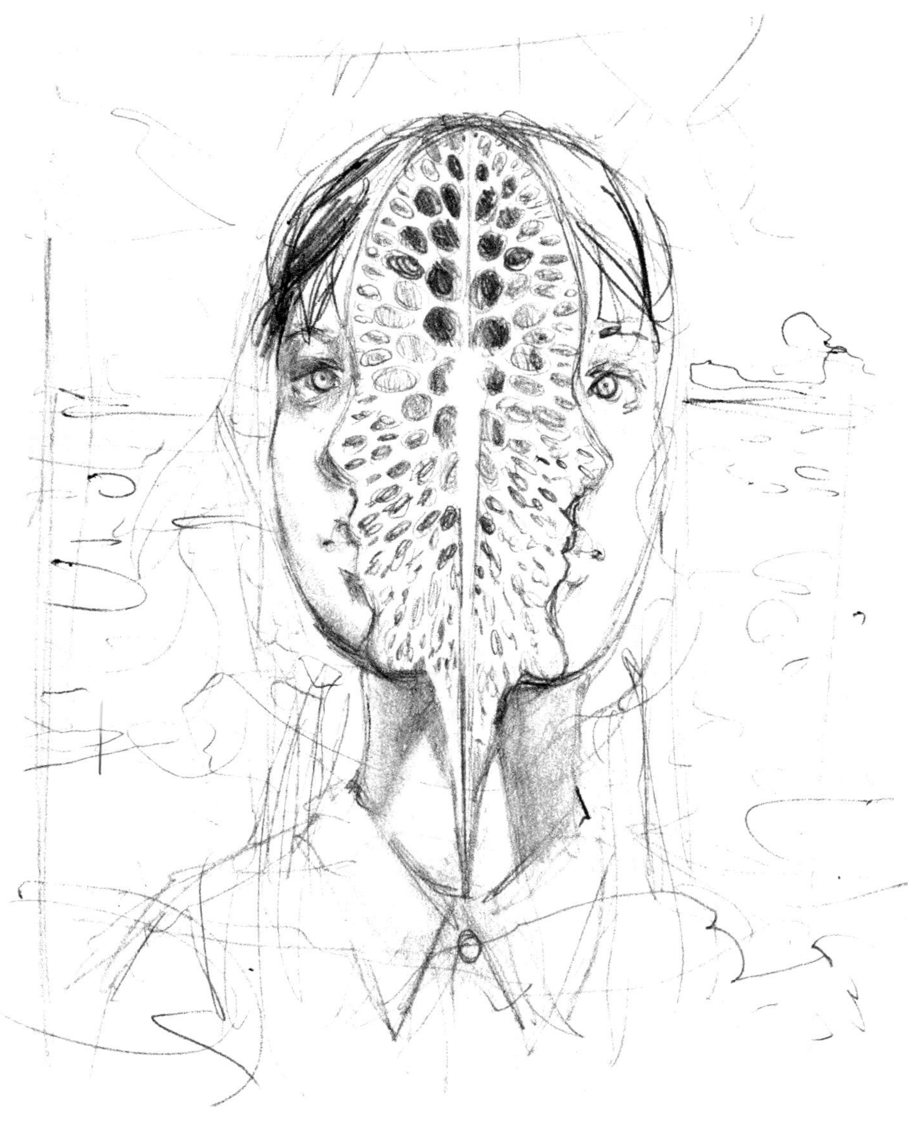

Hivemind (detail) + Study

2018

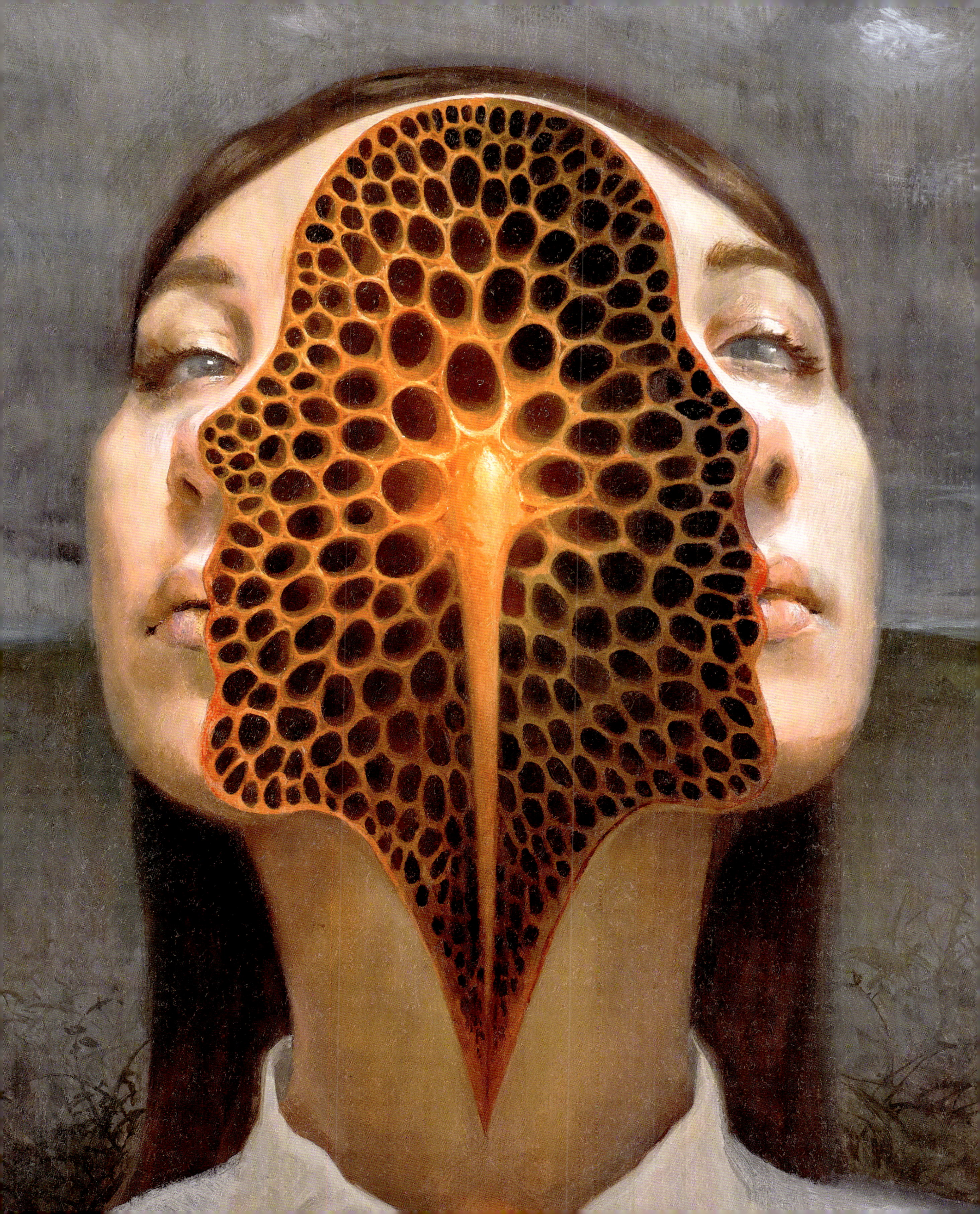

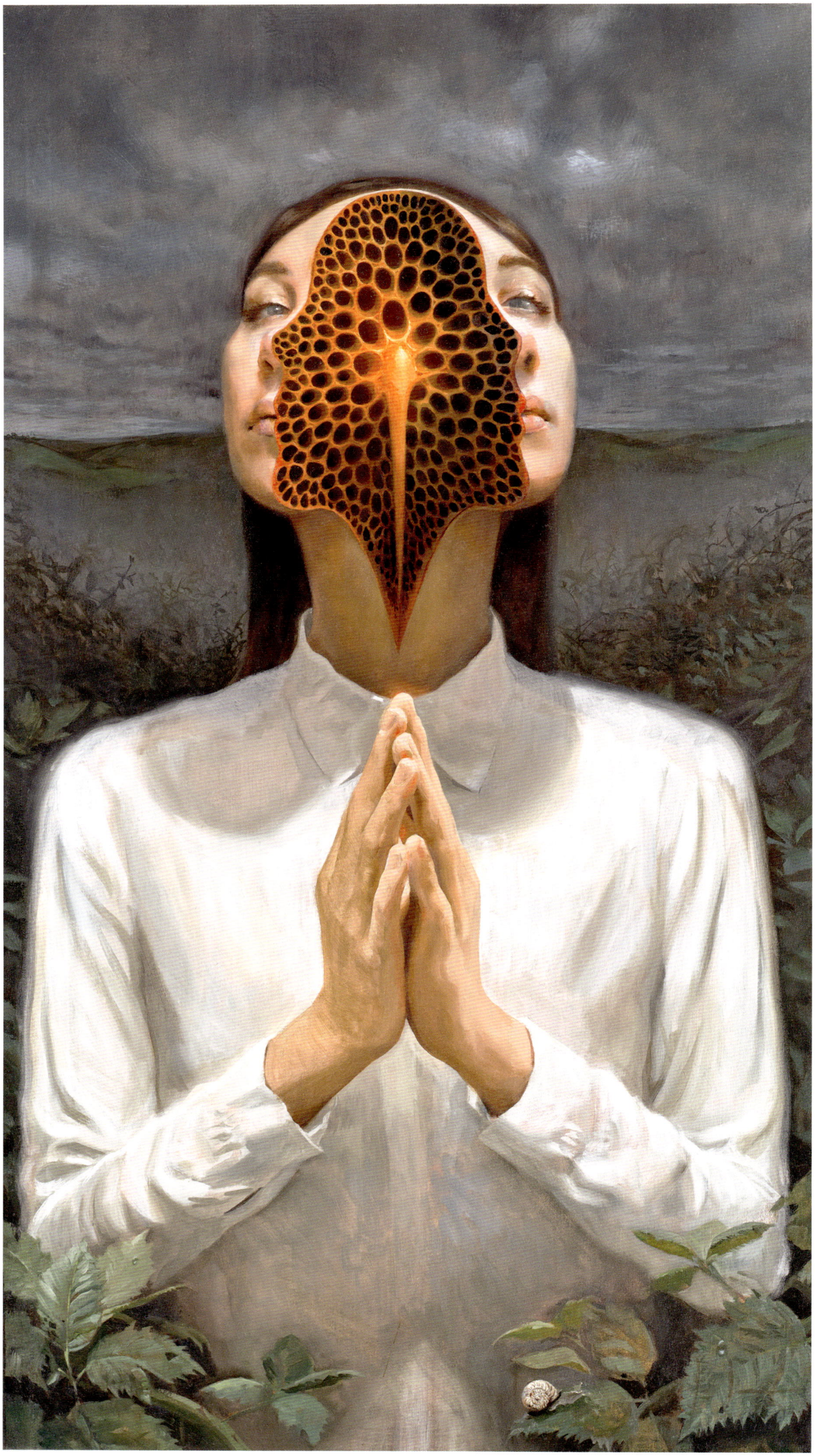

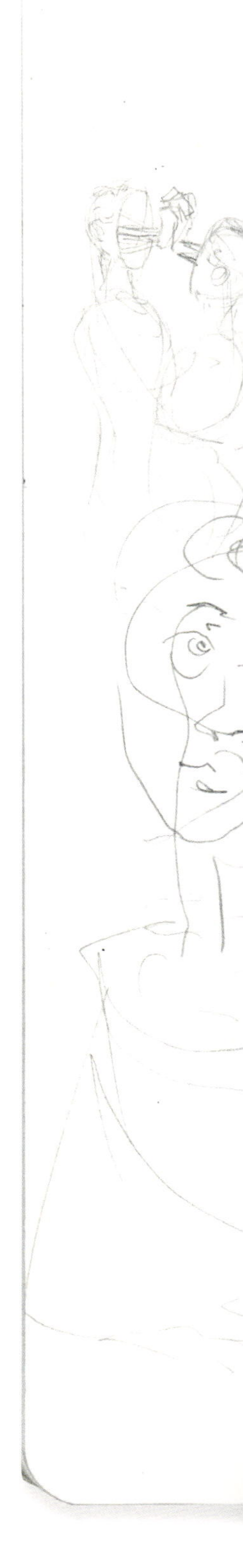

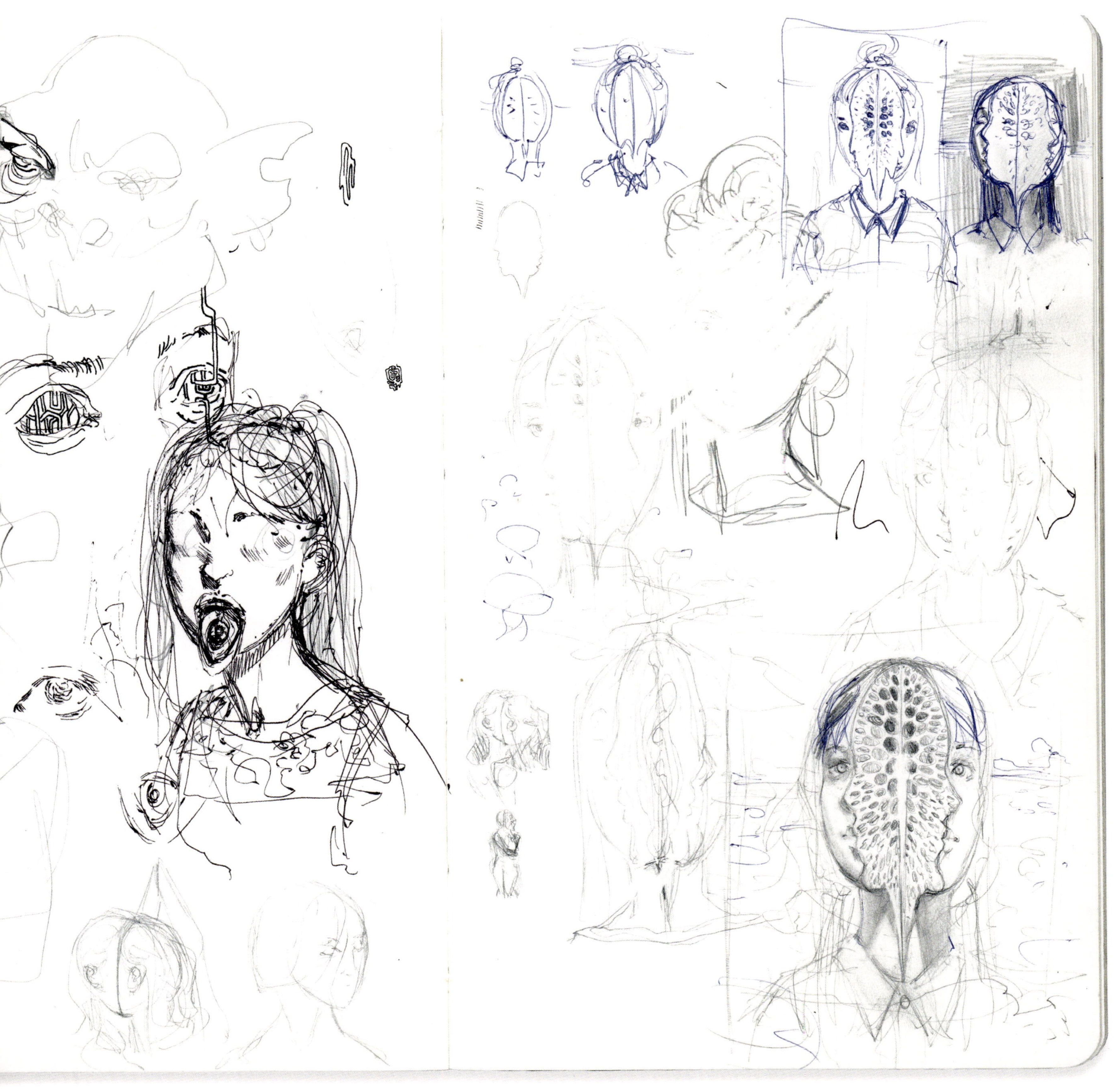

Hivemind + Study
2018

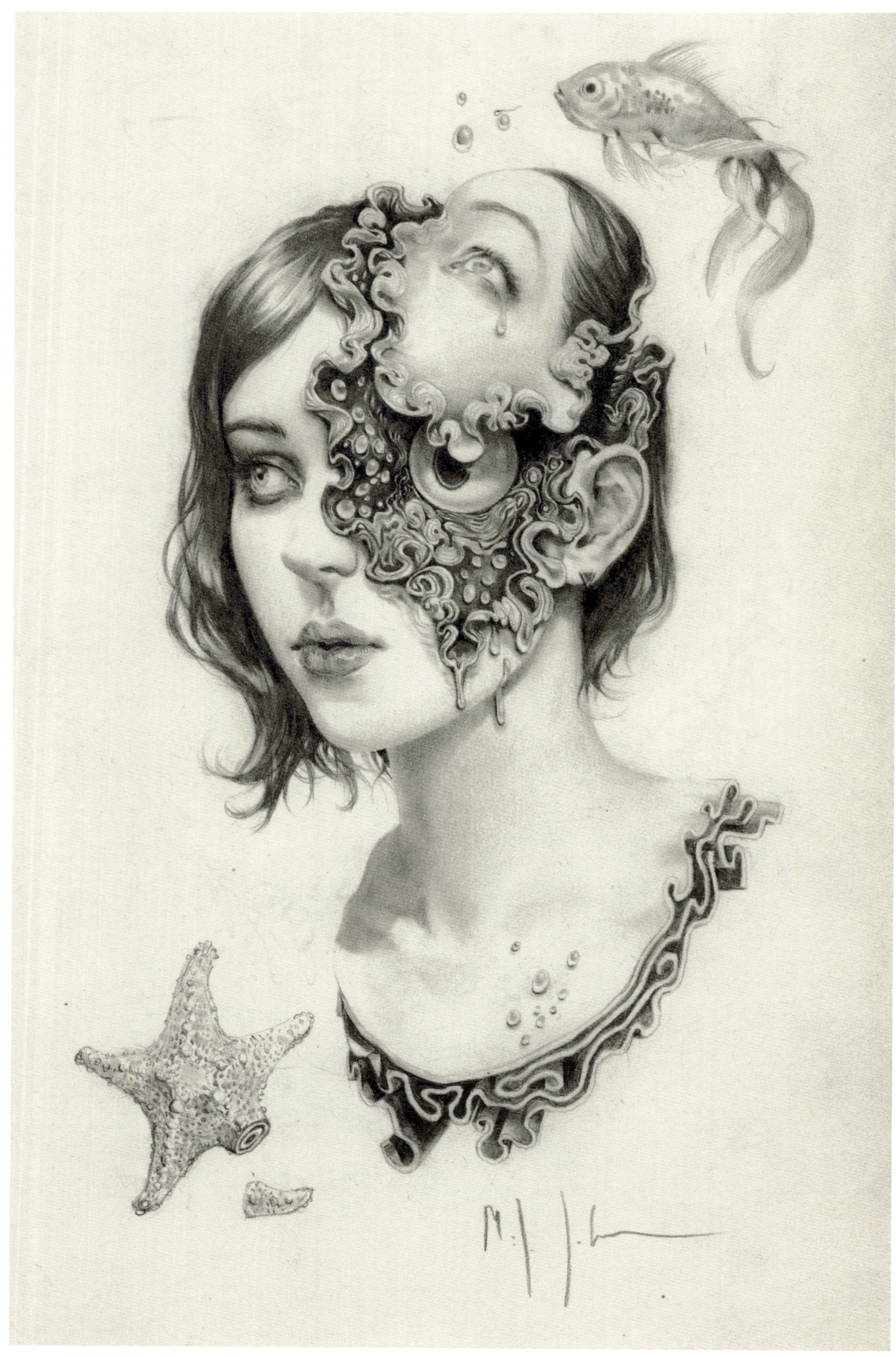

Evil Eye
2016

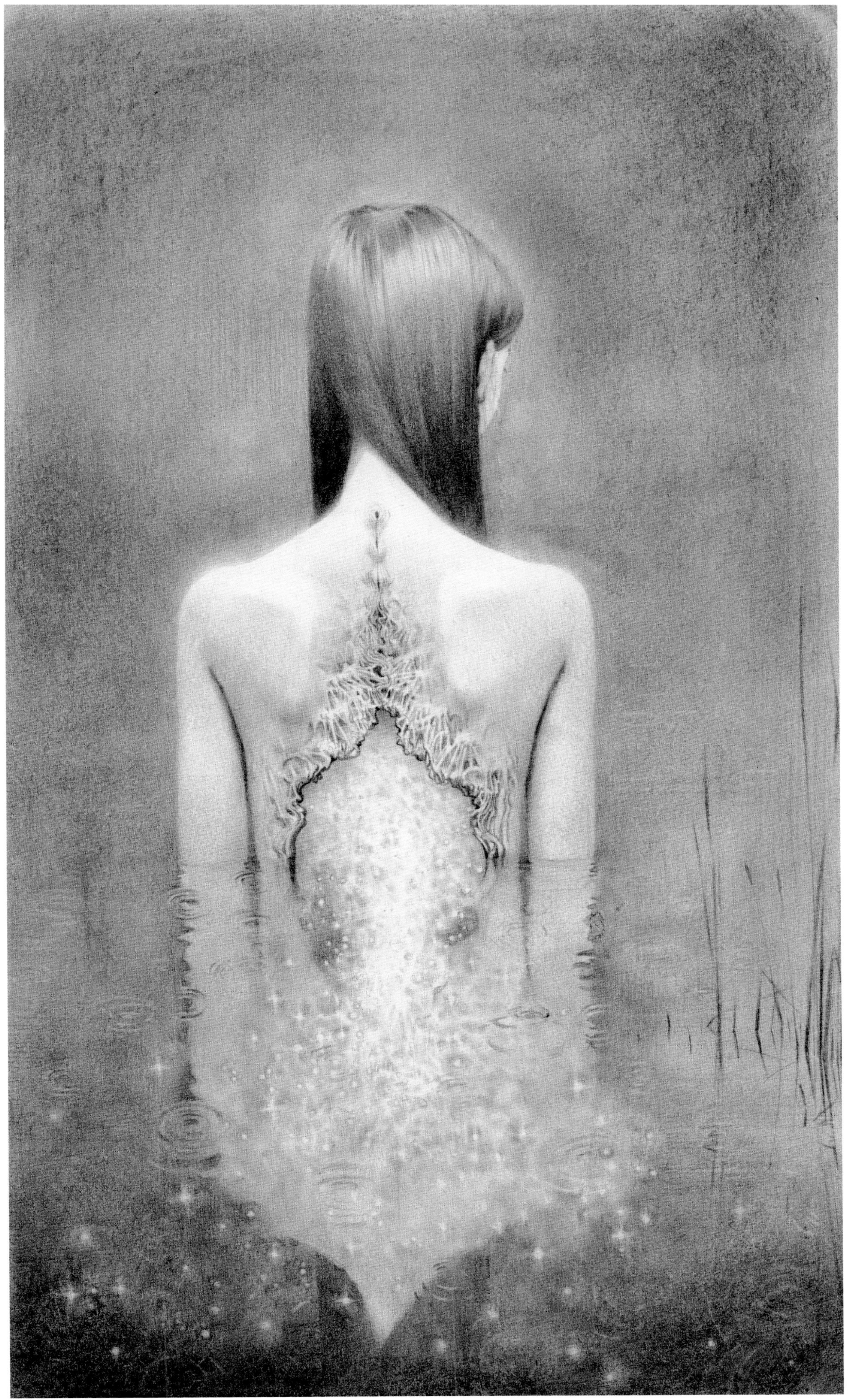

Wound
2016

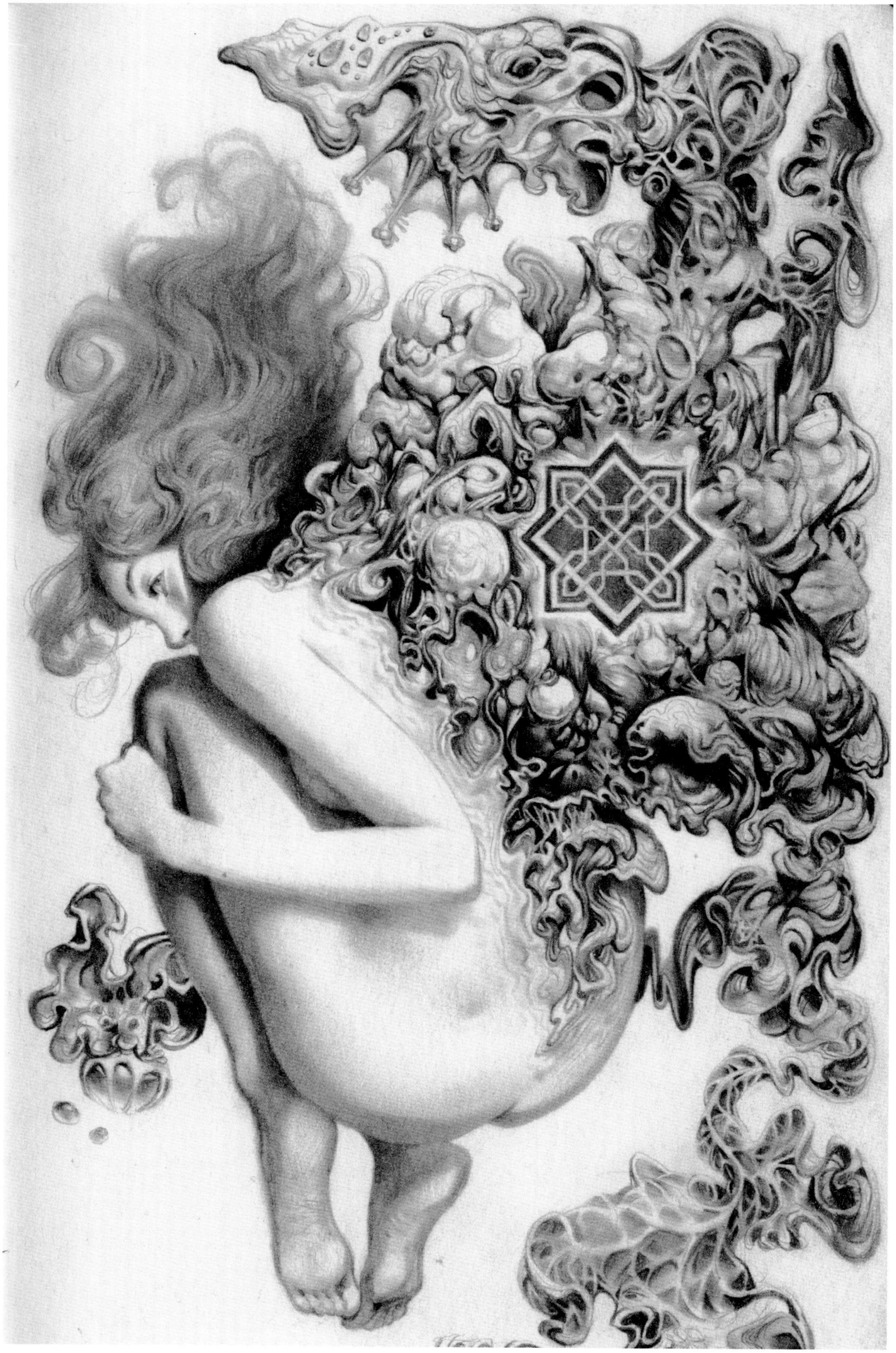

Morphology

2016Z

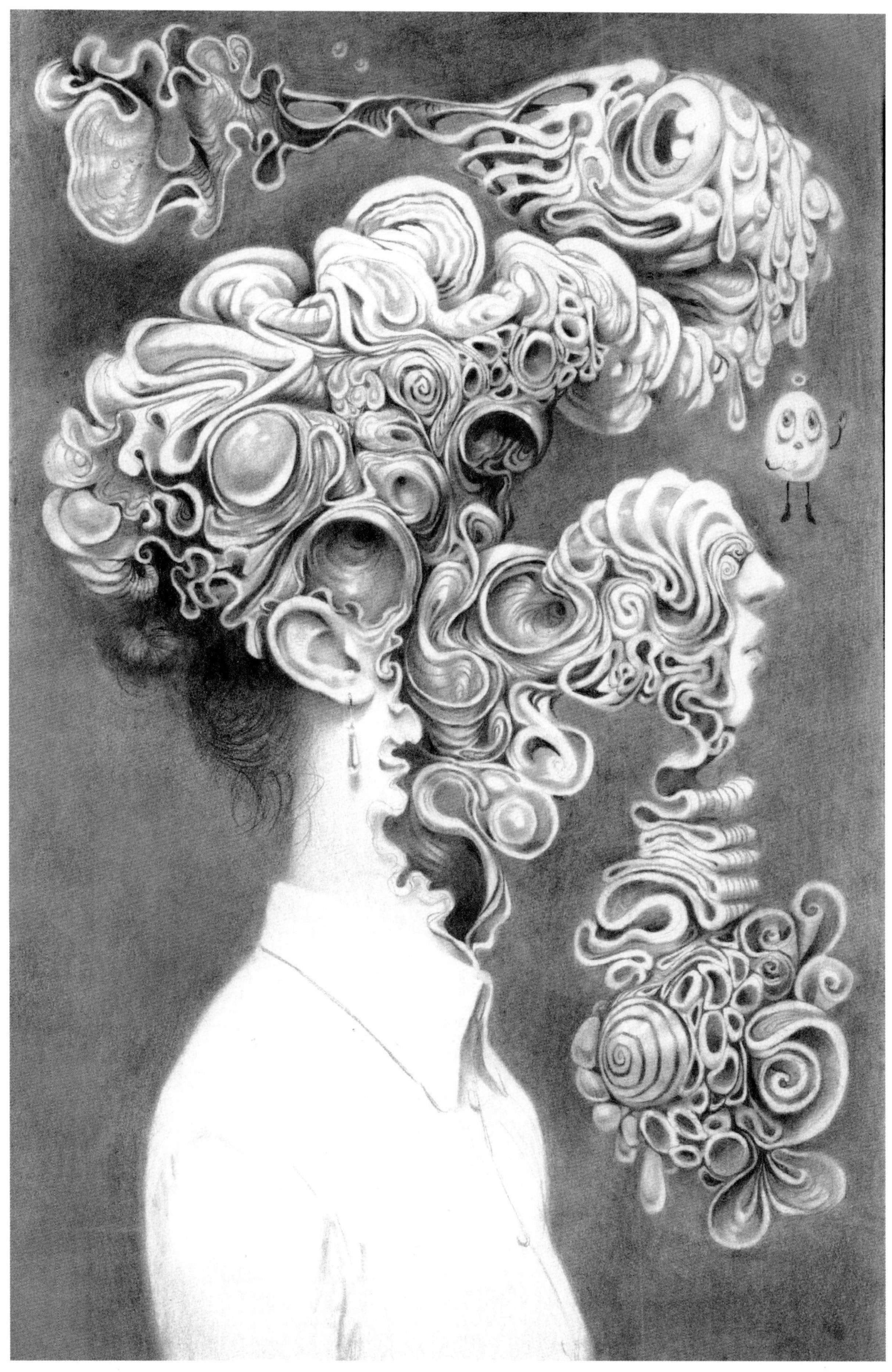

Egg Angel
2017

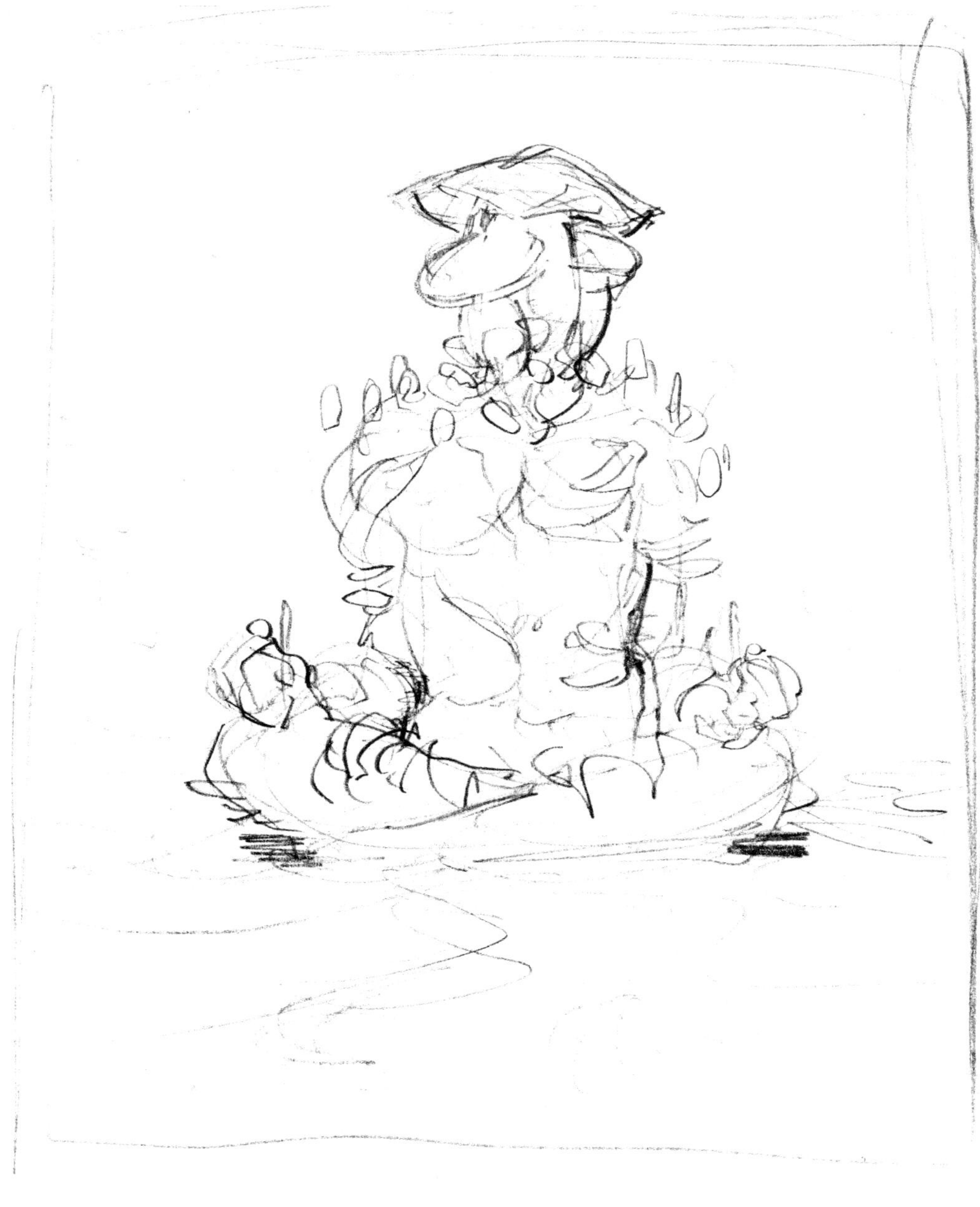

Mycelial Man + Study

2018

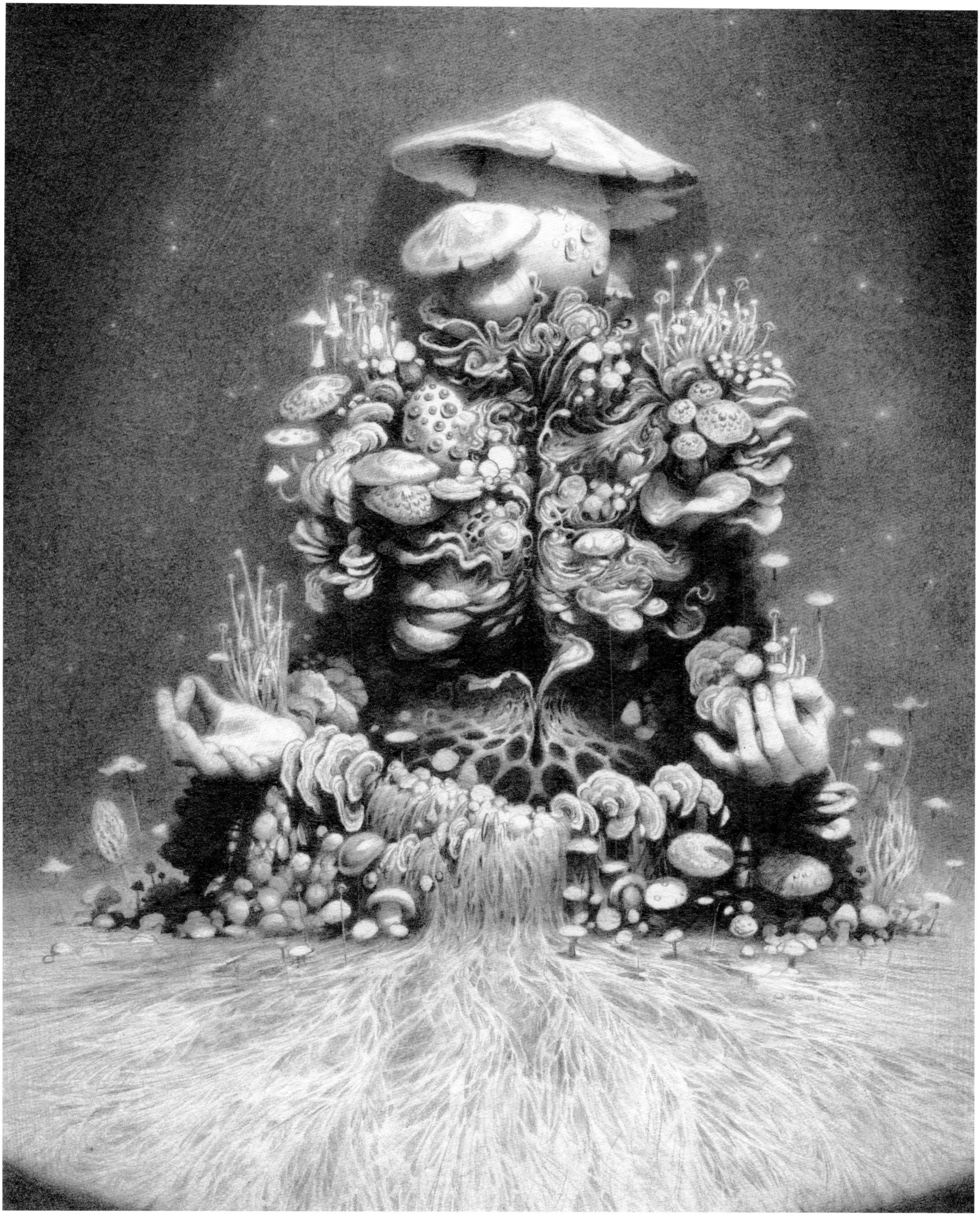

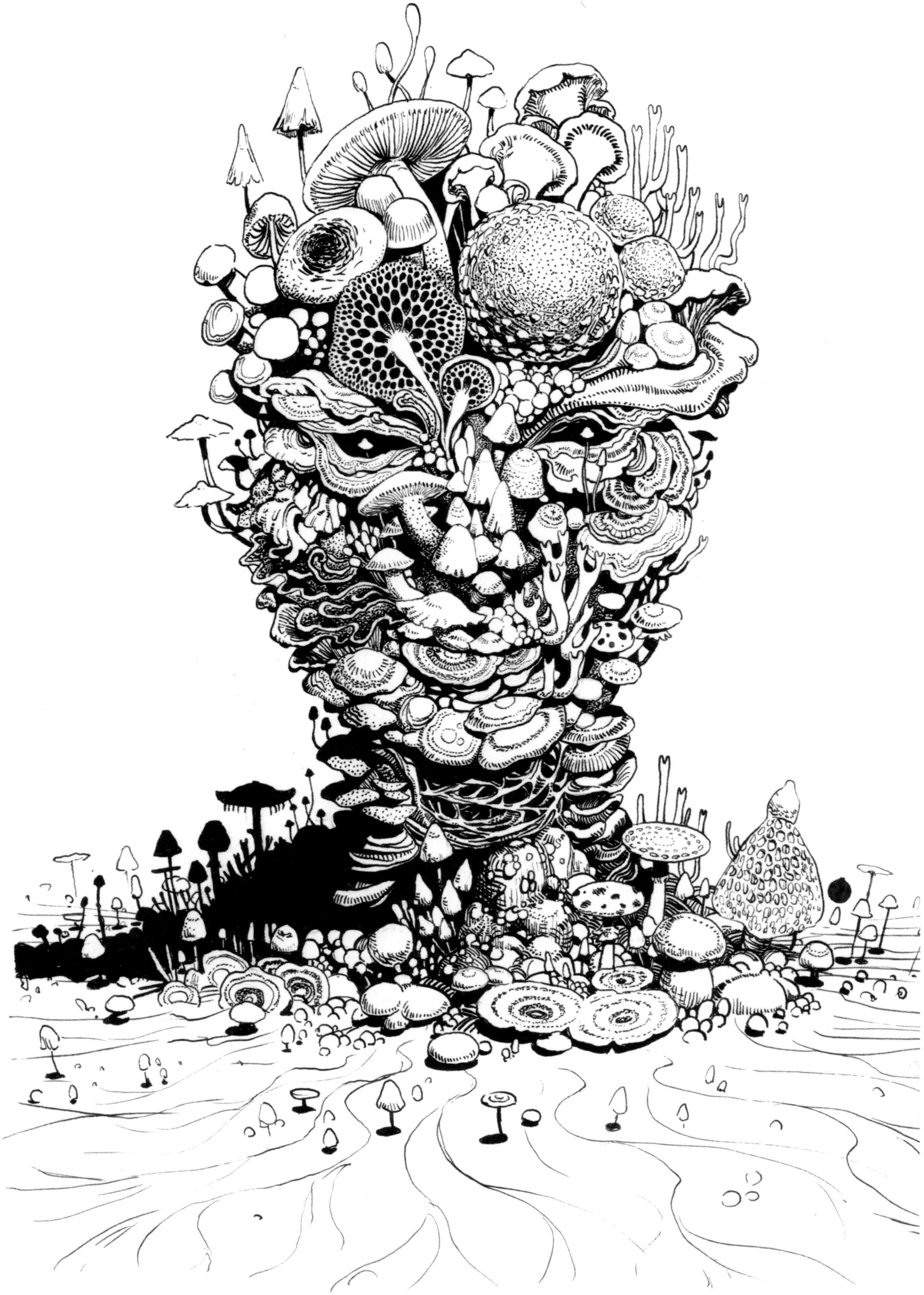

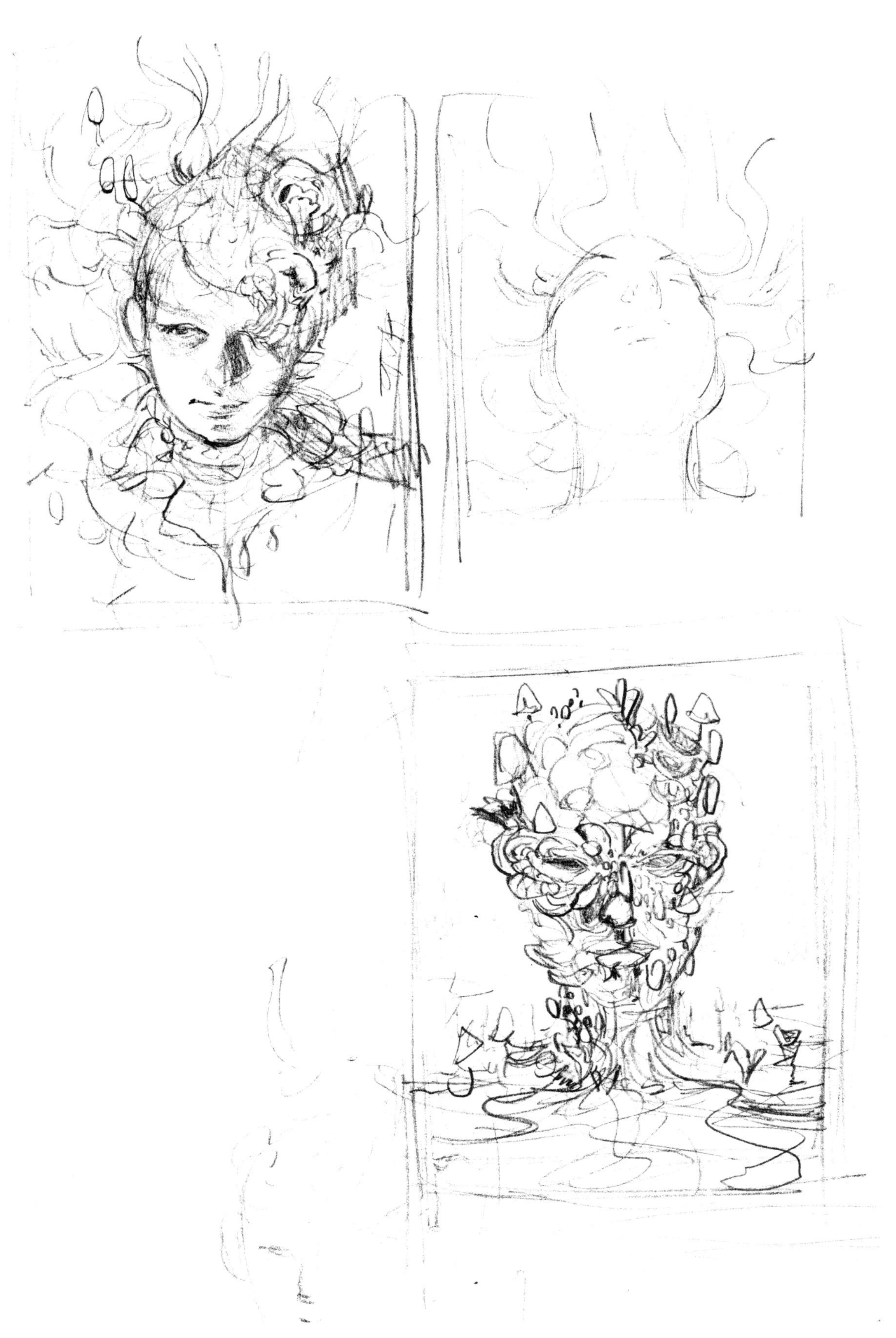

Beksinski Homage (detail)
2016

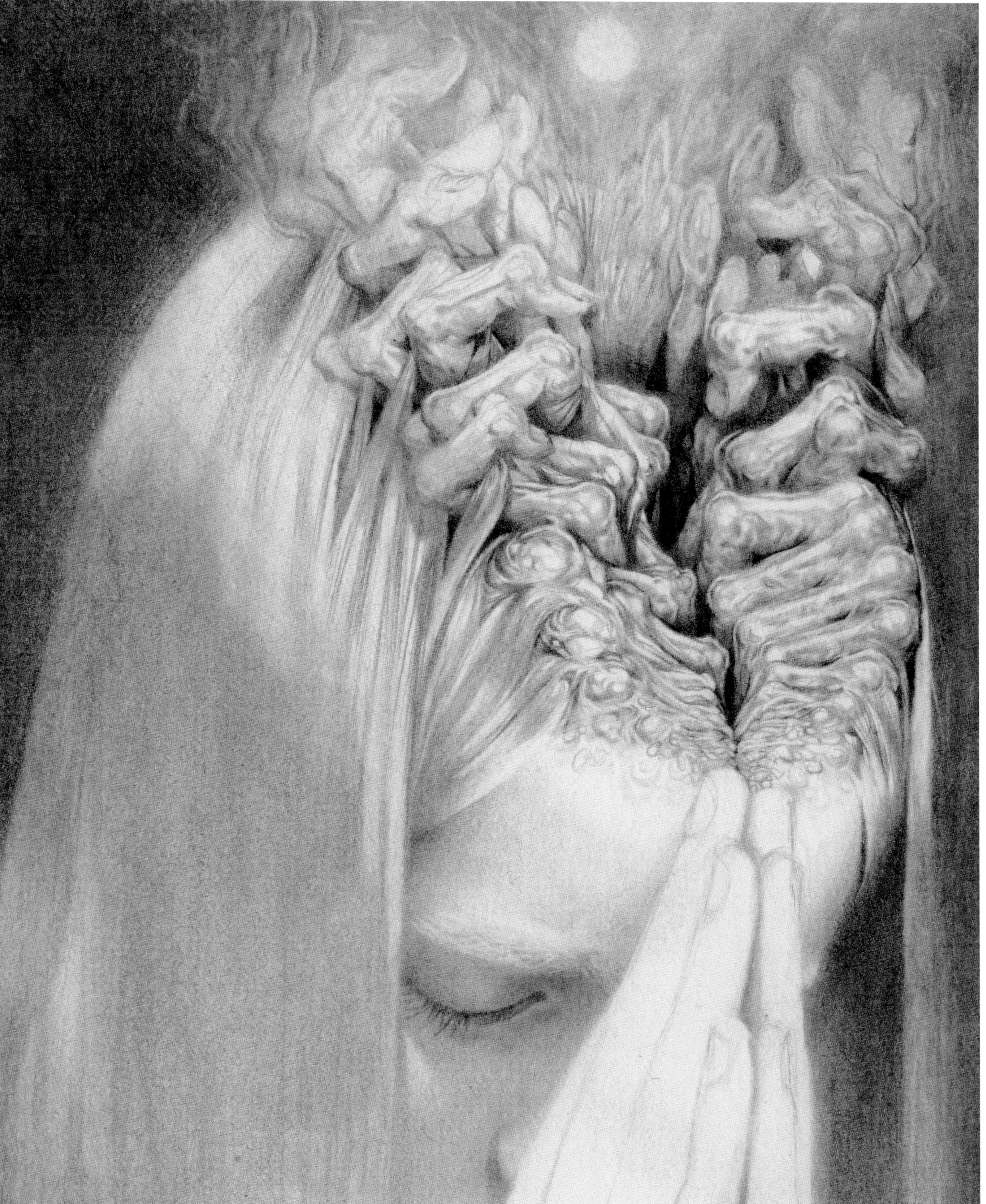

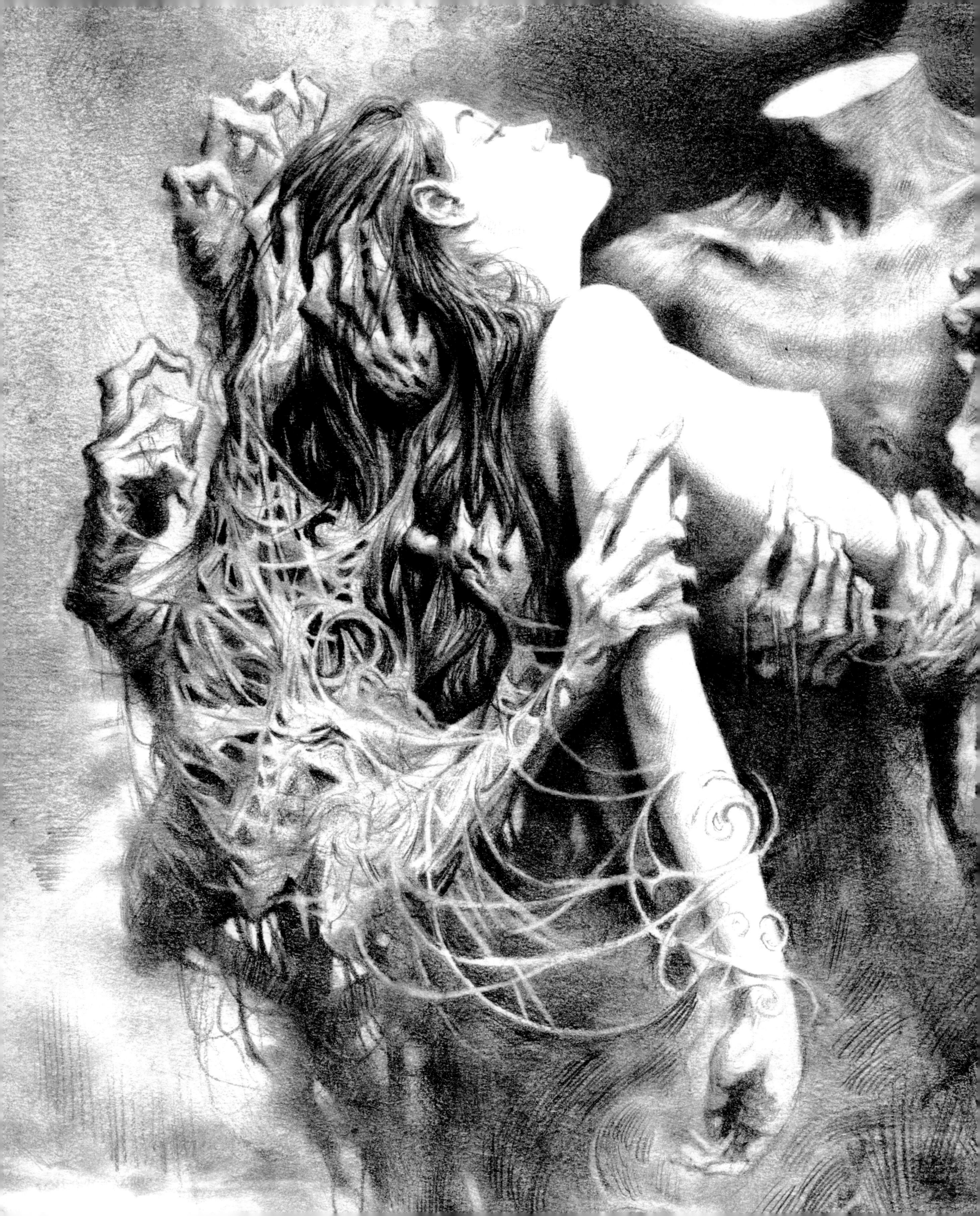

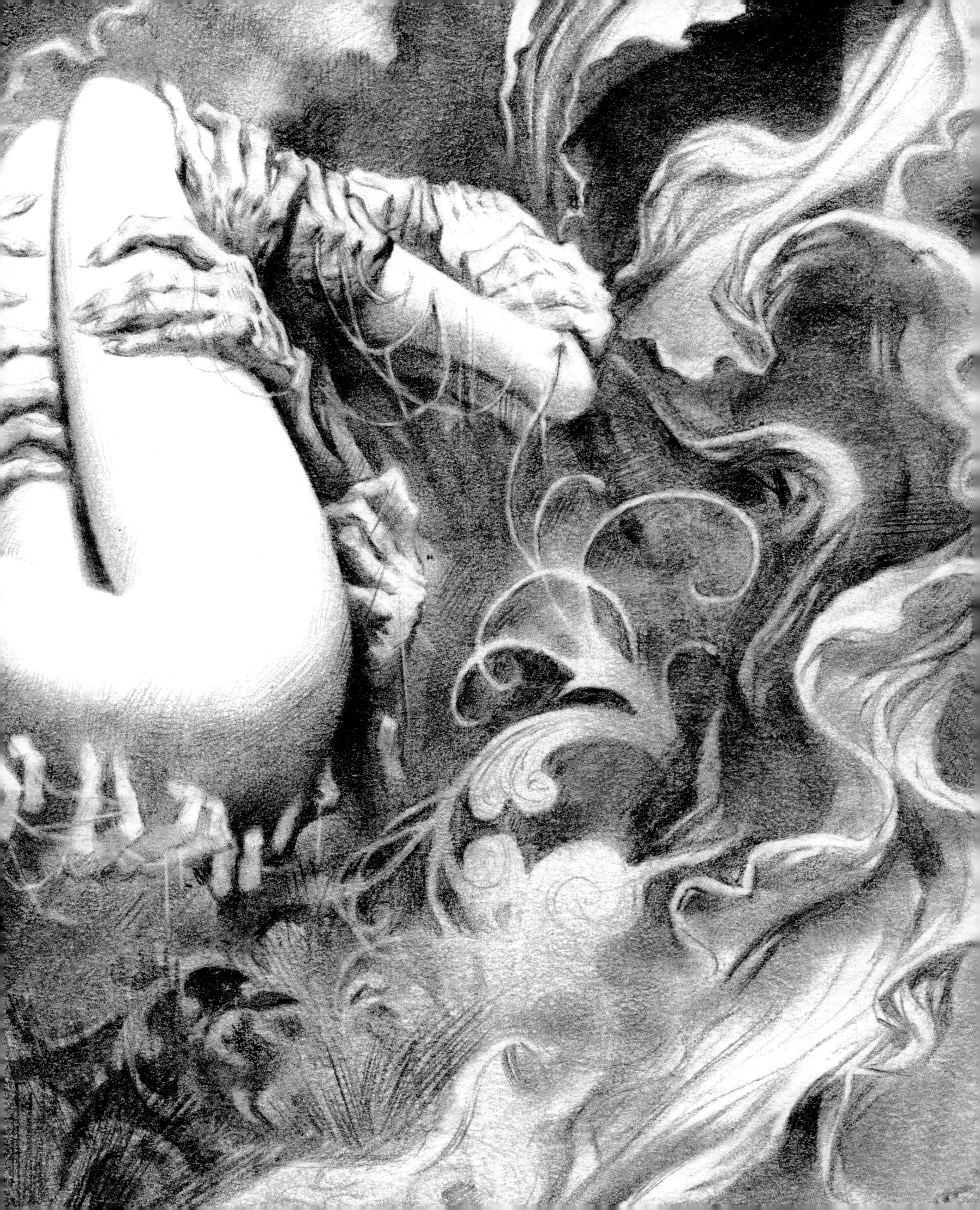

Hands
2015

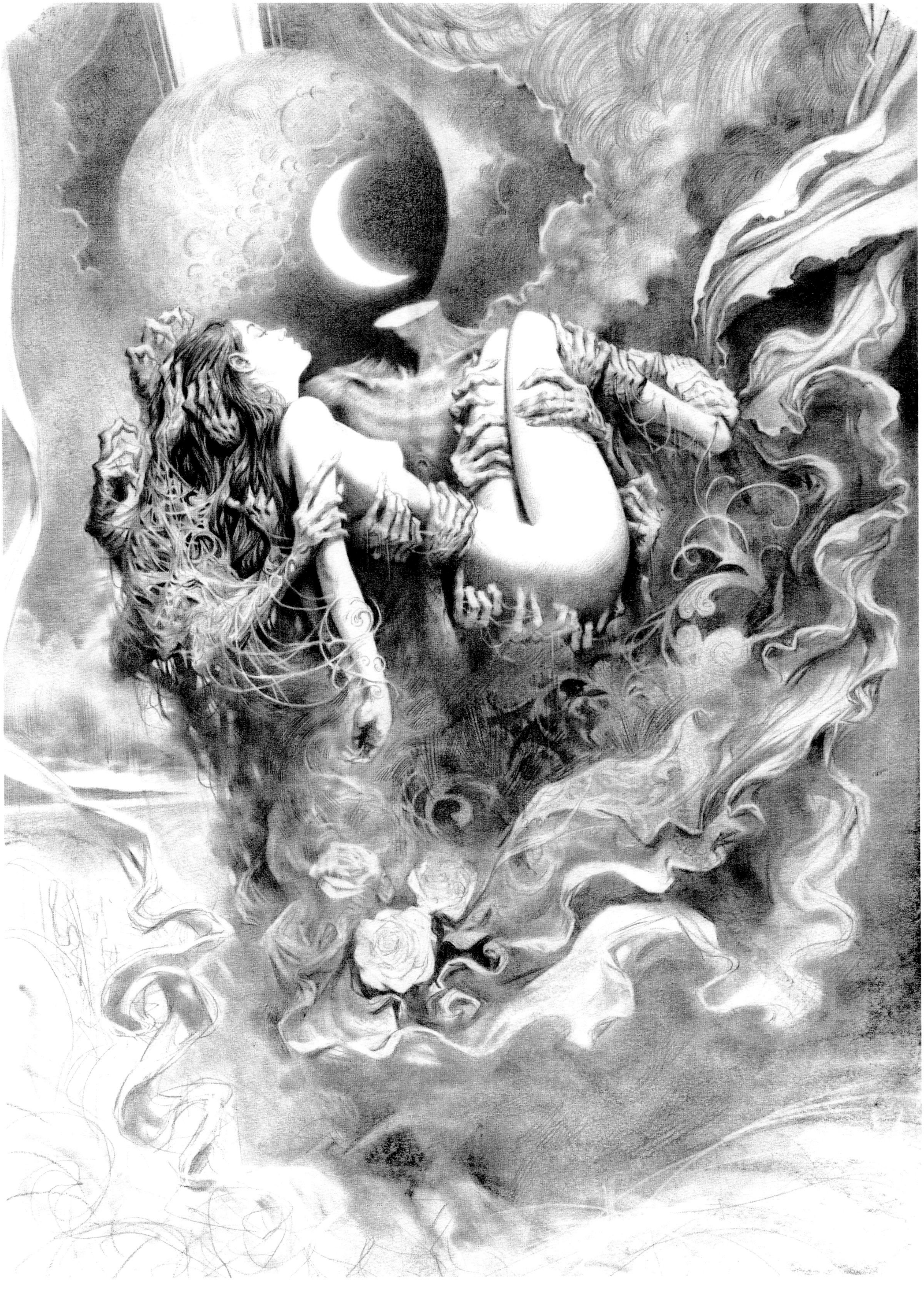

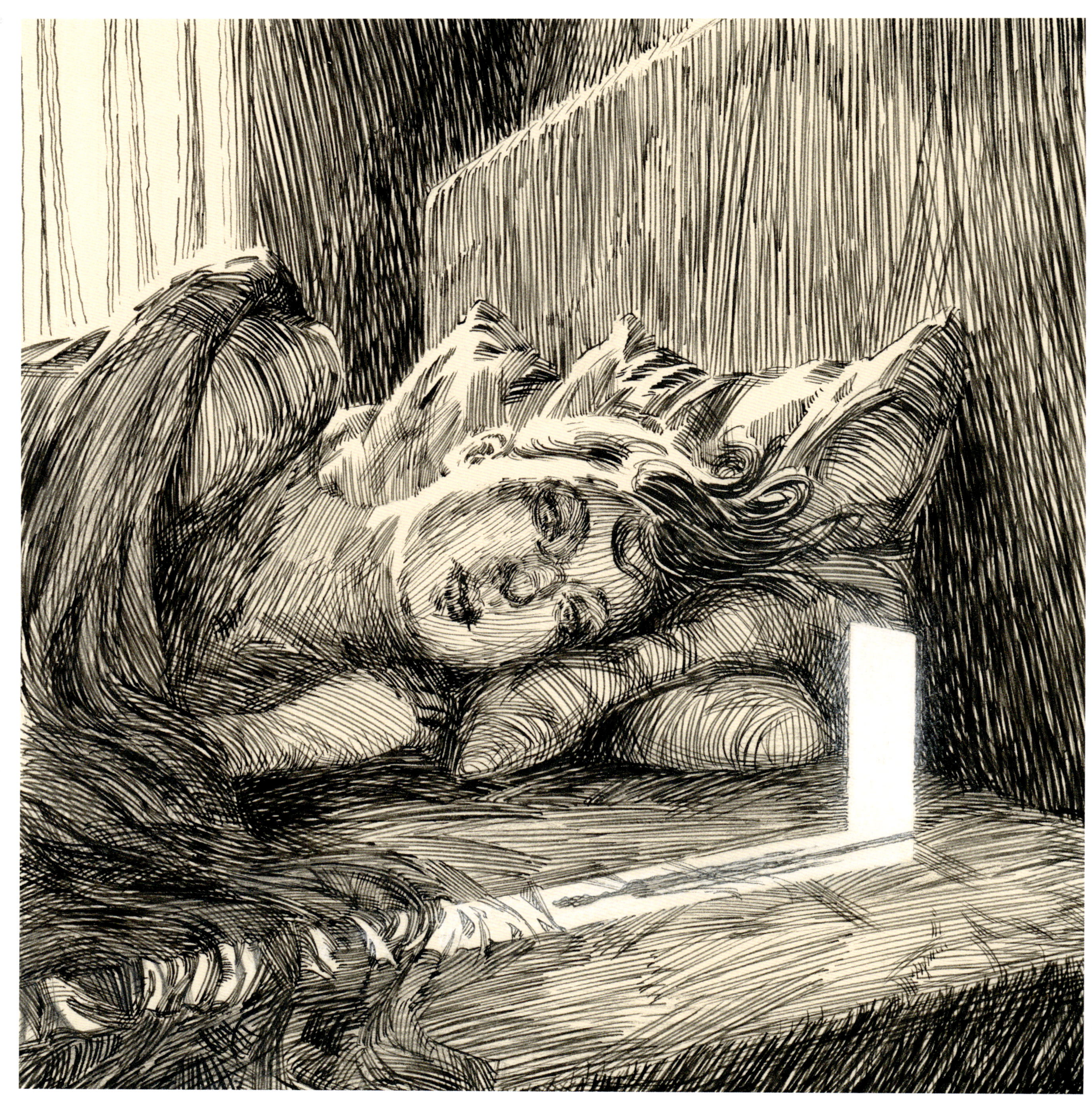

The Arrival

2021

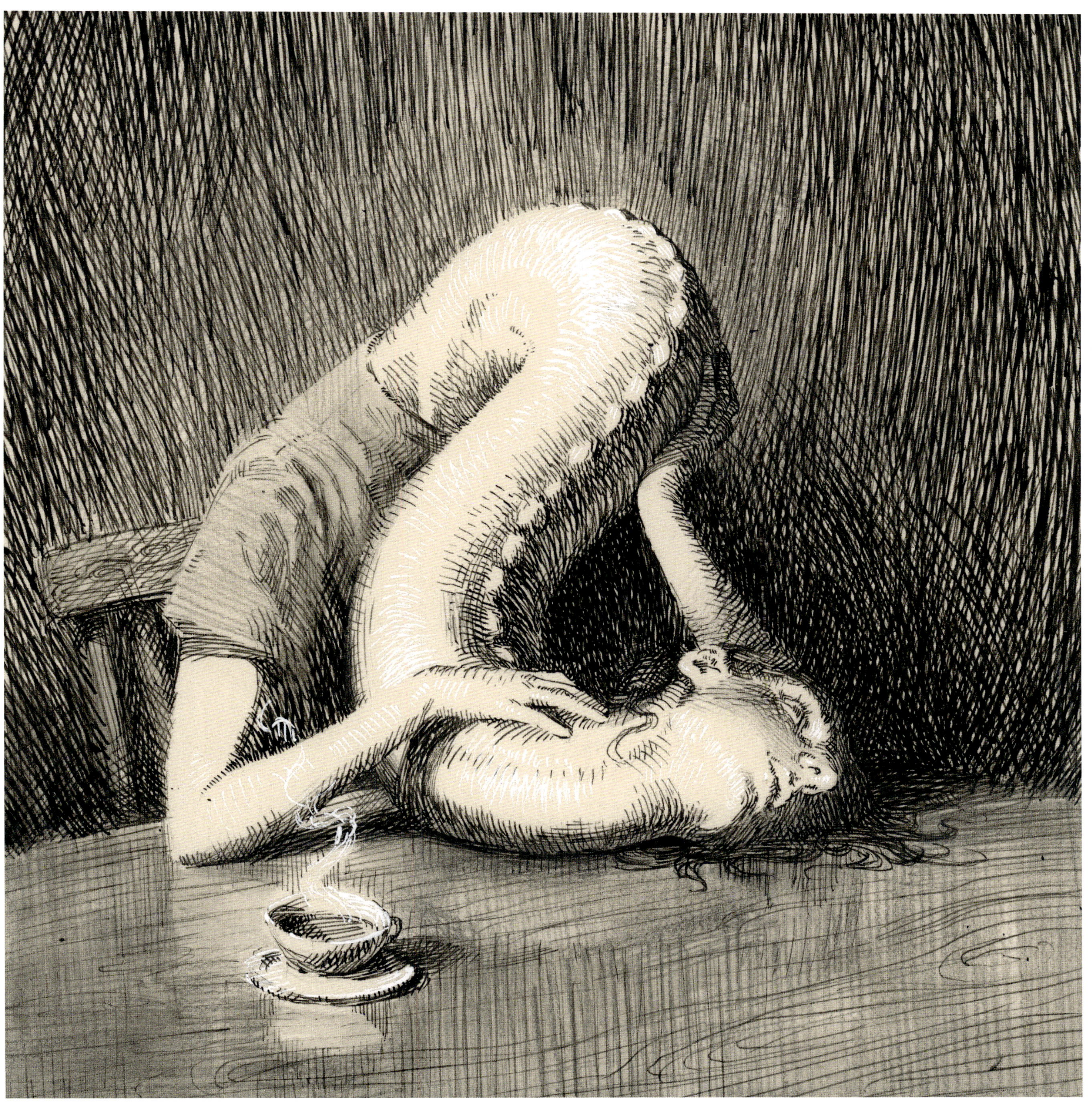

Sore Neck
2021

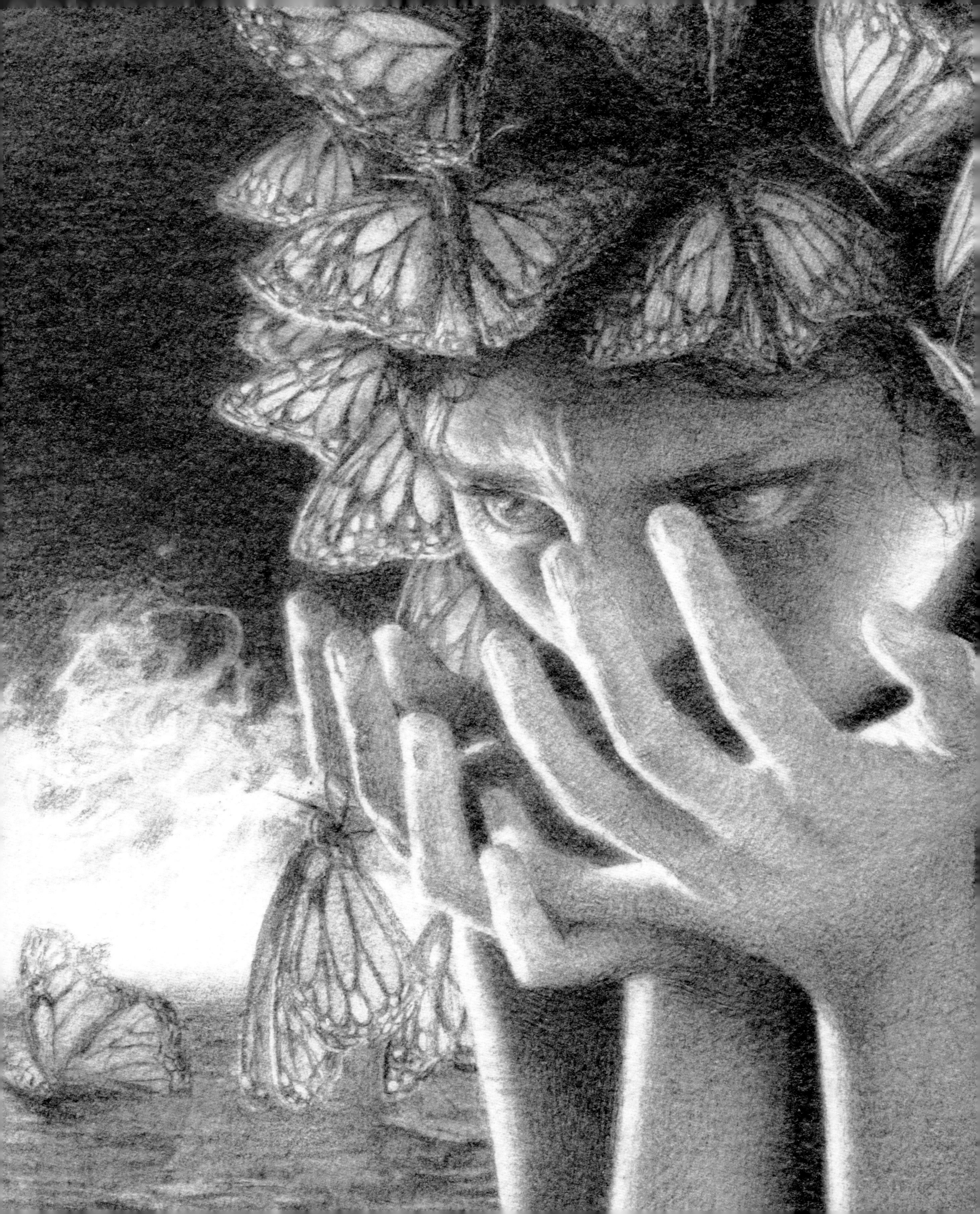

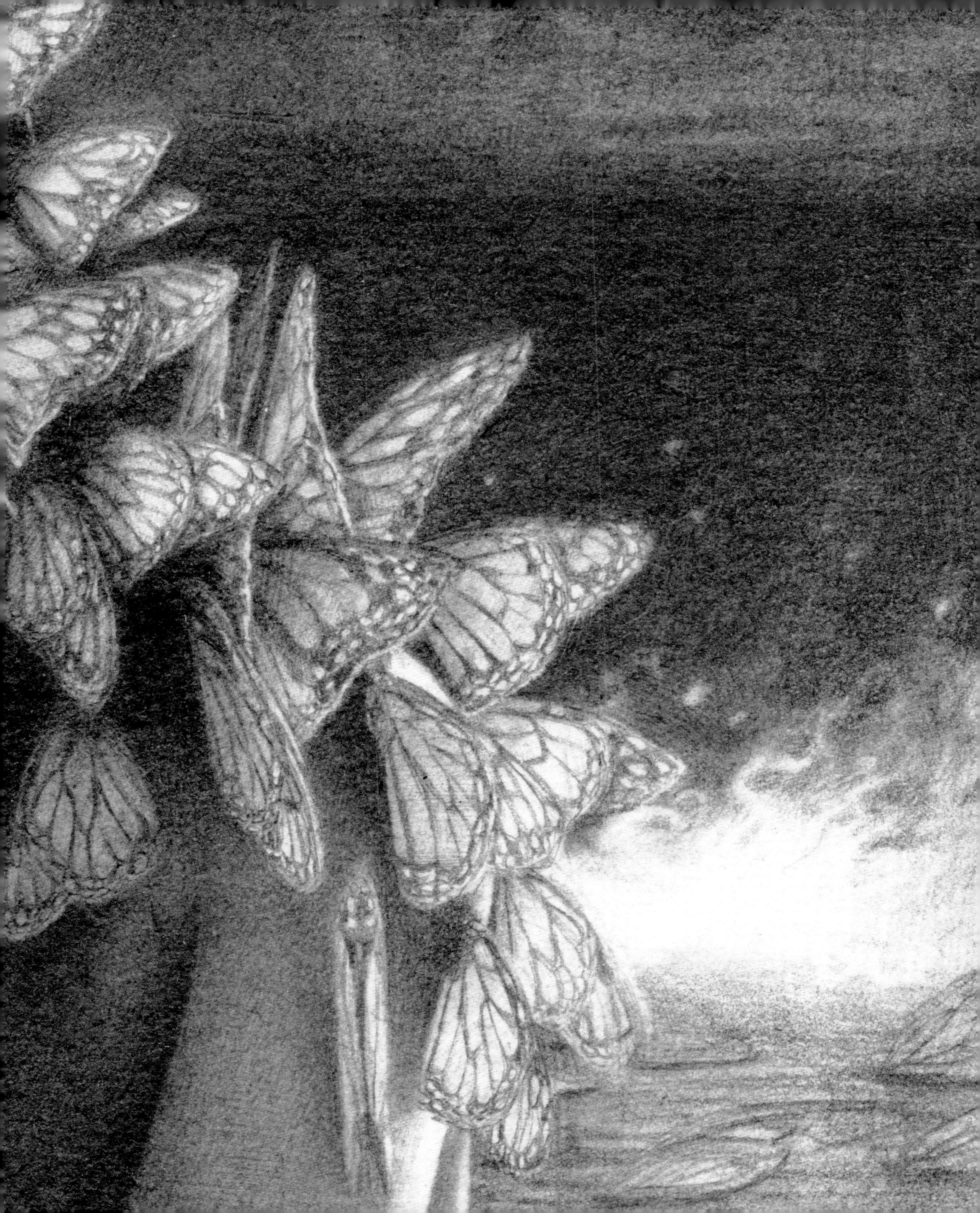

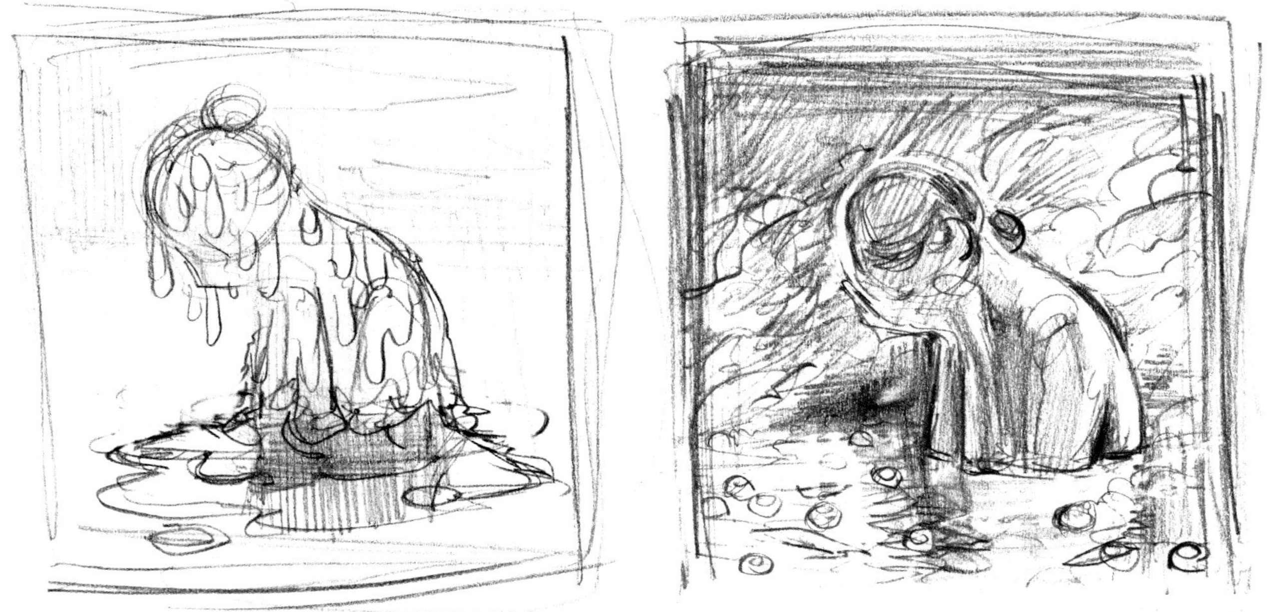

Last Chance + Studies

2019

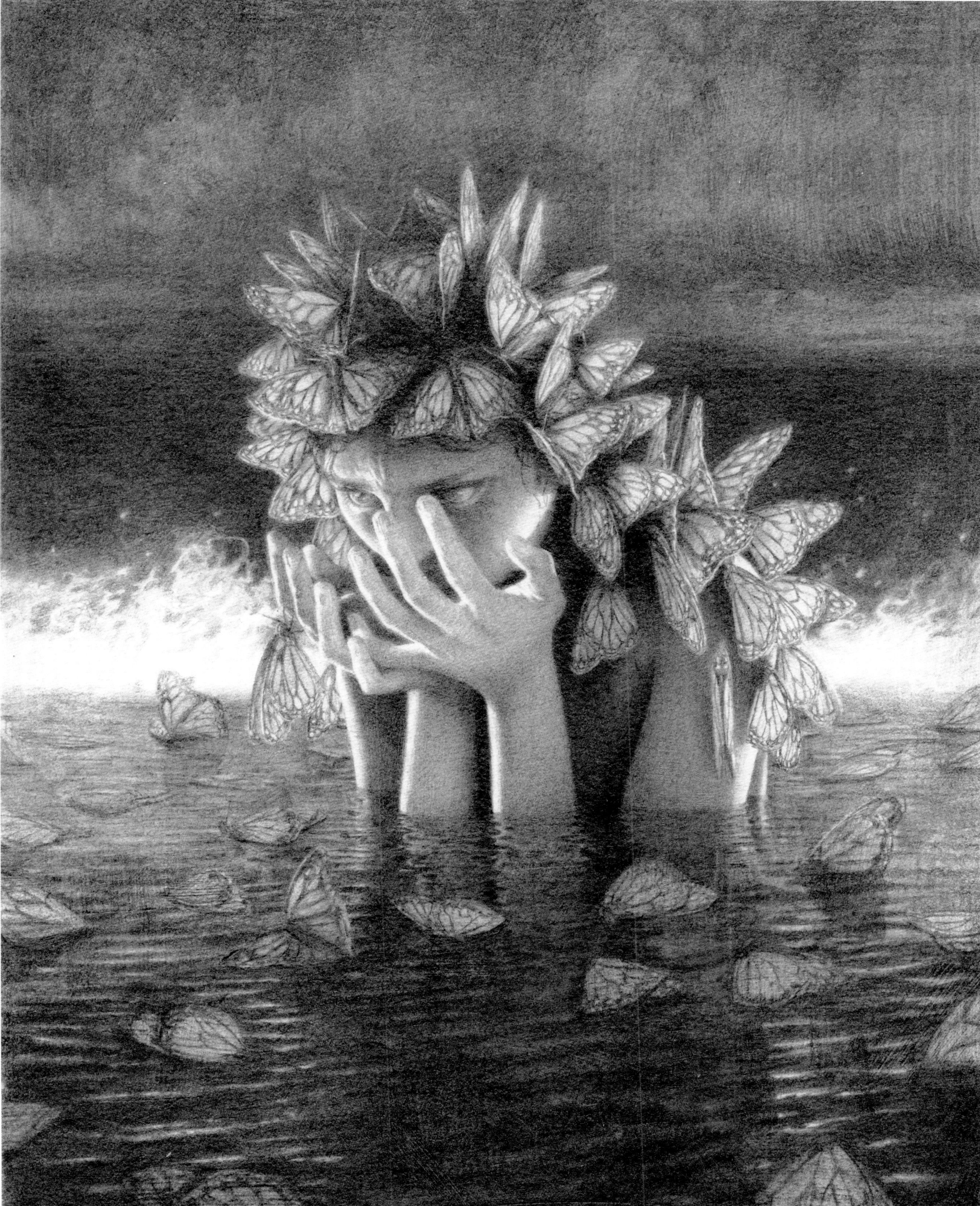

Shame
2020

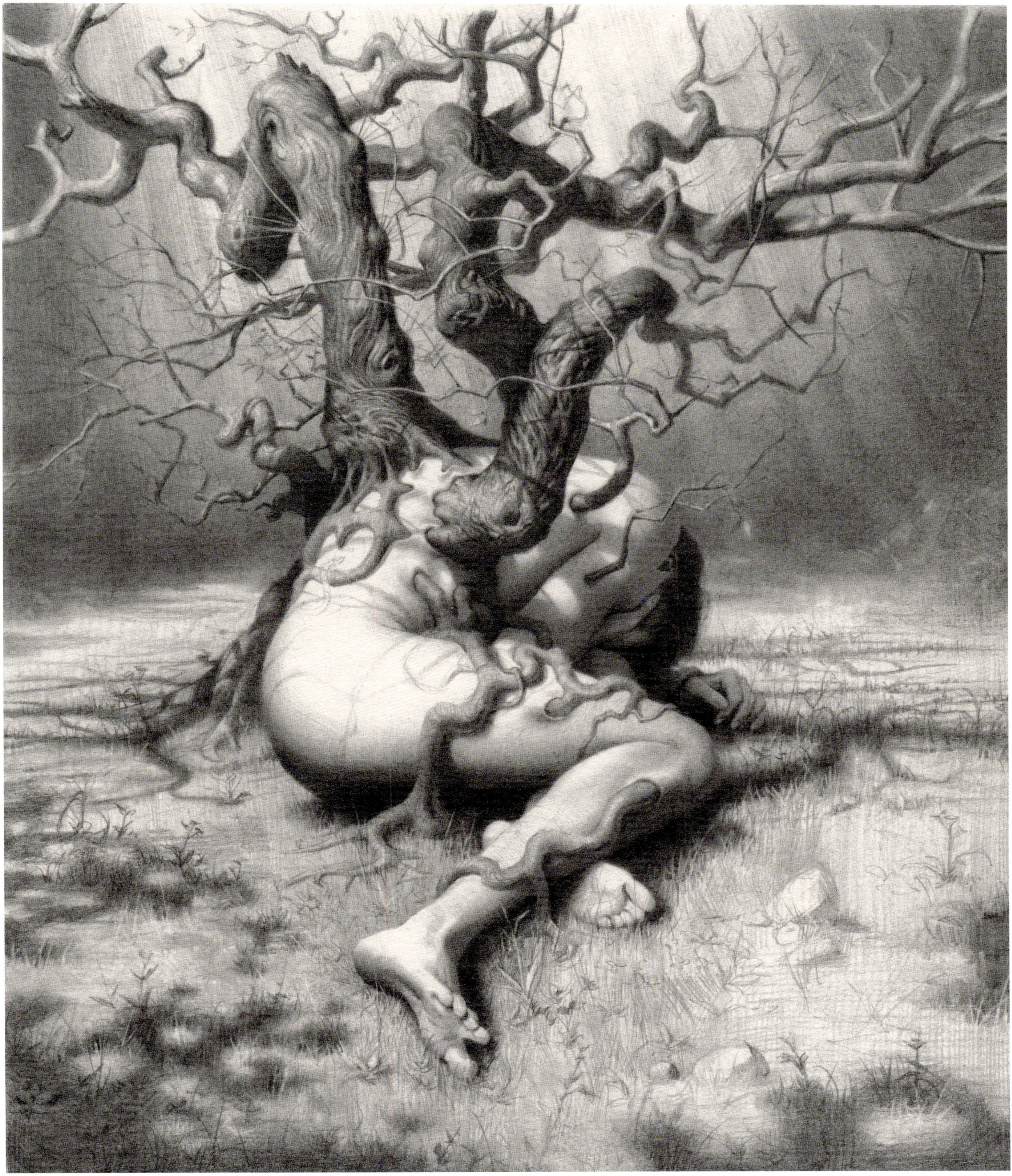

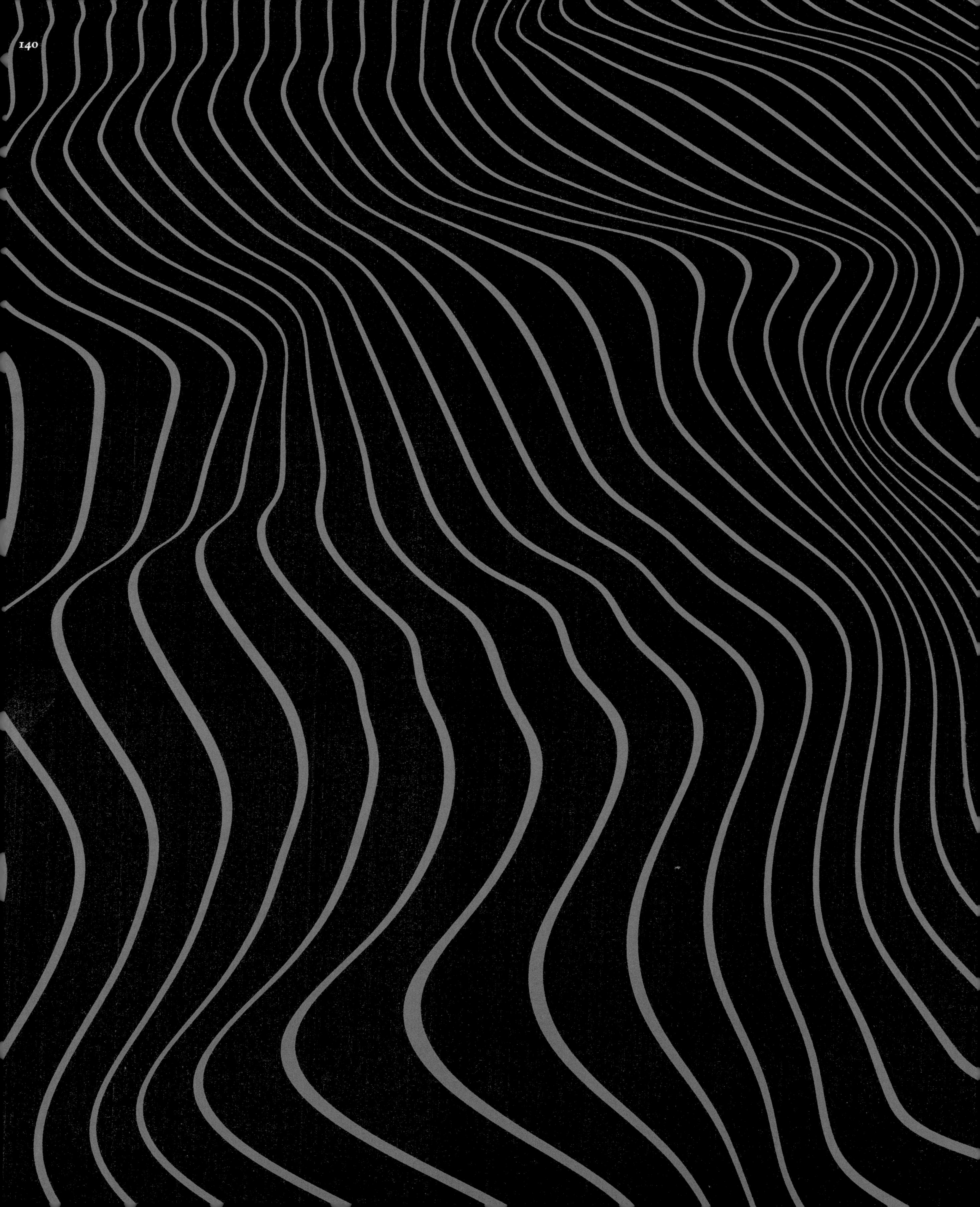

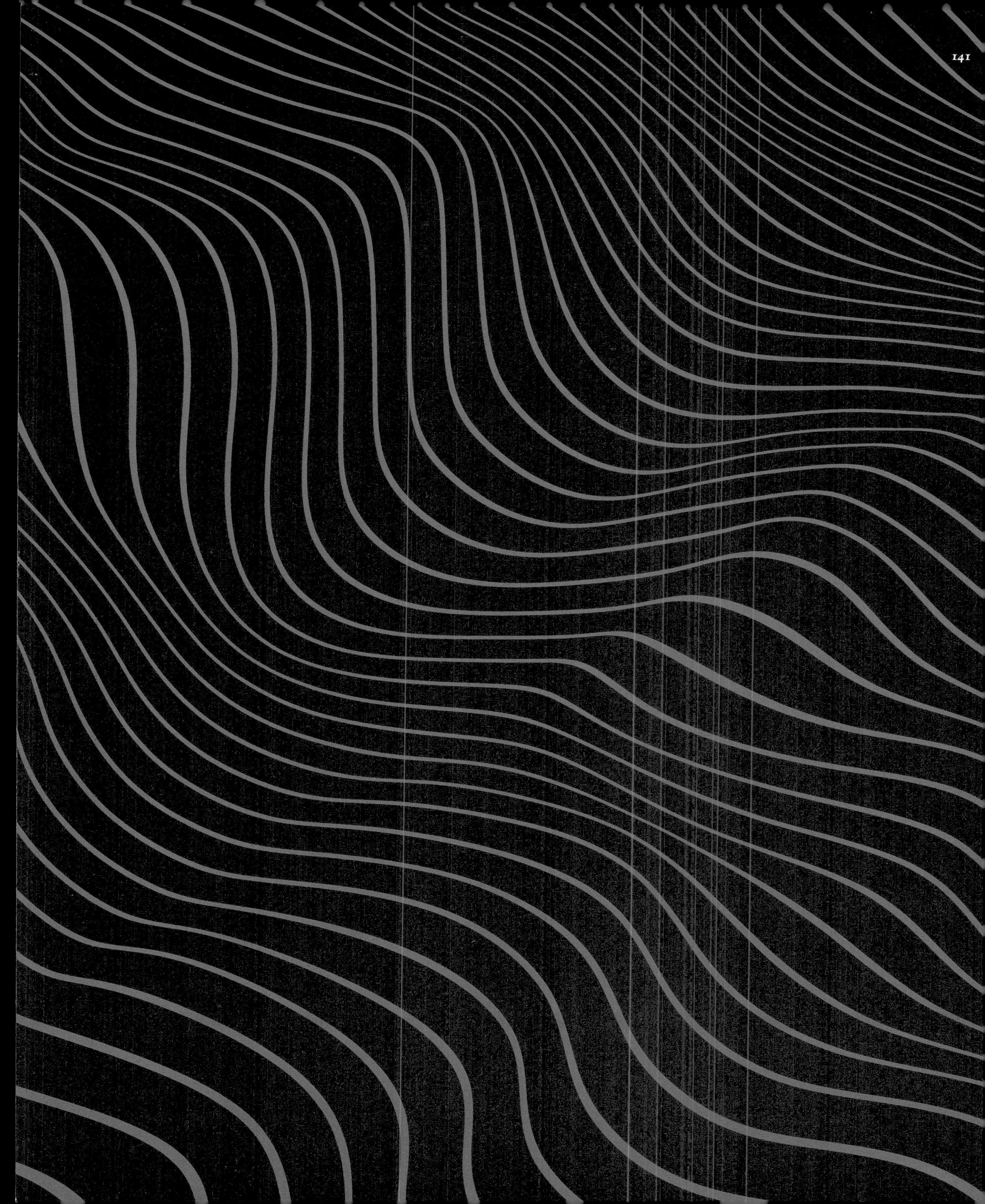

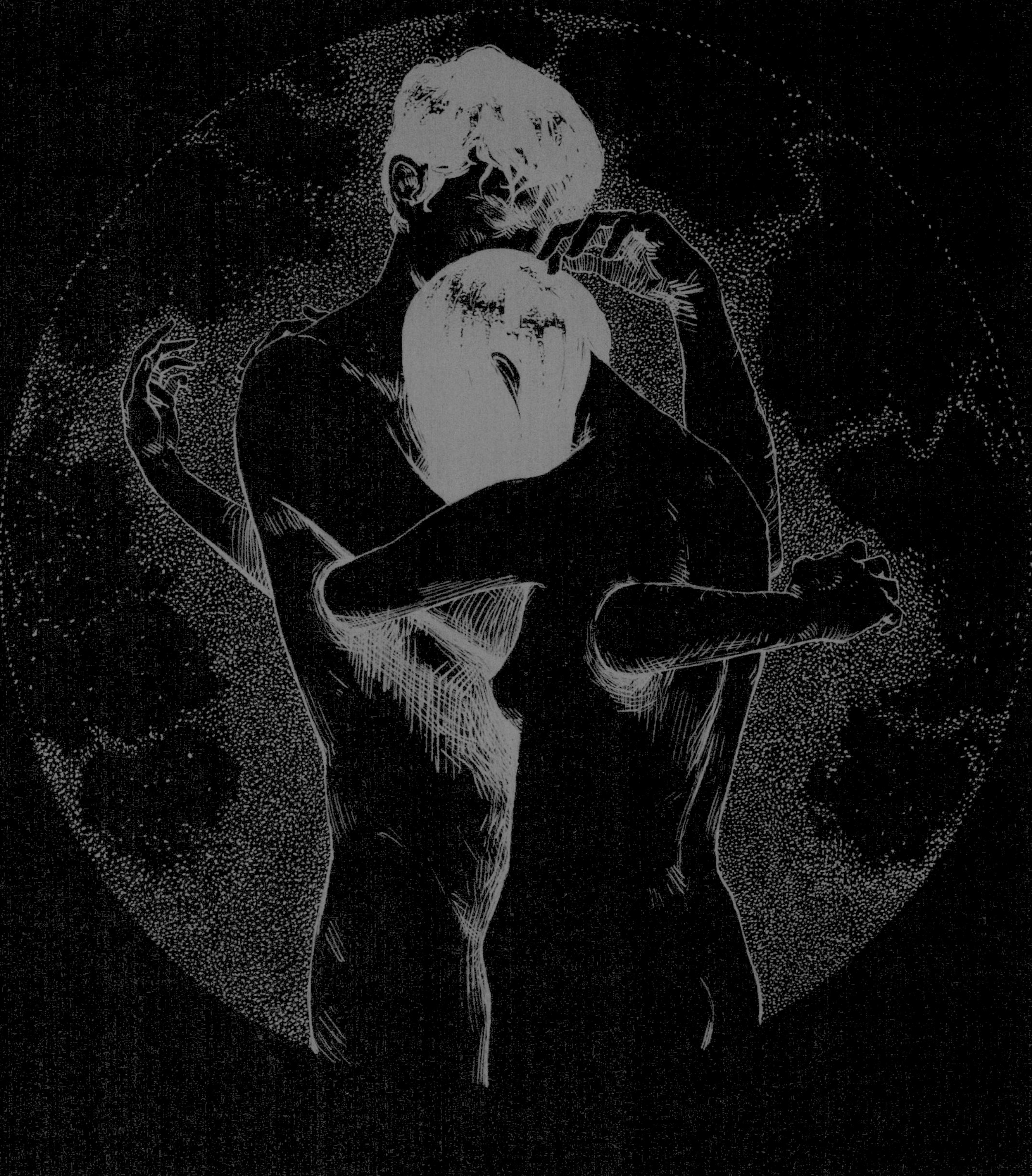

Boundaries (Ink)
2019

III

Storm

Boundaries (Study)
2019

Boundaries (Pencil)
2019

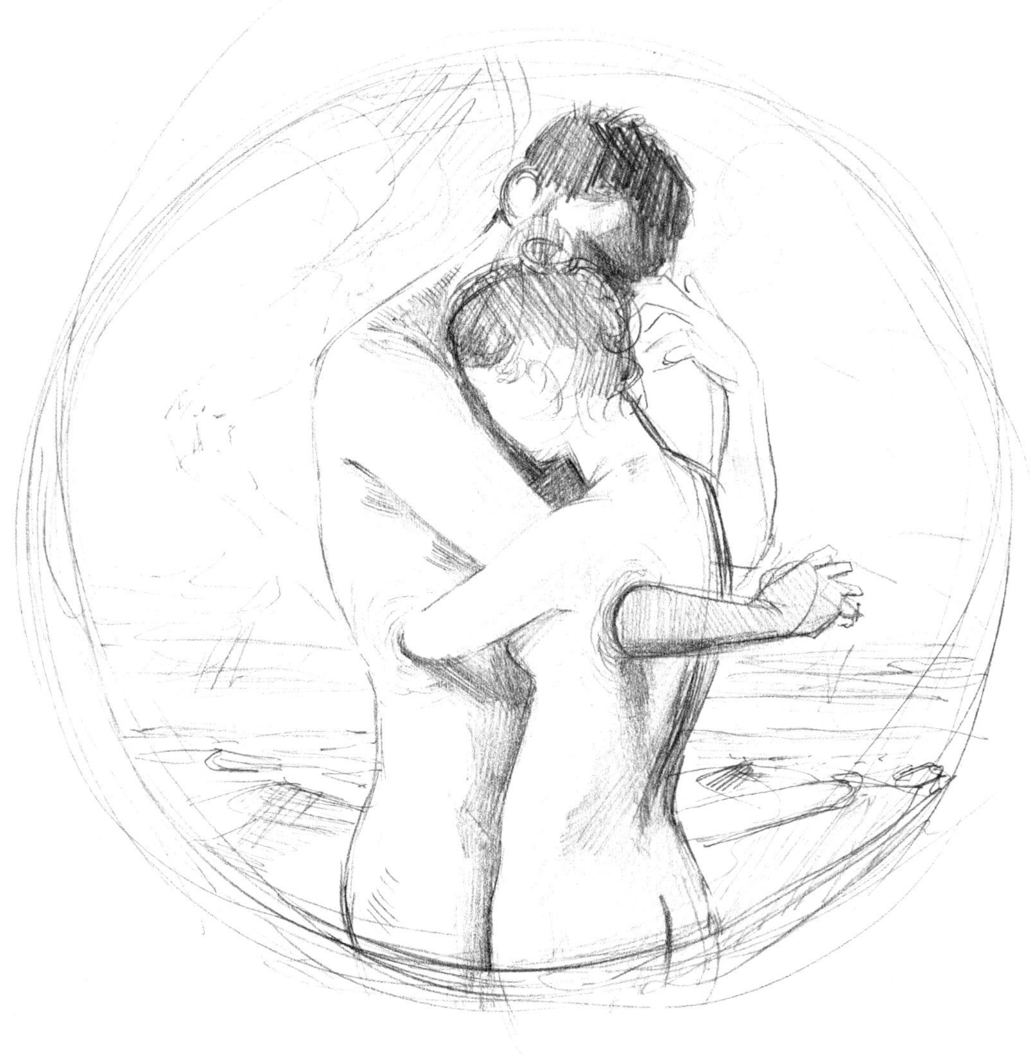

Connection/ Disconnection

In one sense we are alone in this life, our direct experience of the world and the full access to our own mind is a gap we can never fully bridge with another. Yet in another equally real way, we are all here together. We are emergent from the same underlying unified reality. The material and energy that composes our bodies was once part of the same superheated cosmic soup swirling around all together in the big bang. This section of the book covers reflections on this apparent duality between being alone and being together, and the full spectrum of experiences that come from my deep desire to feel connection with others.

Nostalgia is another theme I often draw upon. I find the passage of time and how it affects our relationships strange. At some point in our lives, another person can be the singular focus of our attention. A friend or a lover who you might confide in and share your most intimate thoughts may one day become another stranger. It can be an uneasy feeling that gnaws away in the back of my mind when I'm with my closest connections. *Surely, we won't fade out of each other's lives?* These questions of intimacy in the context of impermanence are a recurring theme in my work.

Ultimately I am drawn to the tragic and the bittersweet. I am moved by the bravery of people, by the way we can support and love each other in the circumstances we find ourselves in. In an impermanent world, every love story must end in sorrow. I think the shadow of death sets the stakes that underlie our connections in this world. Loneliness, both in and out of relationships, aches more in the context of knowing this is how we are spending our limited time. It also adds to the joy of finding someone with whom you connect deeply, knowing how unlikely it was that you met and acknowledging how precious it is for somebody to share a piece of their life.

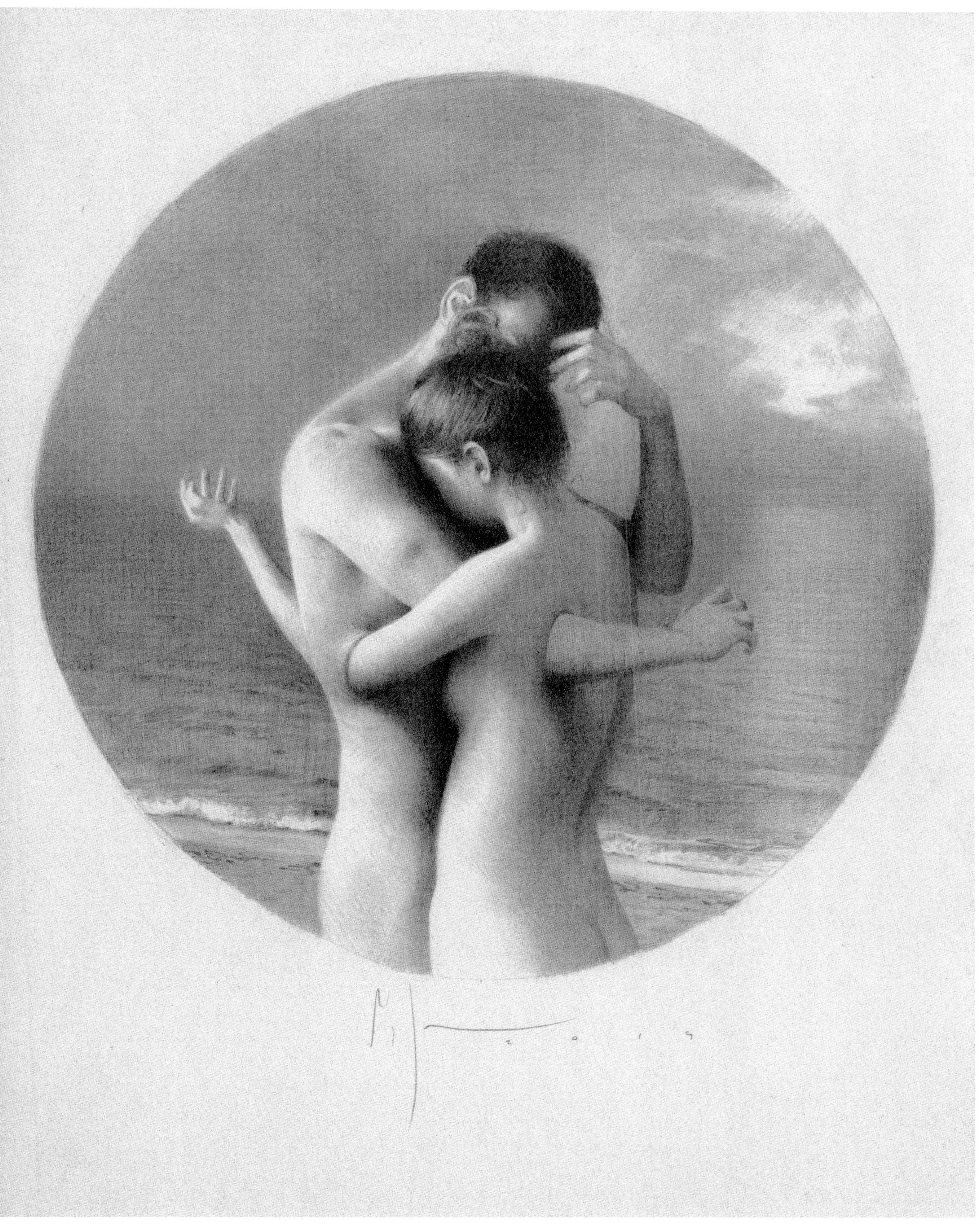

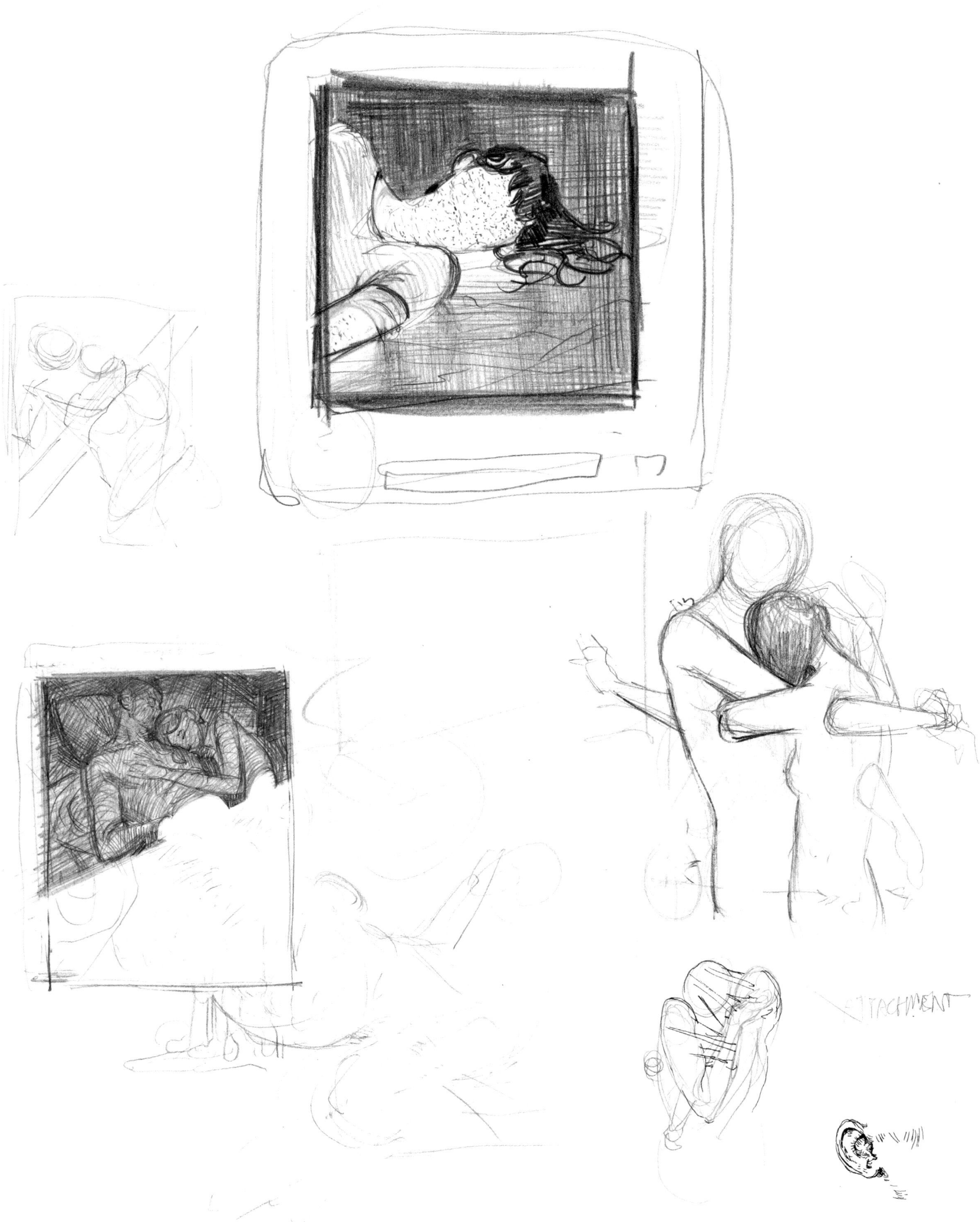

Studies for Boundaries
2019

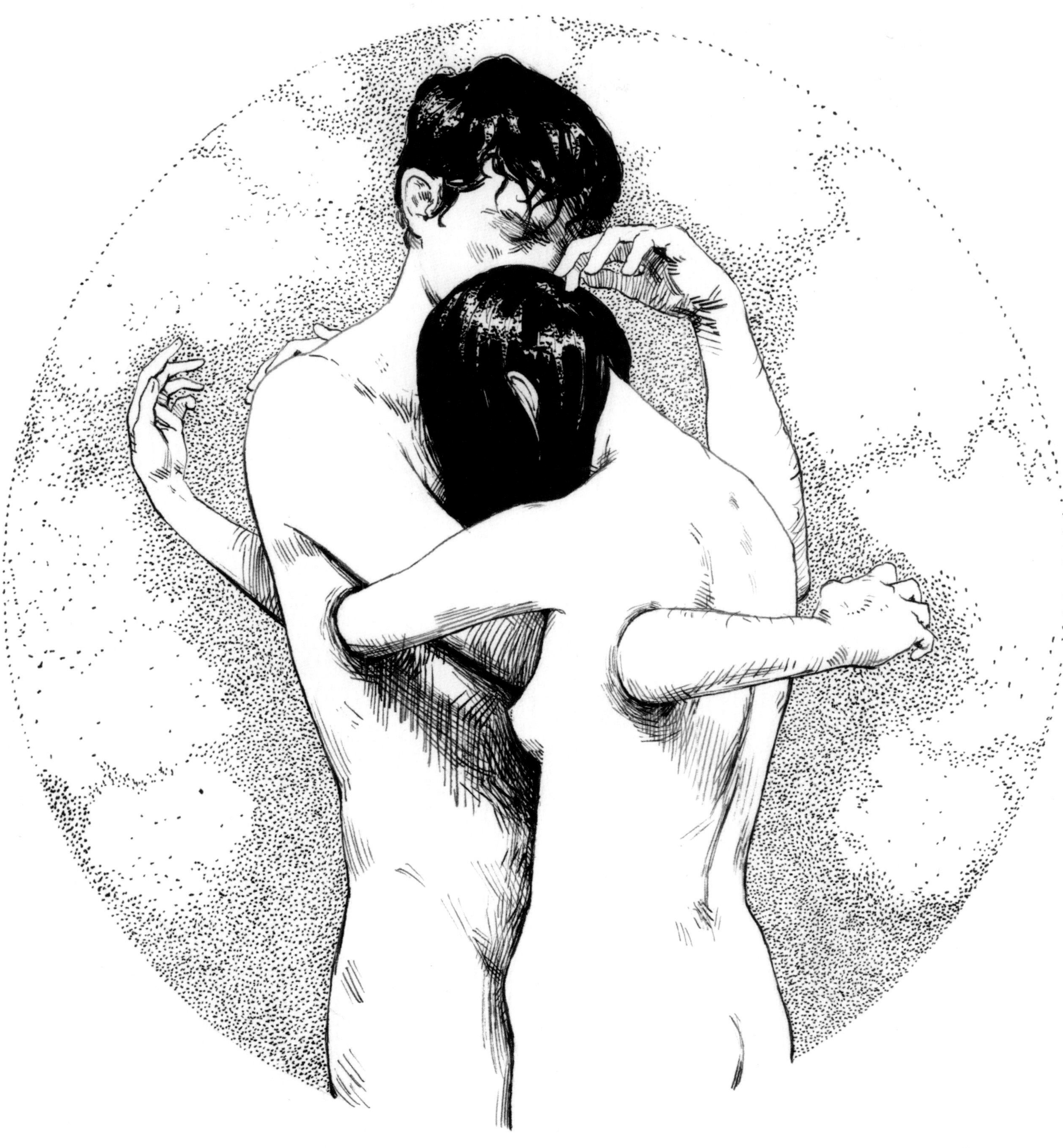

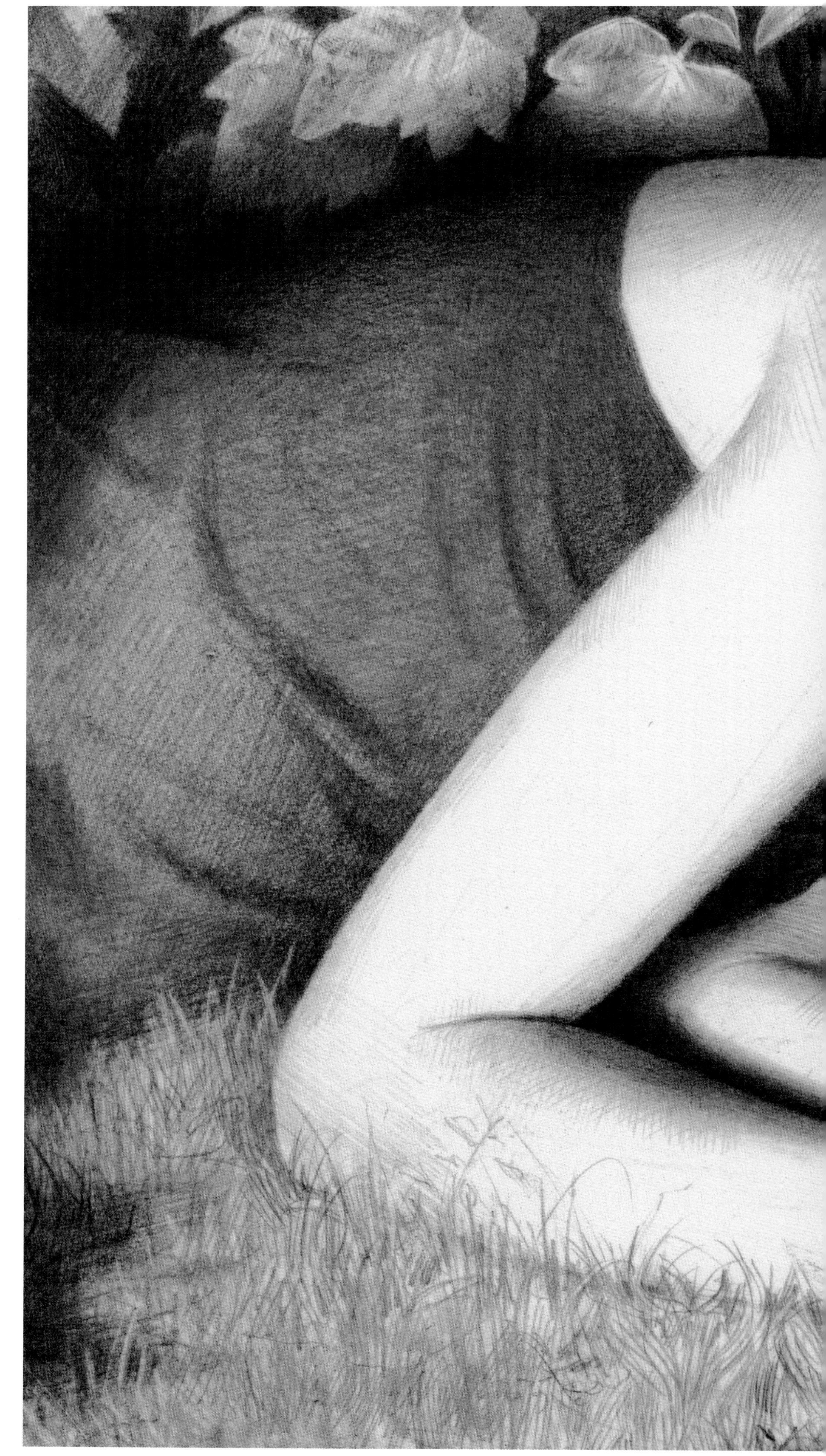

I Still Remember (detail)
2022

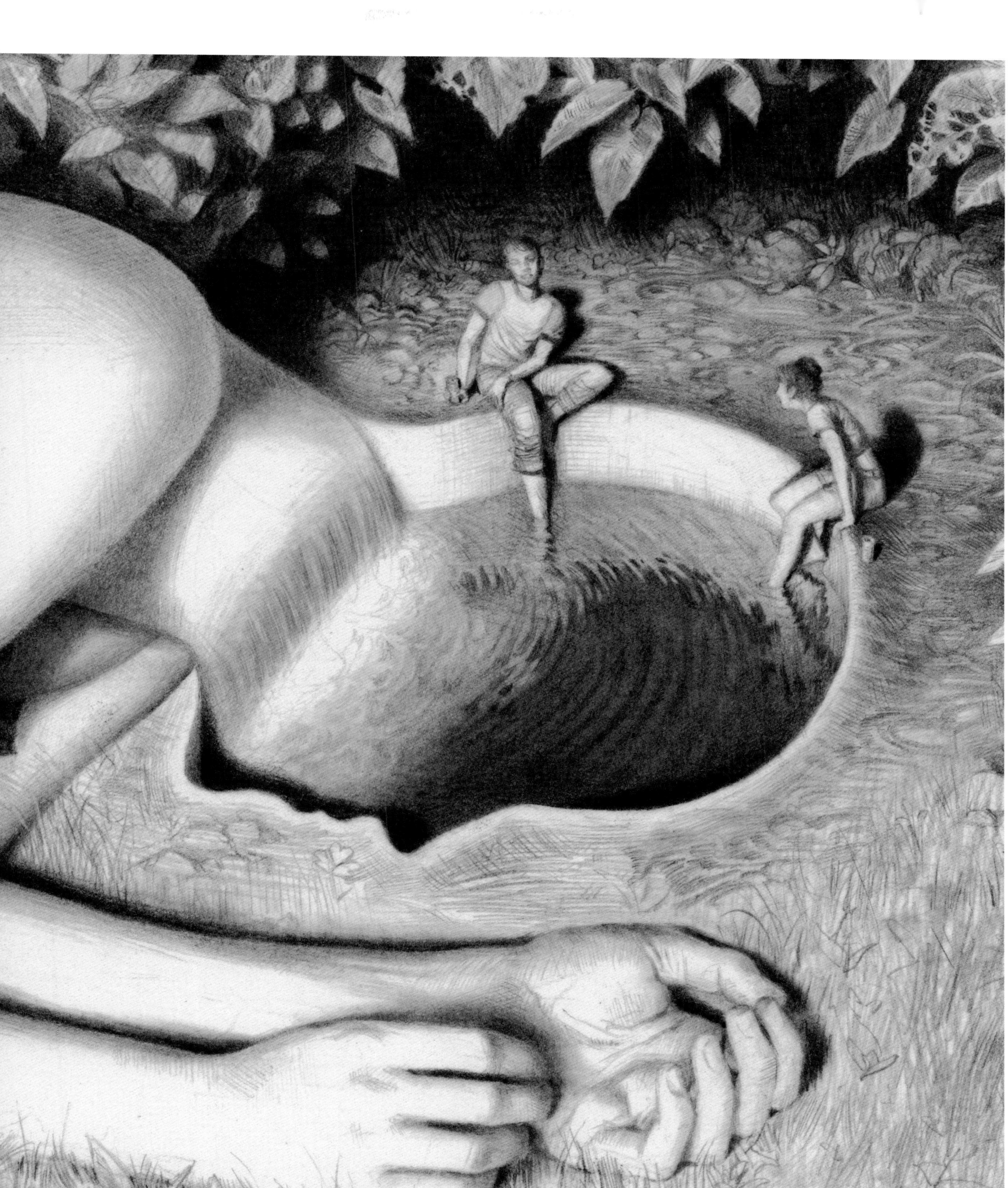

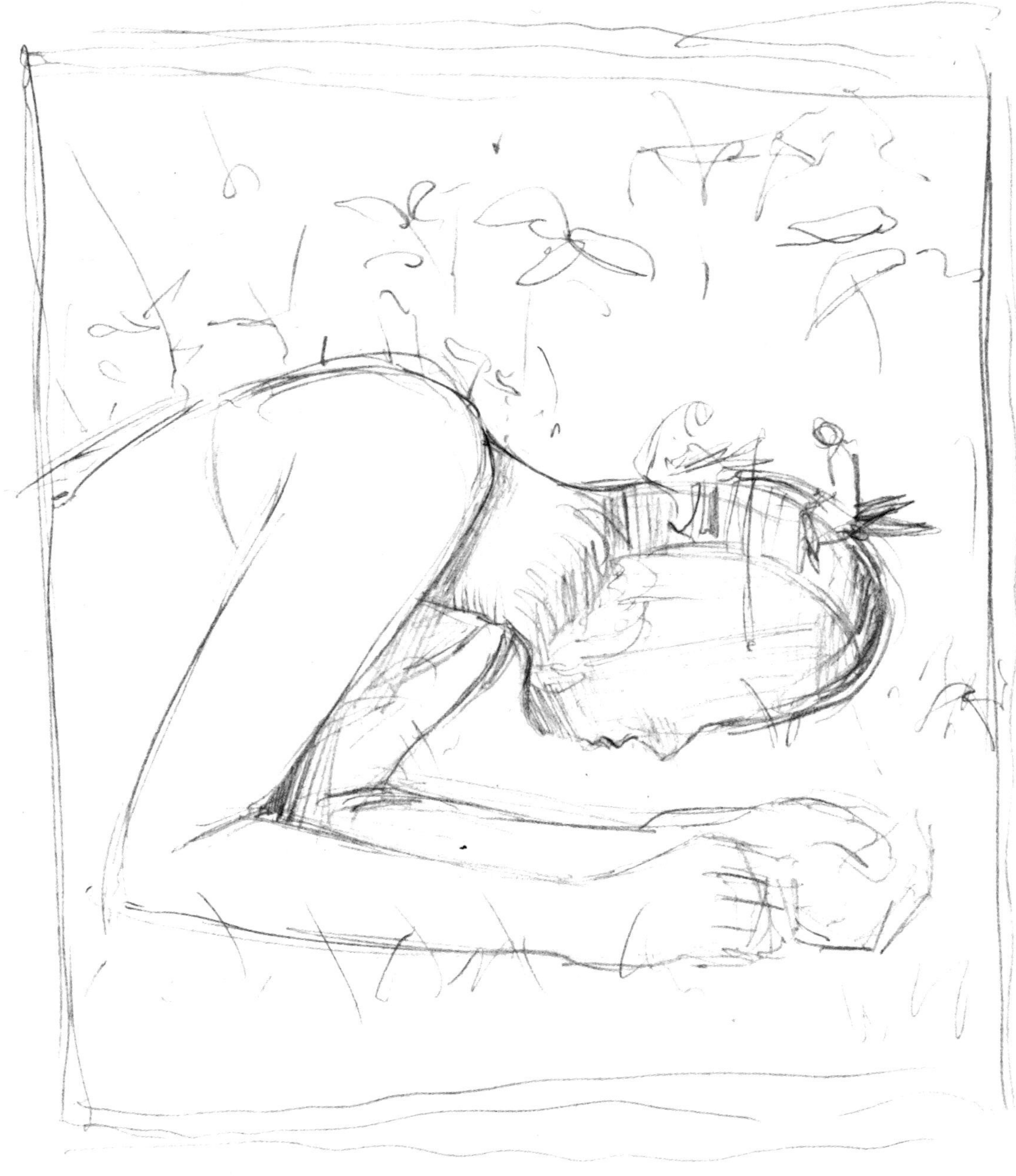

I Still Remember + Study
2022

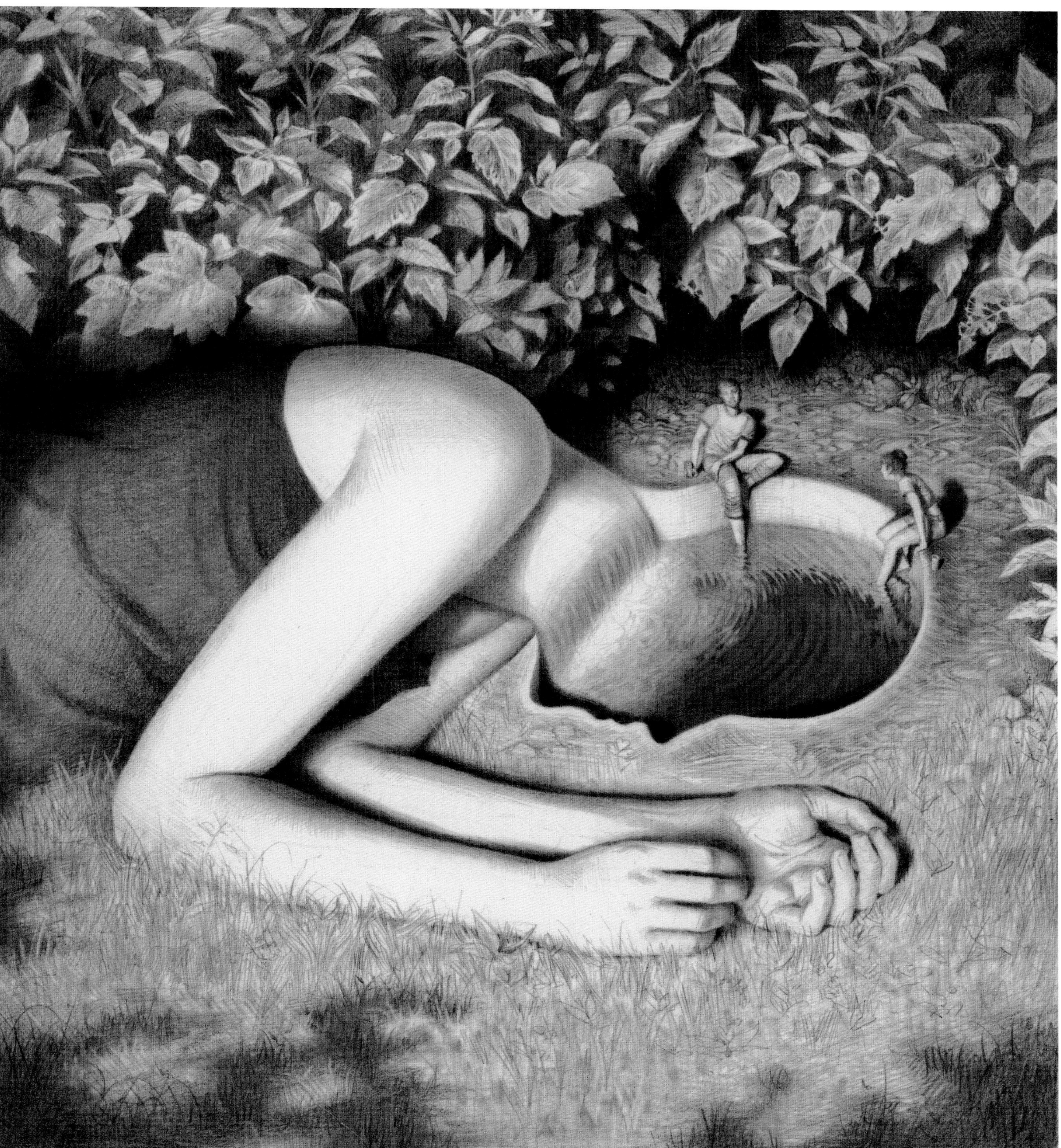

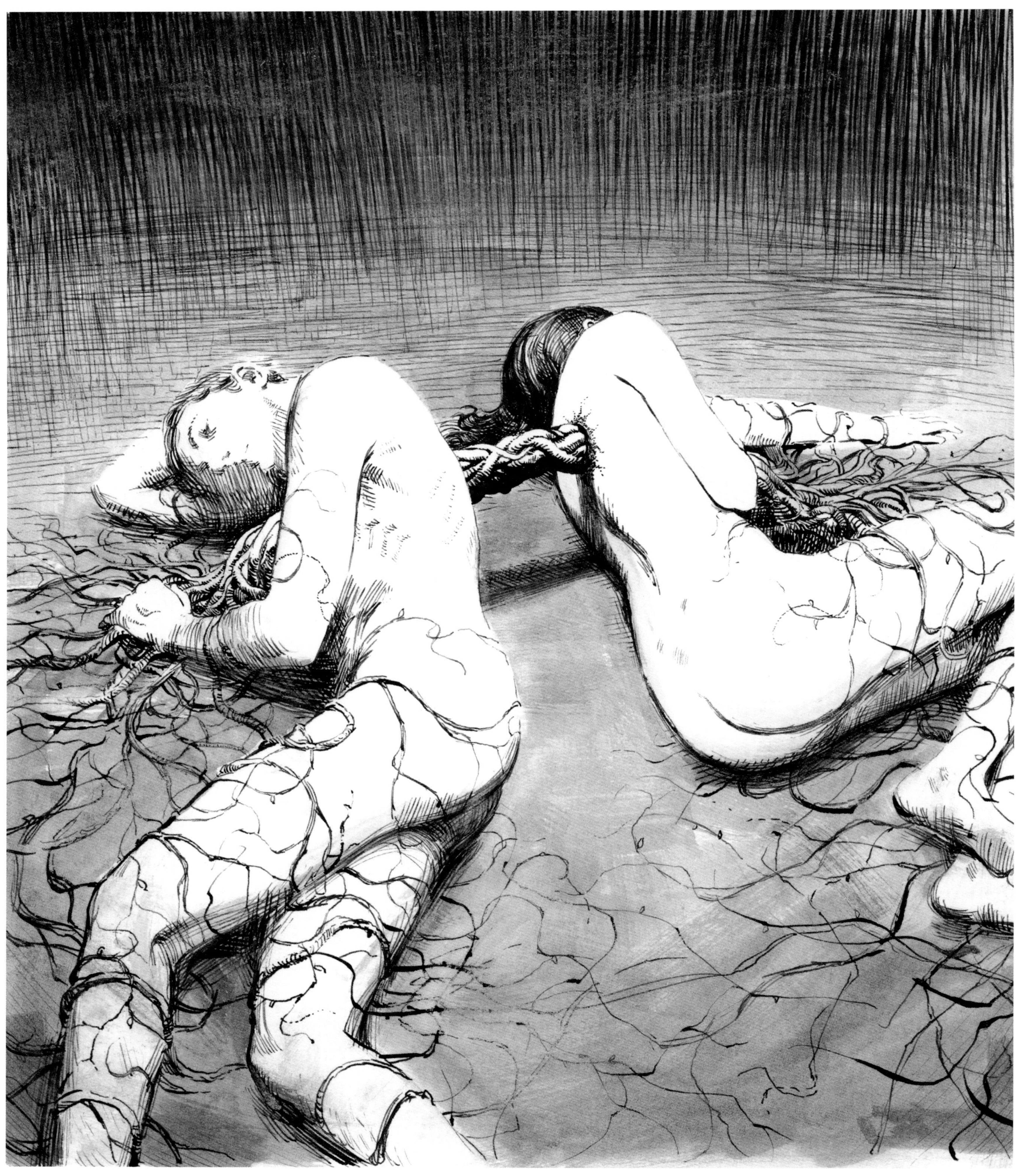

Attachment

2021

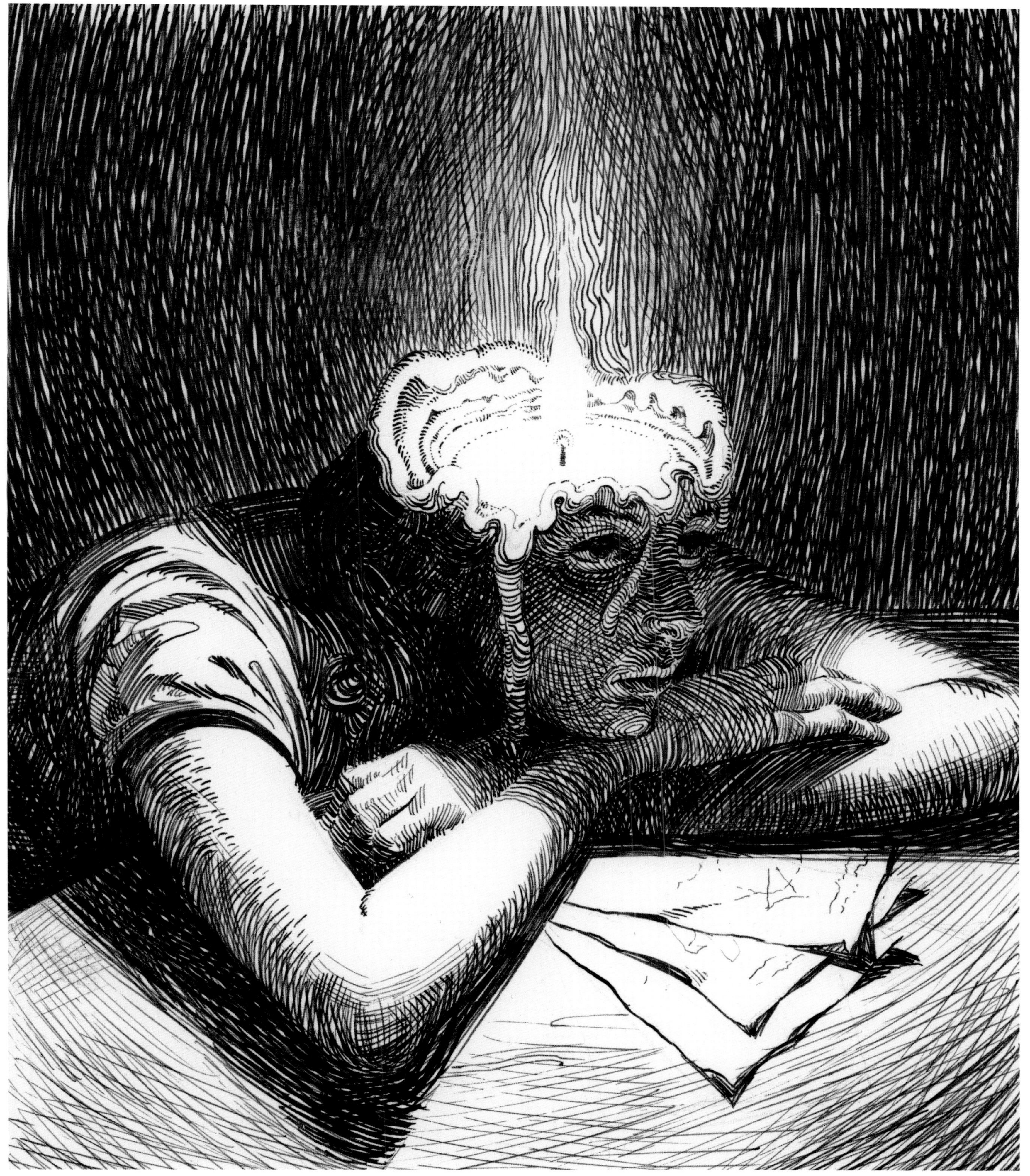

Burning The Midnight Oil

2020

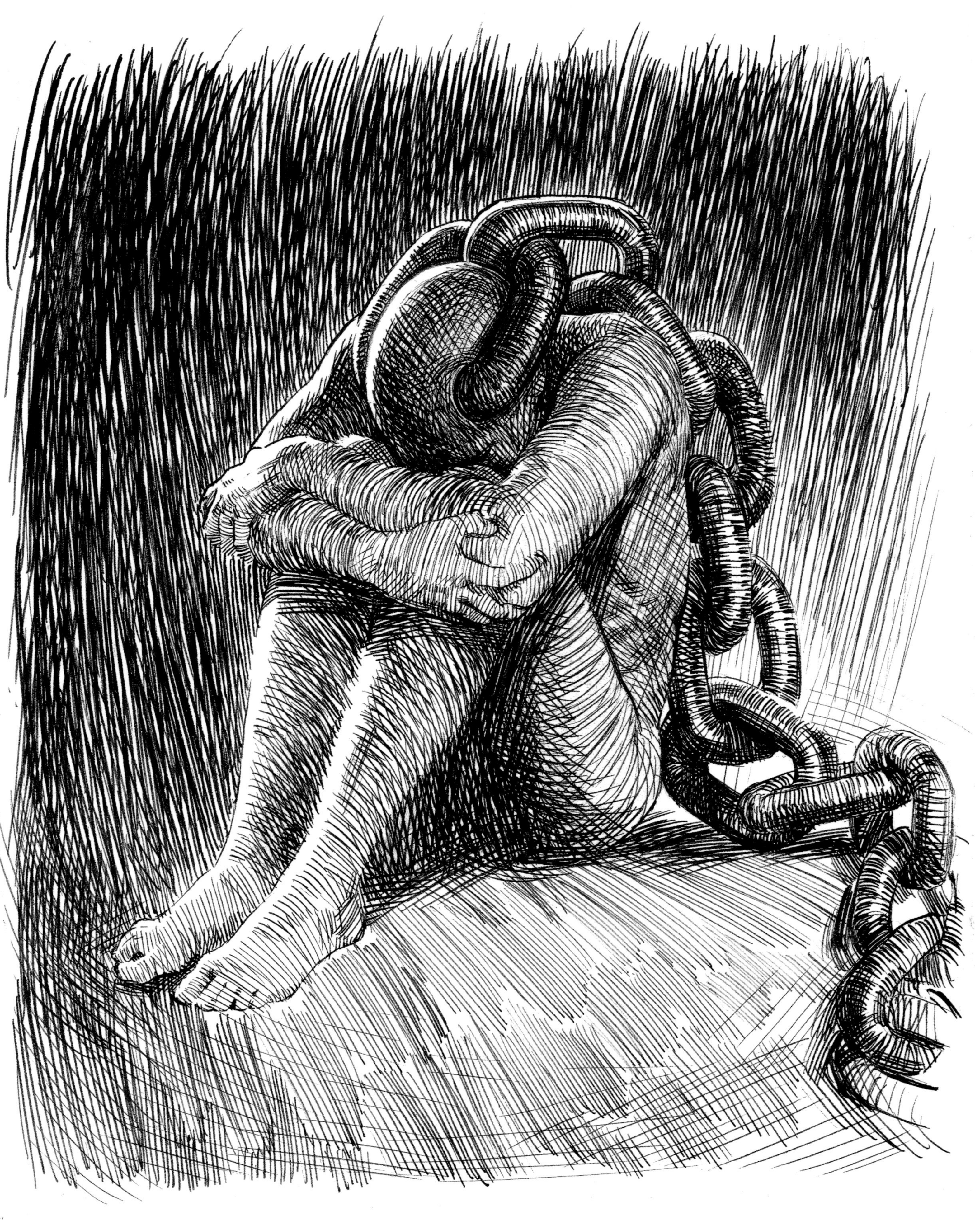

Chained
2019

Brain Chain (detail)
2017

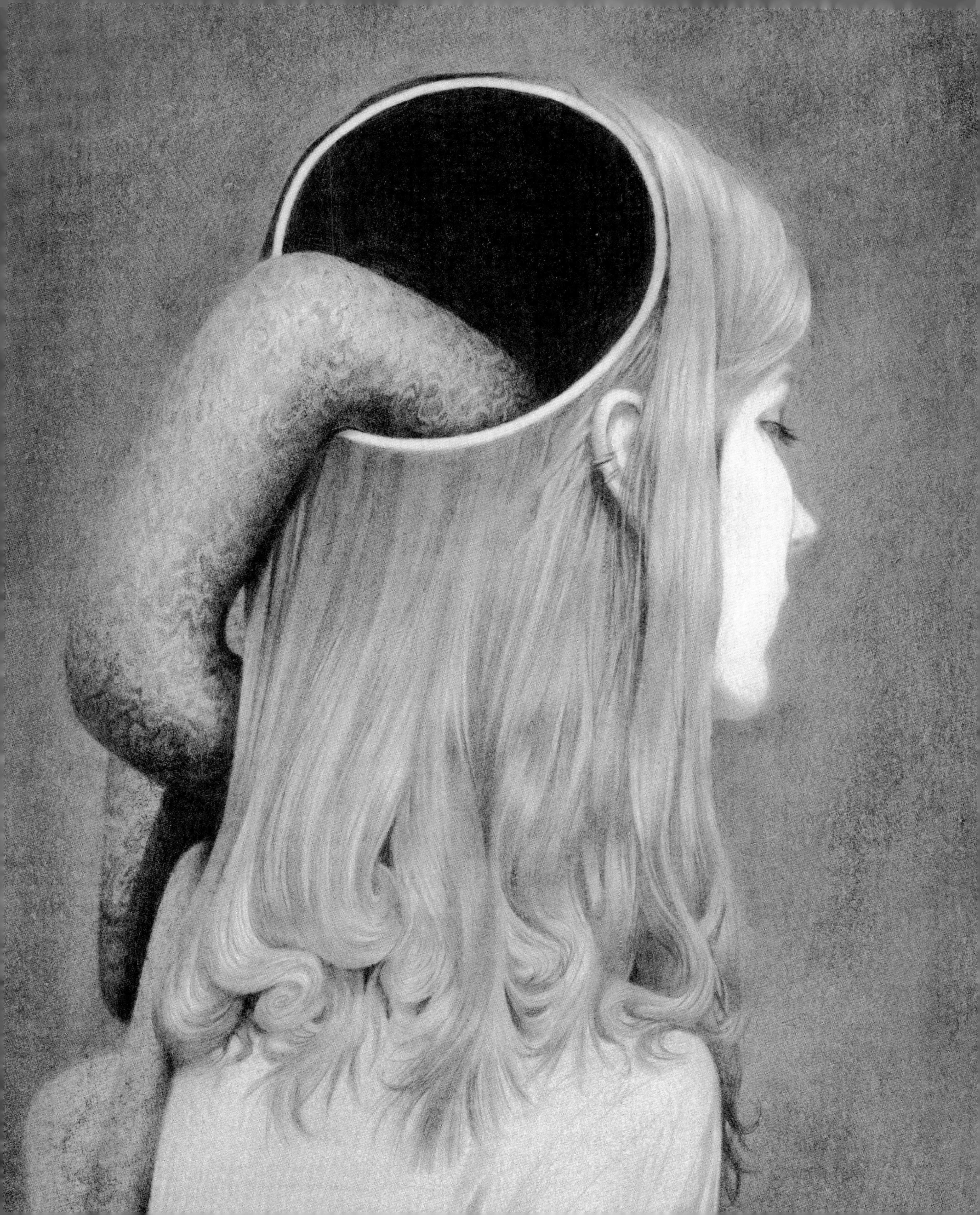

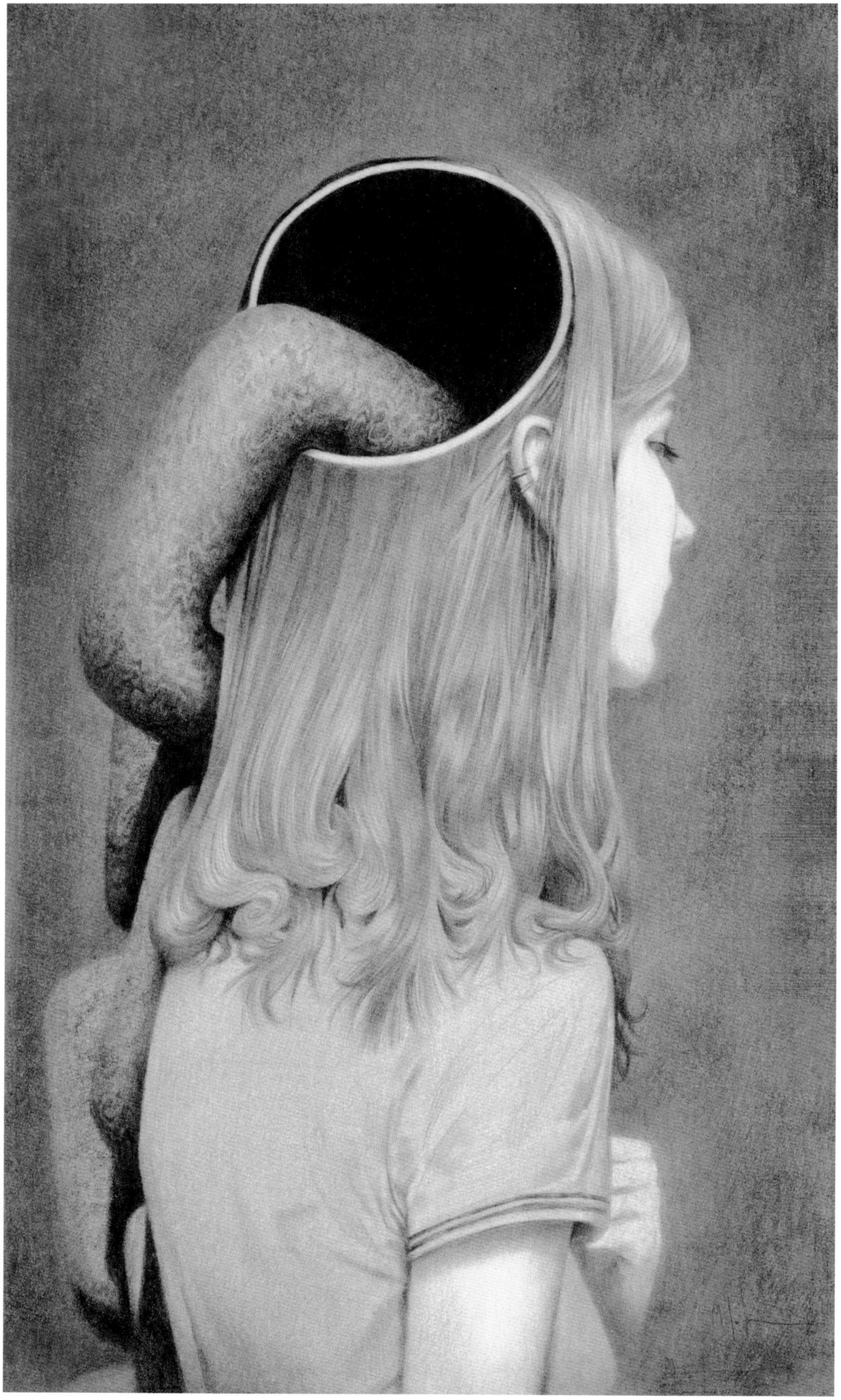

Brain Chain
2017

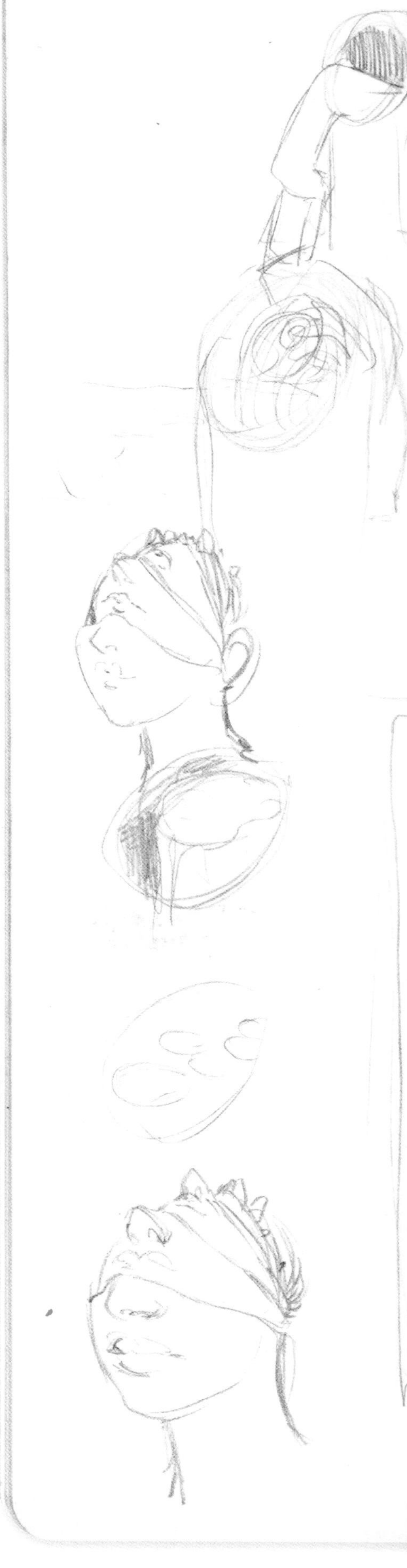

Studies for Brain Chain

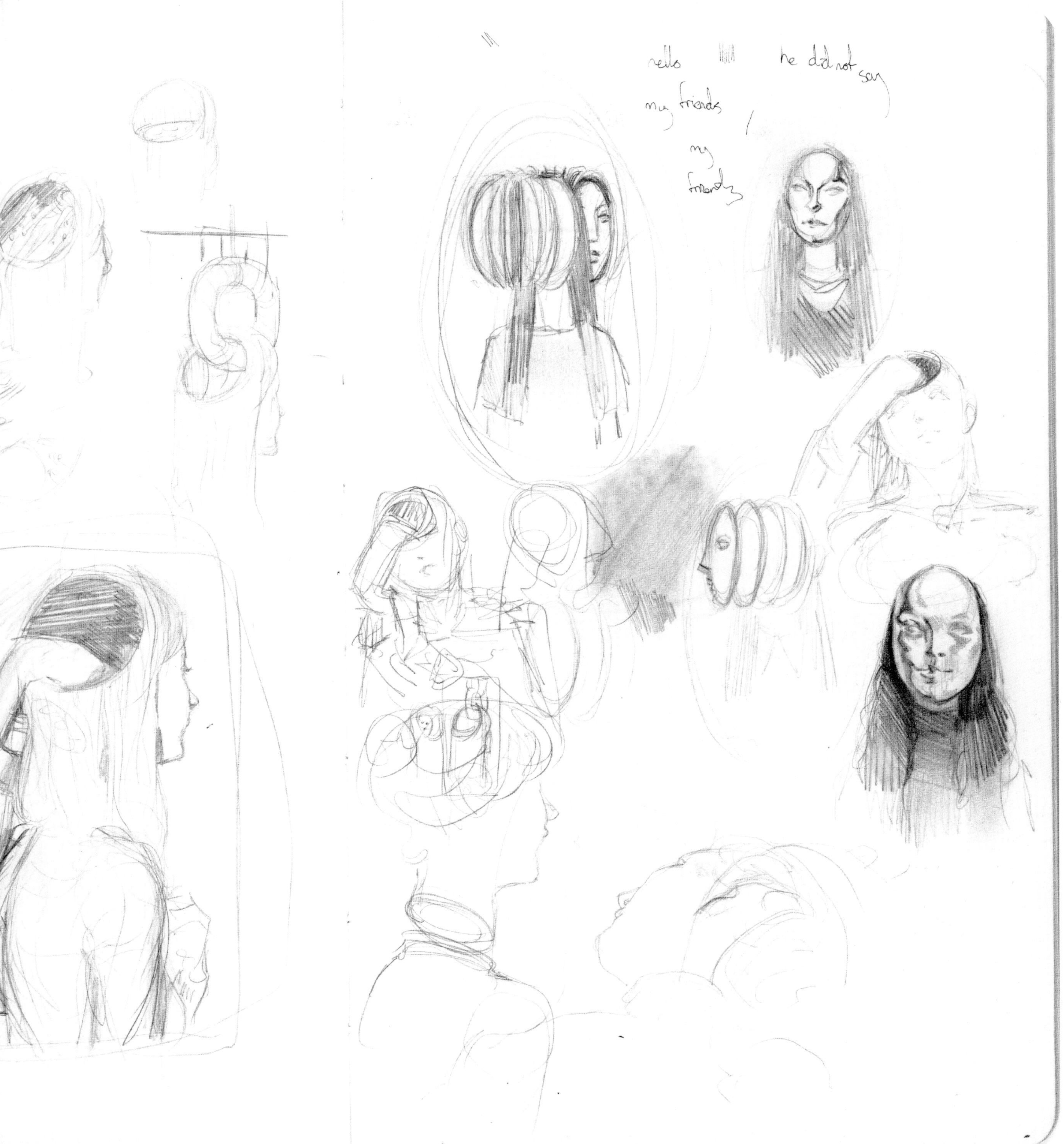
hello
he did not say
my friends
my friends

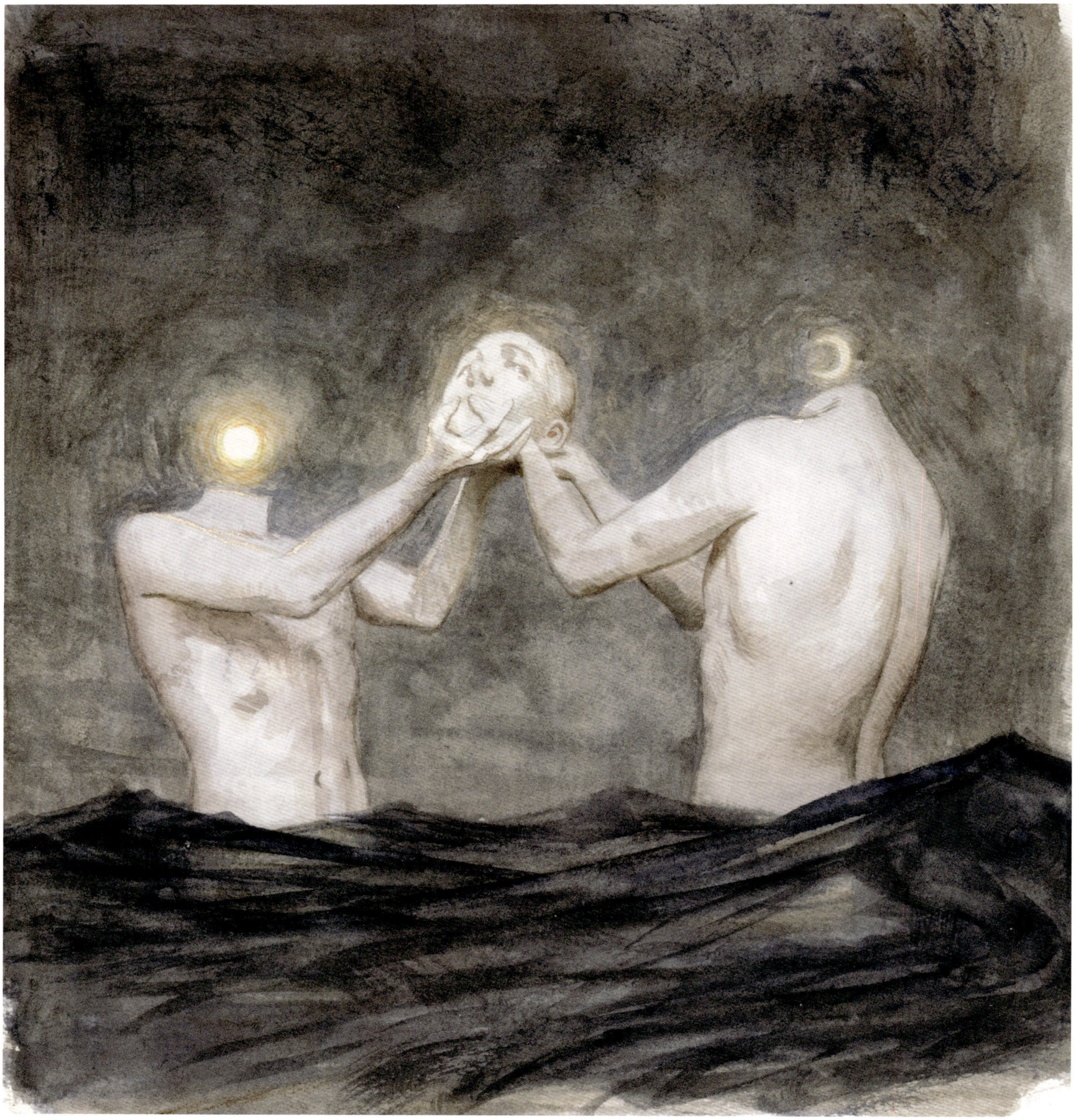

Union of Opposites

2020

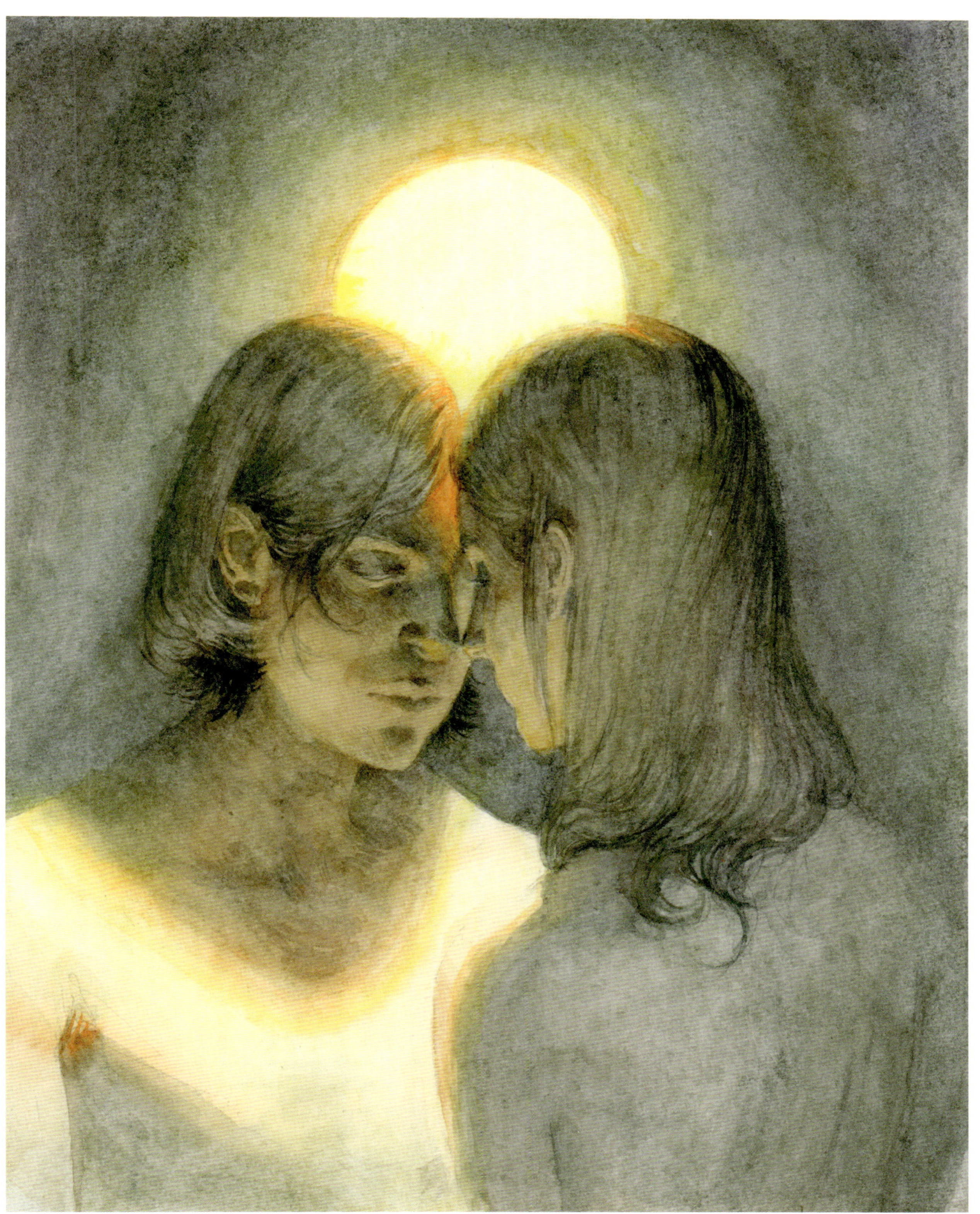

We Shared A Sunrise
2020

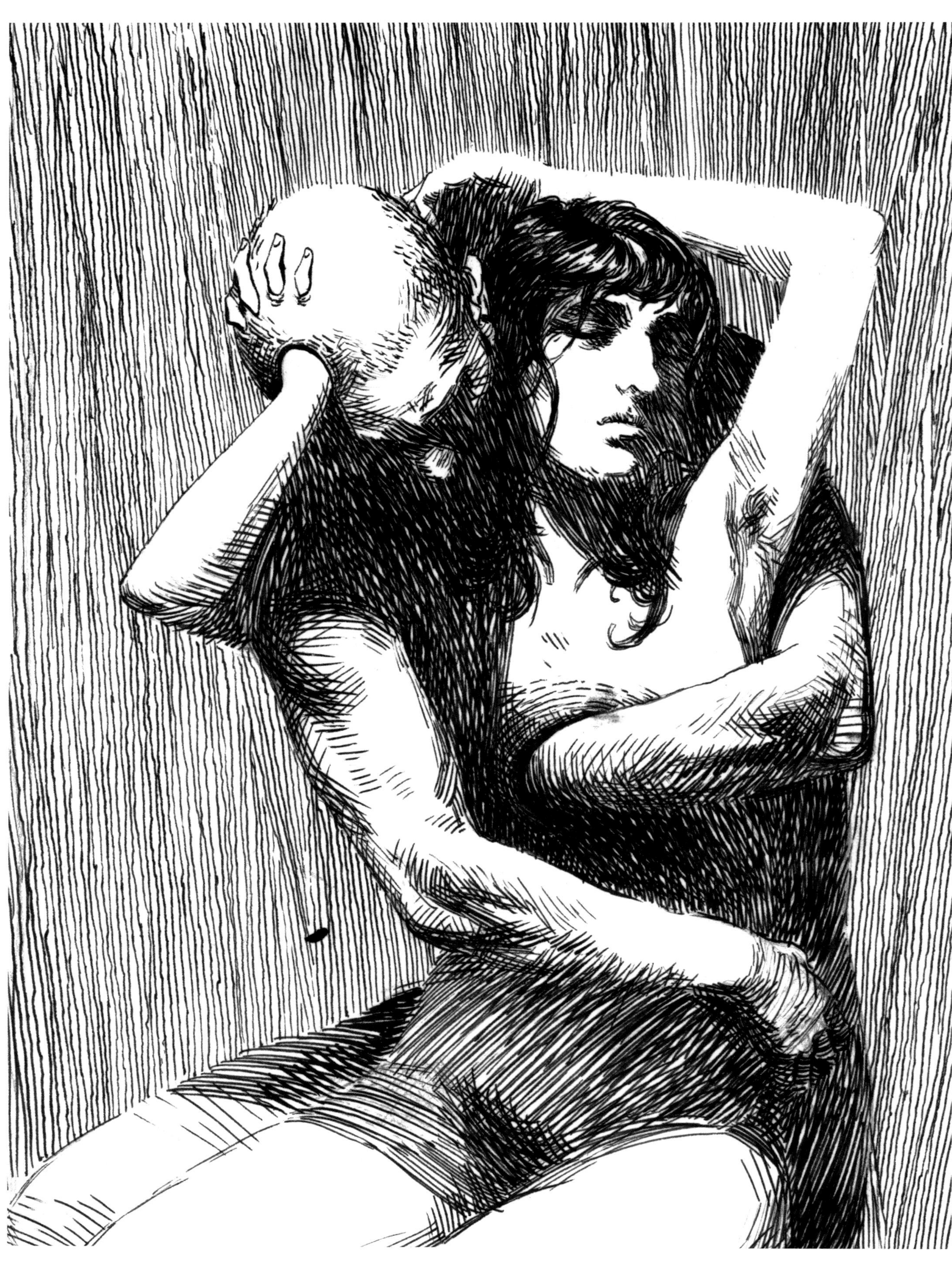

Embrace
2024

Bound
2023

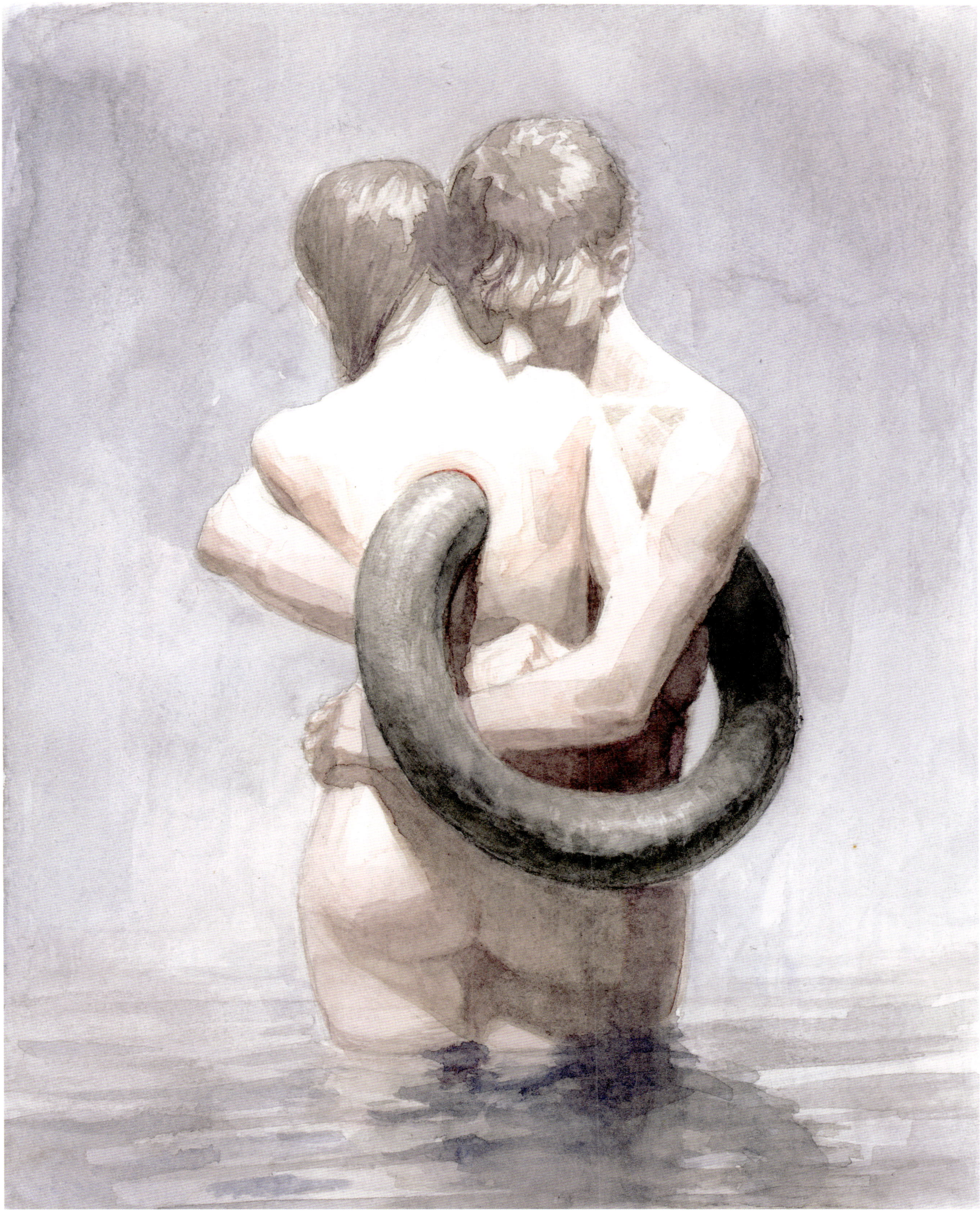

Shelter
2018

I've always felt like this drawing is one of the clearest examples of how fluid an image's meaning is, and how much more it is a mirror for the viewer than a fixed one way communication from the artist to the audience. My intention was to try and create an image that could have two equally plausible yet opposite interpretations (there are of course infinitely more than two), like a psychological version of the famous rabbit and duck optical illusion. Some see a protective male figure, using his own body and being to shield this woman from the world, others see an empty and damaged man filling a void in himself with her and ominously consuming her. My belief, as I have stated elsewhere in this book, is that regardless of what an artist tells you an image means, there actually is no canonical meaning. It is always formed fresh in each new experience of being beheld. I actually don't have the power nor the right to dictate what my work means. Once I've made it, my work is over. If I have succeeded, then the image will take on its own life independent of my intentions.

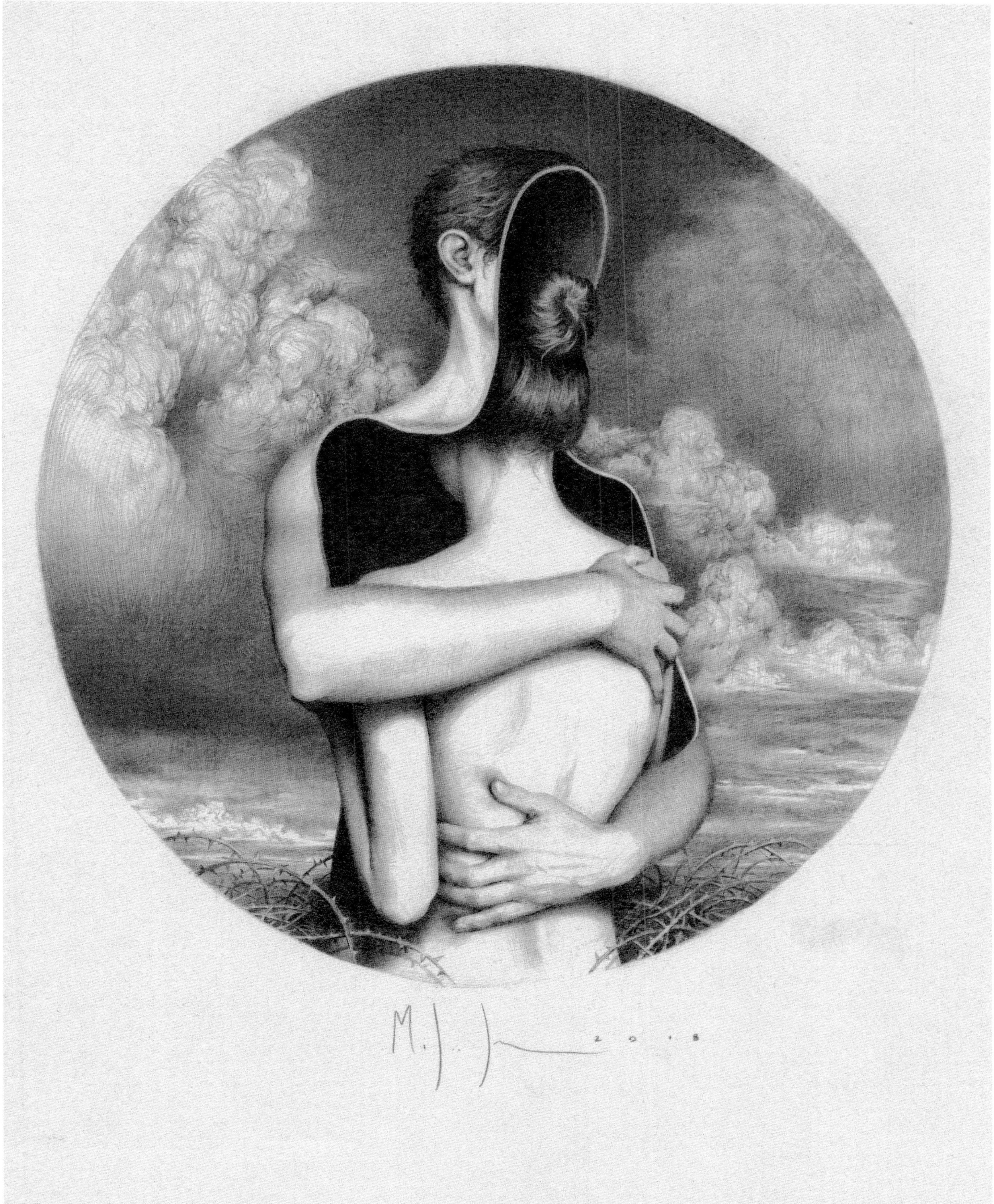

Even once you have narrowed down your focus from the overwhelming infinity of the blank canvas and you have a fairly well established sketch, you still have a further infinity of small changes to play with. The exact positioning of the arms, the position of the fingers, the background elements, the hair styles, the lighting etc. All of these elements are still functionally limitless in their possibilities. This is where the metaphor of distillation comes into play. To make these choices, I have to experiment drawing my sketch over and over and seeing how the changes affect my reaction to the image. Certain changes seem to dilute and introduce noise, whereas others seem to intensify and clarify focus.

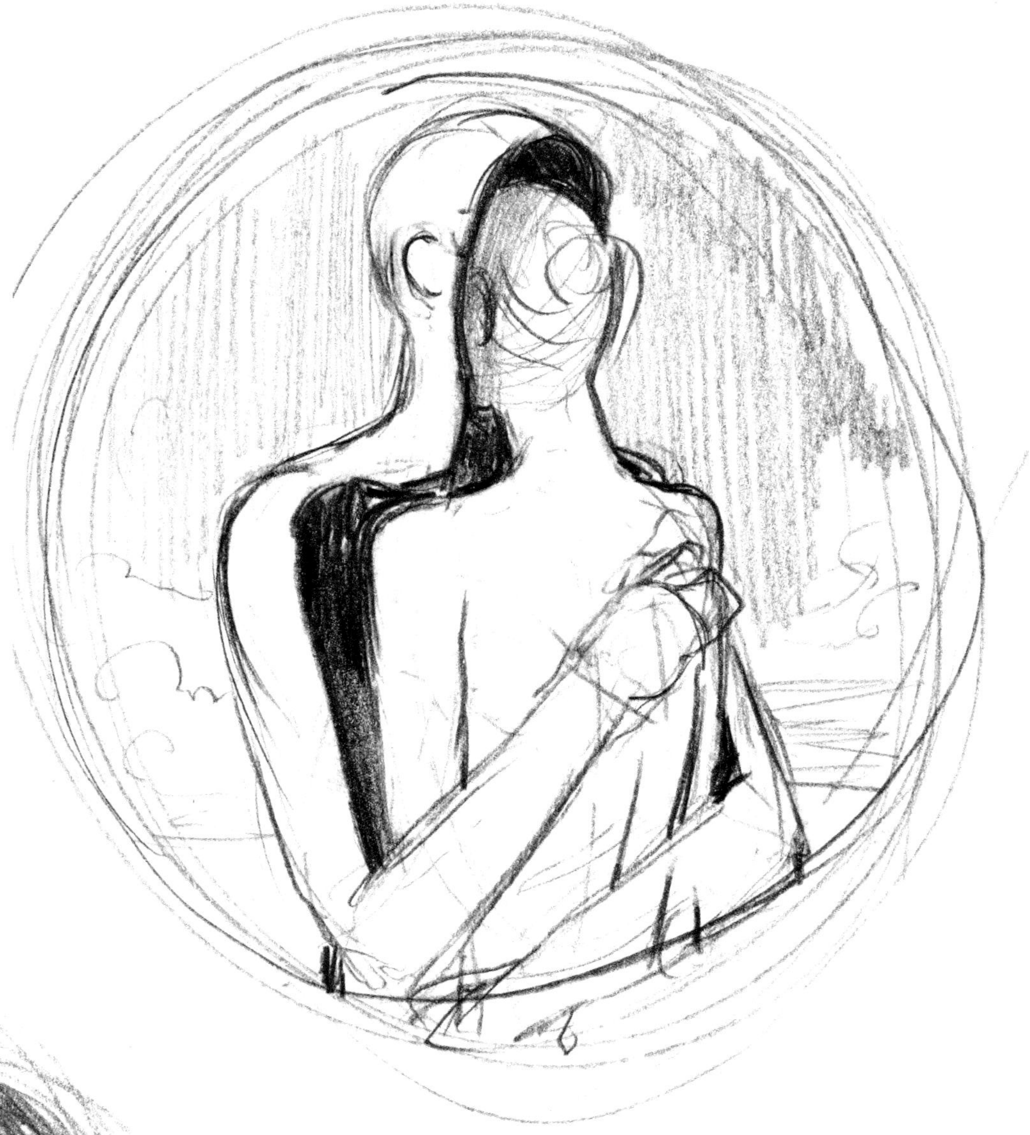

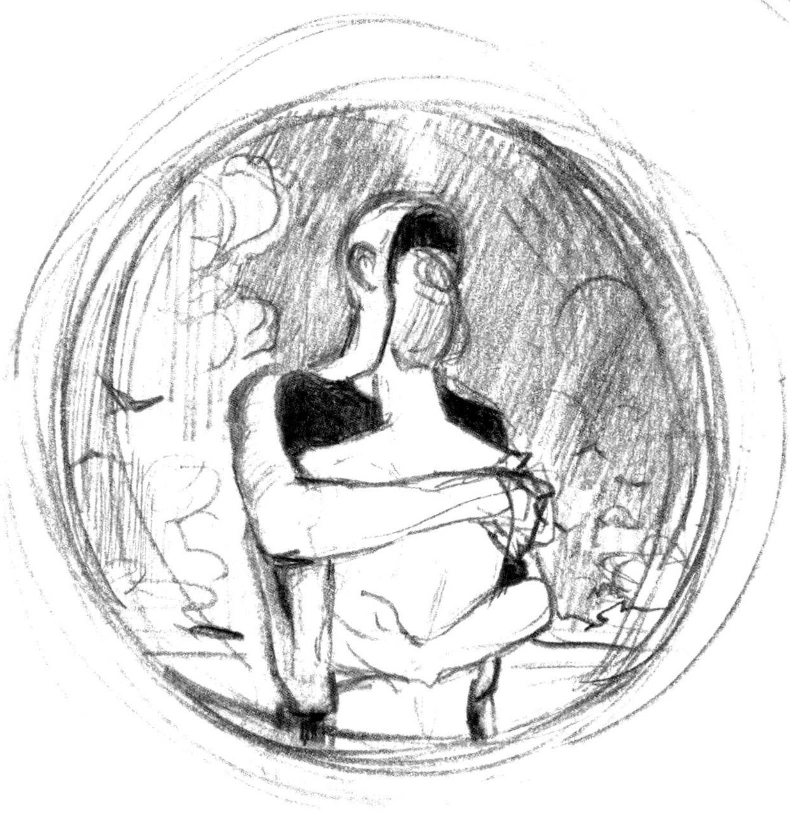

Studies for Shelter
2018

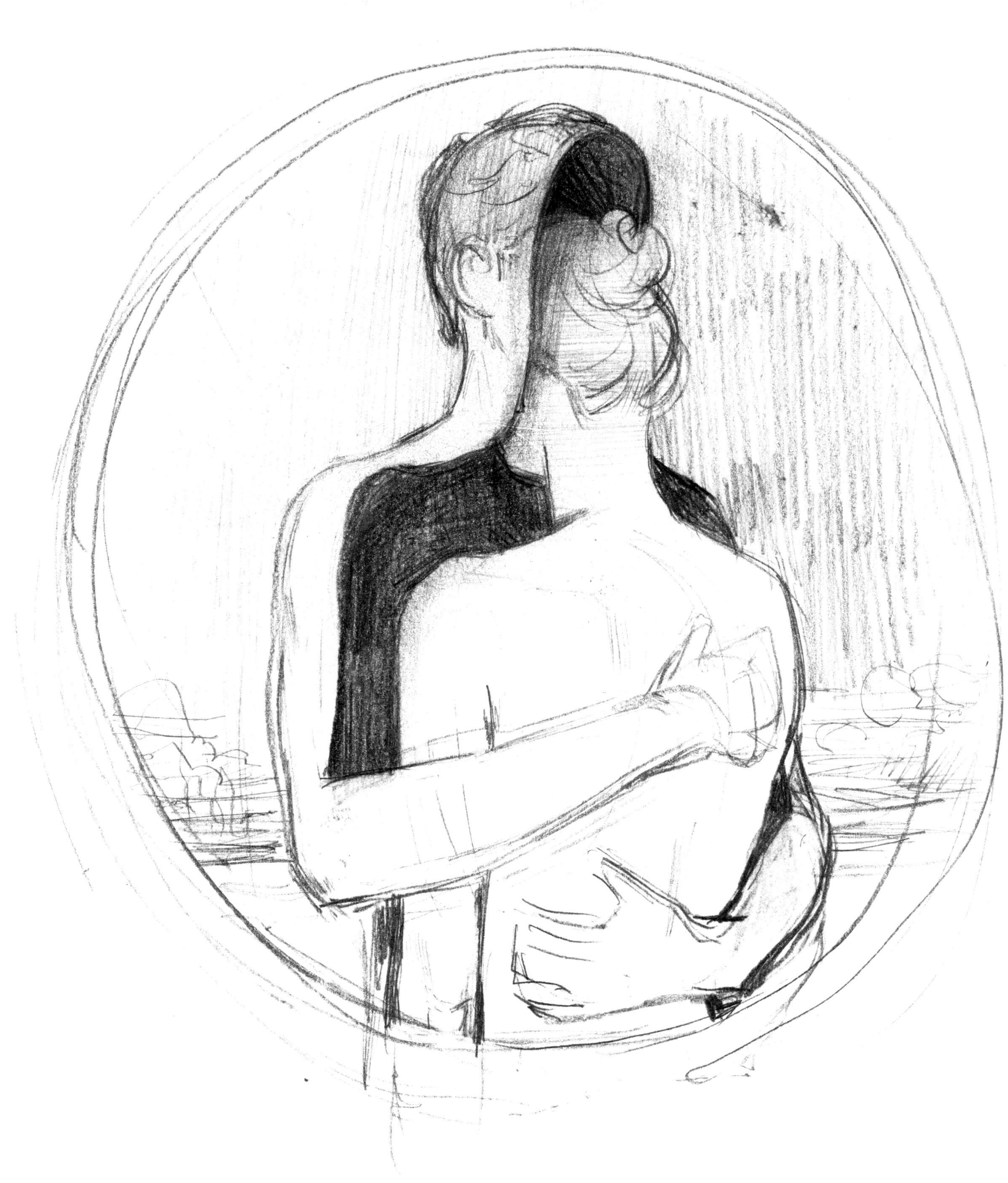

Untitled
2024

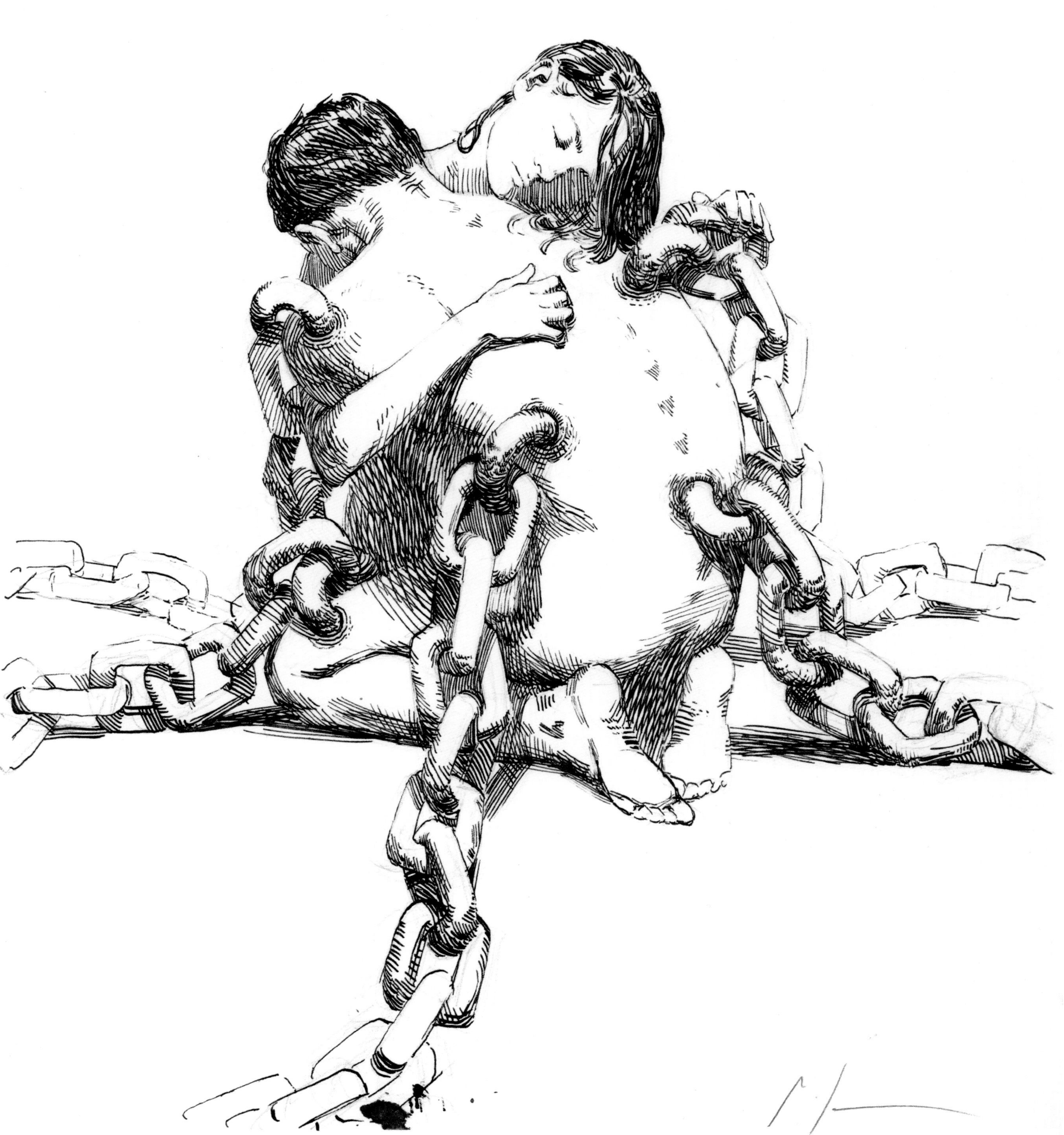

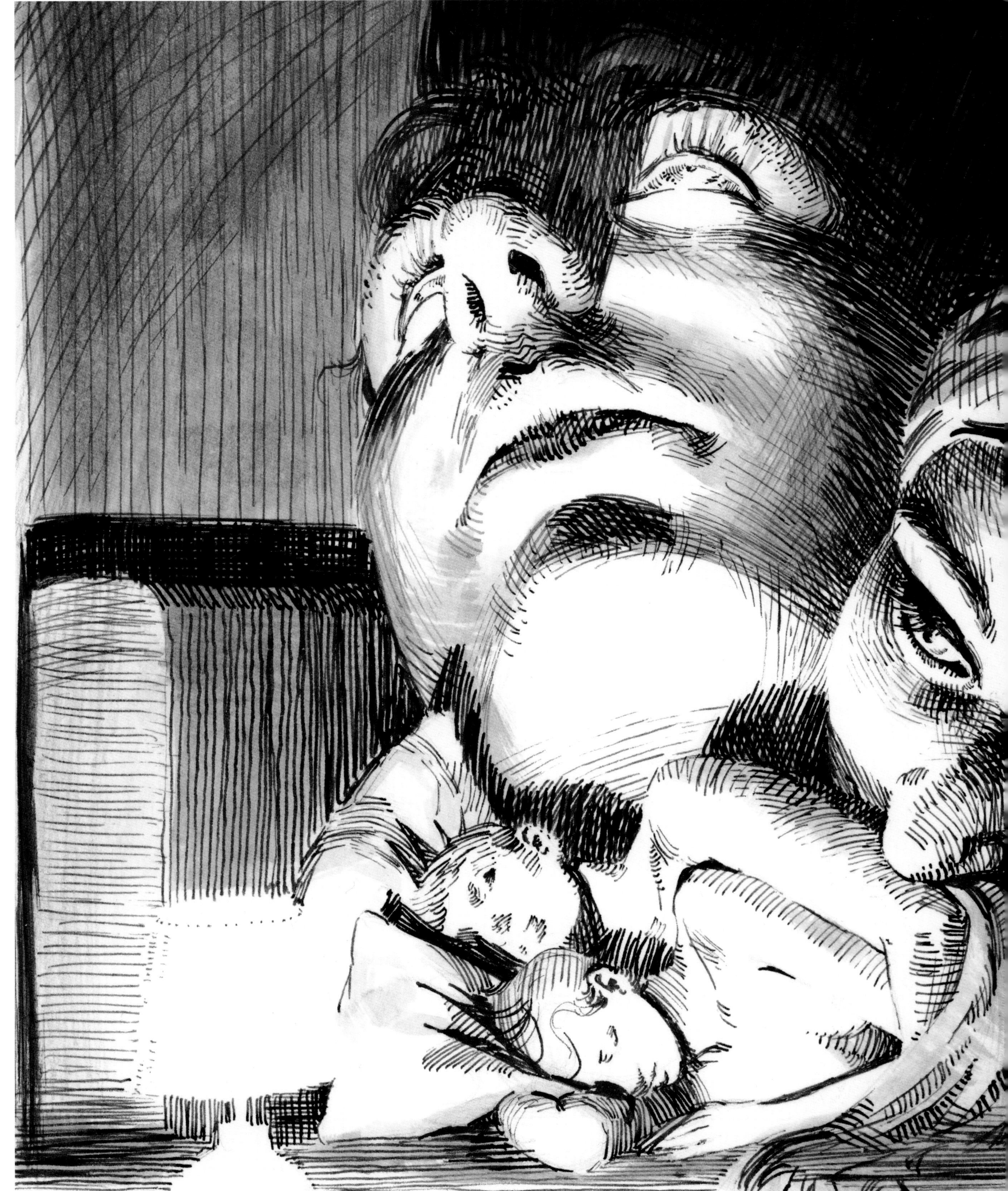

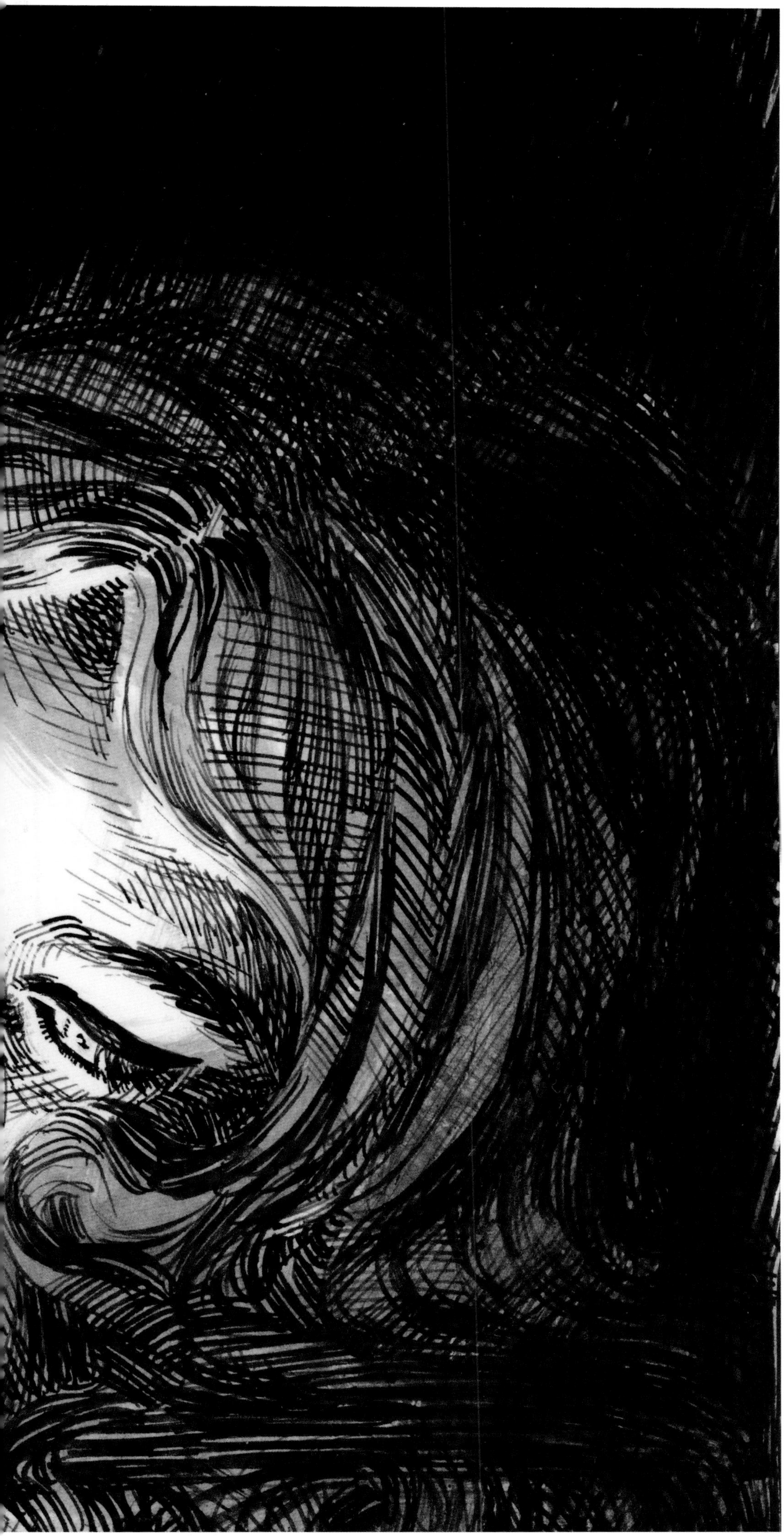

Night Terror (detail)
2021

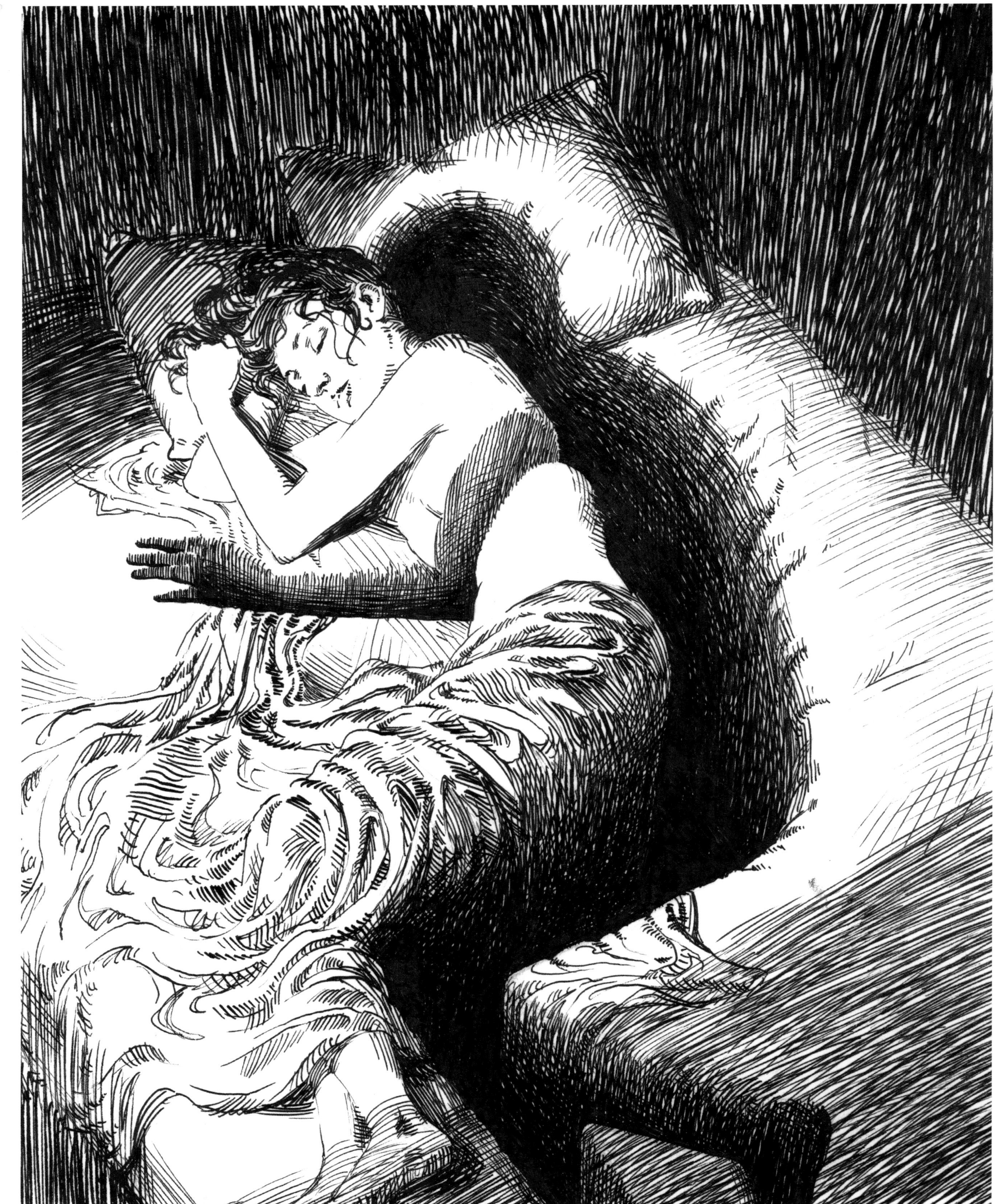

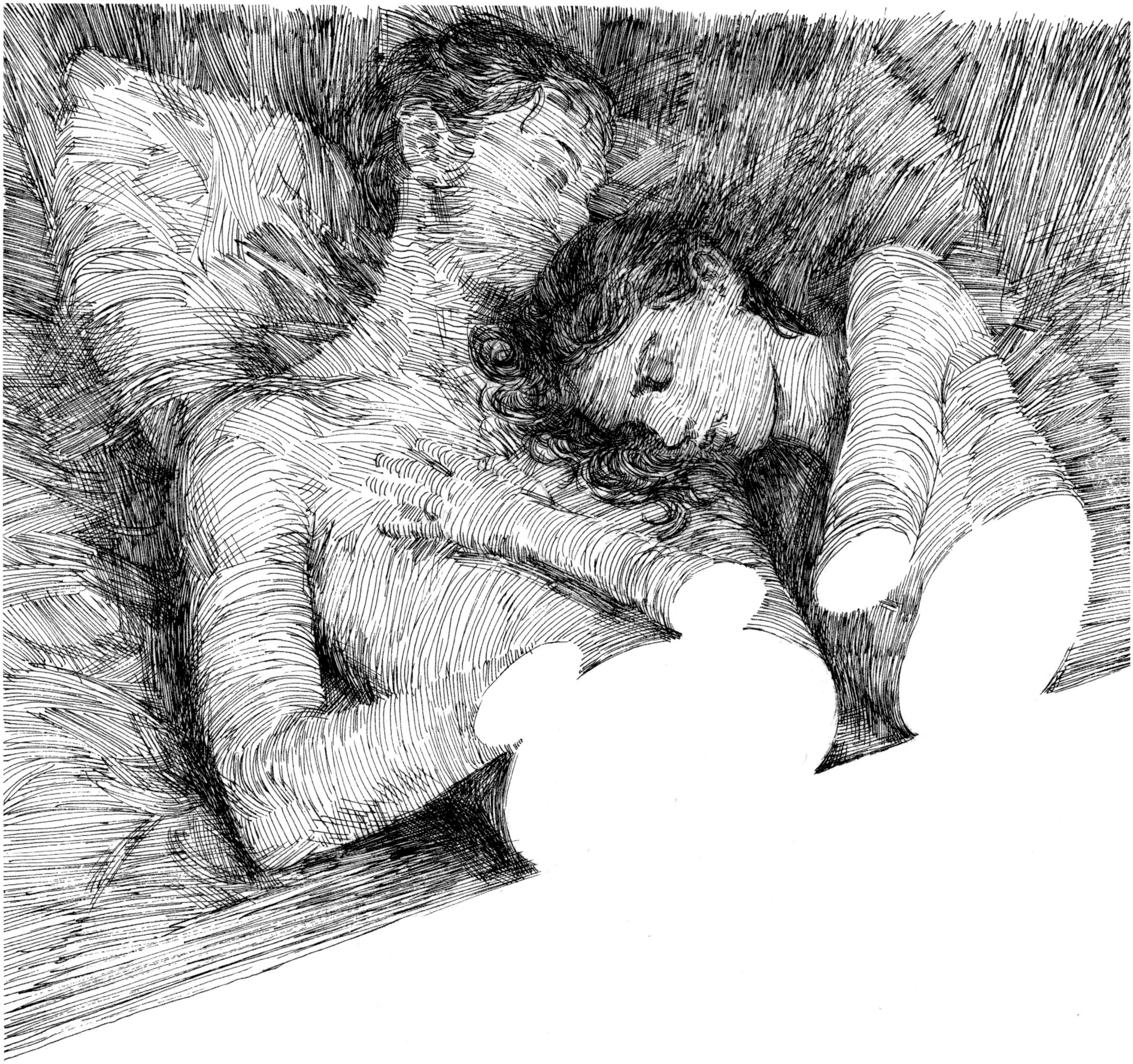

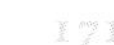

Memories of Mr. Nobody
2024

Erased by The Light
2018

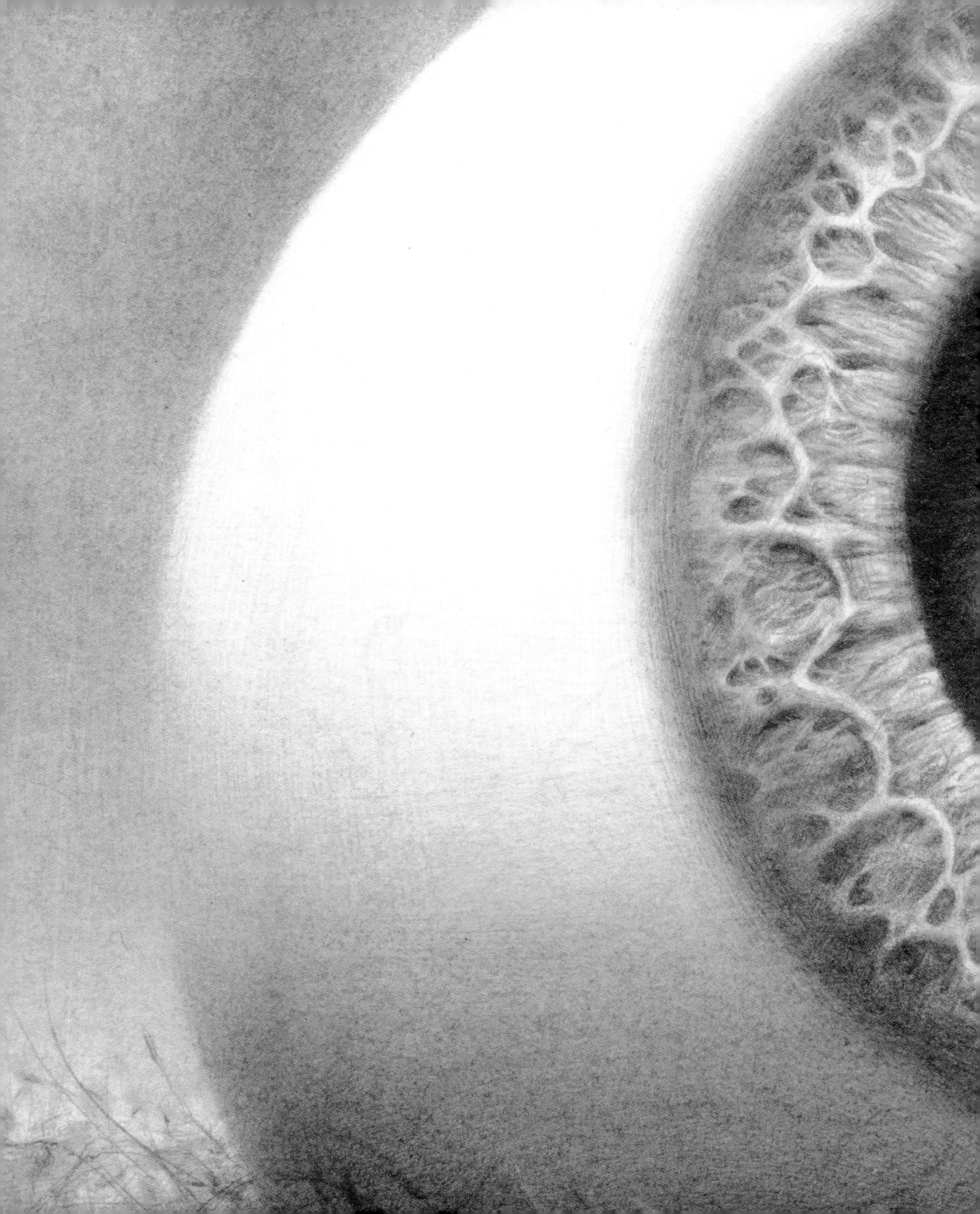

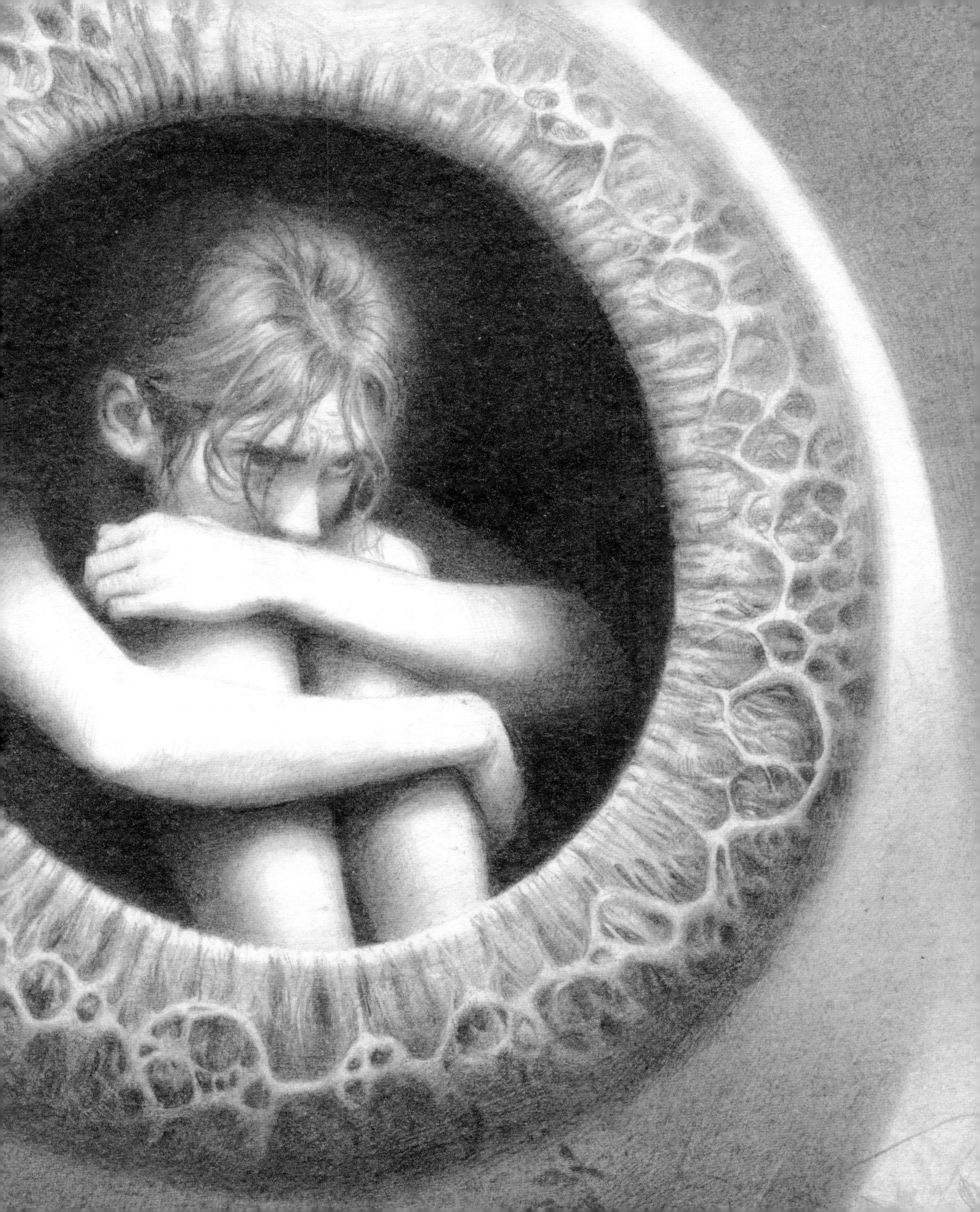

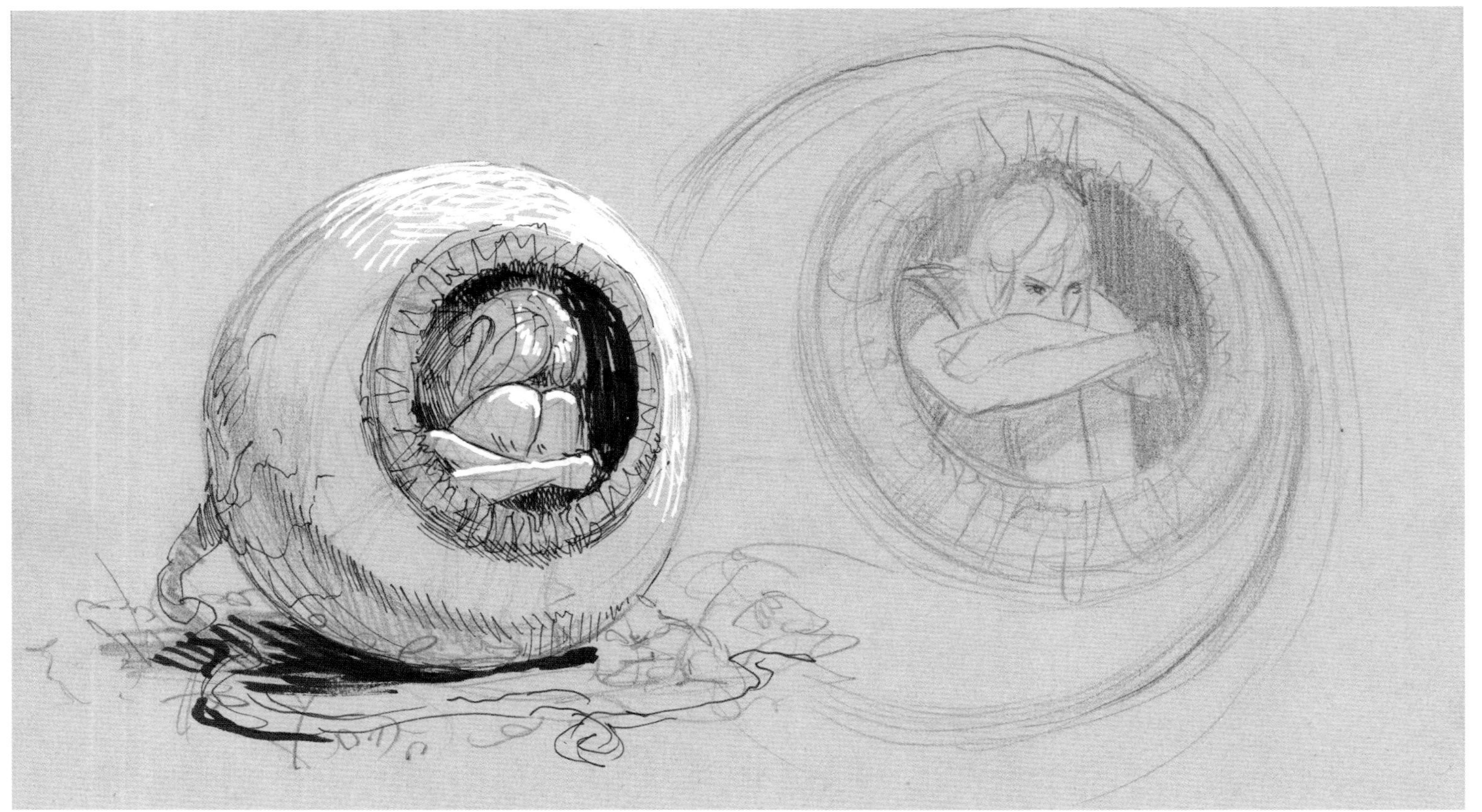

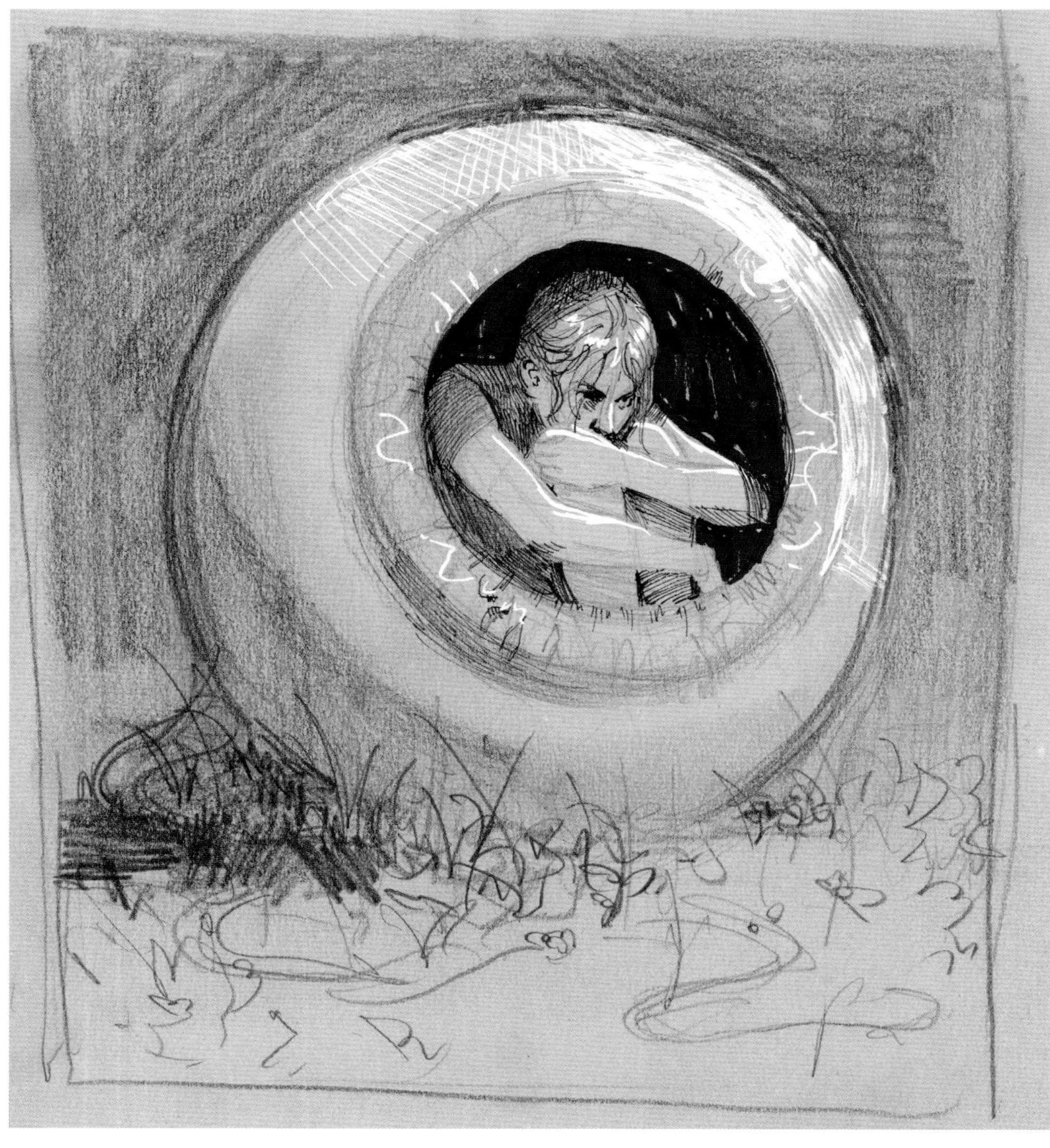

Myopia + Studies
2021

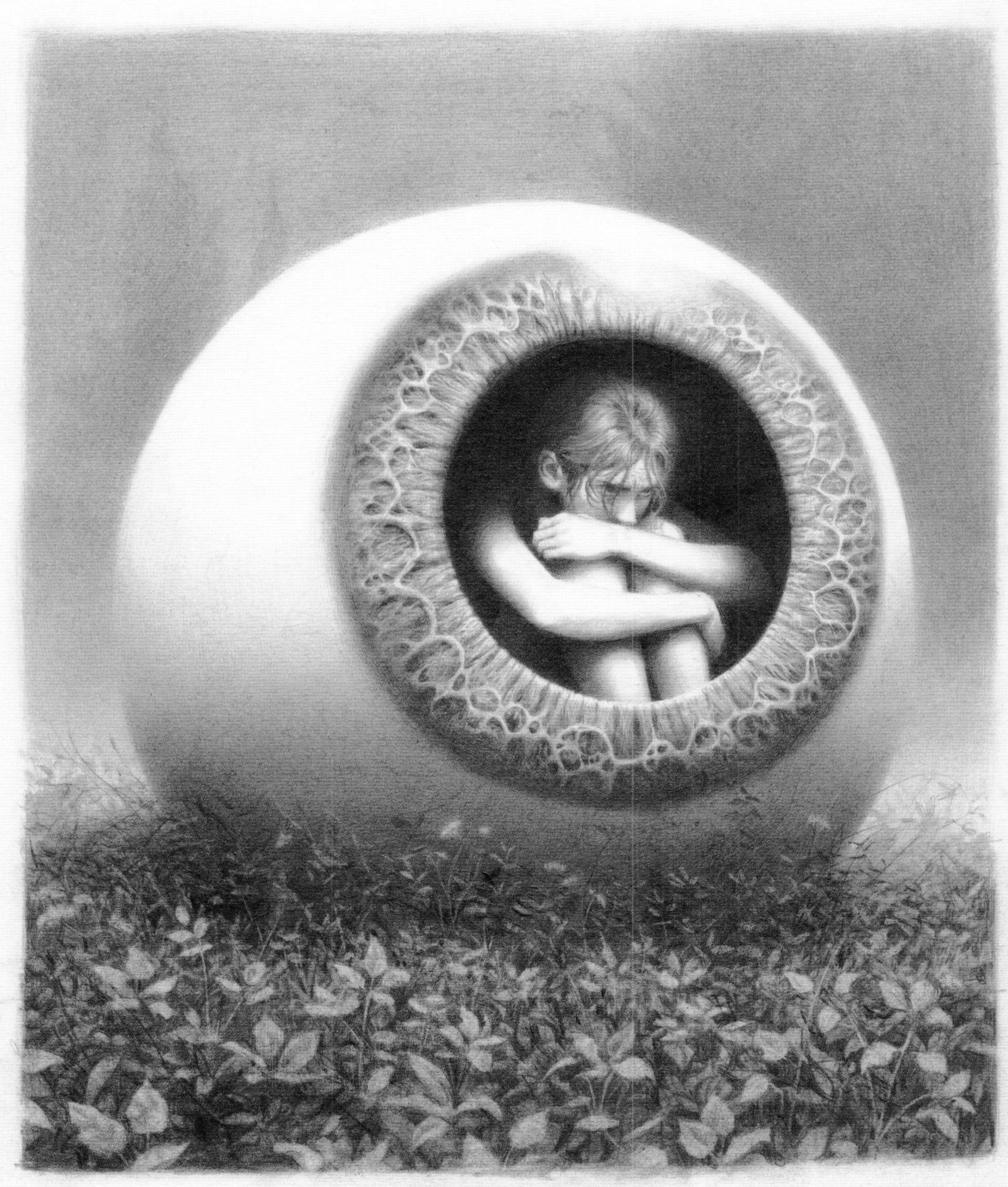

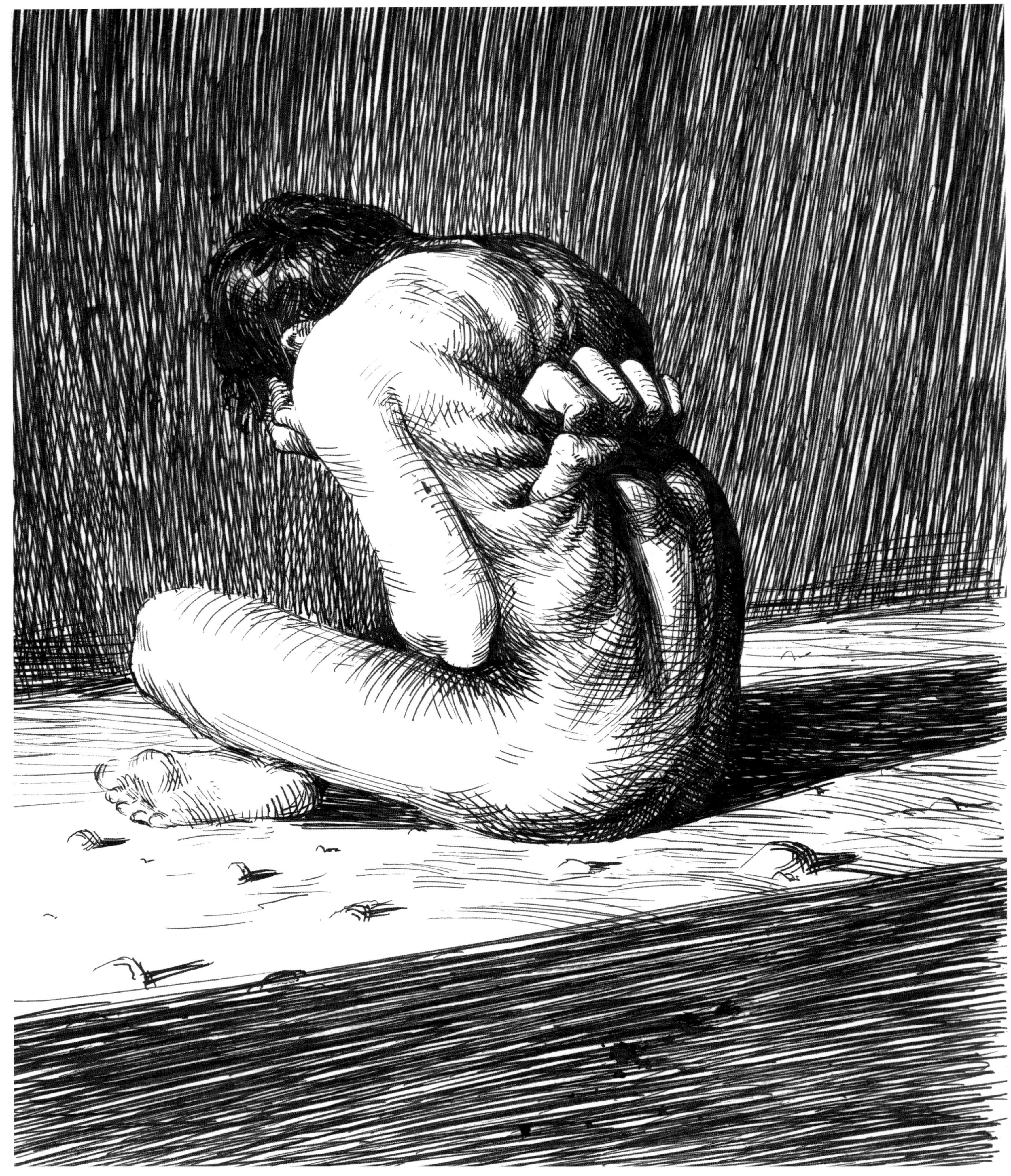

Tension
2023

Cardiophobia
2020

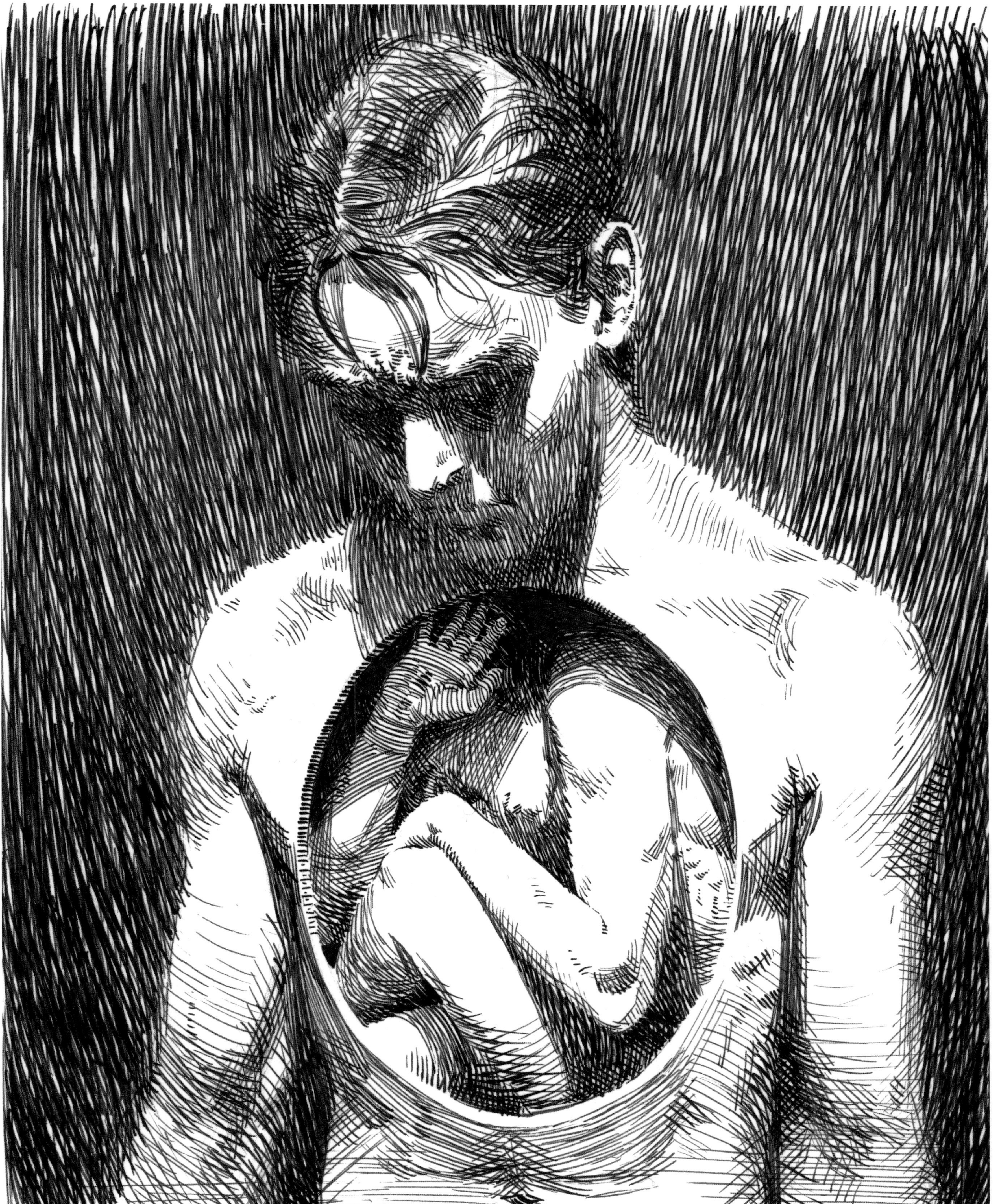

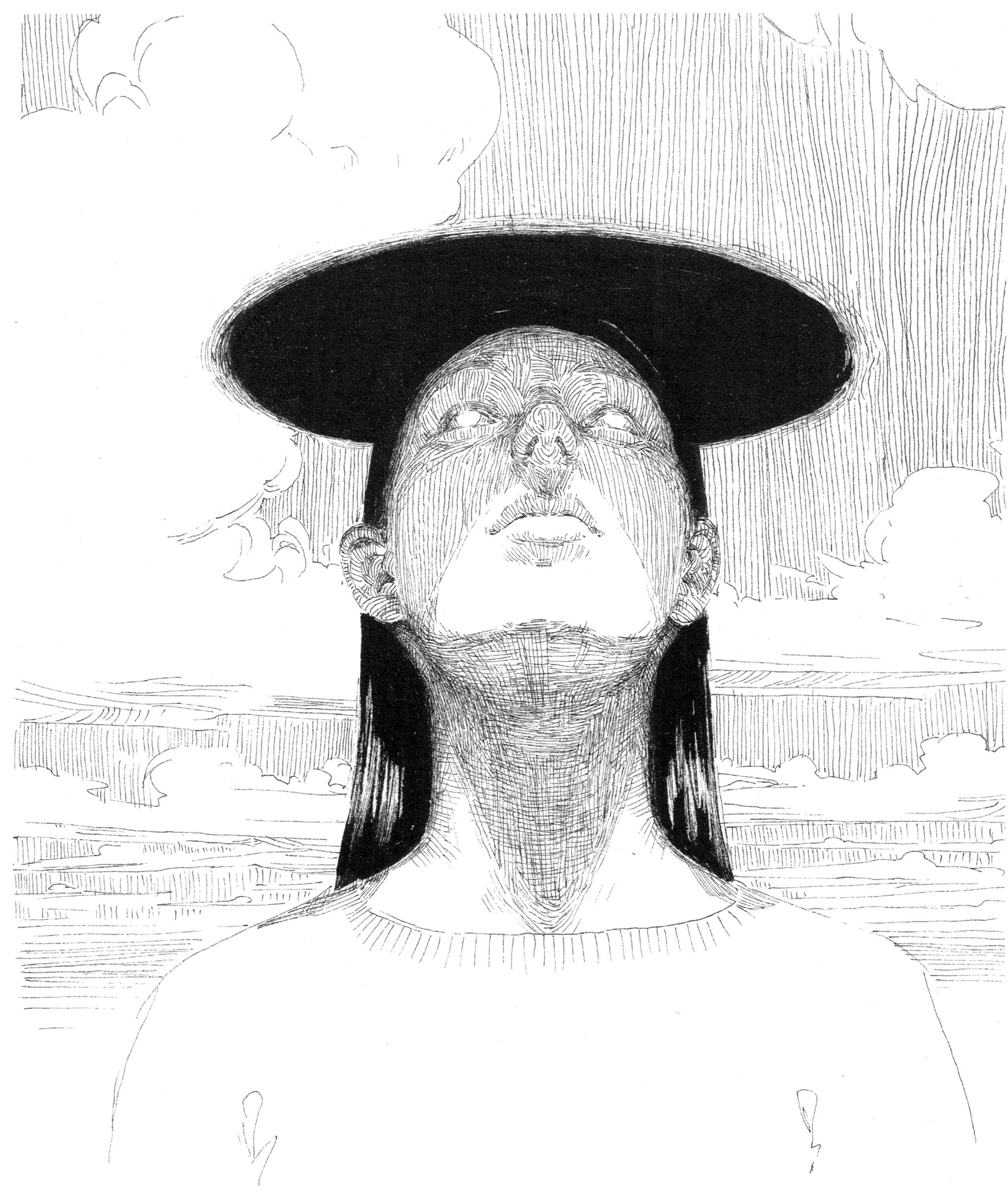

Void Fascination

2019

Loner
2022

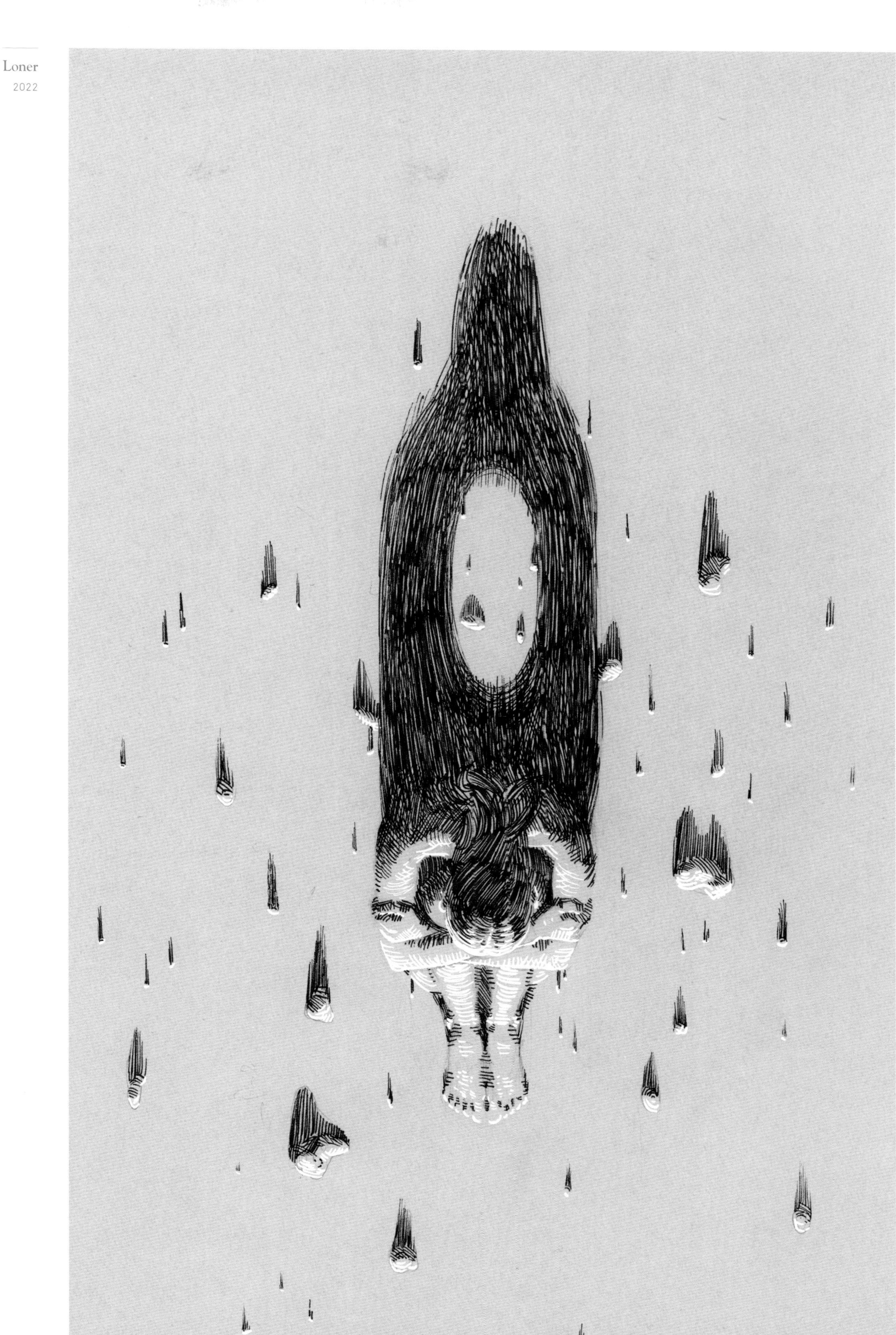

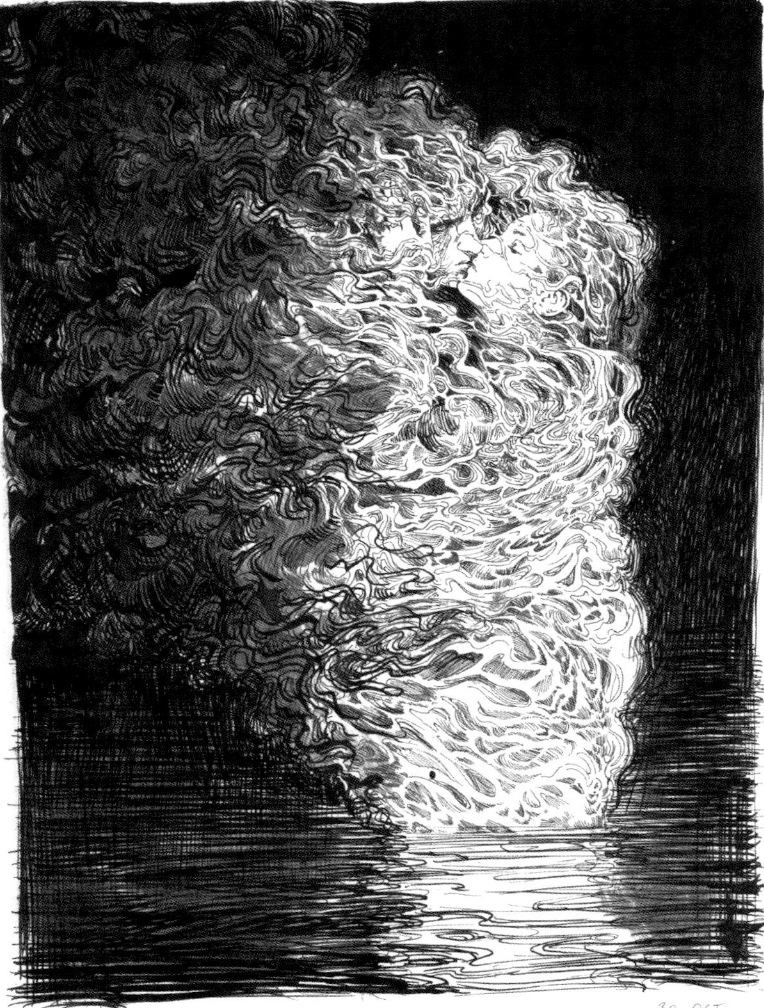

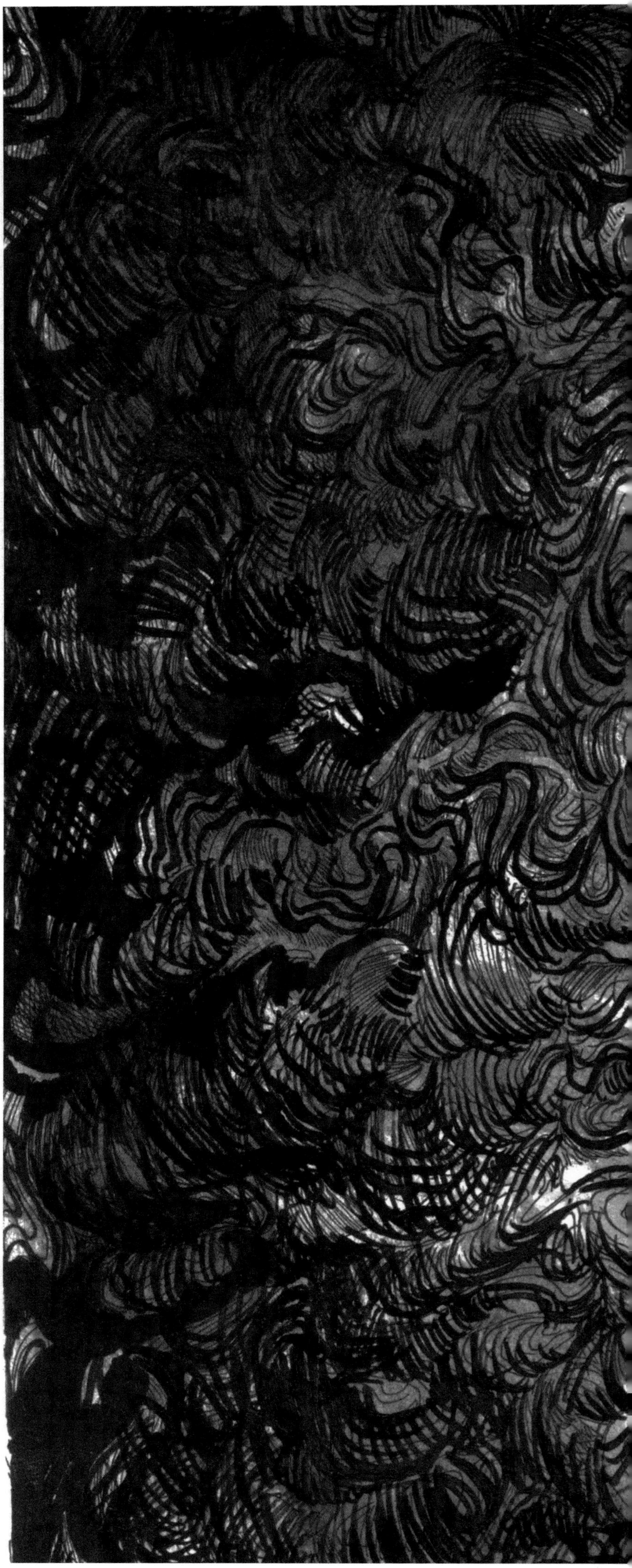

Love in The Final Days + Detail
2019

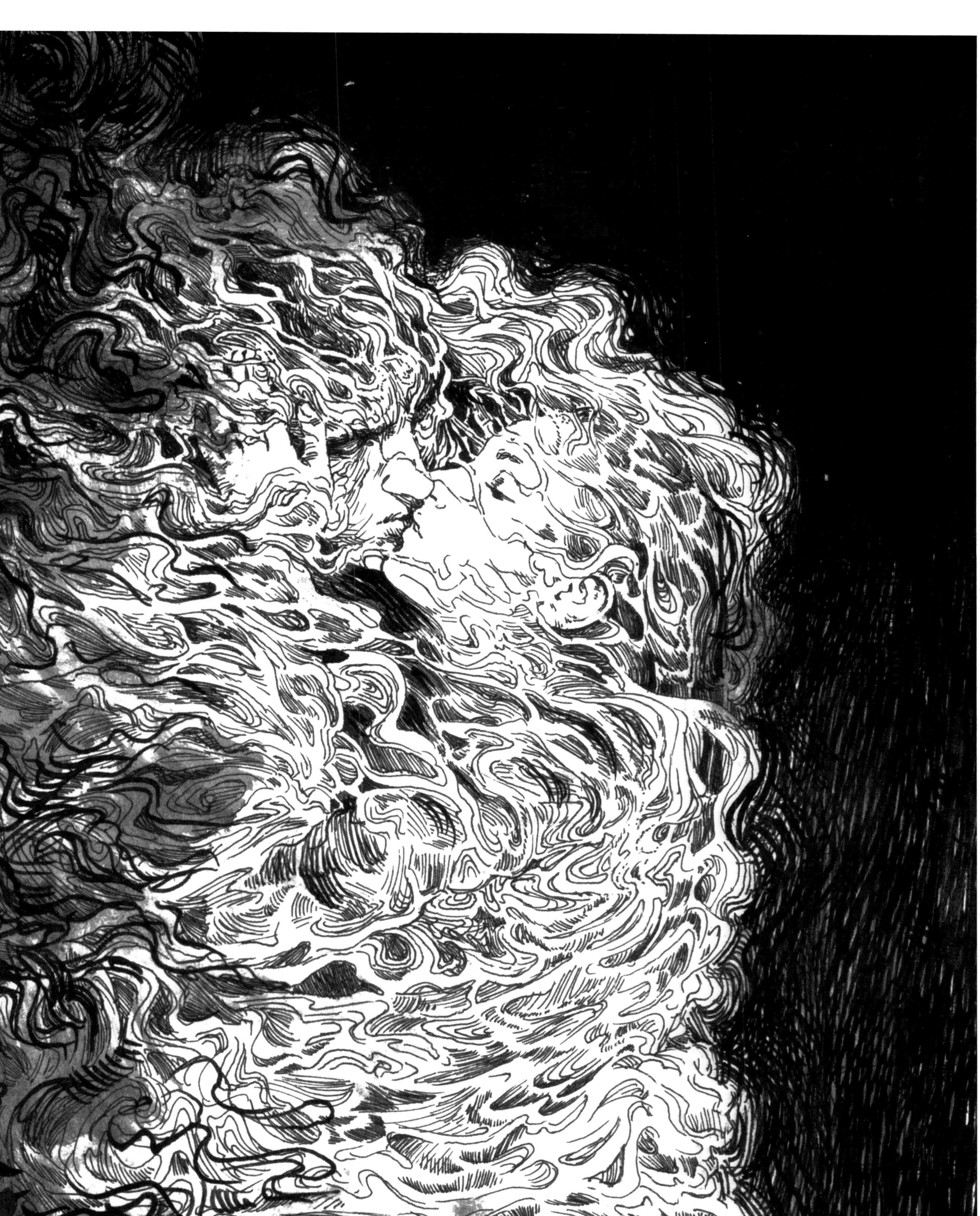

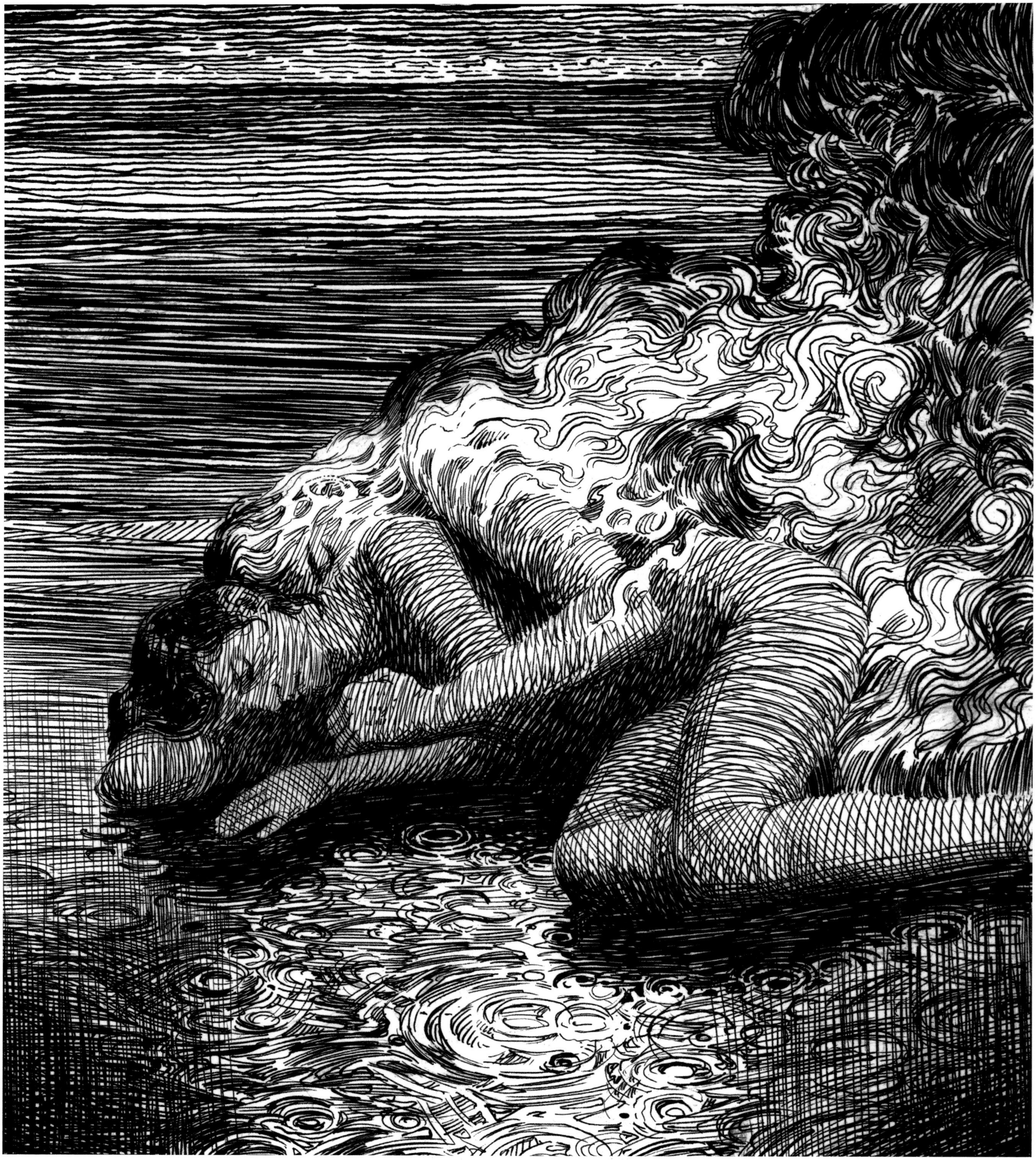

Smoulders

2022

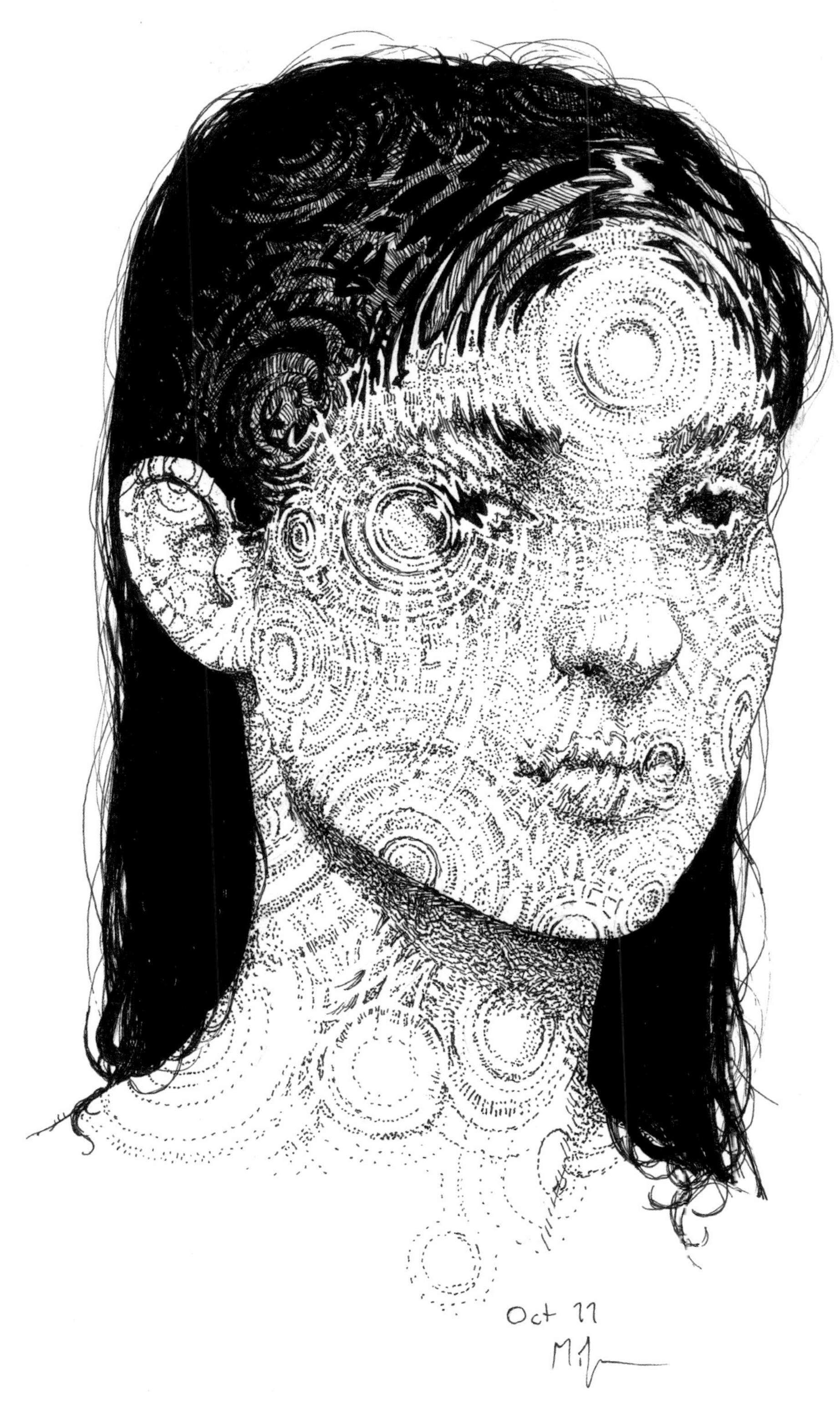

Unreachable
2018

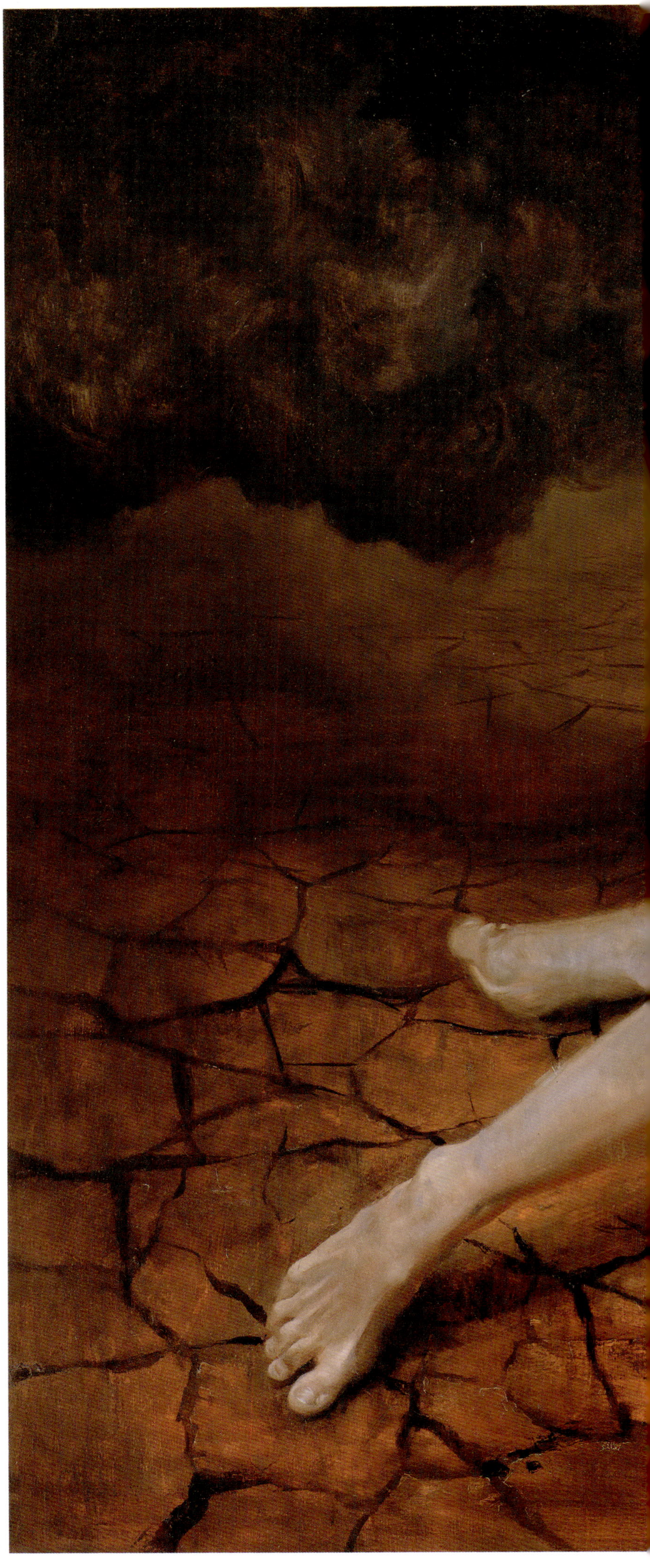

Agony
2018

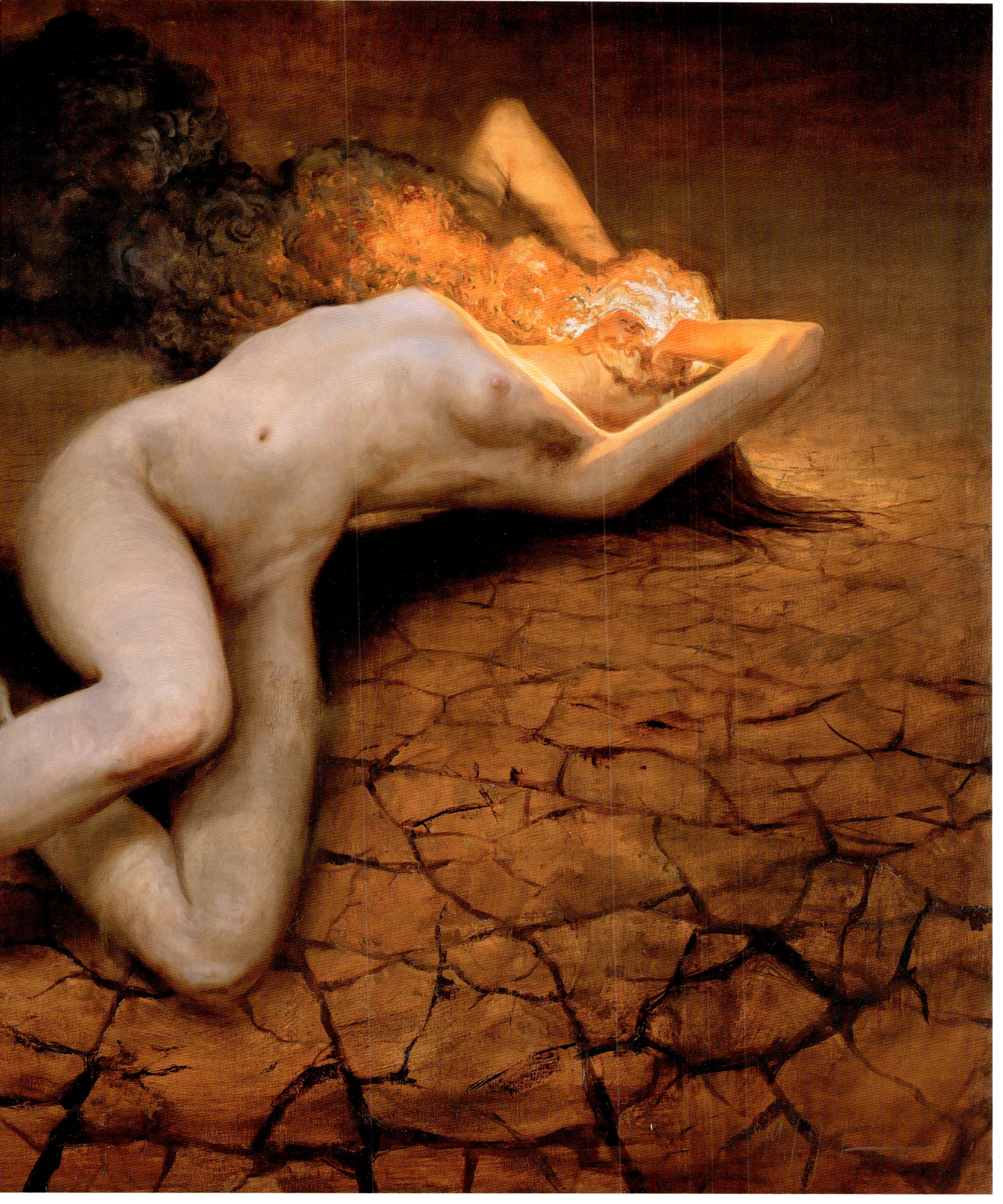

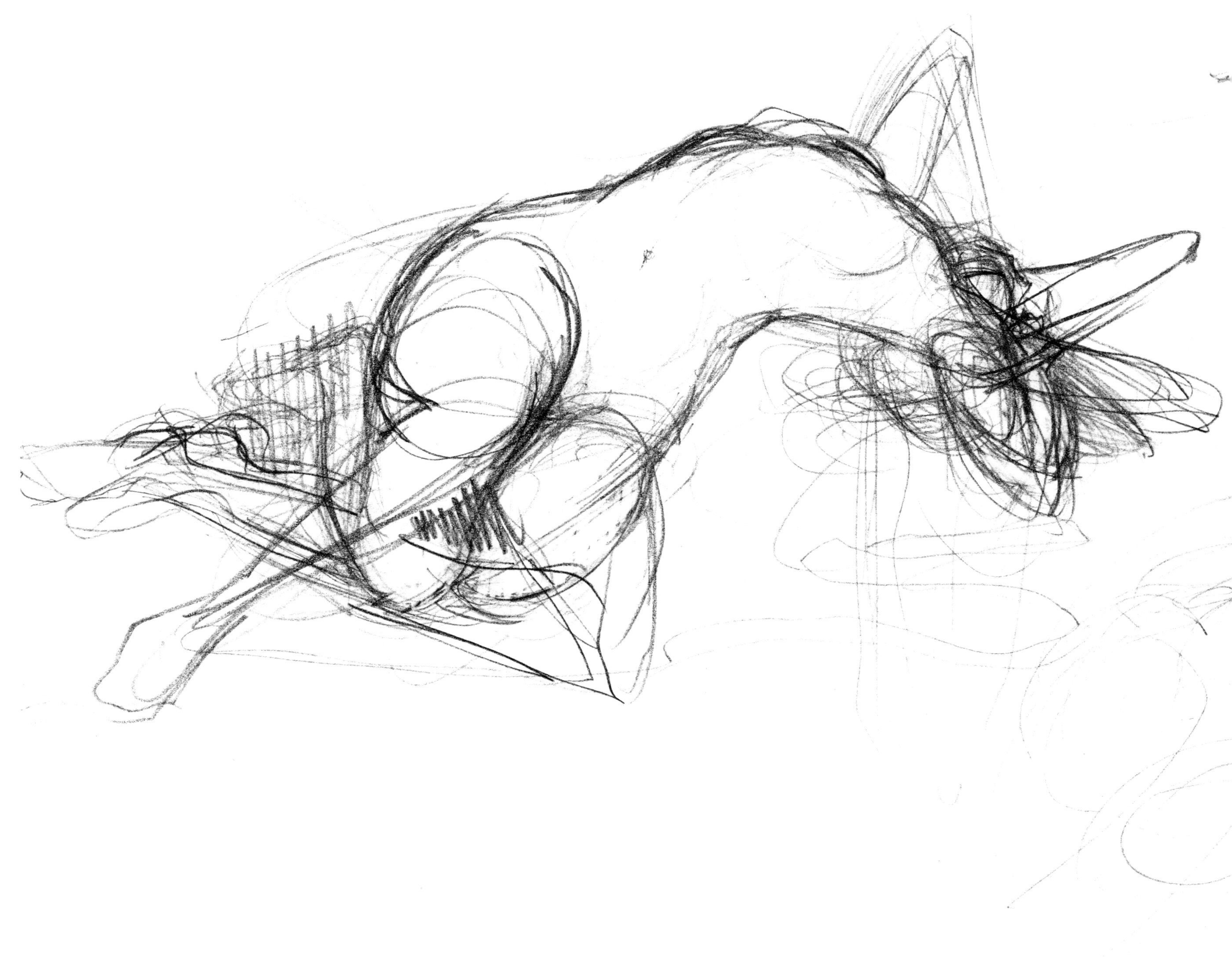

Sketching

Studies for Agony & Guilt
2018

I feel that it is interesting to talk about "*Agony*" and "*Guilt*" together, as their origins are intertwined. In exploring how they came about I can illuminate a few aspects of my creative process.

Sketching is, at its core, about overcoming the inertia required to make anything at all. If I wait to have a good idea before I start drawing, I simply never sit down to draw. I often tell myself to do an impression of someone who has something to draw. I sit, I open the sketchbook and I move the pencil. Most of what is produced will be discarded, but the trick is to stop feeling this as a disappointment or a failure. It is a necessary part in the strange pipeline between the limitless imagination and the small set of images I will ultimately make in my lifetime. My process is long and labour intensive, so by far the most difficult part is finding something that I am willing to commit a small but significant chunk of my life to.

I often start my images from body language. I am looking for ways to pose and depict a figure that inspires a sense of the inner emotional life of the subject. I am drawn to gestures and shapes that feel simple, iconic, and sculptural. Once I find a pose that feels interesting, I play with distortions of space, scale, perspective, or other out of context and unexpected elements. It is an intuitive process of distilling and enhancing the feeling that is compelling me to work on that particular drawing. I try to make sure that every choice throughout the process of developing the work is done in service of this. Looking for what is needed and losing what is not.

"*Agony*" and "*Guilt*" both emerged from the sketchbook page pictured here. In the top right corner, you can see I was experimenting with two different variations on the same pose: one where the torso was fully extended backwards with the hands on the face and one where the torso is instead curved over. When I drew these variations, I didn't know they would both go on to become fully developed images. It speaks to the strange chronology between sketches and their finished works. There might be months or years between a sketch first showing up in my sketchbook and the decision to further develop that particular motif. It all forms a part of my creative output as a whole.

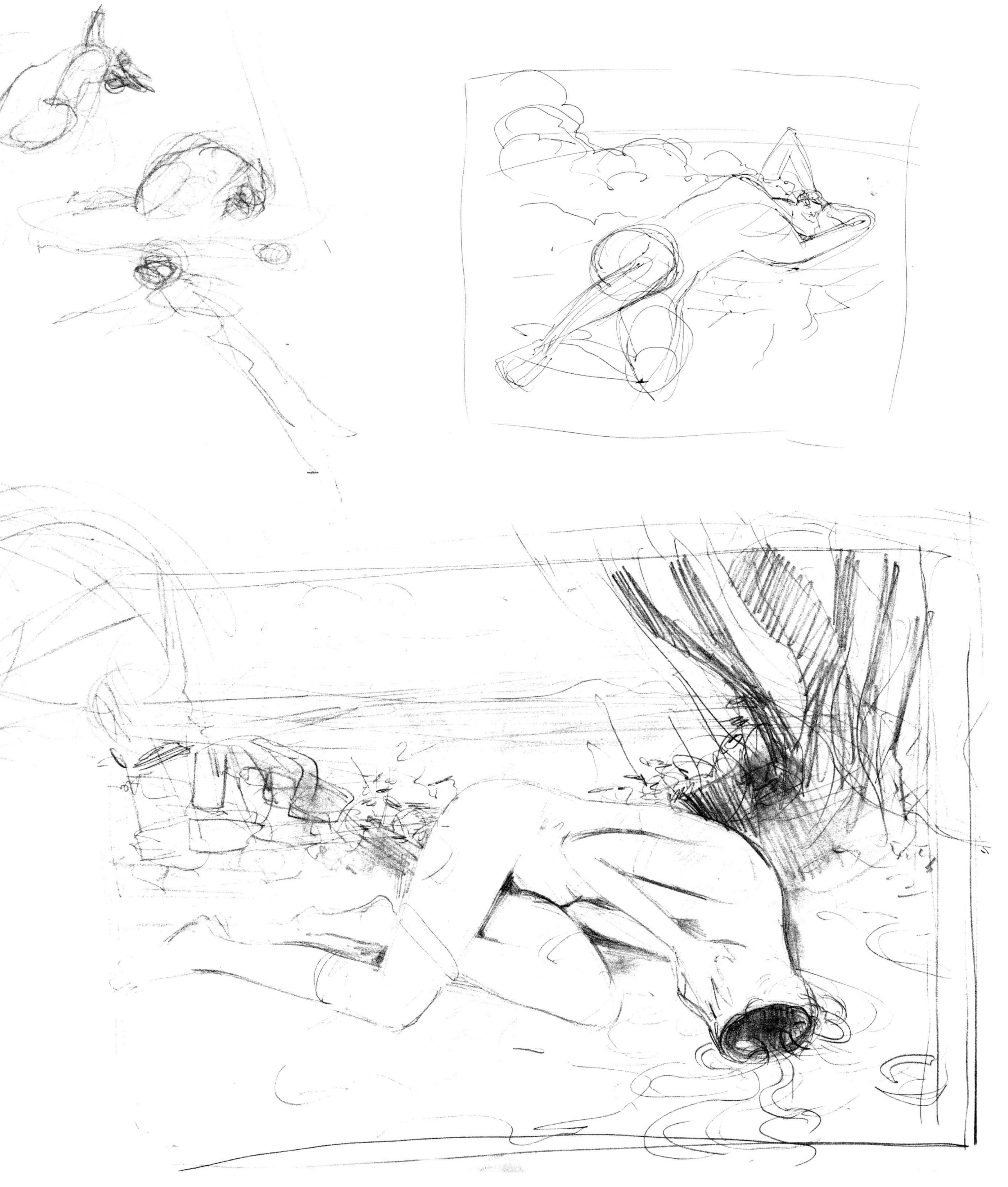

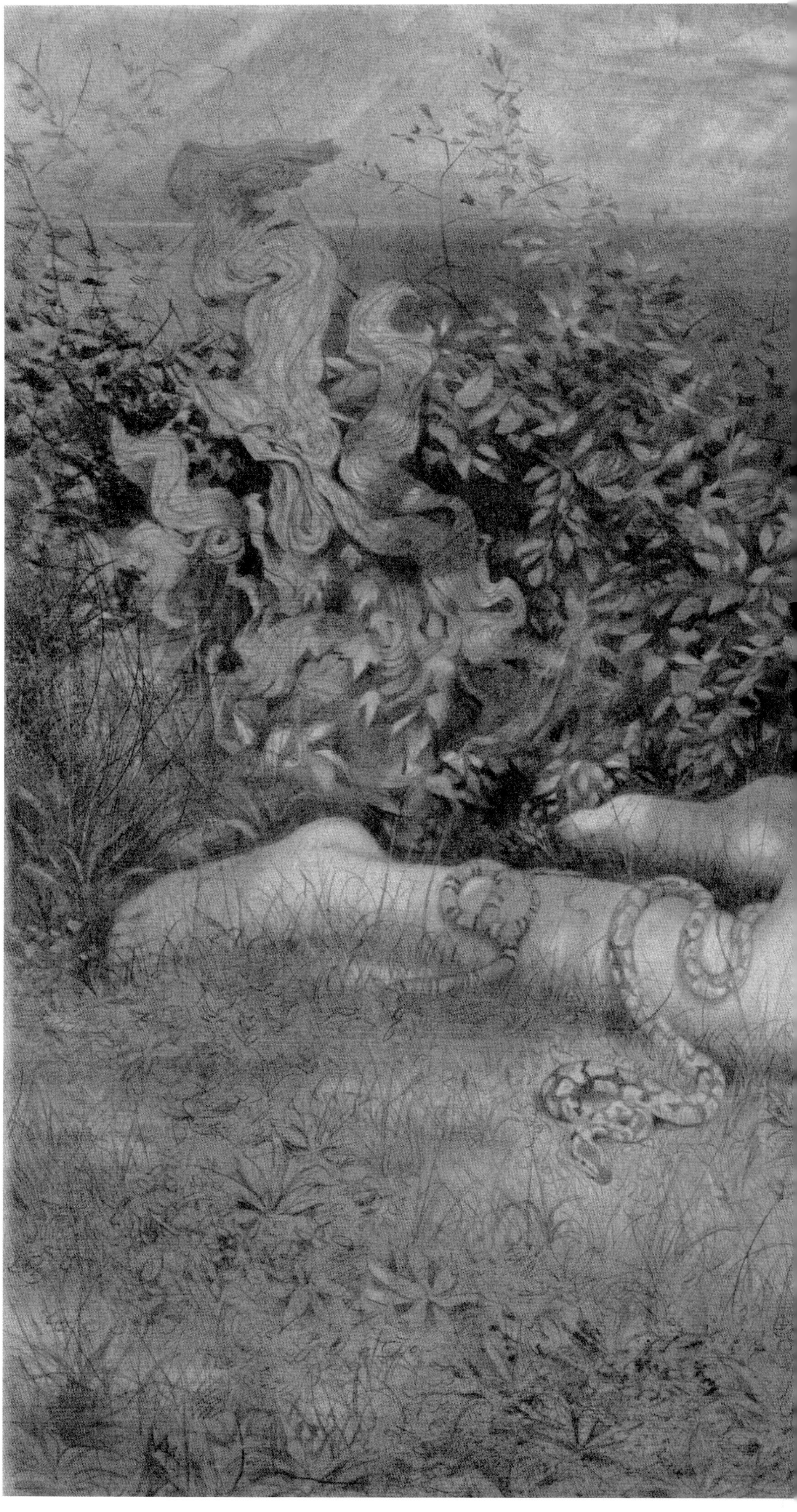

Guilt
2017

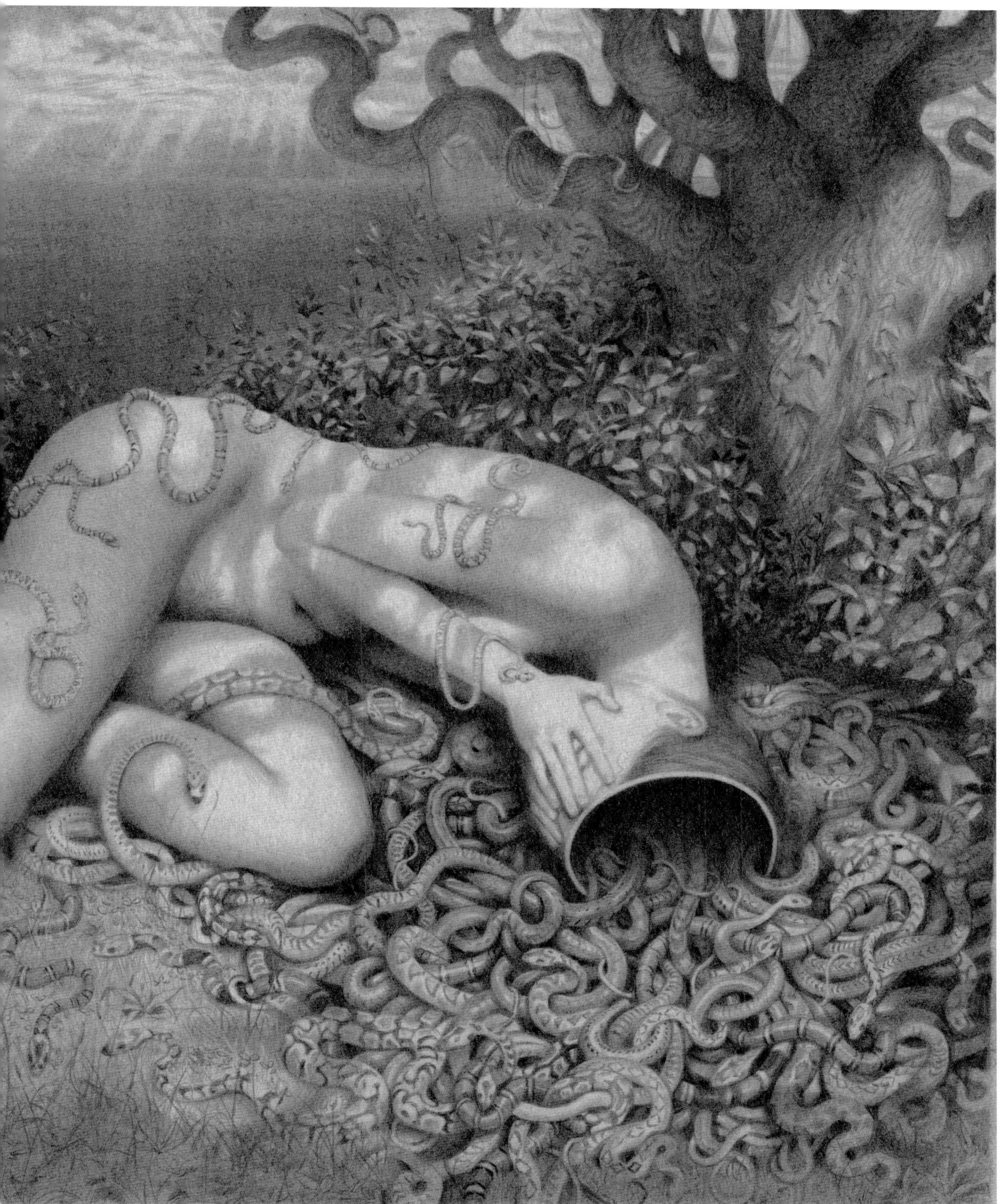

With language, we divide the world into opposites. Light and dark, hot and cold, good and evil. My goal with this painting was to depict the role of this division in our own suffering as human beings. From a broader perspective these opposites can collapse: if there can be no inside without an outside, no life without death, in what meaningful sense do these words actually represent separate things? The painting depicts this linguistic bifurcation of reality as a literal splitting of the whole world, with the human being in the middle both struggling against and being torn apart by their own nature.

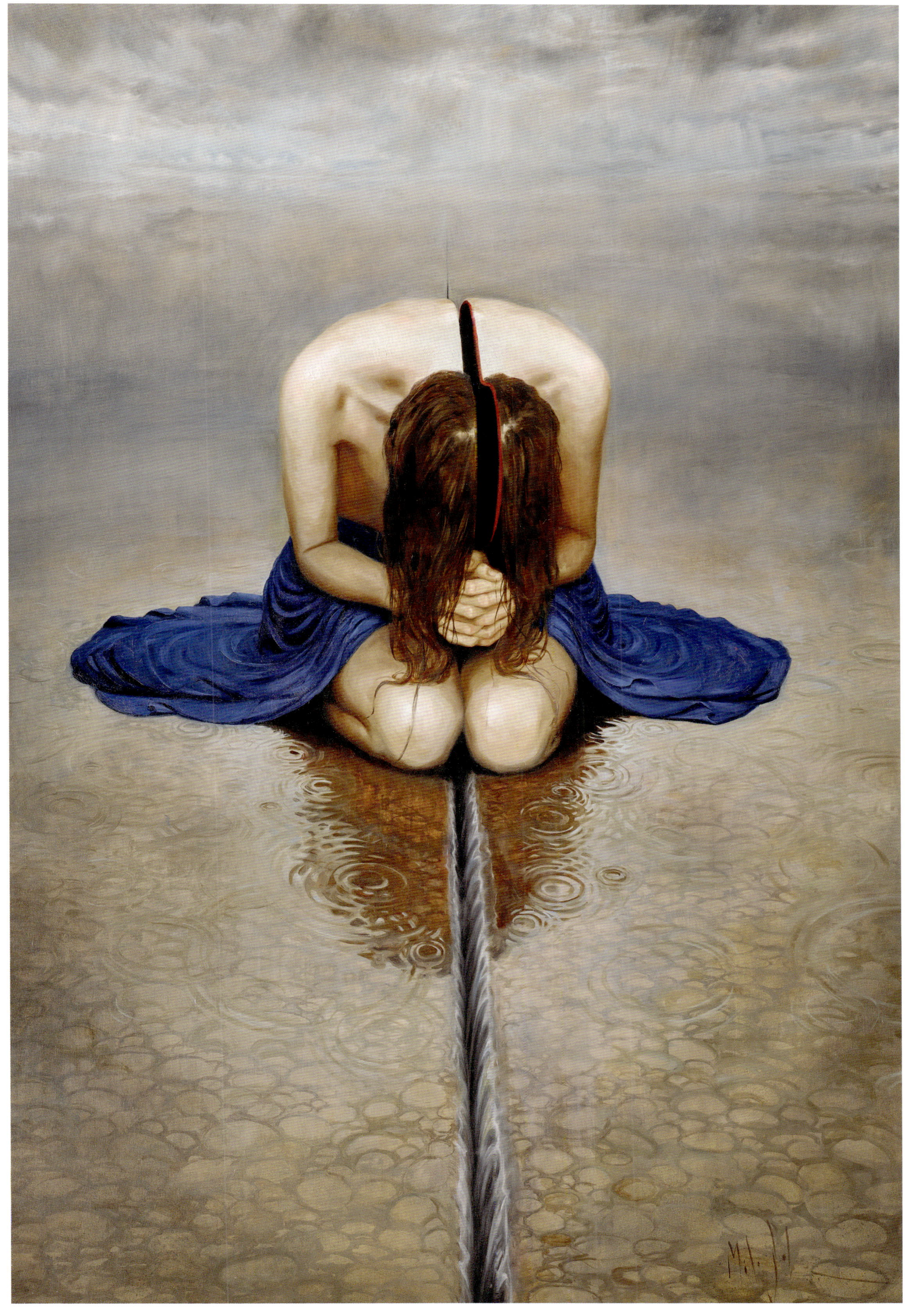

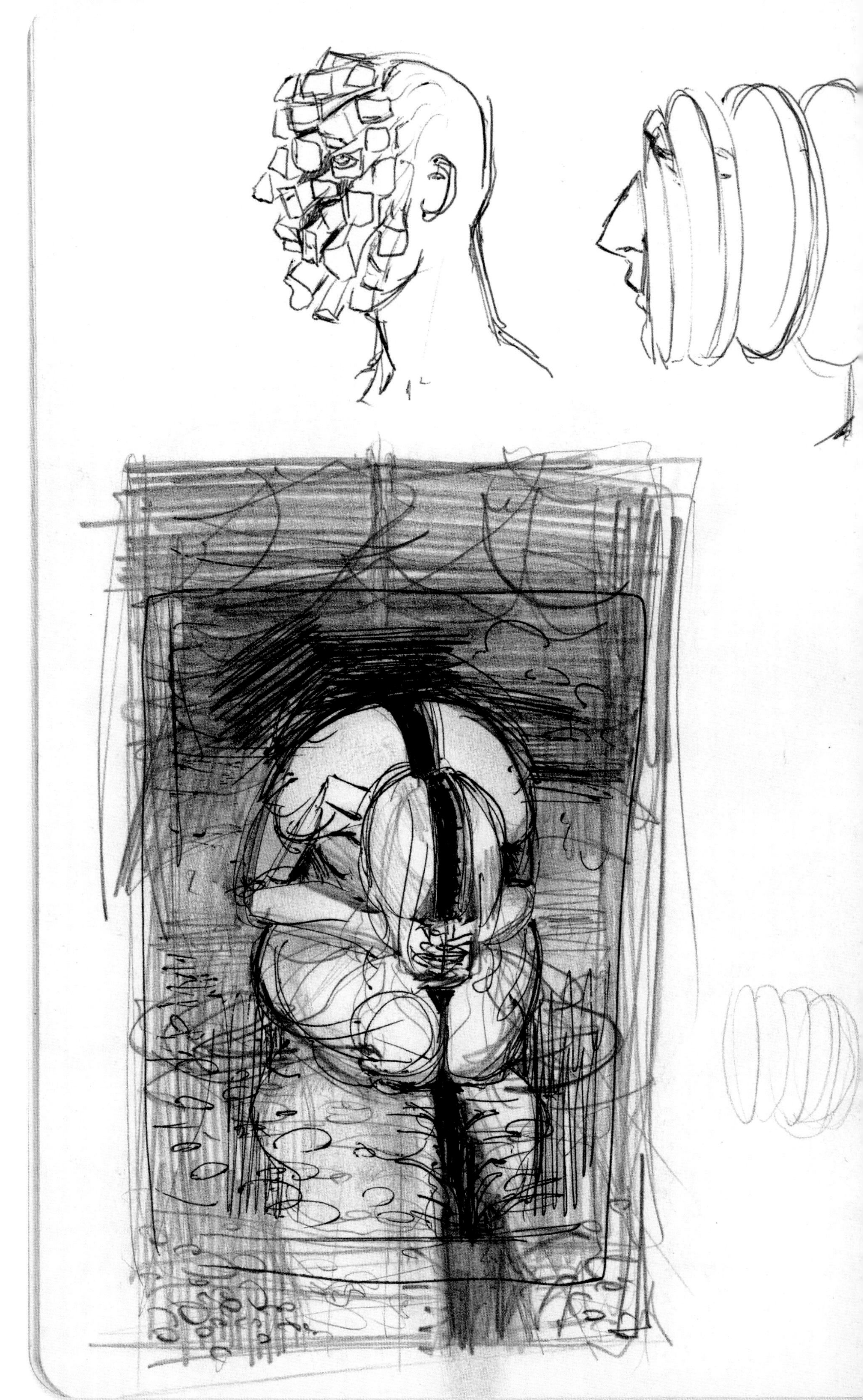

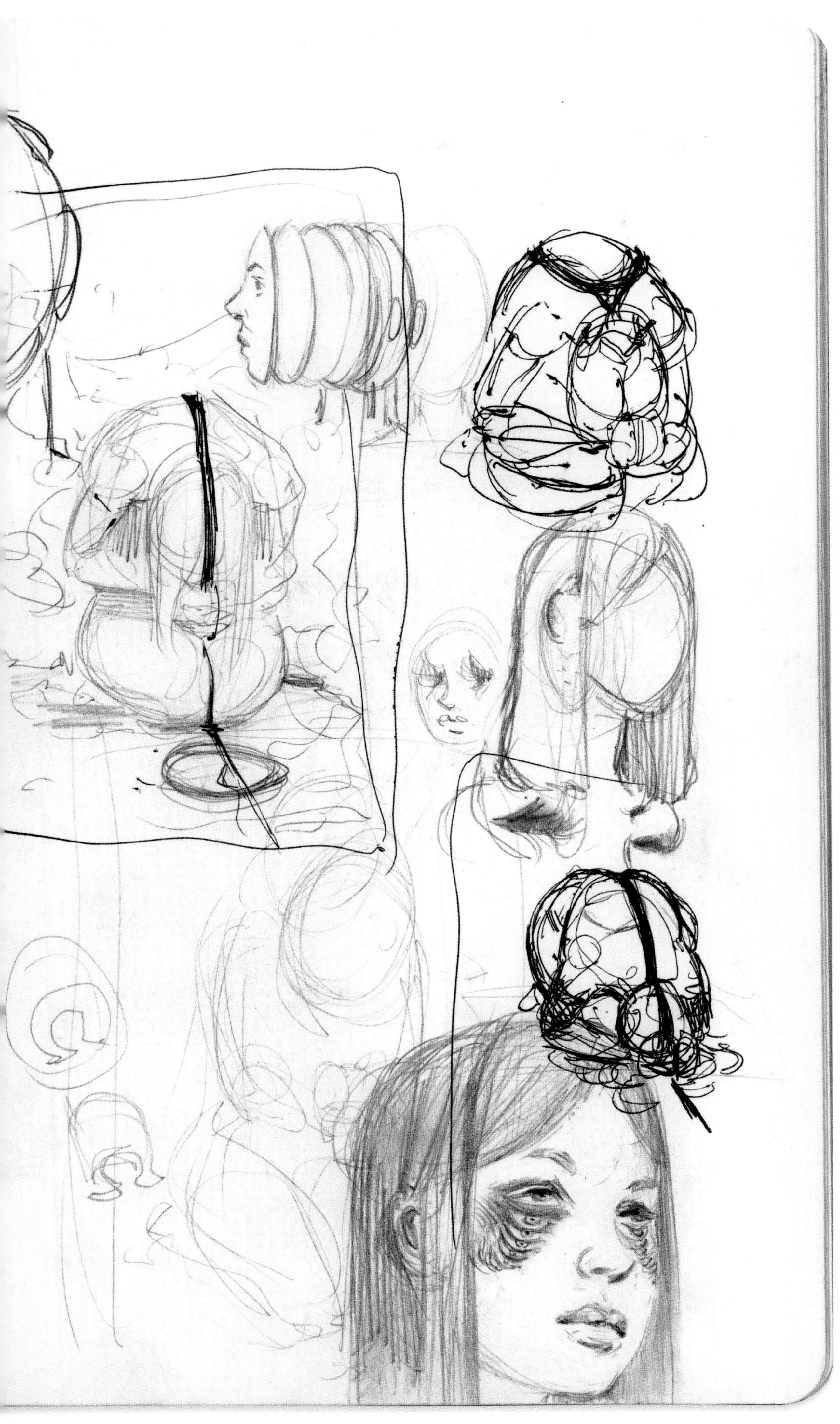

Studies for Dualism
2018

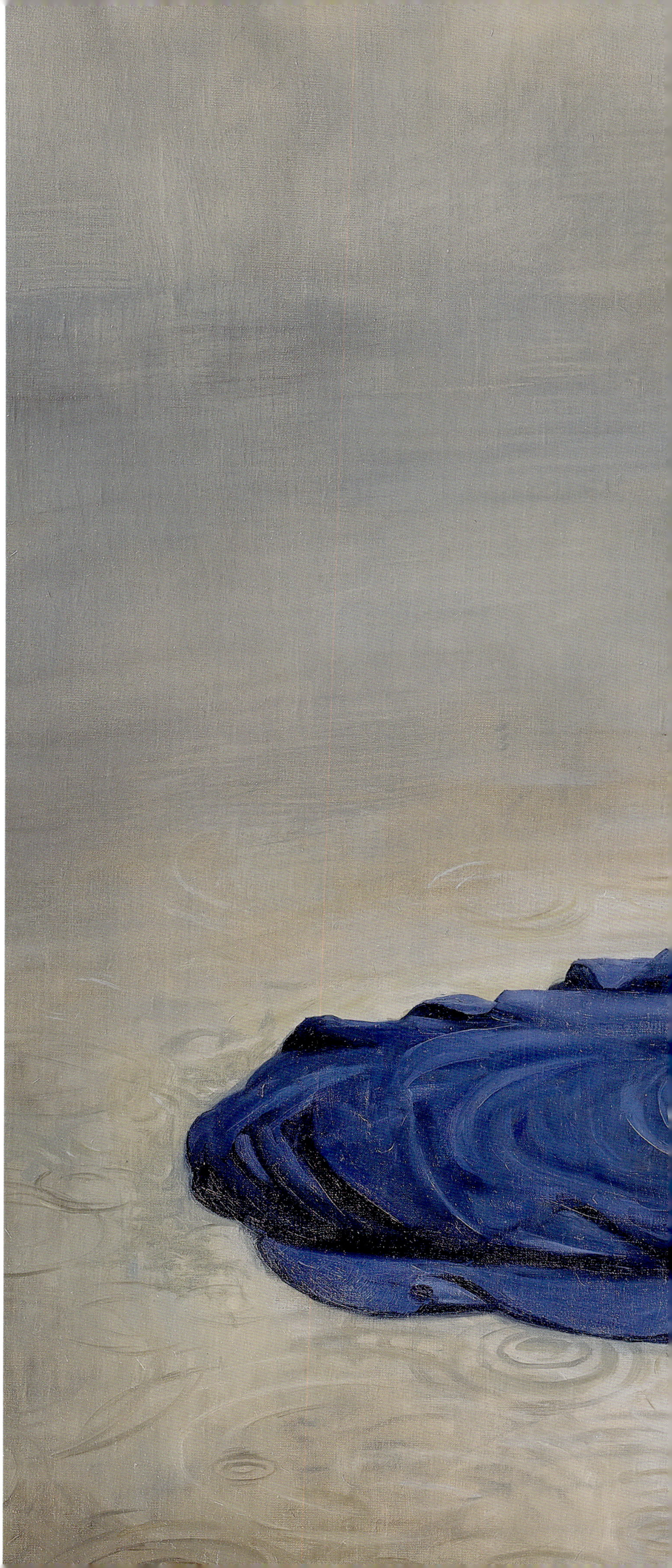

Dualism (detail)
2018

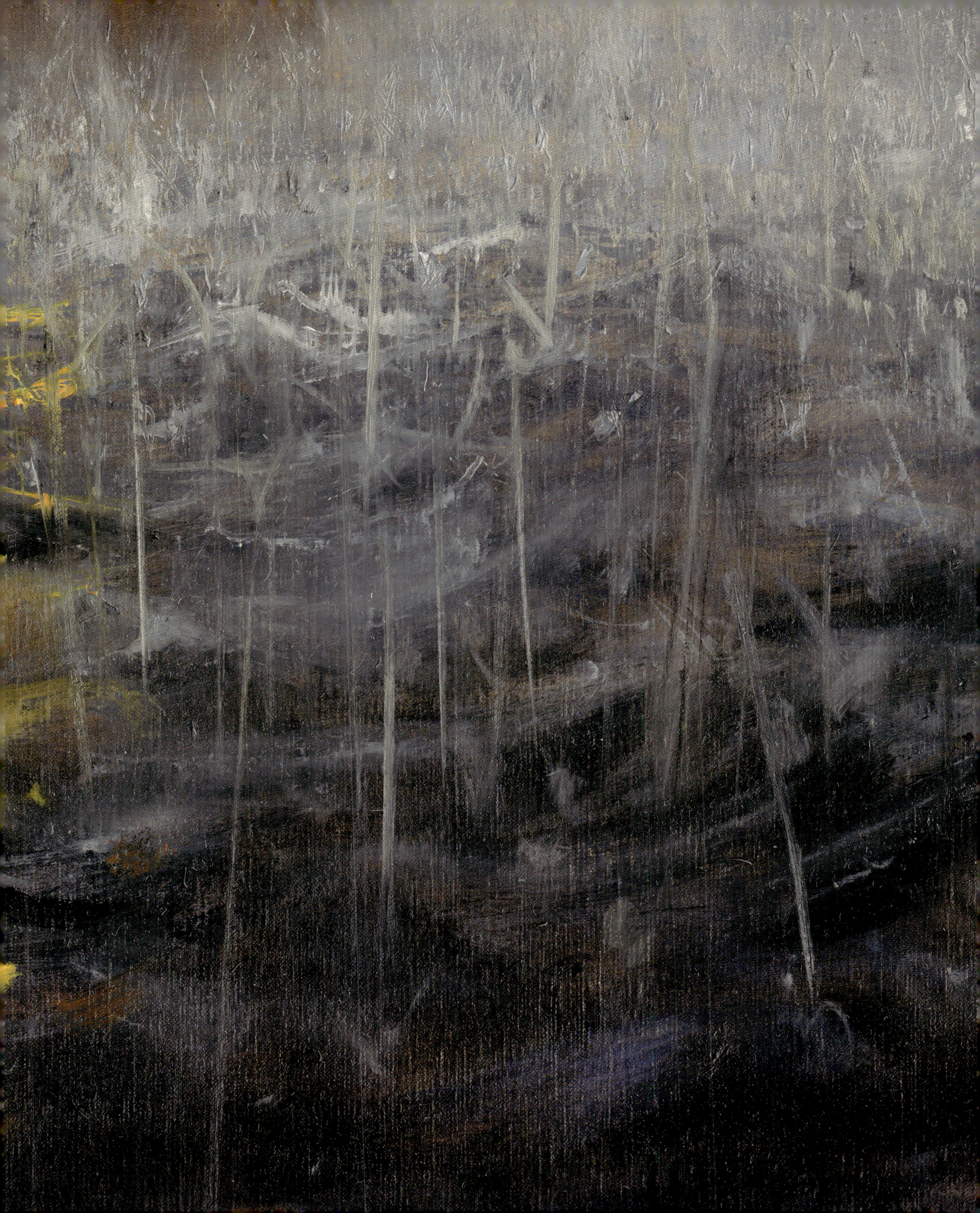

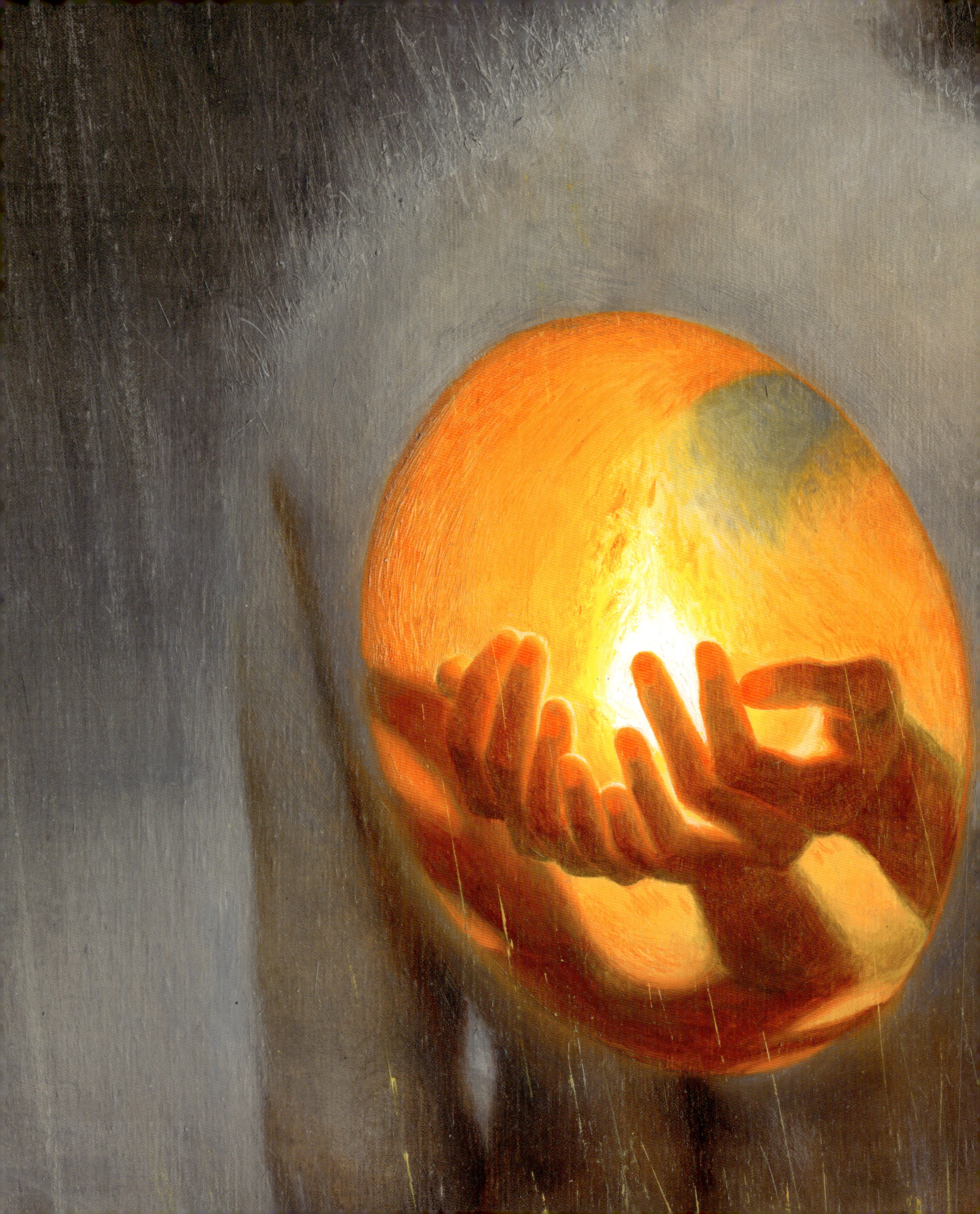

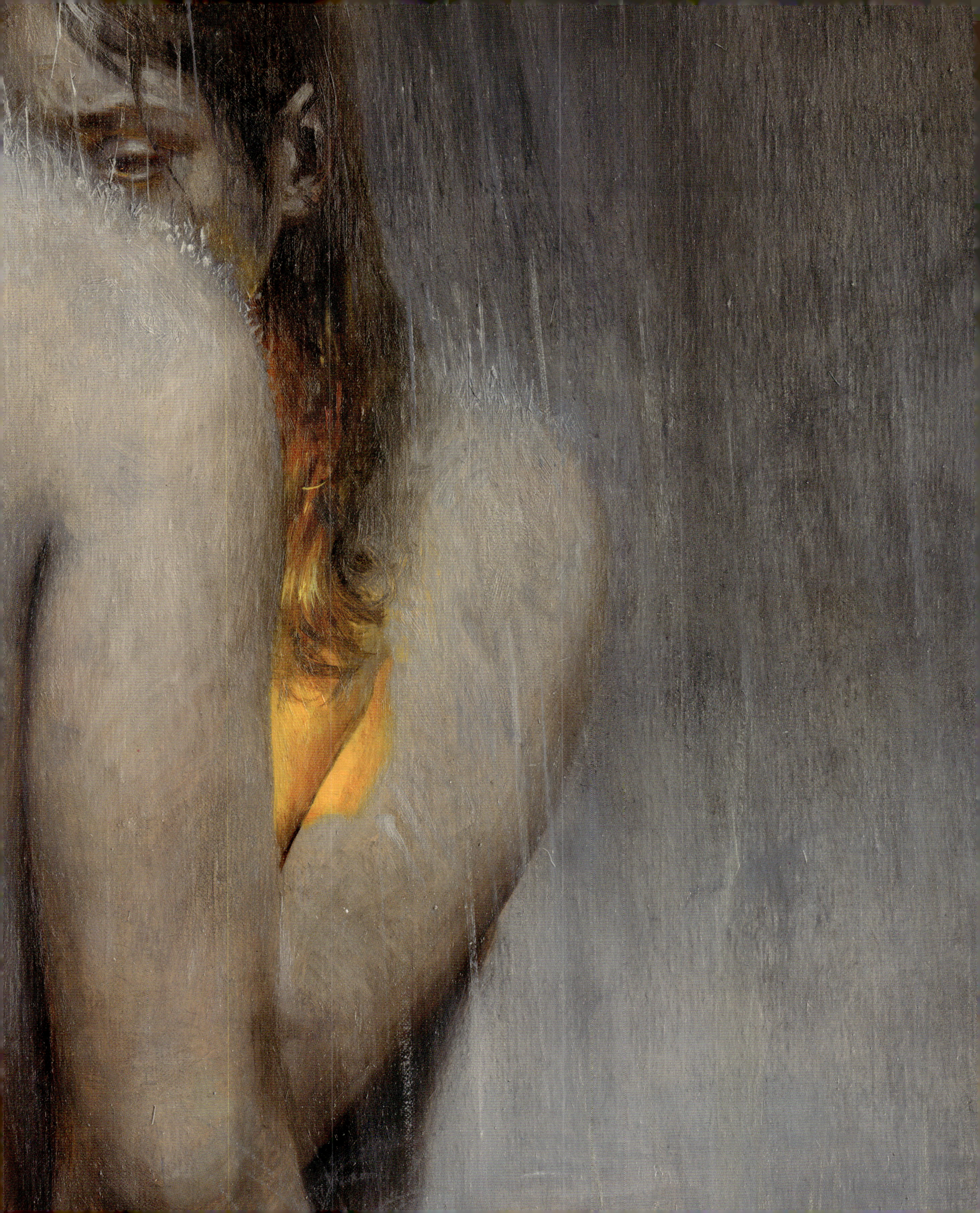

Nurture
2024

I want you to feel the fragility of that small flame, the tender way it is enveloped by her hands and the warmth it brings contrasted against the violent and relentless rain and cold churning waves. The harshness of the world can throw into stark relief the sacred beauty of the small moments of comfort we can give one another. I find great comfort in our capacity to give love and this painting is an expression of the gratitude I feel for those who have done me that kindness.

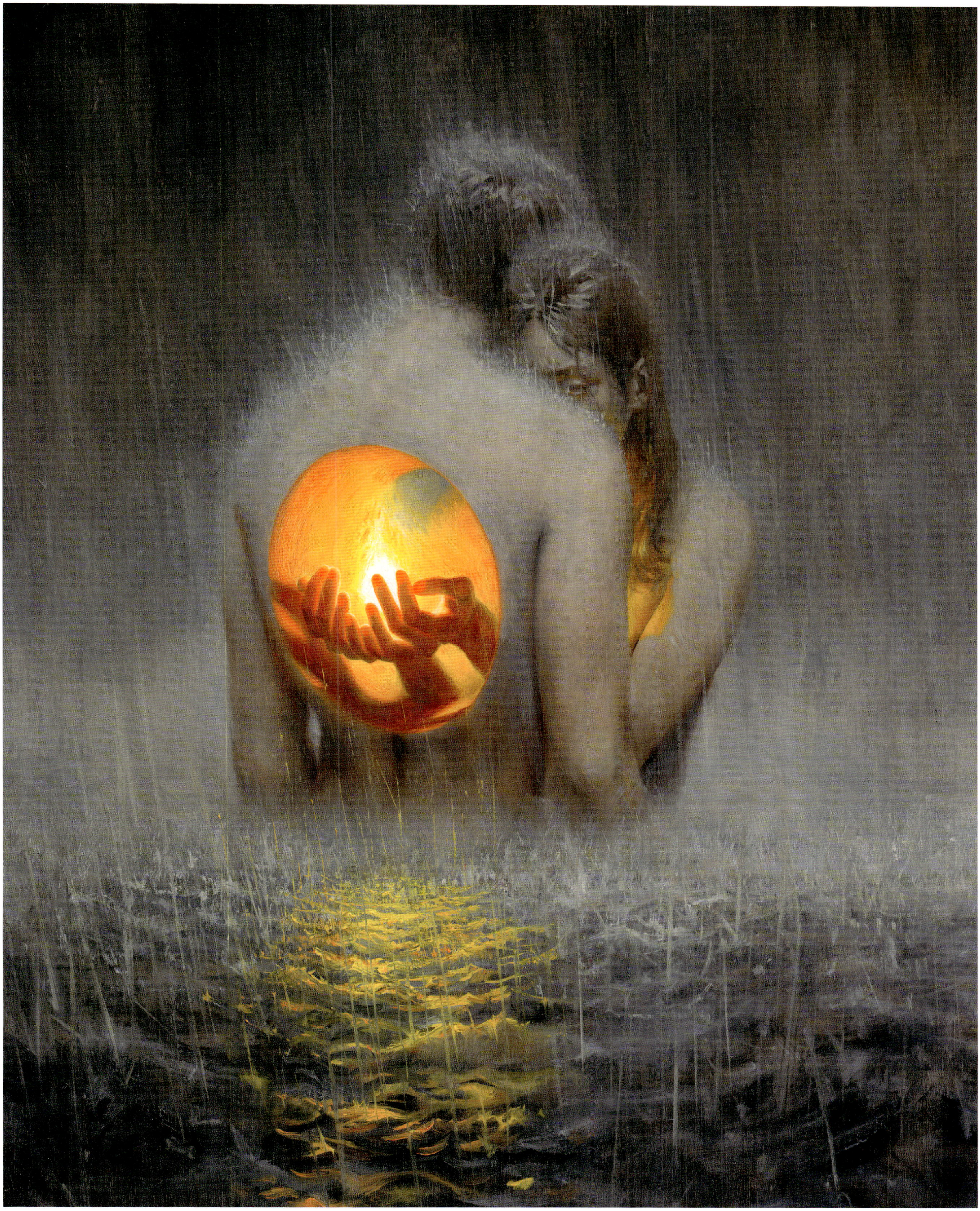

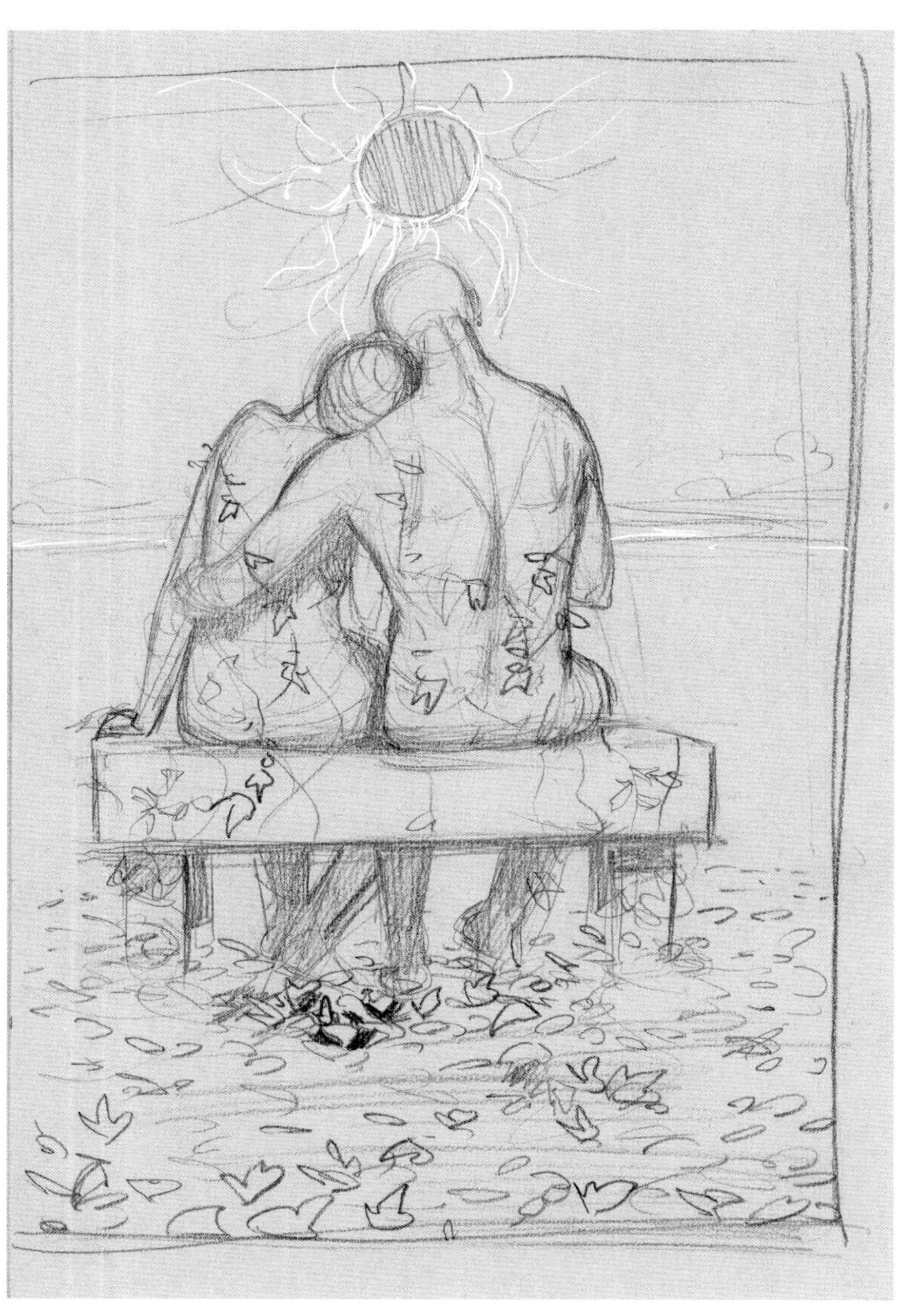

Until The End + Study
2021

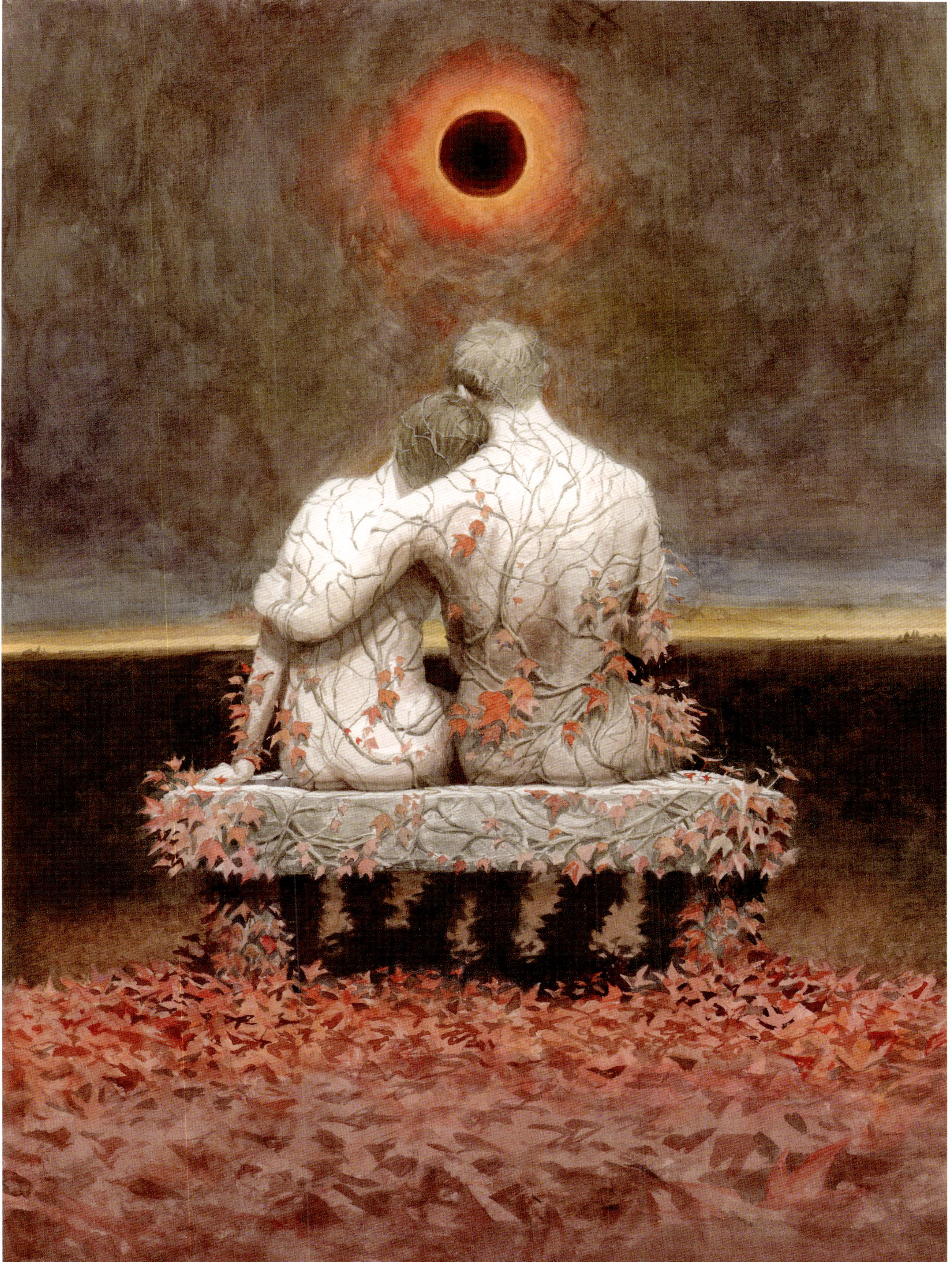

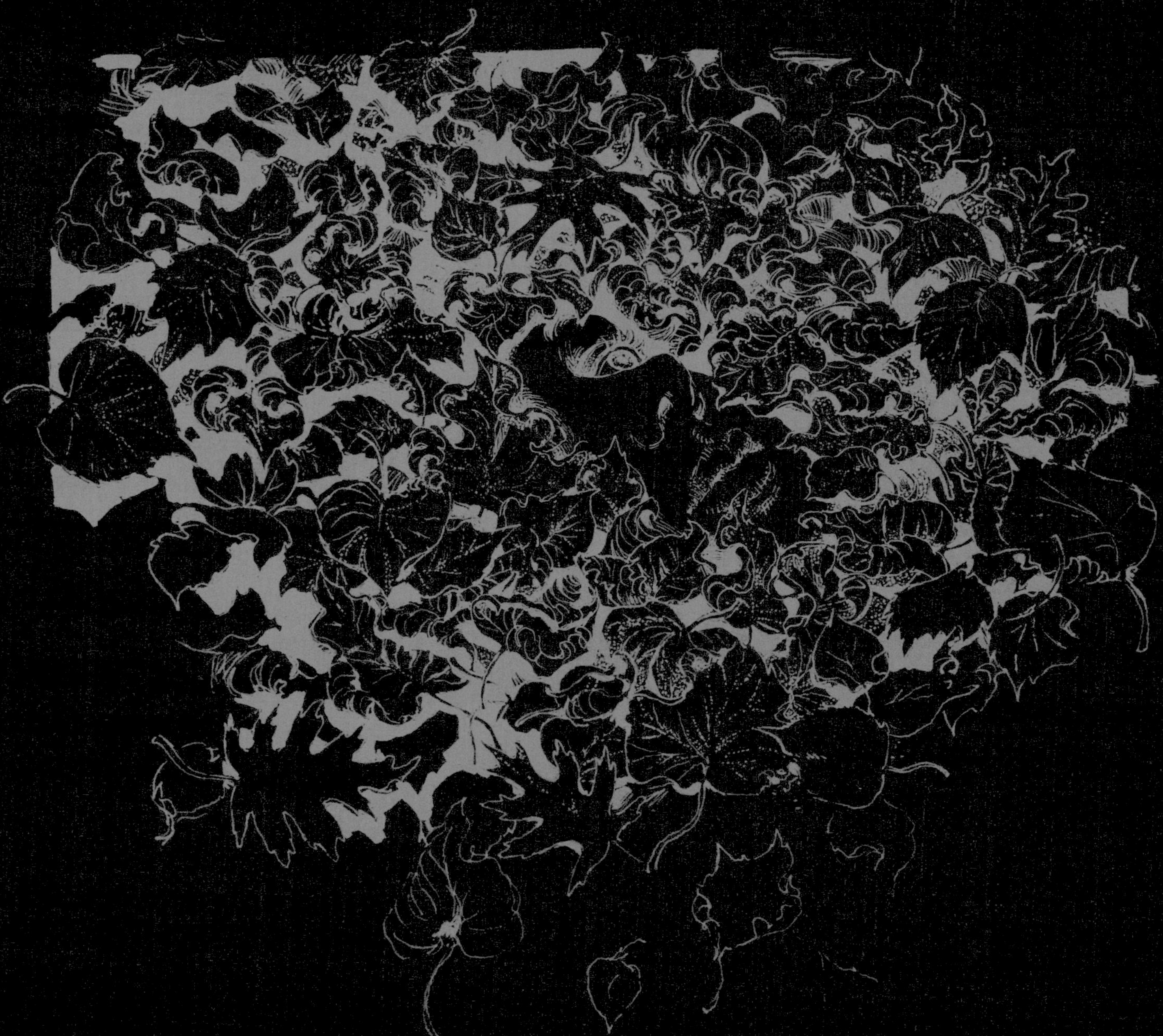

Autumn Mood

2018

IV

Surrender

"These drawings will be erased from the world, but that does not drain them of their meaning."

Impermanence & Renewal

What does it mean to really grasp the finality of impermanence? Everything we touch, all our efforts as individuals and as a collective, everyone that we know and love will all be lost. The constant churning renewal of the present moment is awe inspiring in the classical sense of the word, incredible and terrifying.

Art is my way to try and confront my fears head on. These drawings will be erased from the world, but that does not drain them of their meaning. They occupied a crucial space in my life, the making of them provided me with a journey to undertake. They were there for those that saw them and found some small moment of comfort of recognition in their own experiences. They were a form of conversation I had with other people who lived and died on this earth.

Art is a reaction to the circumstances in which we live. To me it is a necessity, one of the few truly sane activities that human beings can participate in. It will never provide any kind of final answer, there is no painting, song, book, film or any other form of creative expression that will finally reveal the big secret. I believe that the value lies in the simple bonds of existential solidarity. There have been times in my life where I have felt so overwhelmed by the sheer maddening nature of reality. To hear a beautiful song, or to see a powerful painting, is a reminder of the inherent vitality and possibility afforded to us by being alive. The world must be good if it can contain this within it.

I am drawn to images of relief, giving in, dropping the struggle for a moment. What awaits us when we slow down and step away from the busyness of the world? Stillness, light and precious moments of peace, the merging of our bodies and minds with nature. The rush of cold water over your feet in a mountain stream, the wind on your face on a dark shoreline. Sunlight that traversed the cold depth of space and narrowly found its way through a forest canopy to warm your skin. The feeling of solace amidst the carnival of reality. These are the moments of stillness and connection where I feel most at home in the world. These experiences defy the need for explanation, for me they are inherently meaningful and upon reflection have always been the things that allow me to find the determination to begin again. My artwork is my avenue to reify these fleeting feelings into something concrete, they are a form of worship.

On Having No Head
2020

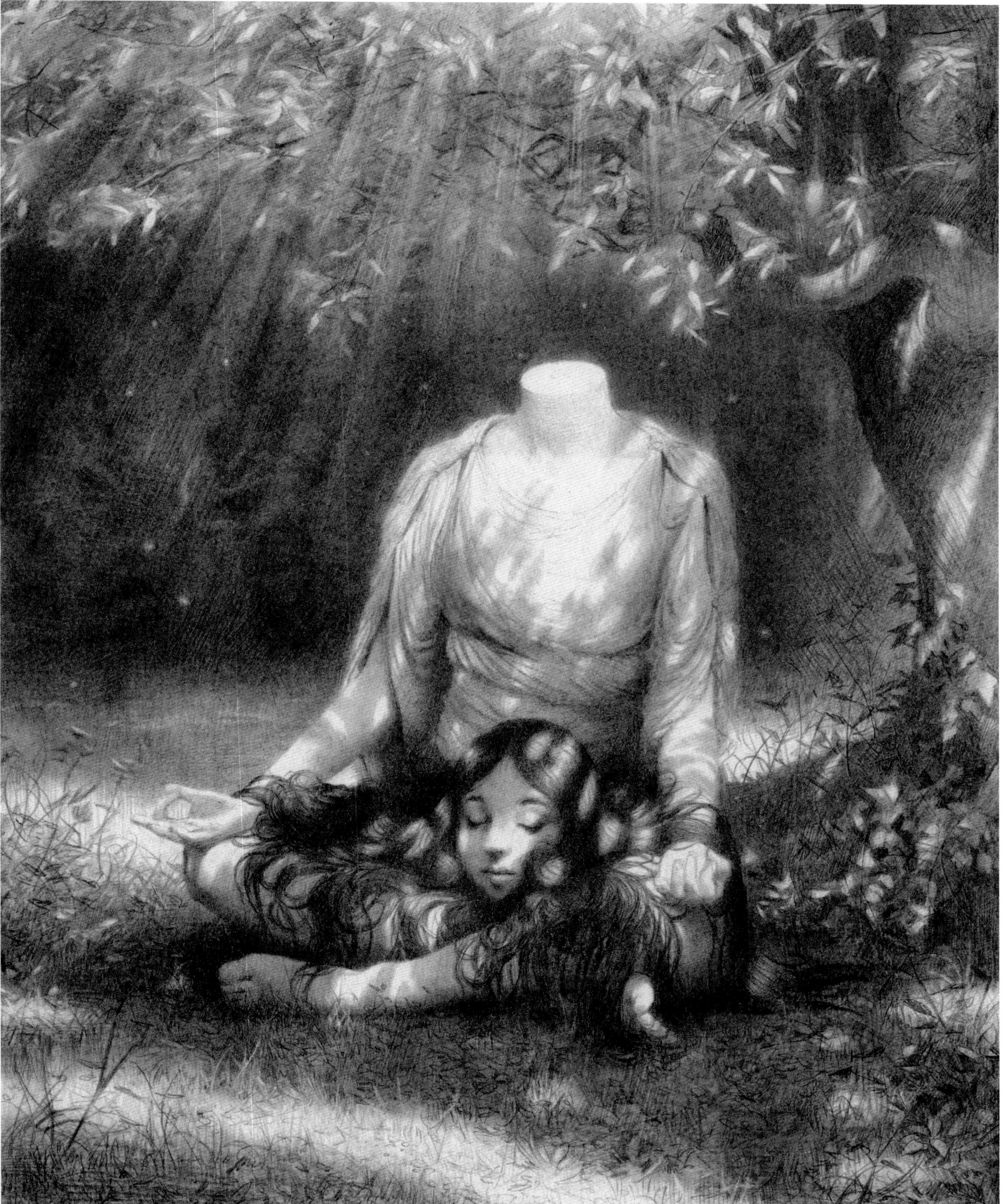

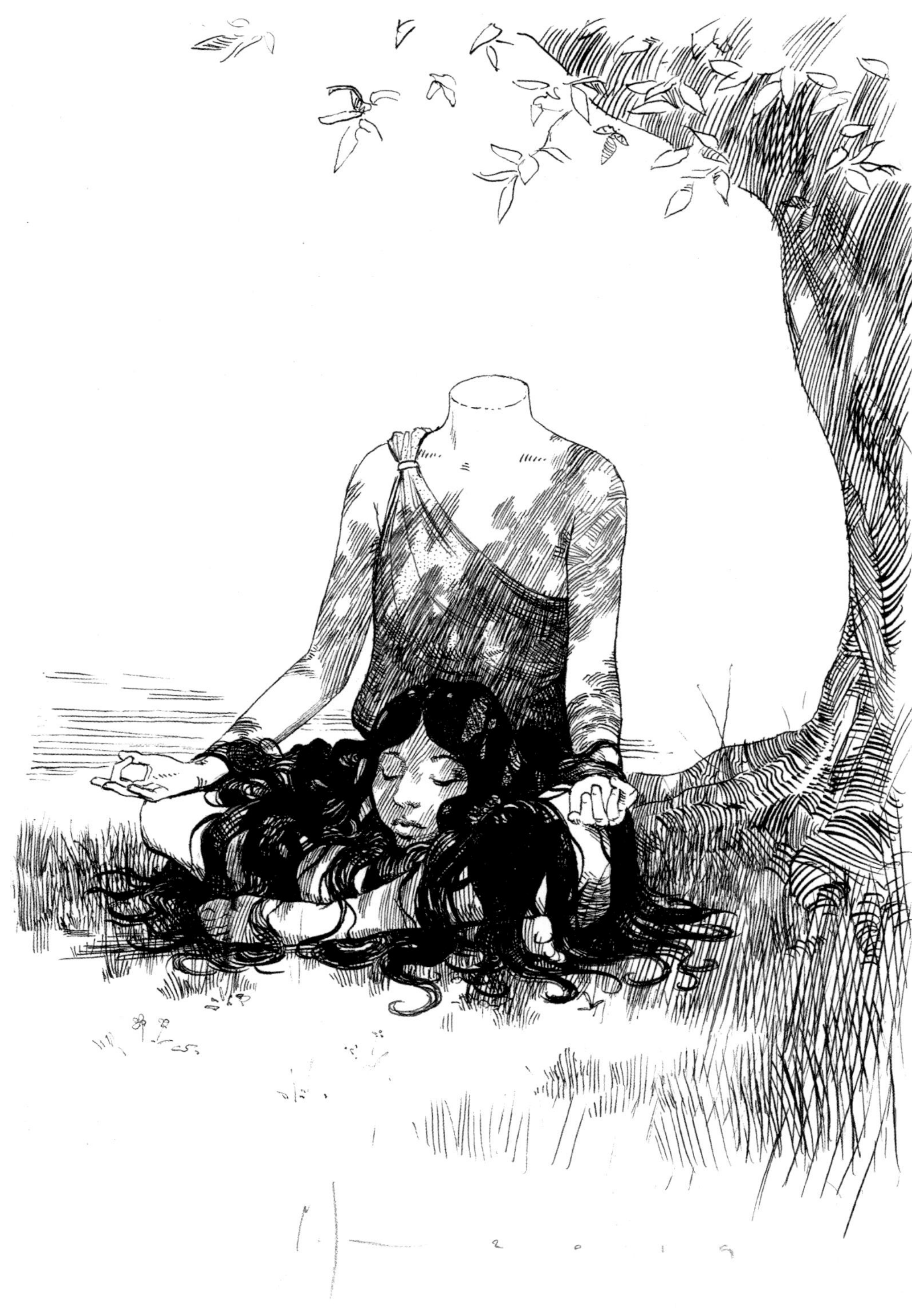

On Having No Head (Ink Study)

2020

Float

2019

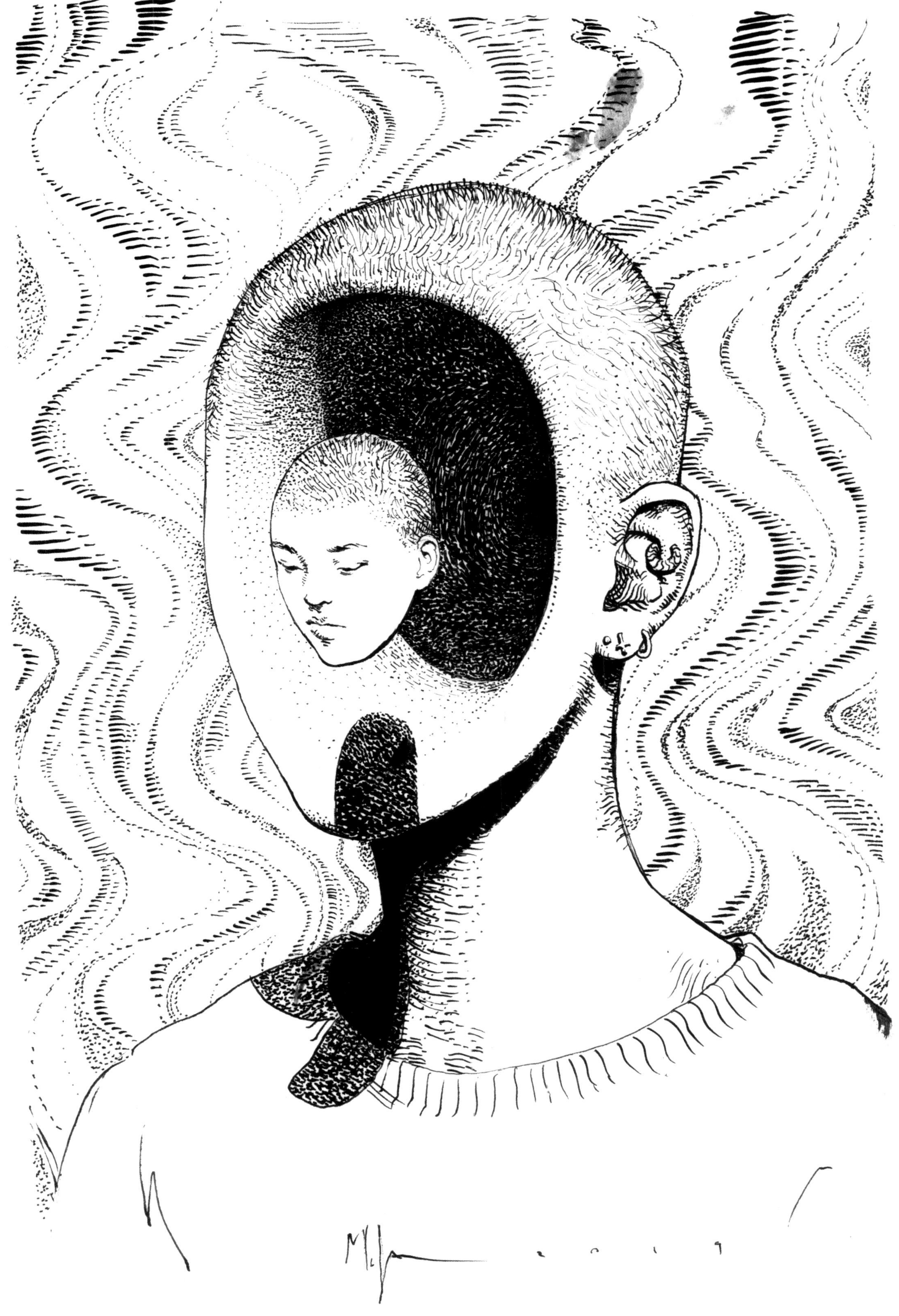

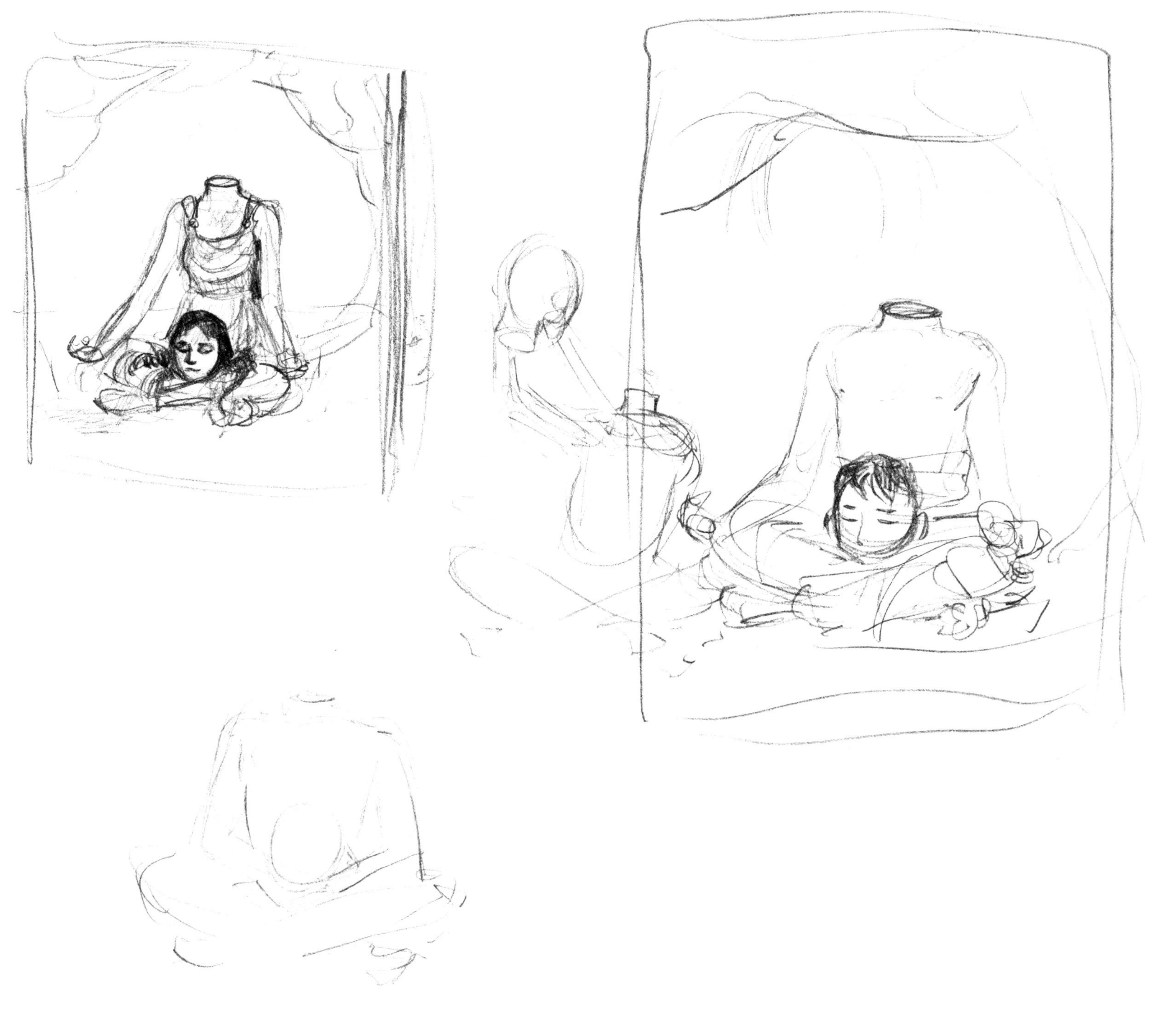

Studies for On Having No Head
2020

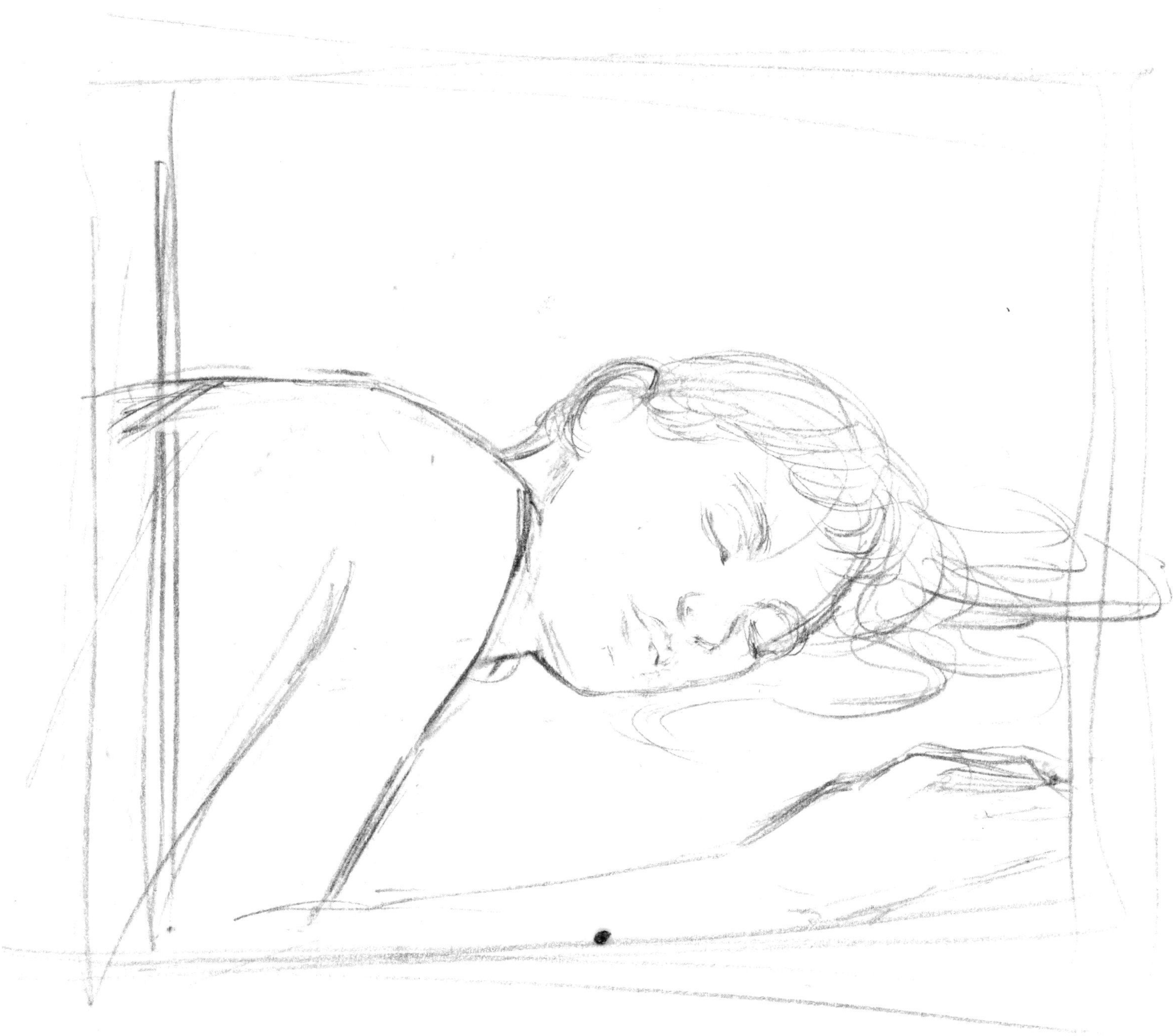

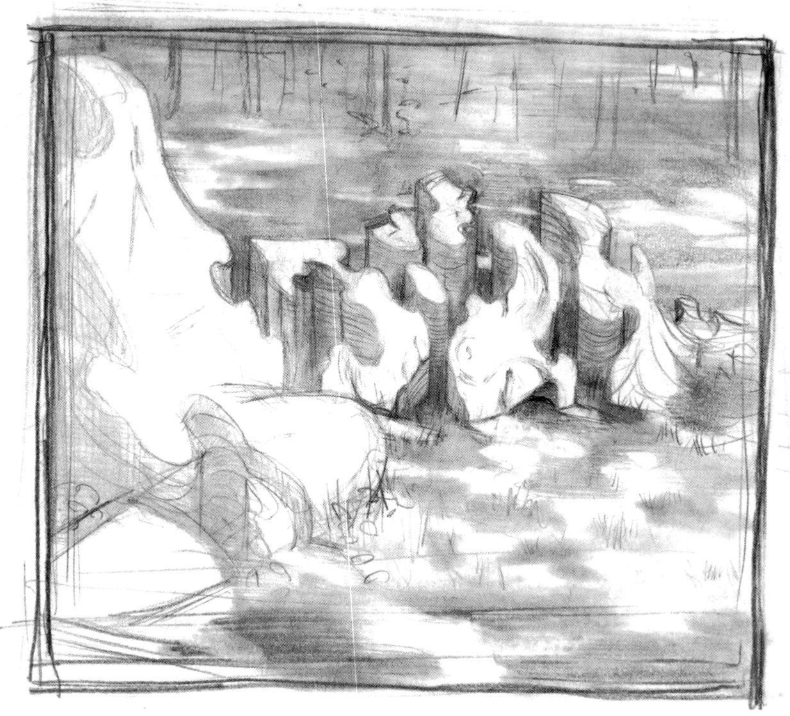

Studies for I Only Exist in The Light
2018

Dappled Light Study

2018

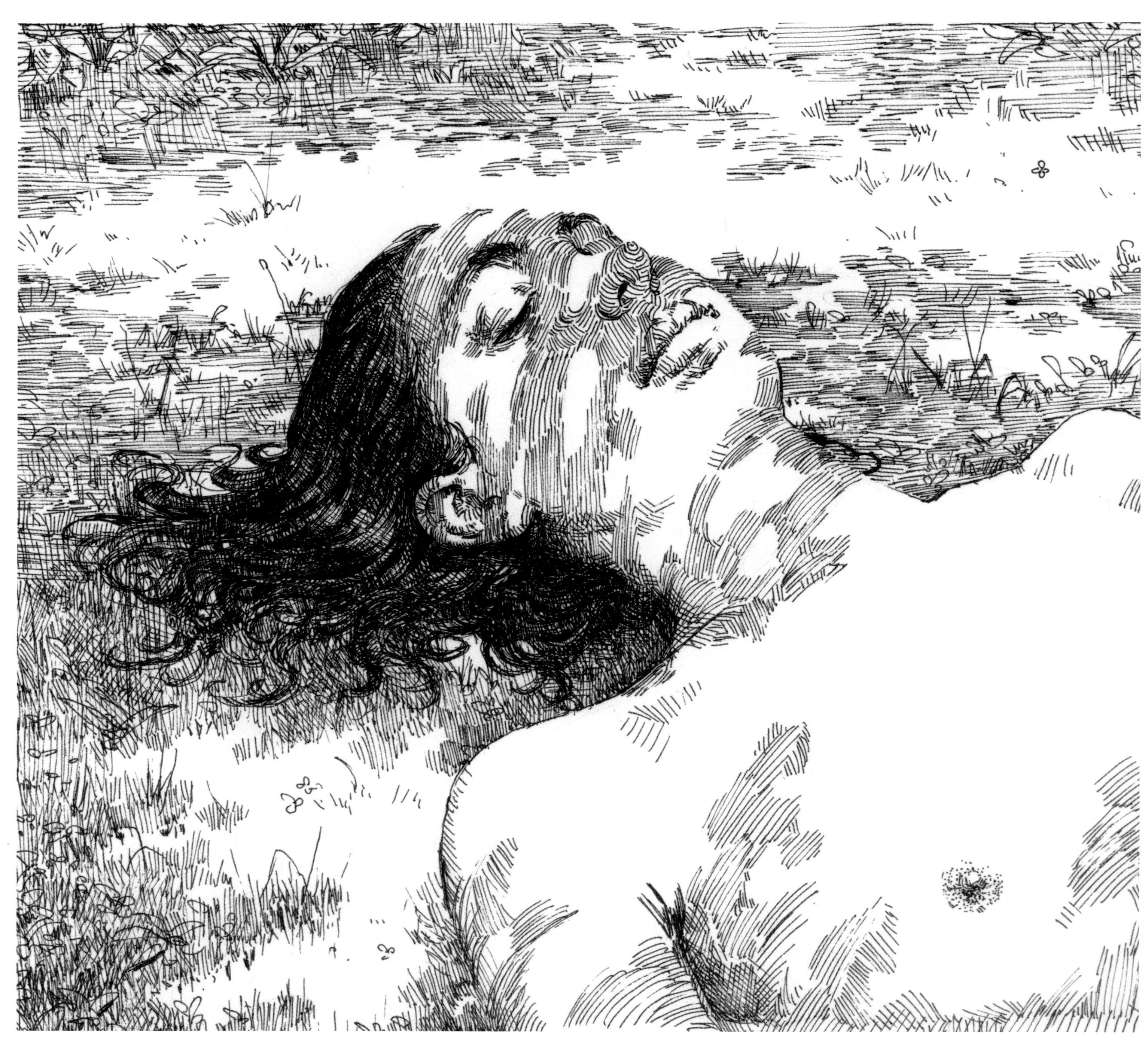

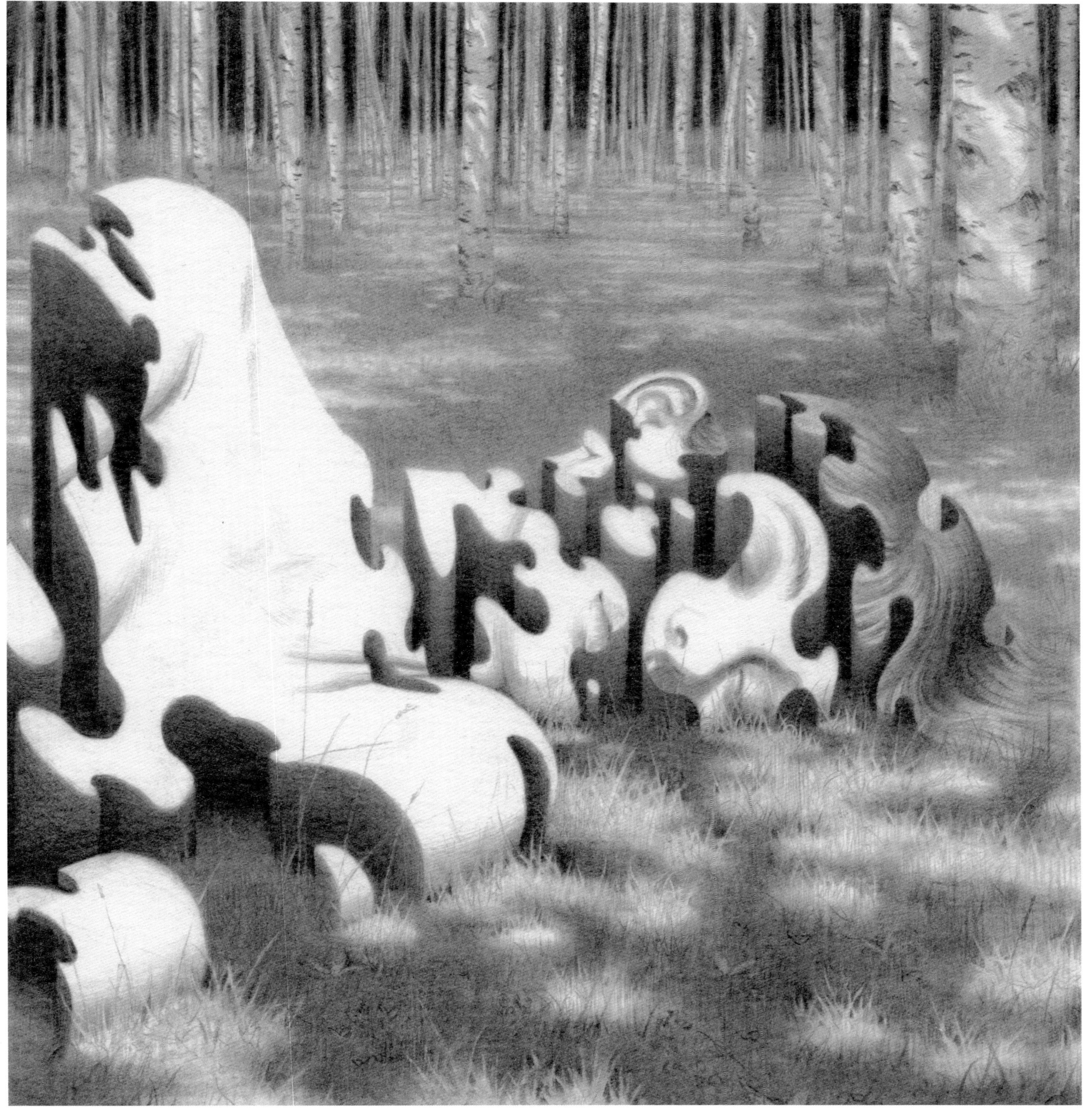

I Only Exist in The Light
2018

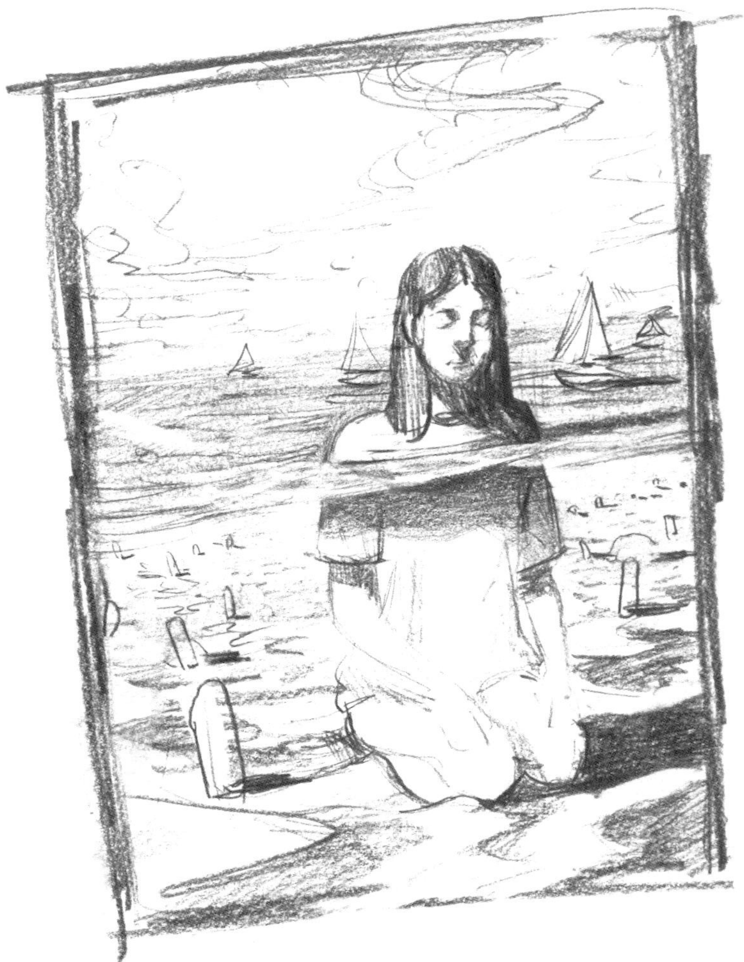

Shoreline + Study
2020

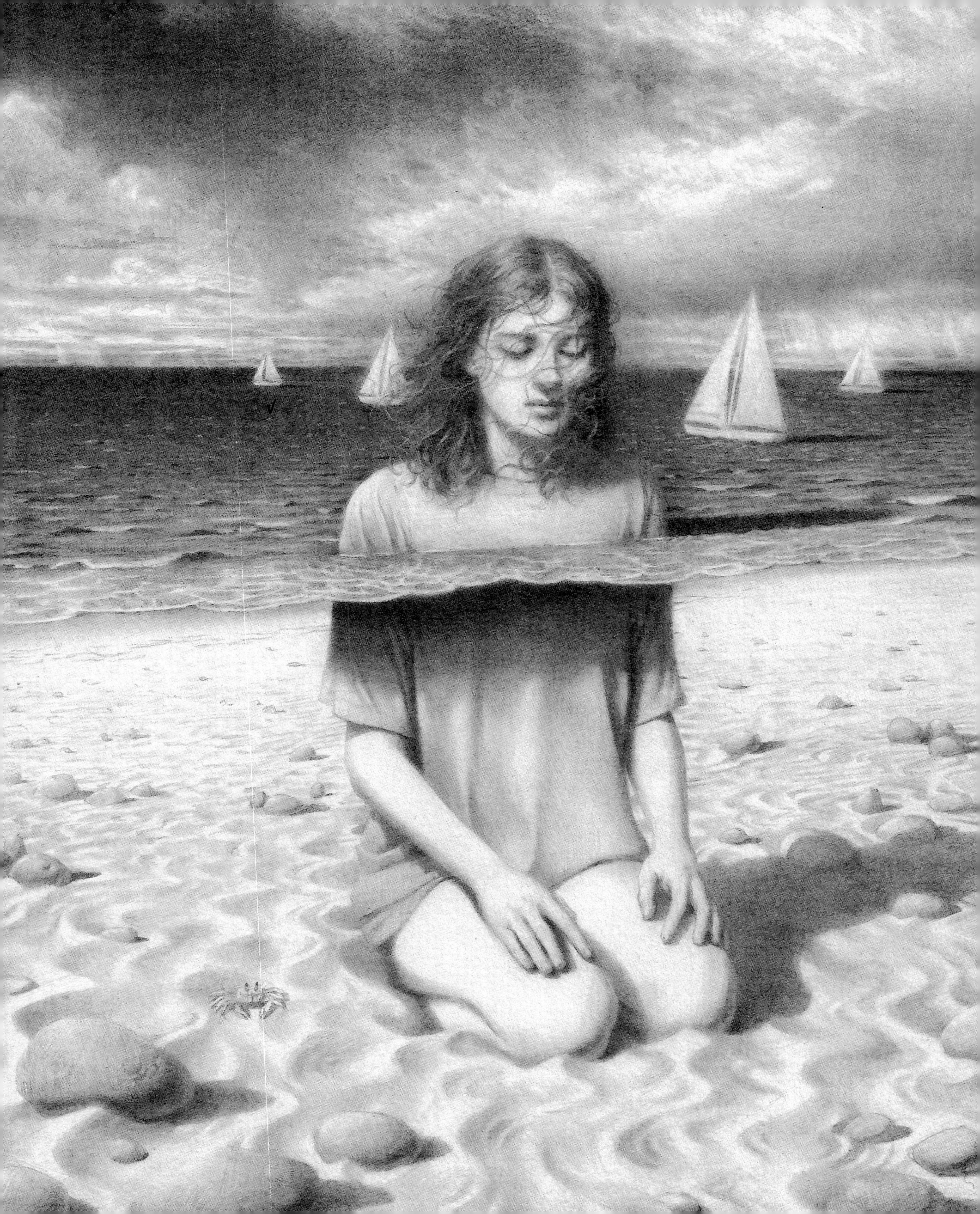

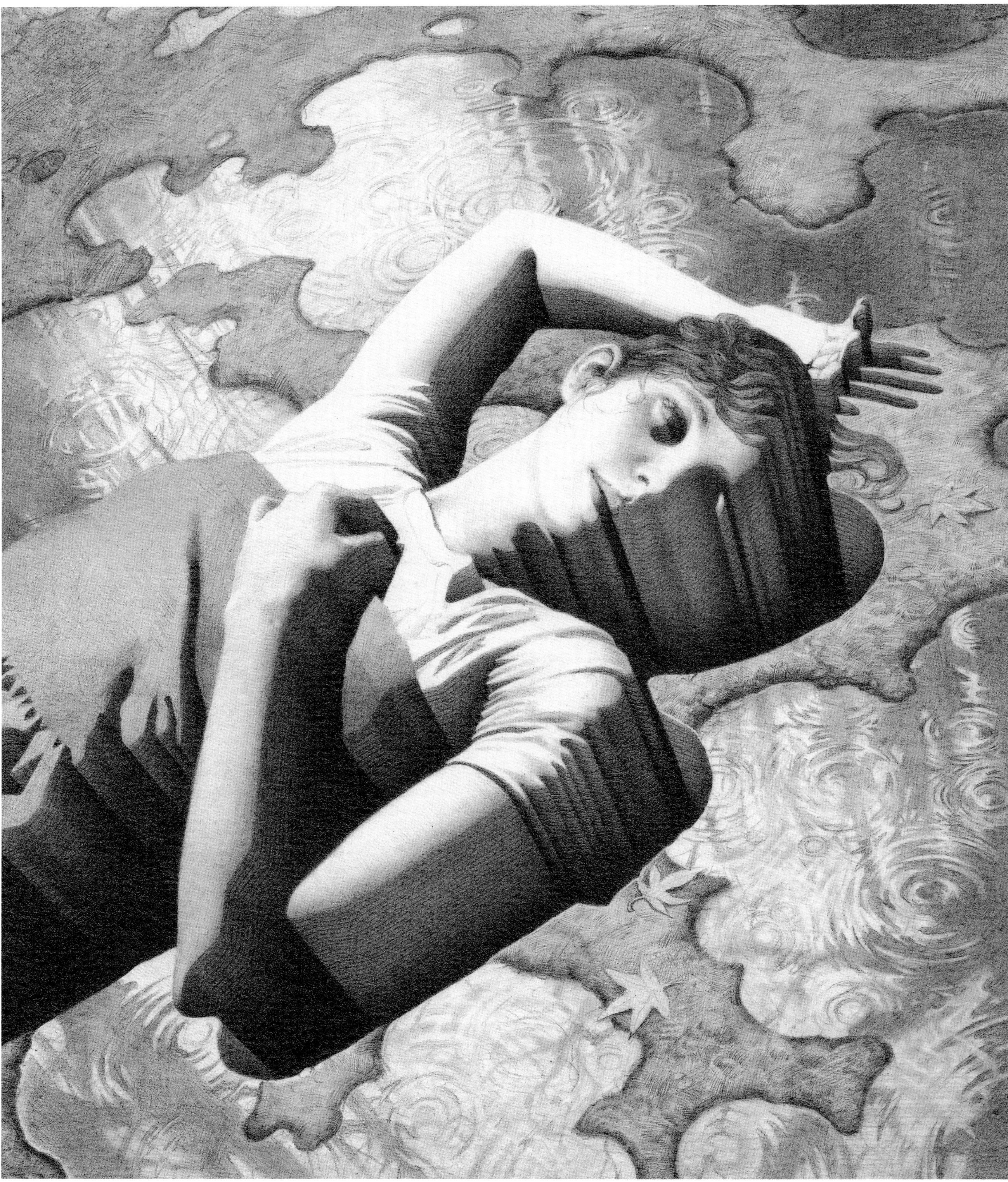

The Shadow
2018

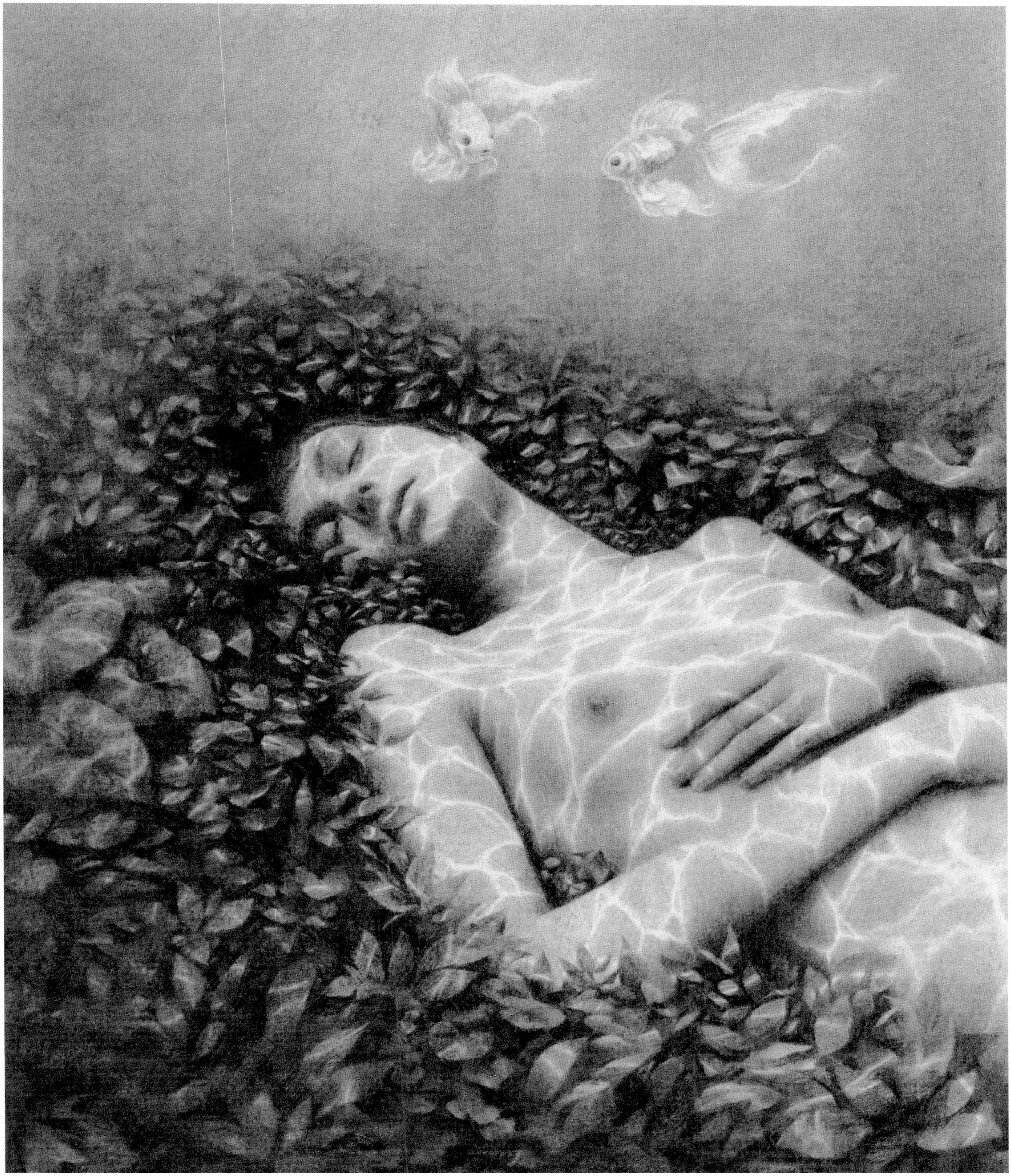

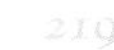

Peace is Possible

2018

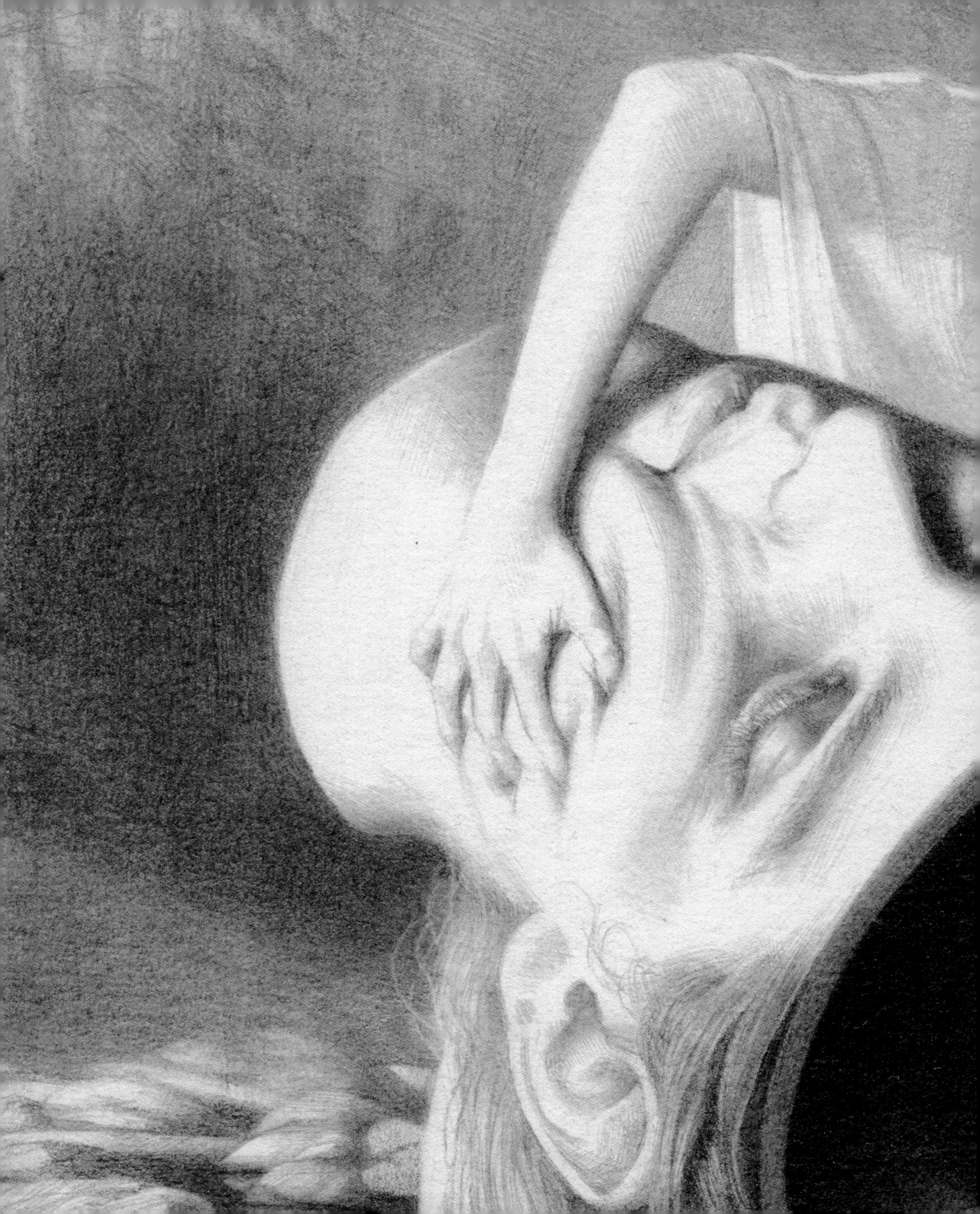

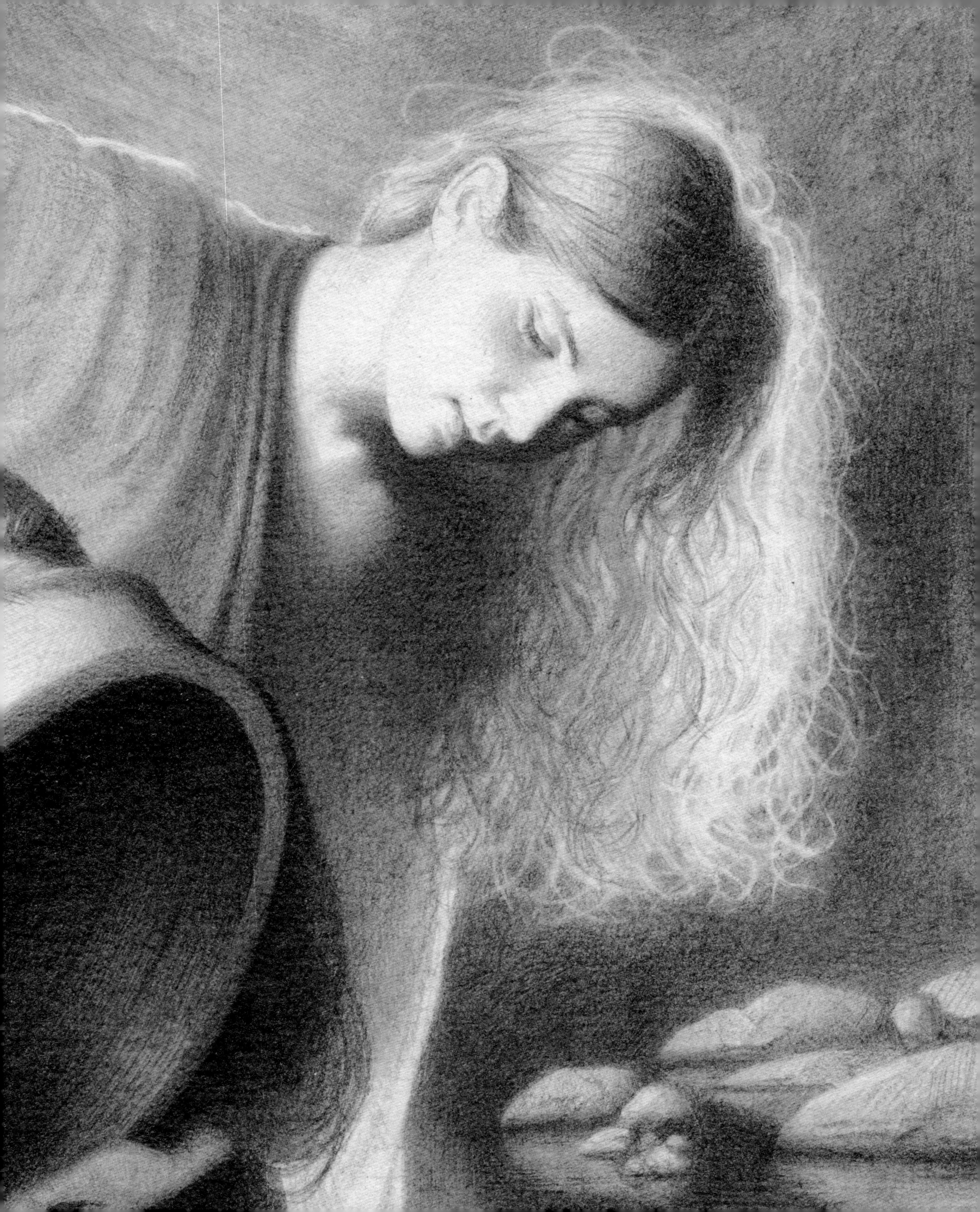

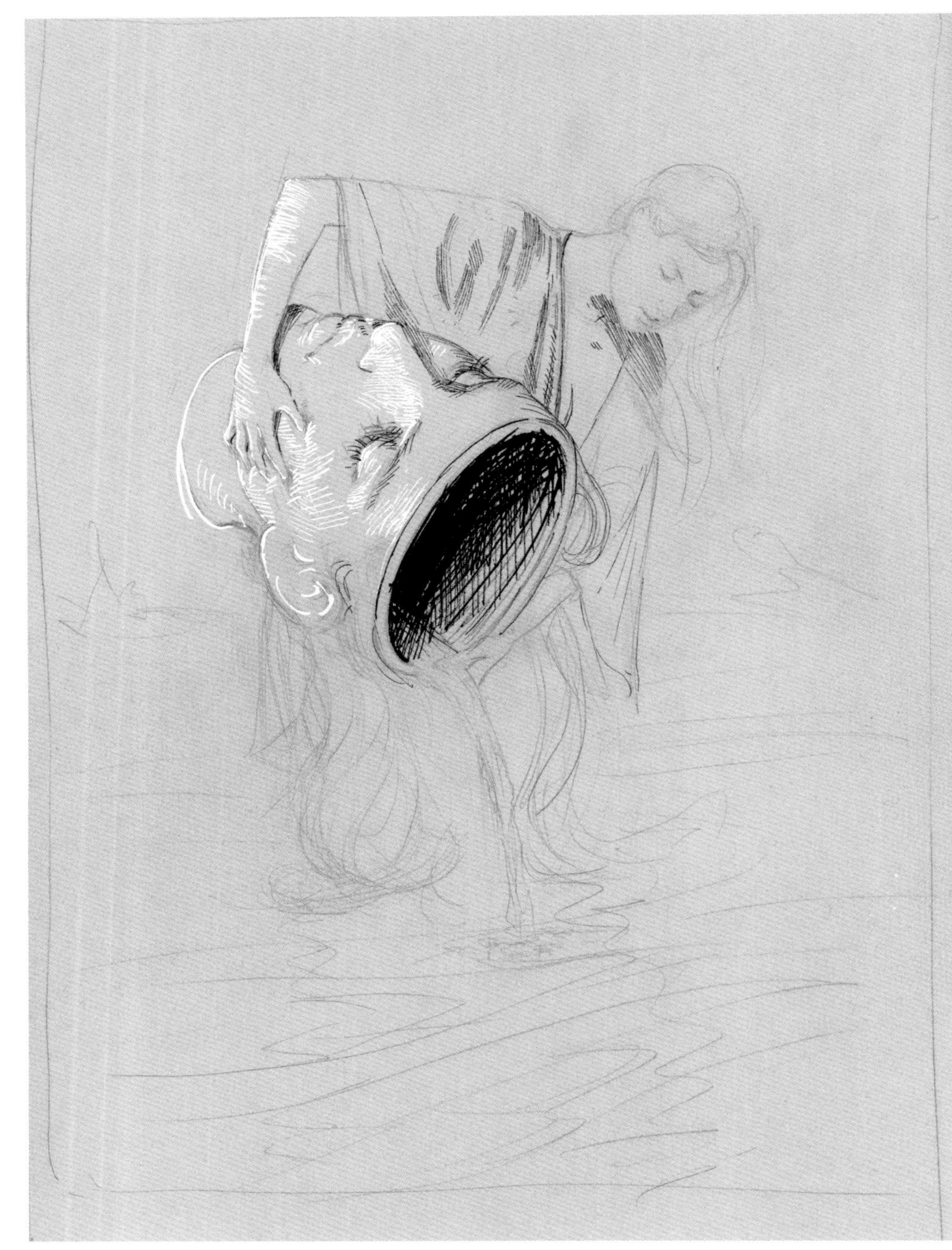

Stream of Consciousness + Study

2021

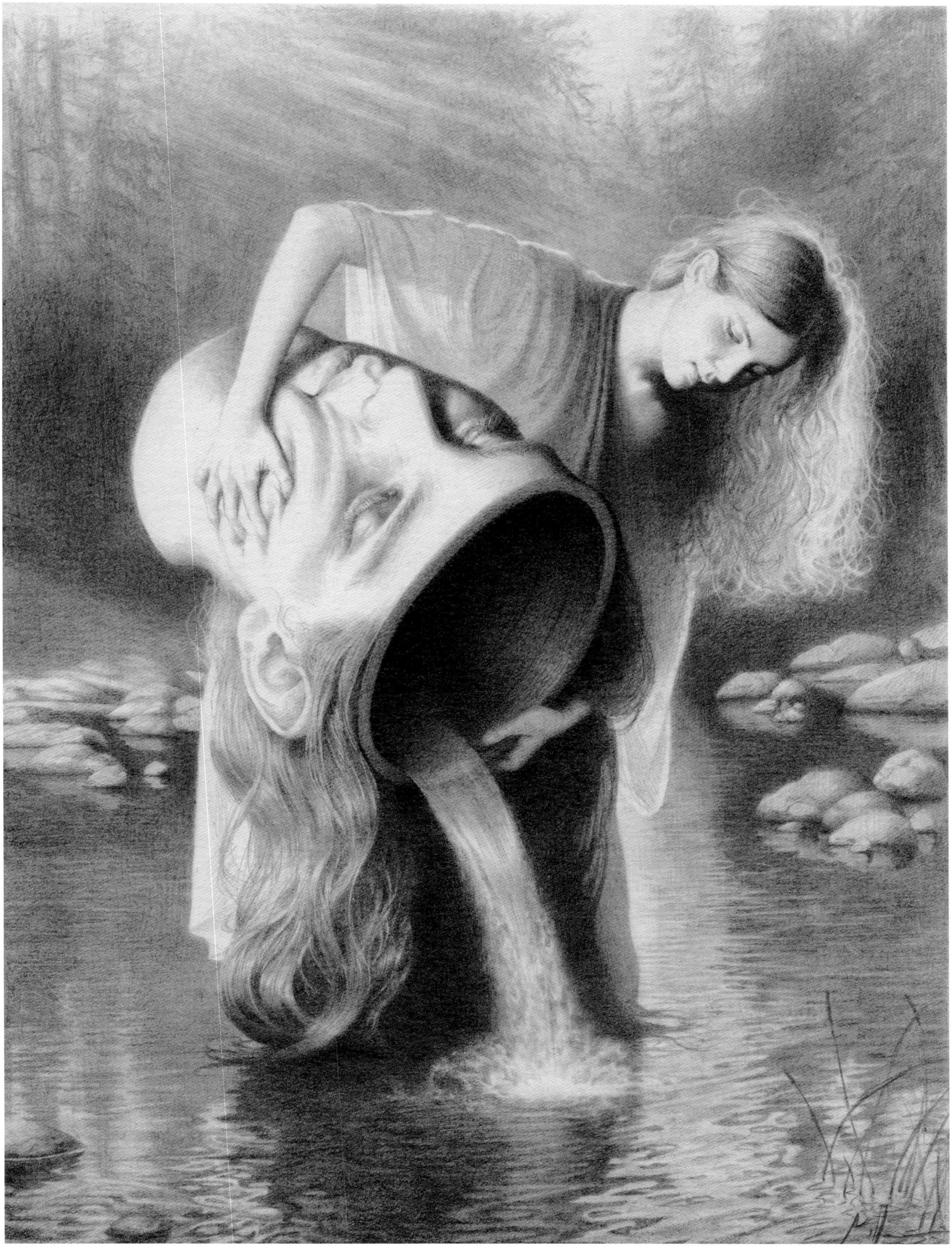

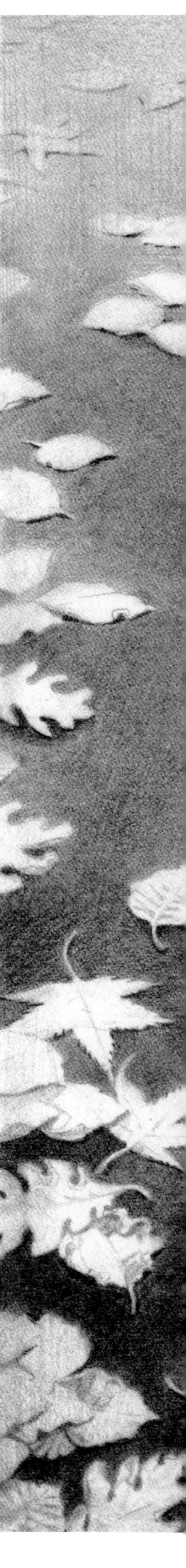

Surrender
2017

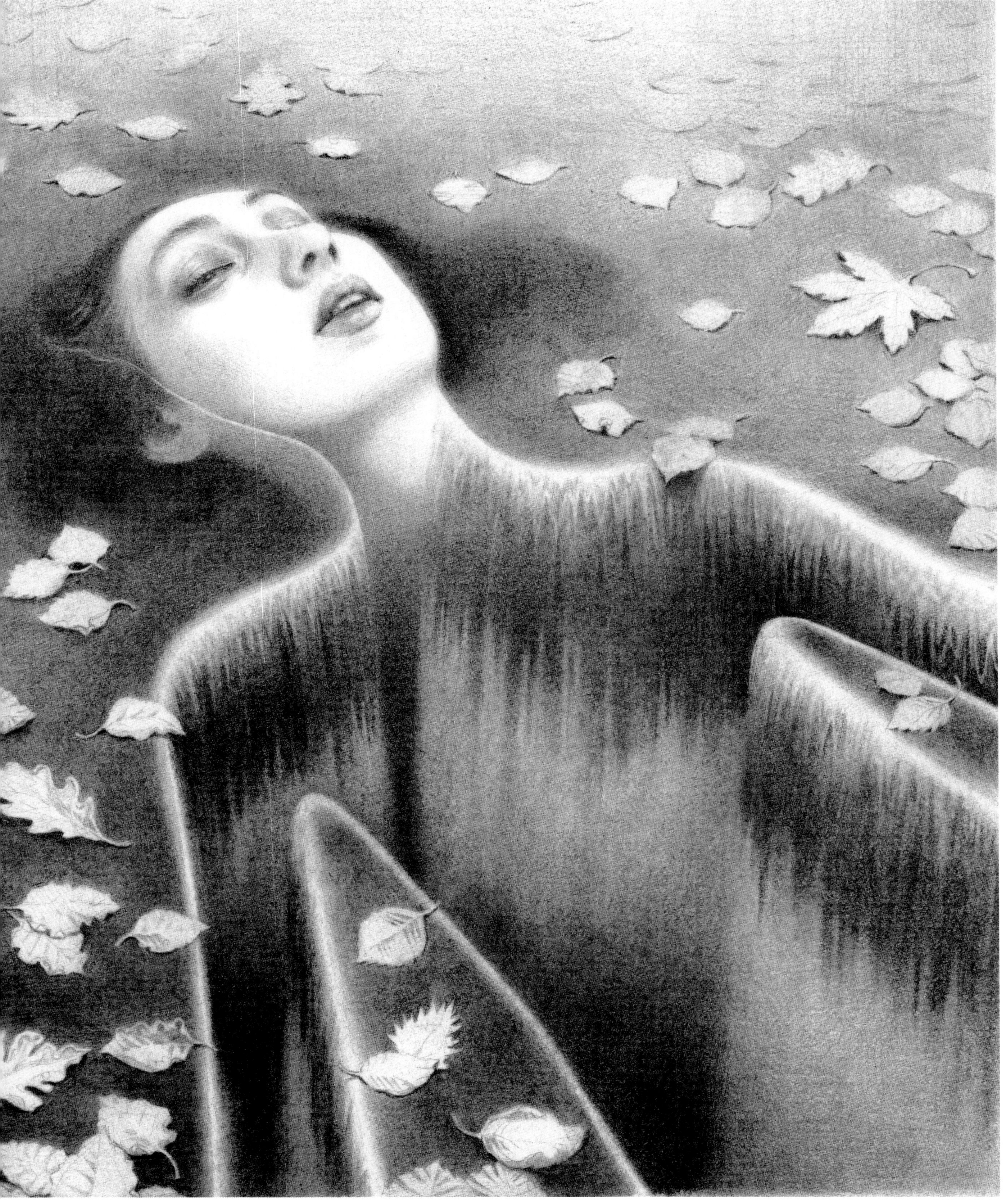

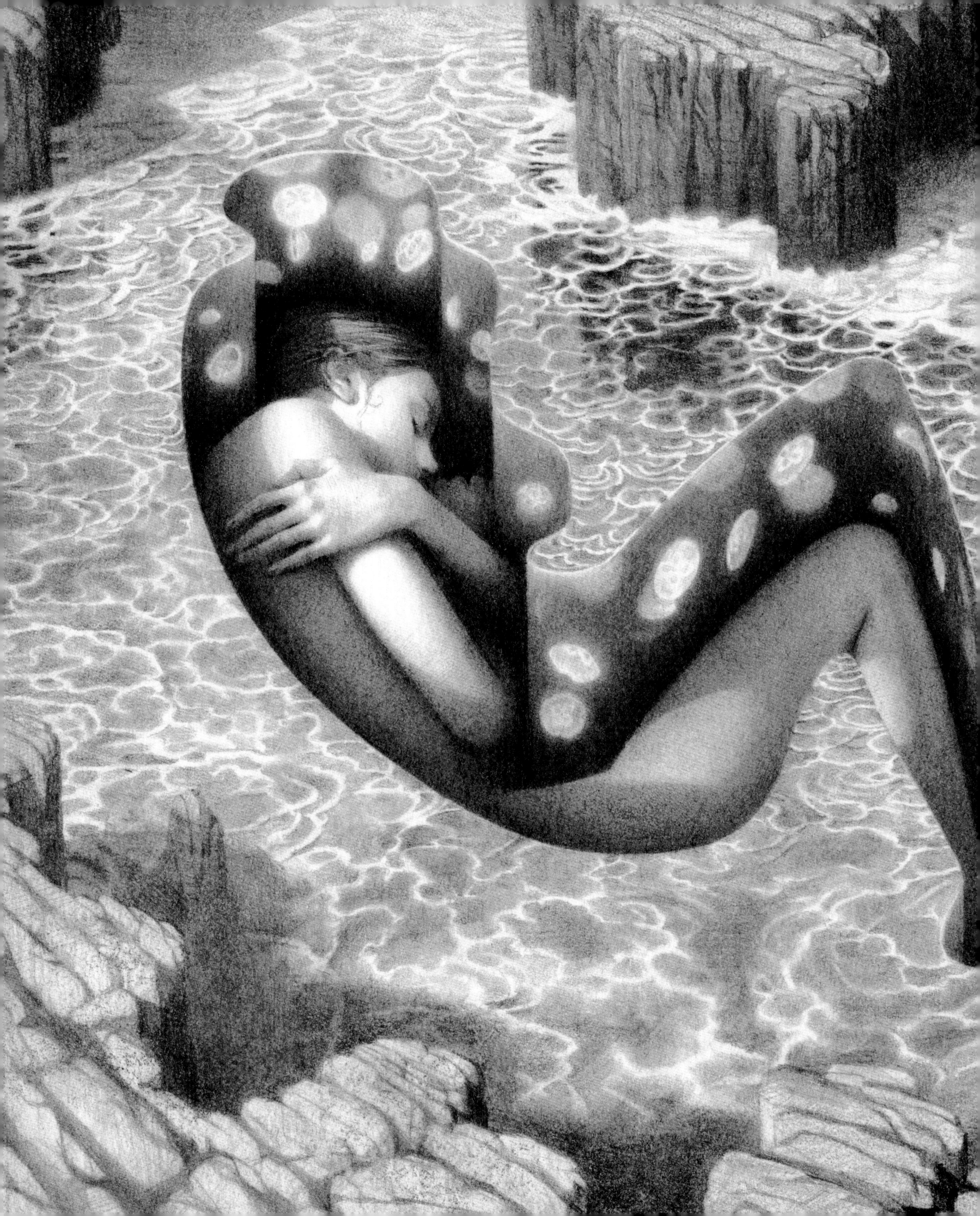

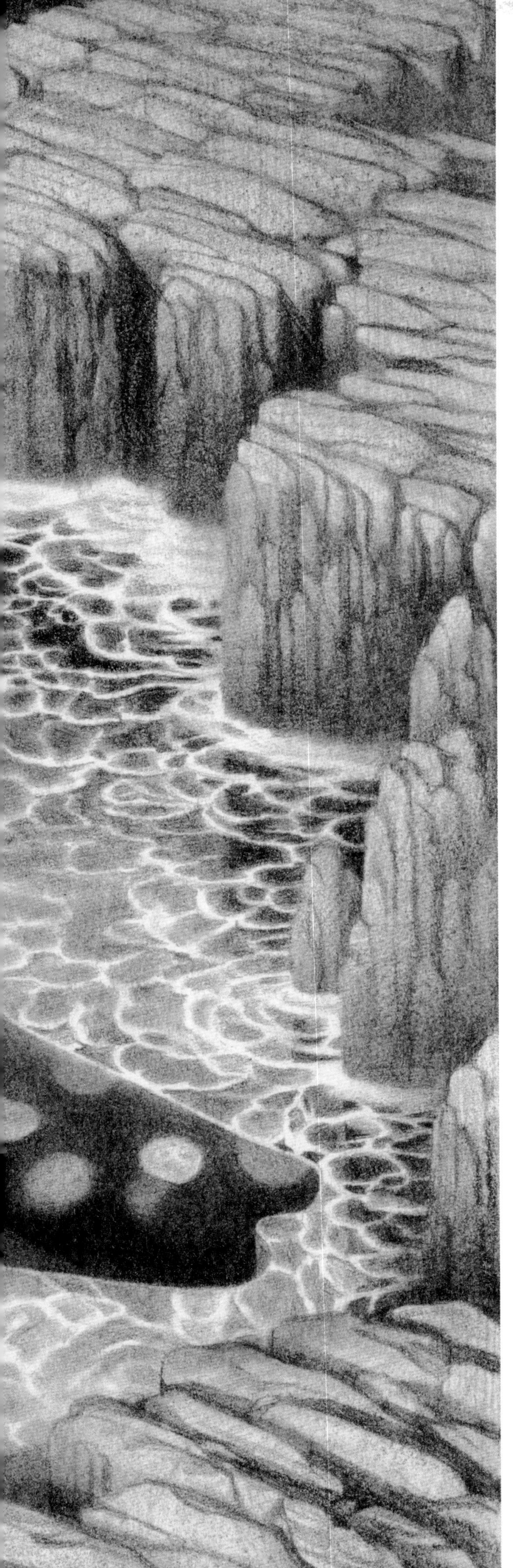

Solace
2018

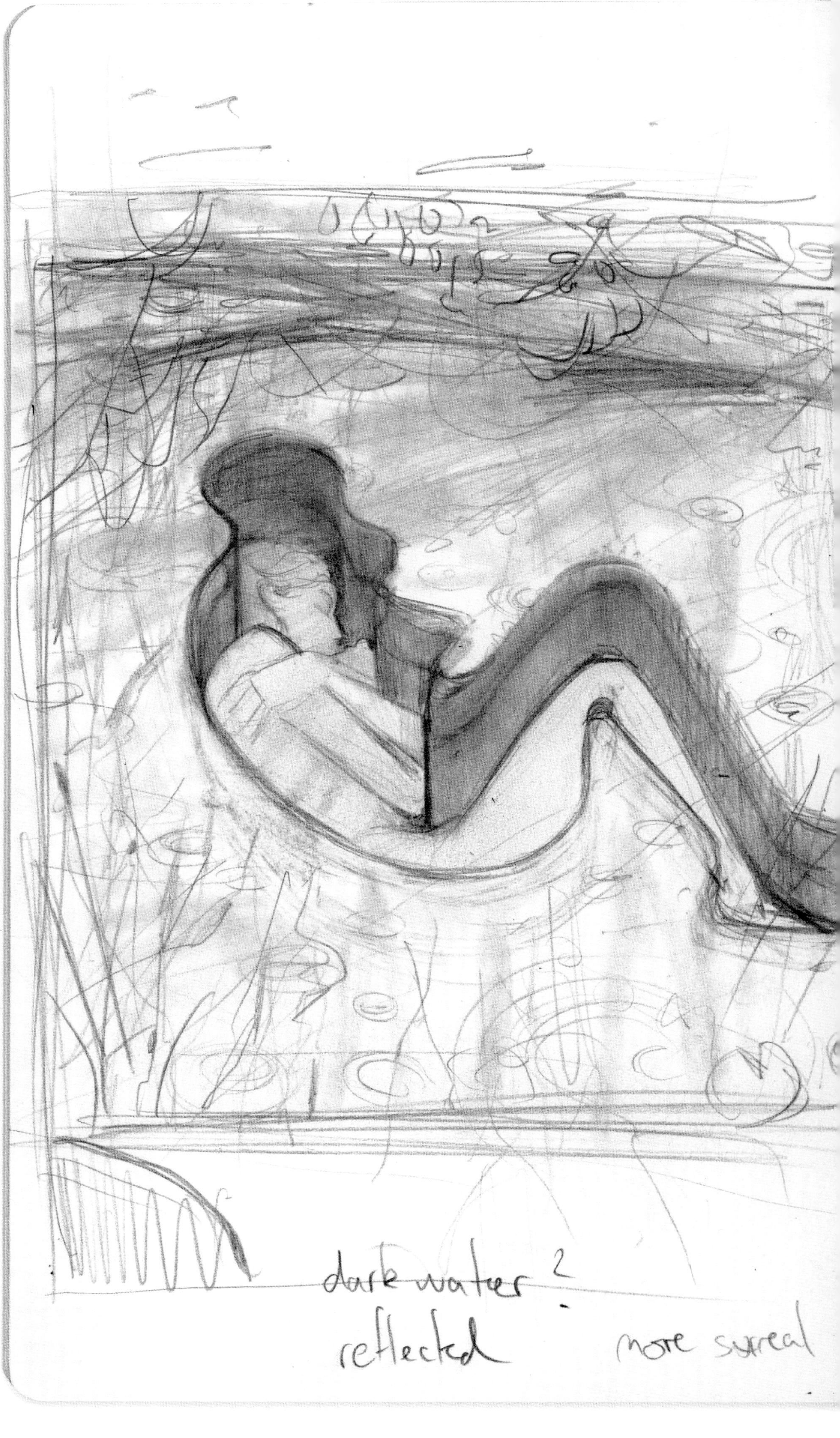

Studies for Solace
2020

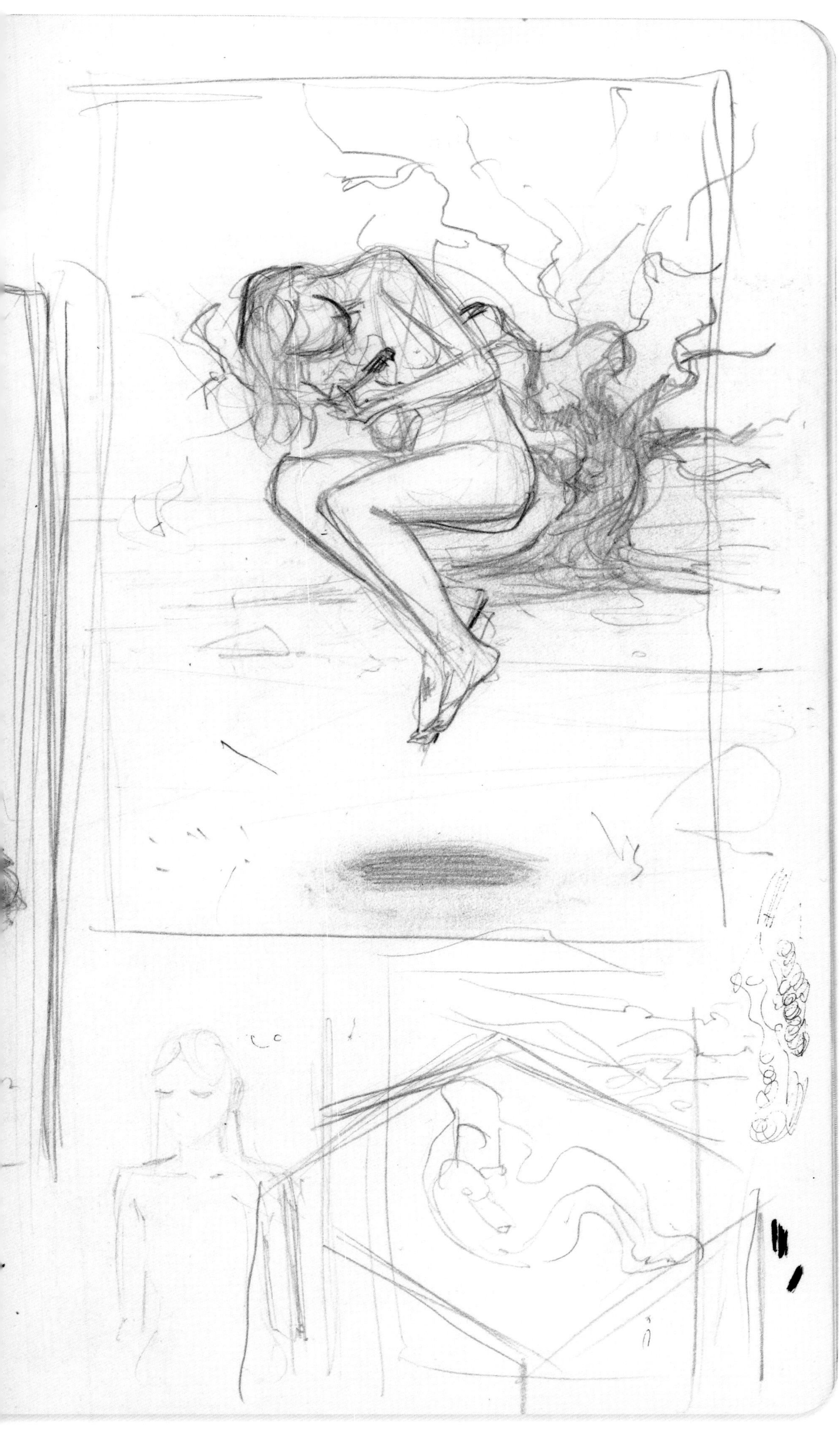

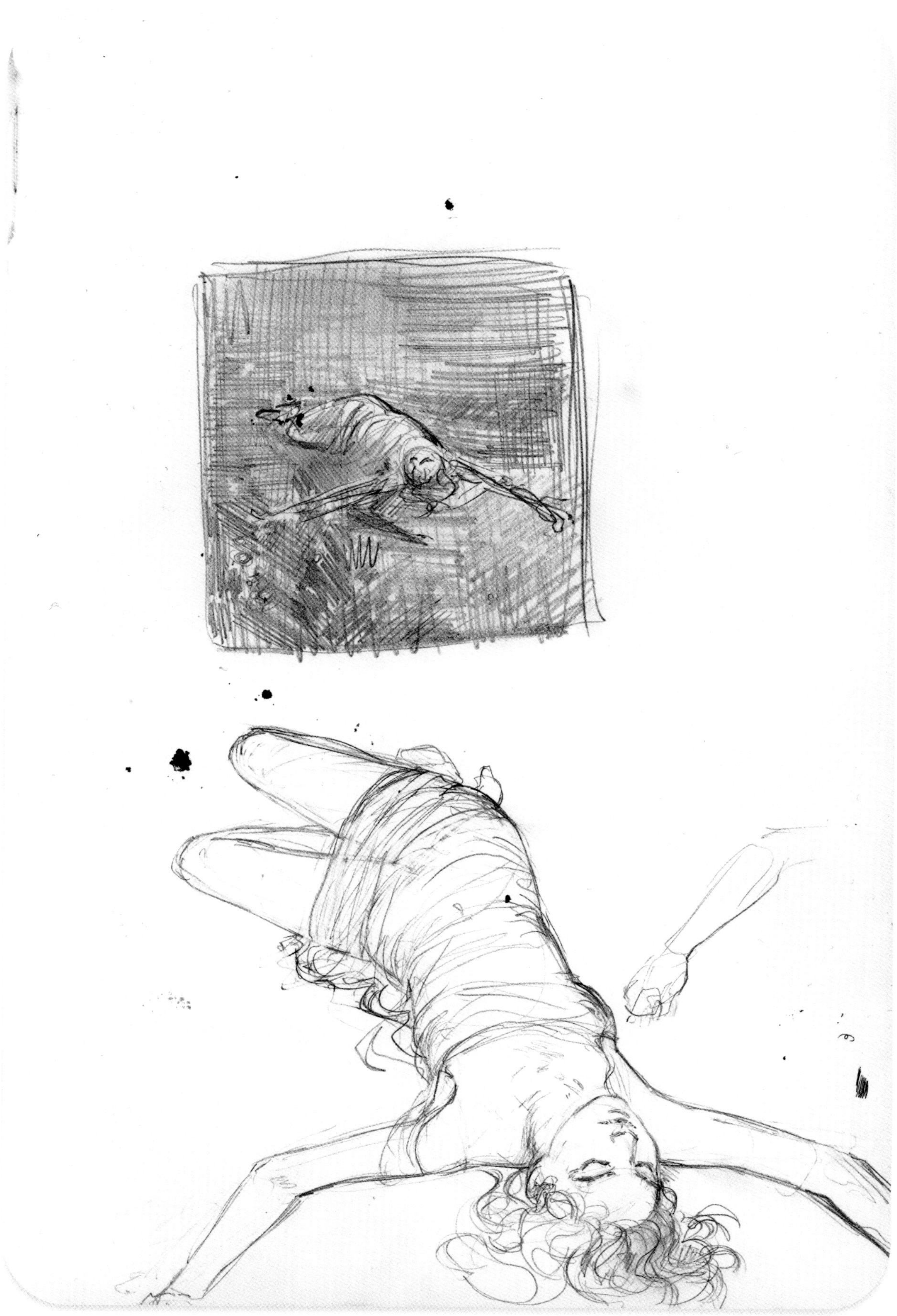

The Weight + Study
2018

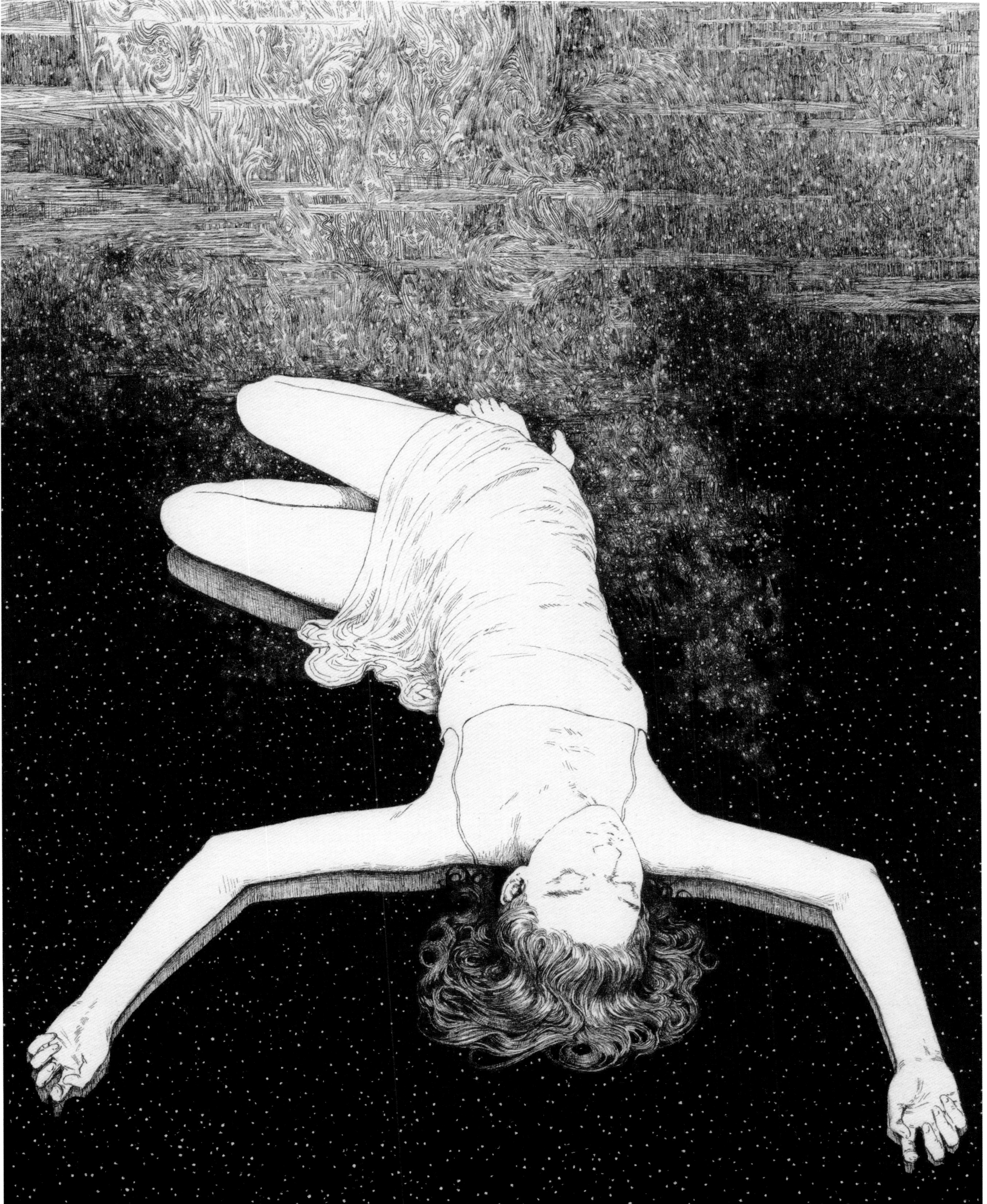

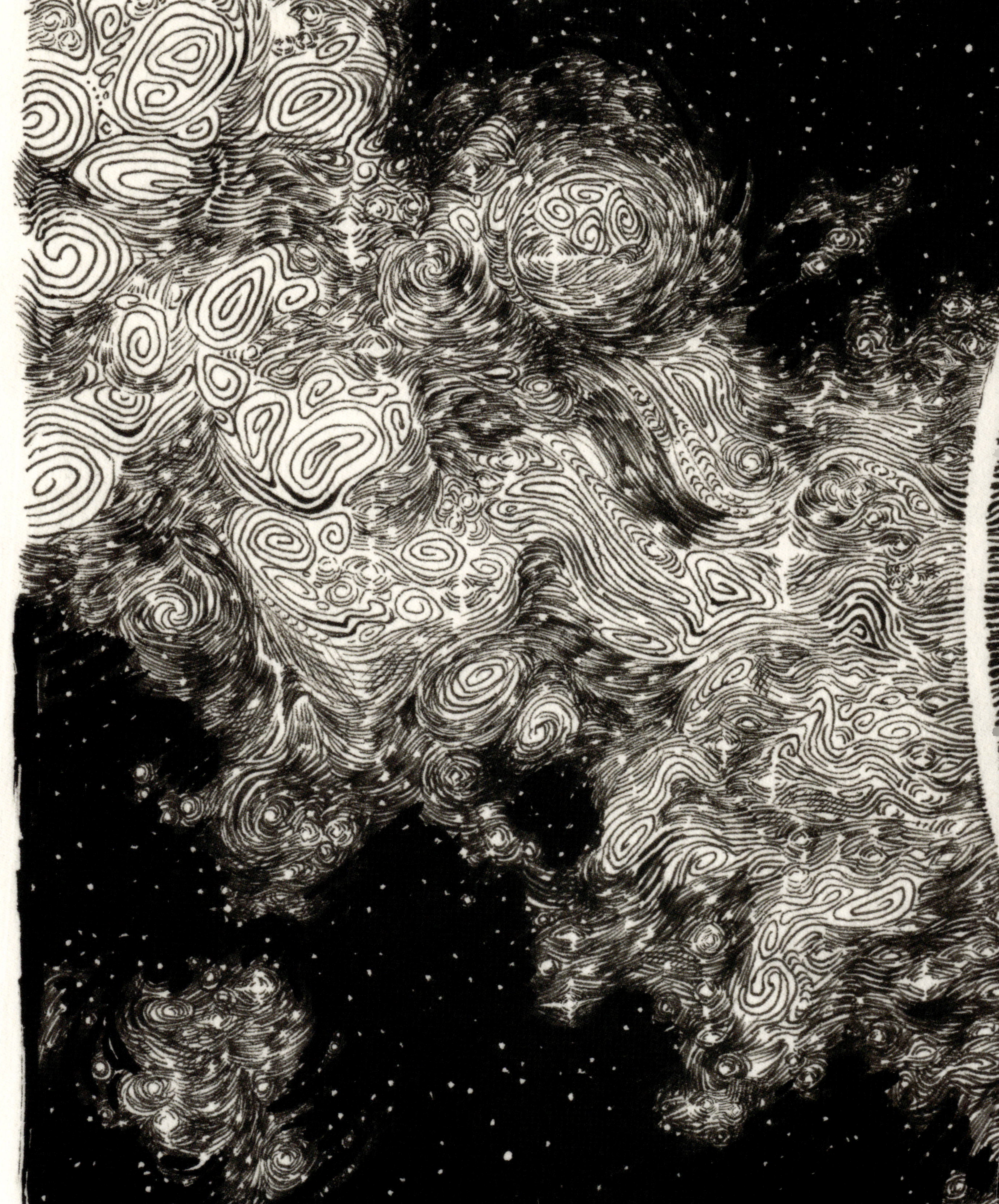

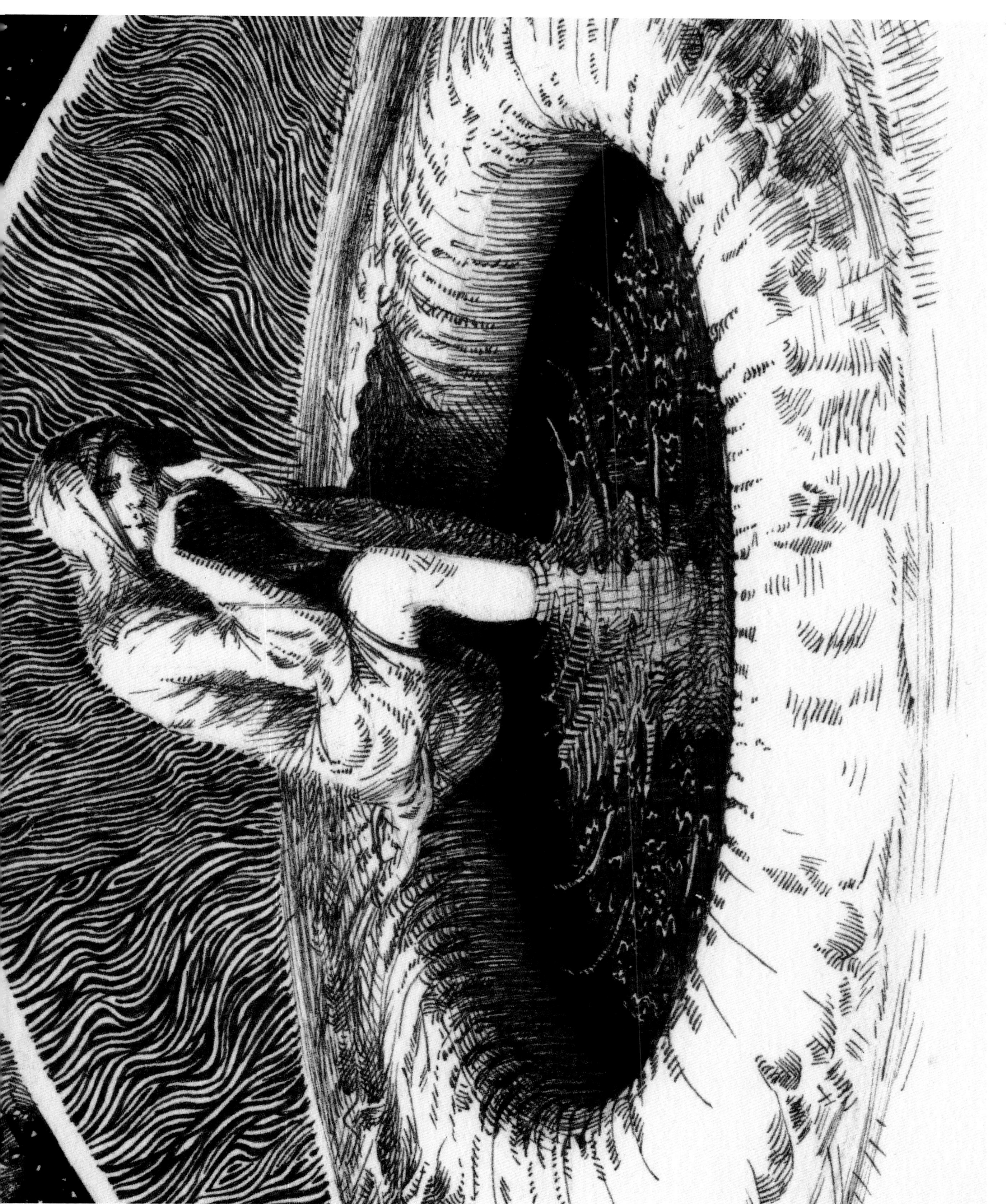

Psyche Bathing in an Eyeball

2021

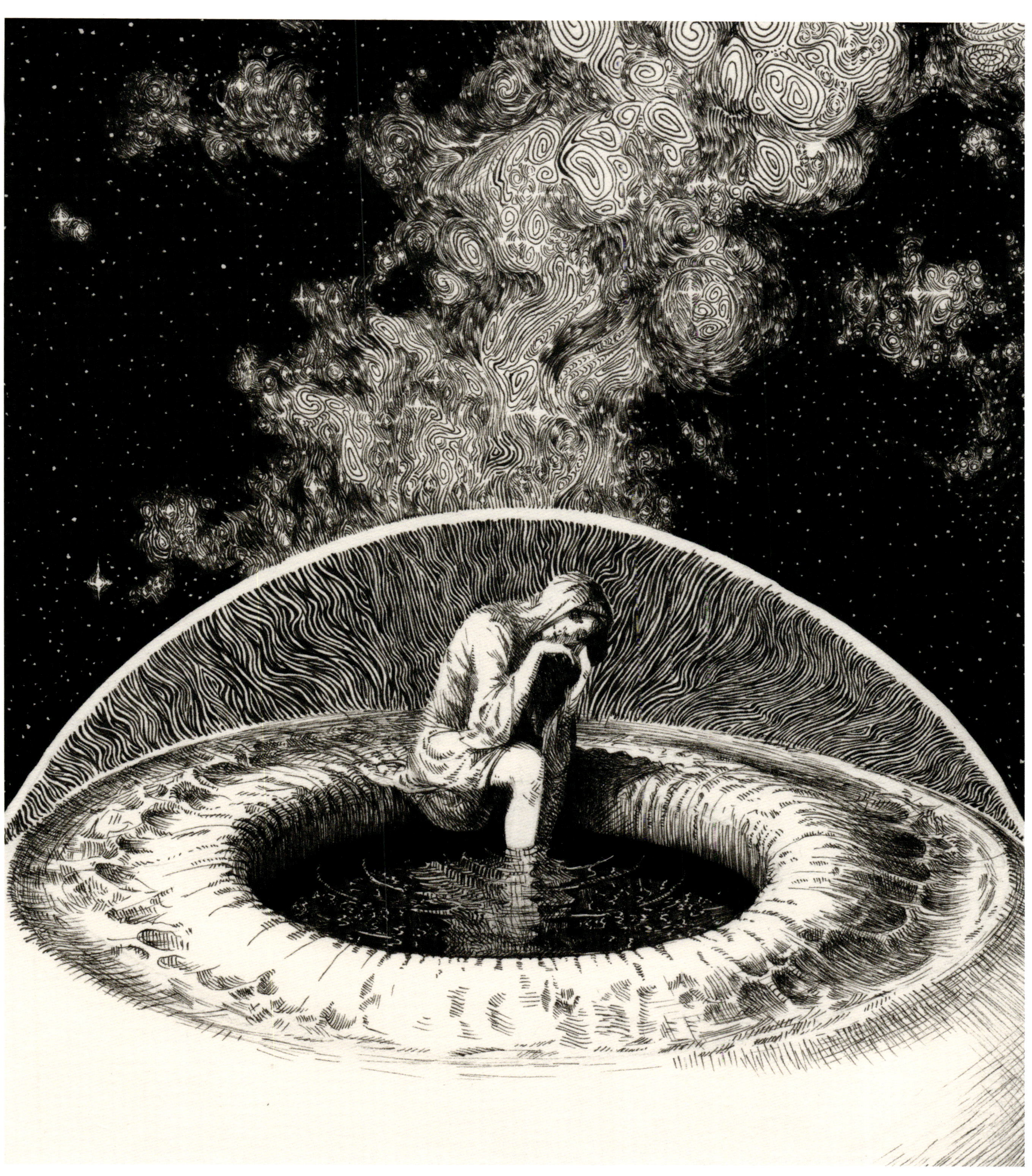

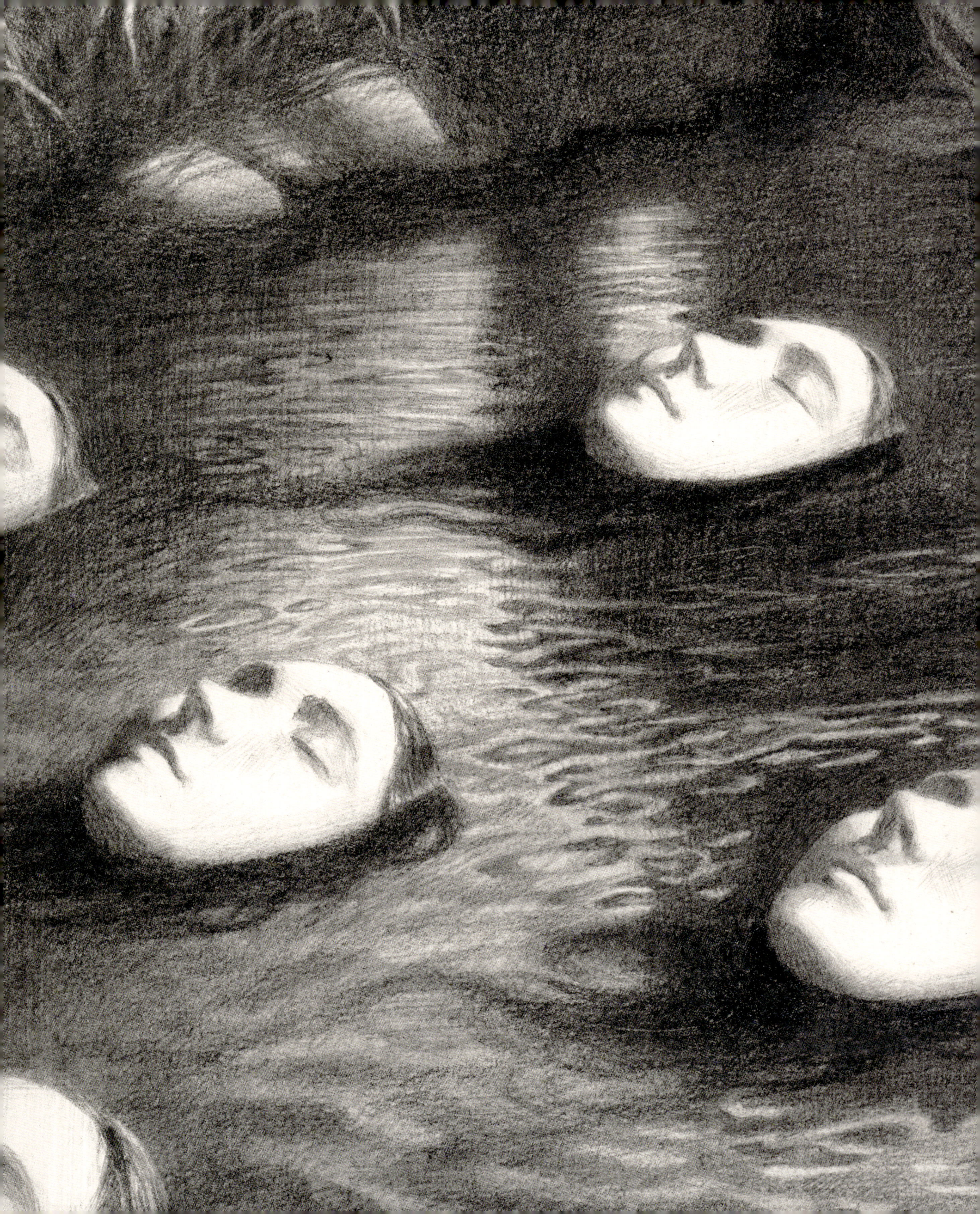

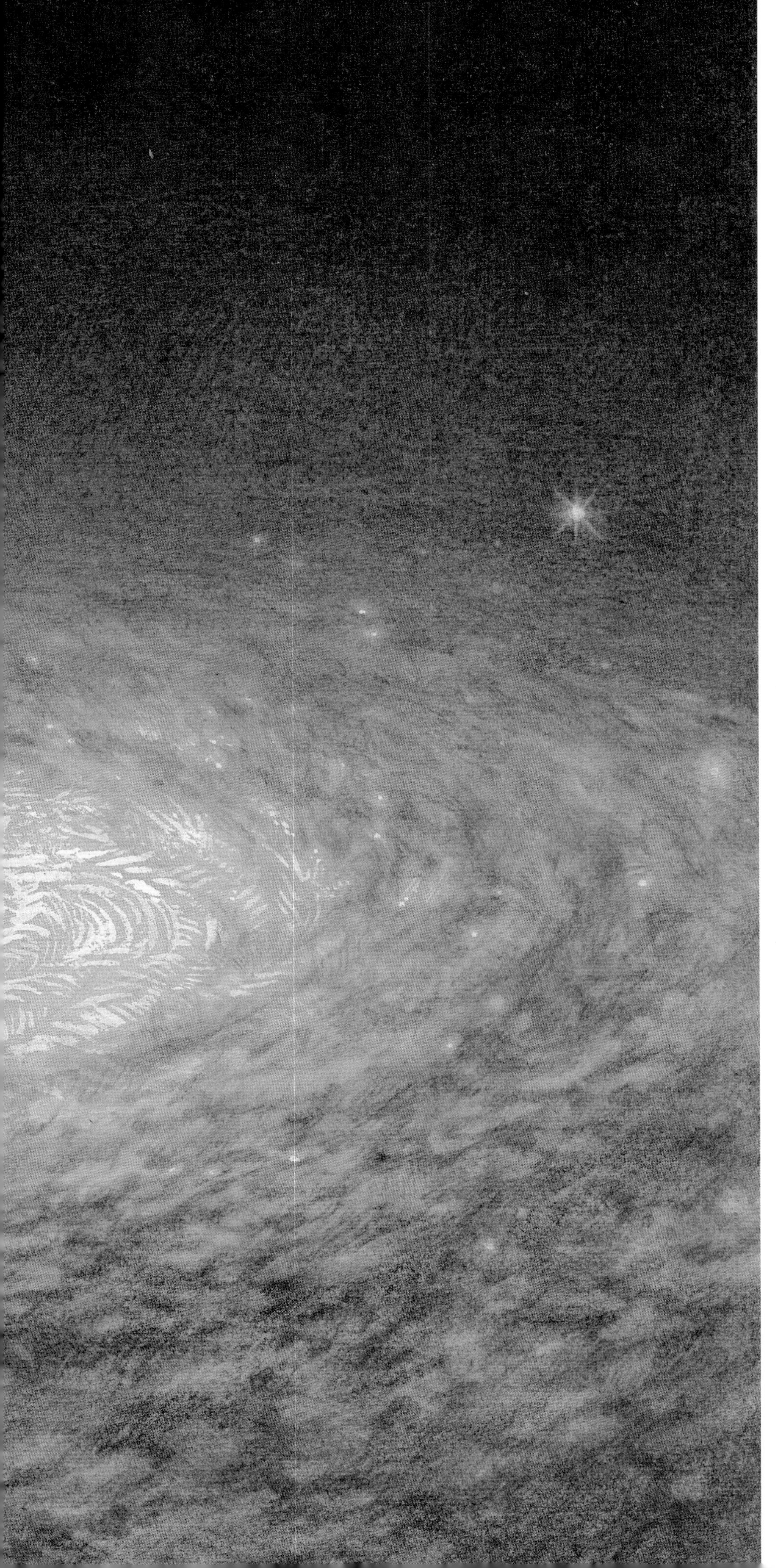

Entropy (detail)
2020

Entropy
2020

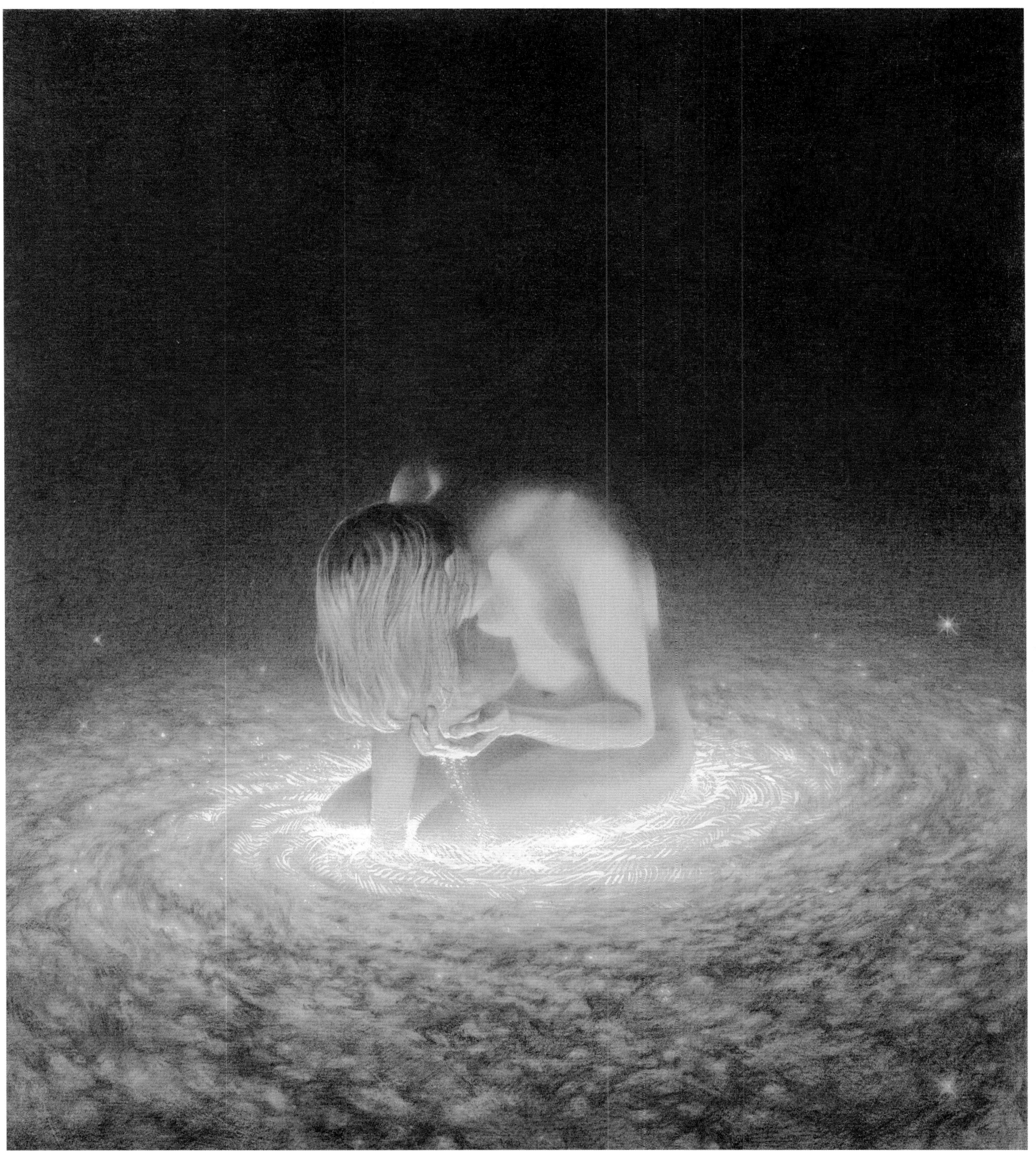

Epilogue

Two years ago, I became a dad when my two wonderful girls were born. I ended up taking an entire year off of work—twins will do that to you. I am grateful to have had the opportunity to do so, I can't think of many other reasons I would have and it has given me a lot of time to reflect on who I am and what I do. It feels right to be compiling this book together now as it feels like the conclusion to a chapter in my life both personally and artistically. The challenge I am wrestling with now is how to integrate the seismic shift in my identity that becoming a parent has imparted on me into my work going forwards.

When I see all of this work compiled together, it feels a little strange. This book represents the best of my efforts over a nearly ten year period. I don't know whether it feels like a lot of work or surprisingly little. Any one of these drawings or paintings sometimes represents months of labour. Overall I am content in the knowledge that I gave all I was capable of giving for who I was at the time.

I am betting my livelihood on the belief that human creativity matters. In a world that demands of us more—more efficiency, more productivity—I take great pleasure in the subversive joy of doing things the slow and difficult way. When I spend hours slowly building a subtle gradient in graphite to create just the right feeling of atmosphere, or painstakingly drawing things by hand, I savour the delight of refusing to optimise. As the world becomes more alienating, less human-scale, I believe the power of things made for the intrinsic joy of creation grows day by day. So many of us experience a crisis of meaning in our lives, for me the path of the artist has been where I have found that vital connection to reality. Each of these drawings is like a fossil of thought, each brushstroke or pencil mark is evidence of a living, feeling consciousness that has left its mark on the world. It all represents the desire to say something while I still have the chance.

Dedication

I would like to dedicate this book towards my children Hilma & Ofelia, who have ushered in a new and vital chapter in my life. This book represents the creative story of my adulthood before I met you, and I hope that one day this book might help you to know another piece of me. I will love you always.

I would like to give special thanks to Saga Frid, my partner and the mother of my children. You have been with me through so much of the creation of the contents of this book, and much of it would not be the same without you. Your belief in me, your love, and your taste and vision has been a huge part of my development as an artist and as a person. The amount of times I have been stuck on a drawing or a painting and you have helped talk me through it and been an essential collaborator, model, and muse is unquantifiable. Thank you.

I would like to thank my family for believing in me and supporting me through my education as an artist. Mum, you always nurtured and encouraged my creativity, I have no doubt none of this would have happened without you. Dad, you passed on a love of music and culture that has always been a cornerstone of my aesthetic sensibilities. Calum, my memories of childhood are filled with countless nights geeking out over music, comics, movies and games and art. Thank you all.

And to all of you who have ever seen my art, supported me, made this dream into a reality, from the bottom of my heart, thank you. I never take it for granted. All art is made in the spirit of a gift, and if anything I have ever made has reached you, I'm grateful for the opportunity.

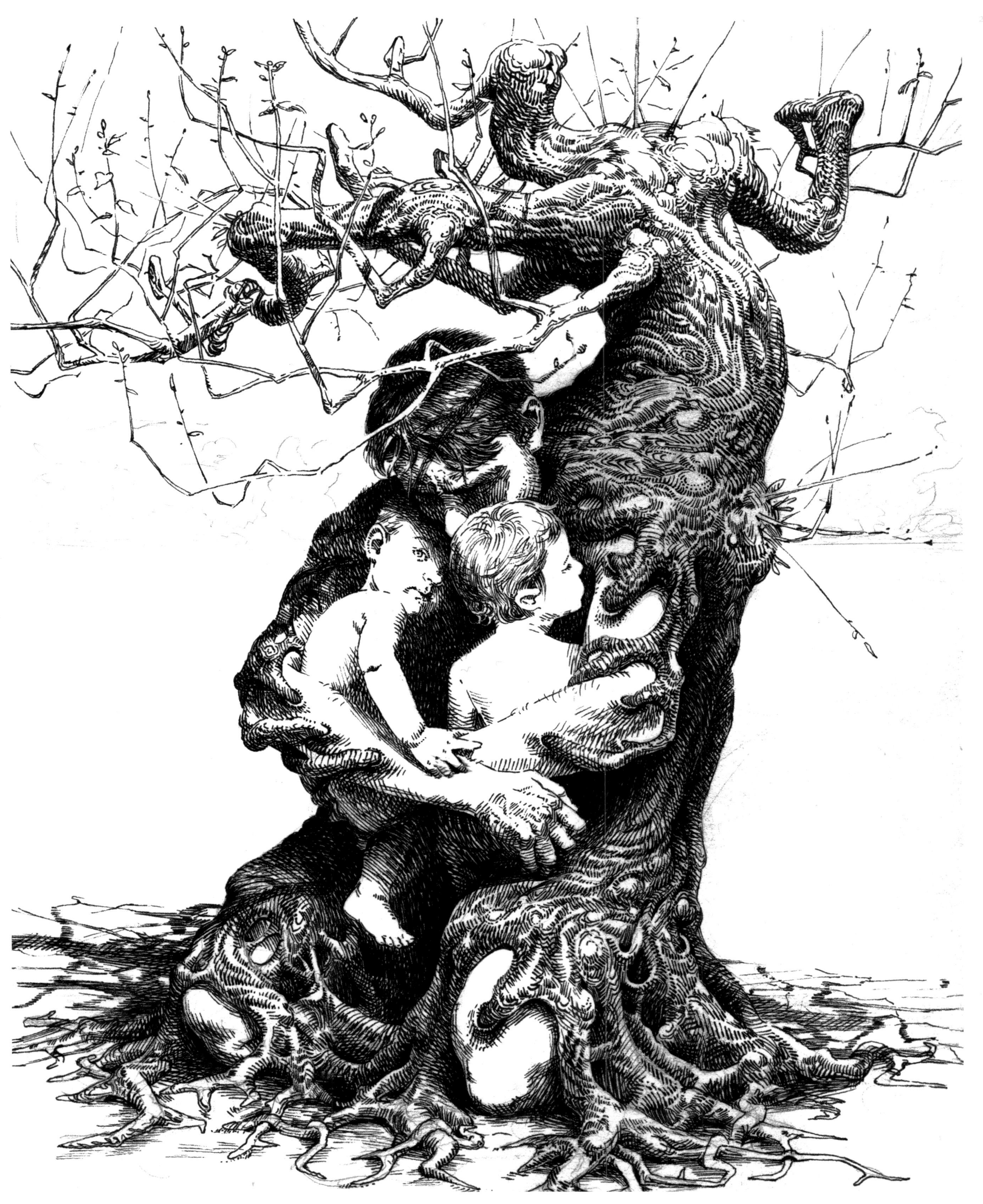

Curriculum Vitae

Solo

2024

Upcoming Solo
Harman Projects, New York City

2018

Interoception
Last Rites Gallery, New York City

Group

2021

Lend Me Your Eyes
Aux Gallery, New York City

Small Works 2021
Beinart Gallery, Melbourne

2020

Miniature Art — A Group Exhibition of Miniturists
Beinart Gallery, Melbourne

2018

Dreamer, Lover, Maker, Fighter
Beinart Gallery, Melbourne

Moleskine Project VI
Spoke Art, San Francisco

Suggestivism
Spoke Art, New York City

Hi Fructose Presents: Art of the Mushroom
Oakland, California

13th Hour
Last Rites Gallery, New York City

2017

Forbidden Thinking
Last Rites Gallery, New York City

Small Works Summer Show
Beinart Gallery, Melbourne

13th Hour
Last Rites Gallery, New York City

2016

Moleskine Project V
Spoke Art, San Francisco

2015

Moleskine Project IV
Hashimoto Contemporary, San Francisco

2013

Moleskine Project III
Spoke Art, San Francisco

Fairs

2023

Art on Paper
Harman Projects, New York City

2021

CONTEXT *Art Miami*
Hashimoto Contemporary, Miami

Art on Paper
Aux Gallery, New York City

2023

Miles Johnston: Works on Paper II
Aux Gallery, New York City

Teaching & Workshops

2023

Quarantine: Fire Walk with Me, Lazaretto Island, Maó, Menorca, Spain

2018

La Galarie Roja, Discovering your Inspiration, Seville, Spain

2015–PRESENT

Primary Instructor at The Swedish Academy of Realist Art (SARA), Simrishamn, Sweden

Biography

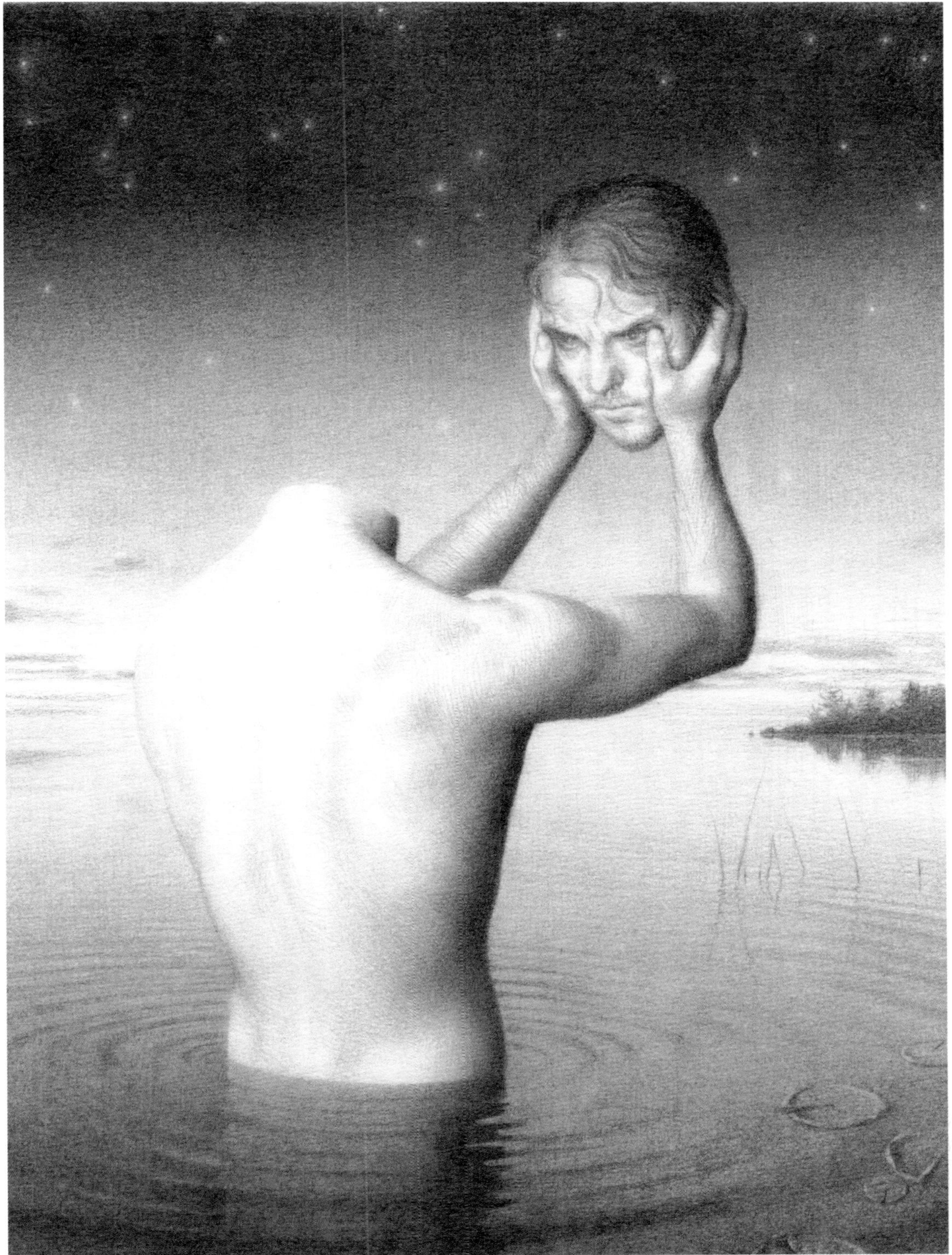

Self Reflection
2020

Miles Johnston was born in the UK in 1993. His childhood and schooling was primarily in Hampshire, England, though some early years were spent living in Brunei, Borneo. He graduated from the Swedish Academy of Realist Art in 2014, where he also worked as an instructor from 2015-2021. His pathway into the art world involved building a direct connection with a global audience through the internet and social media. Since then Miles has taught workshops, exhibited internationally and collaborated with major musicians. His work can broadly be categorized as contemporary surrealism.

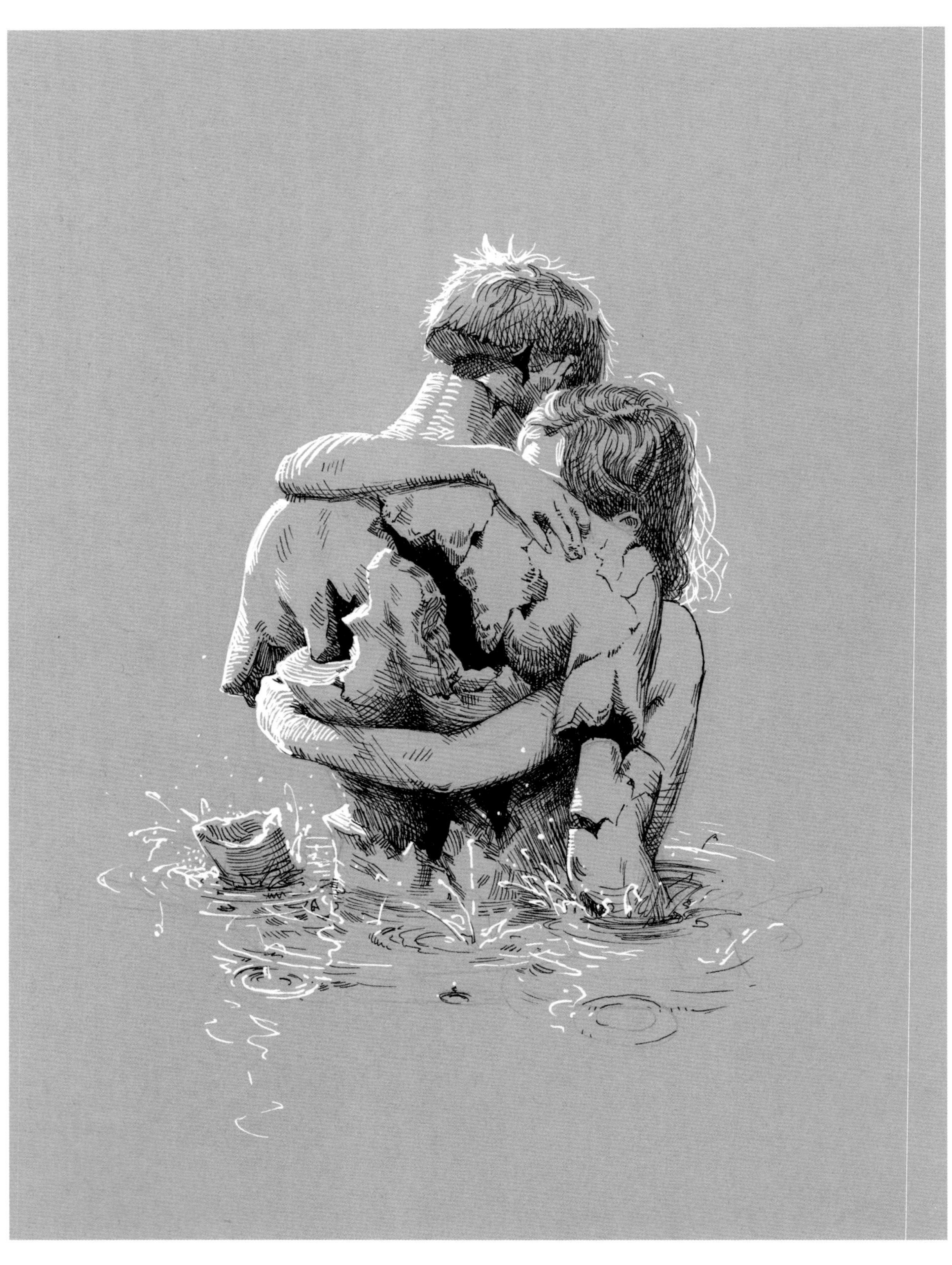

Crumble
2020

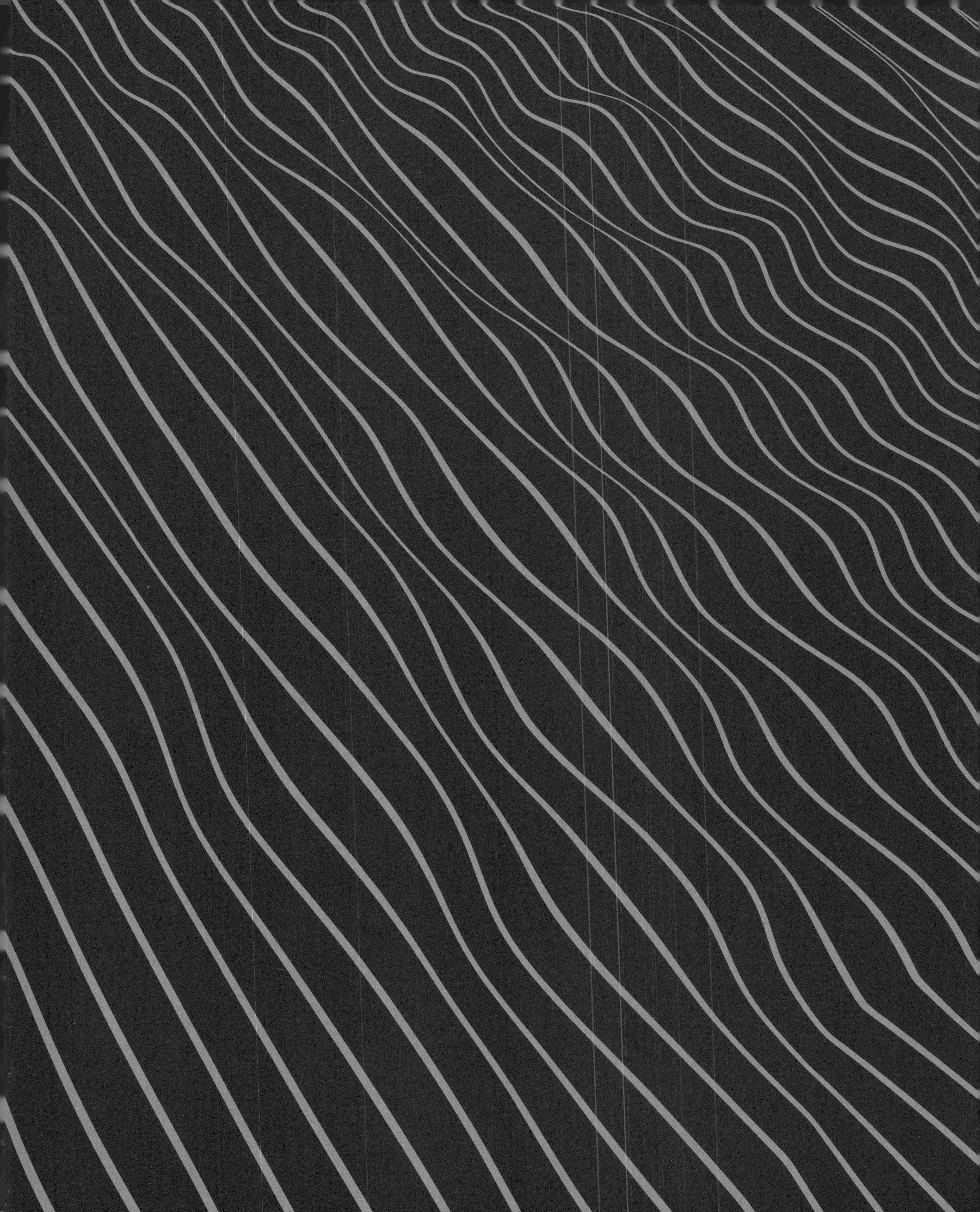